STRATEGIC ISSUES
MANAGEMENT

STRATEGIC ISSUES MANAGEMENT

Organizations and Public Policy Challenges

Robert L. Heath

SAGE Publications
International Educational and Professional Publisher
Thousand Oaks London New Delhi

For information:

SAGE Publications, Inc.
2455 Teller Road
Thousand Oaks, California 91320
E-mail: order@sagepub.com

SAGE Publications Ltd.
6 Bonhill Street
London EC2A 4PU
United Kingdom

SAGE Publications India Pvt. Ltd.
M-32 Market
Greater Kailash I
New Delhi 110 048 India

Printed in the United States of America

Library of Congress Cataloging-in-Publication Data

Heath, Robert L. (Robert Lawrence), 1941-
    Strategic issues management : organizations and public policy challenges /
Robert L. Heath.
      p. cm.
    Includes bibliographical references and index.
    ISBN 0-8039-7034-X (cloth: acid-free paper). — ISBN 0-8039-7035-8 (pbk.: acid-free paper)
    1. Issues management—United States. 2. Industrial management—Social aspects—
United States. 3. Strategic planning—United States. 4. Public relations—United States
5. Industrial policy—United States. I. Title.
HD59.5.H42 1997
659.2—dc21
                                    97-4749

05 06 07 08   10 9 8 7 6

Acquiring Editor:	Margaret Seawell
Editorial Assistant:	Renée Piernot
Production Editor:	Michele Lingre
Production Assistant:	Karen Wiley
Typesetter/Designer:	Marion Warren
Cover Designer:	Candice Harman
Print Buyer:	Anna Chin

Contents

Preface

When I wrote *Issues Management: Corporate Public Policymaking in an Information Society* with Richard Allen Nelson in 1986, the discipline was still being defined. Our analysis featured the conflicting opinions that constituted the dynamics of public policy debate. Public policy struggle characterized the 1960s and 1970s and continued into the 1980s. This contest gave the rationale for building strategic issues management on a foundation that featured public policy debate. Our attention seemed riveted to the concerns of businesses, but it actually centered on the ability of activists, business entities, and governmental agencies to find common ground and create wise public policy. Fracturing disagreements centered on the evaluative criteria and factual information that key groups—activist, business, and governmental—used to judge the ability and willingness of businesses to meet prevailing expectations of how the private sector should perform. Some combatants in that debate even concluded that business as such was the problem.

Now, I have become convinced that the contest is not limited to opinions but must include the management of public policy resources. An organization—private or public—may only be able to solve a problem between itself and one or more stakeholding public by spending resources to increase the quality of a product, service, or activity. Communication may not suffice to reconcile the differences that lead to the struggle. Sides engage to contest facts, opinions, and policies but eventually negotiate and agree on various policy settlements.

The agenda for issues management scholarship and practice seems to stress two vital goals. One is to elevate issues management in the strategic planning and management efforts by staff and executives. To add value to the organization, this can be done by managing resource allocation and creating harmony with key stakeholders in the public policy arena. Harmony demands the creation and maintenance of mutually beneficial relationships. People often hold conflicting opinions. They must find those points in their zones of meaning where their interests align with others. A contest of ideas is one means by which people come to one mind. People can collaborate in decision making and derive a mutually beneficial outcome but for different reasons.

The second goal is to refine the assumptions that guide the professional practice and academic inquiry into issues management. The objective is to build on a communication rationale for issues management while featuring a resource management paradigm. This second requirement is vital to efforts by issues managers to add value to organizations and thereby to earn their status in the leadership cadre.

Addressing this challenge, Renfro (1993) featured the discipline's management contribution:

> The overriding goal of an issues management function is to enhance the current and long-term performance and standing of the corporation by anticipating change, promoting opportunities, and avoiding or mitigating threats. Attaining this corporate goal, of course, promotes the performance and standing of the corporate leadership, both within and outside the corporations, but this is secondary for issues management. (p. 107)

This insight frames the conclusion by Davis and Thompson (1994): "Management's control within the firm is contingent on rules determined externally by state and federal governments, and the allocation of corporate control thus depends on political struggles among management, capital, and various governmental bodies" (p. 141).

This book draws on that conceptual framework to examine the dynamics of public policy resource management, its theoretical and research underpinnings, and its best practices. This analysis is predicated on a central theme: Issues management enjoys prominence in the opinion of each organizations' executives and other community leaders to the degree that its practitioners know how to add value to their organizations while balancing the organizations' interests with the community of key stakeholders and stakeseekers.

Three broad underpinnings support the analysis in this book: systems, rhetoric, and social exchange. By no means alone in their opinion, Long and

Hazleton (1987) observed that "general systems theory portends promise as a meta-theoretical approach for organizing public relations phenomena" (p. 5). Systems theory is based on an information exchange paradigm that all systems seek internal and external equilibrium with other systems. As Bivins (1992) wrote,

> General systems theory is a radical departure from many other organizational concepts because it stresses the universality of organizational principles and the interdependence of all systems. It allows public relations to be conceptualized in its interrelationship with business, law, politics, etc., rather than in isolation. Its unique value also comes from its stress on process as an organizing principle. (p. 366)

Bivins featured the transformational functions of systems (input, throughput, and output) and the cybernetic principle of feedback: "Continuous feedback loops allow organizational systems to coordinate and adjust activities to maintain balance and promote survival" (p. 366).

The cybernetic paradigm that underpins systems theory features the use of positive and negative feedback as the means by which individuals in a system maintain or abandon policies. Thus, Krippendorff and Eleey (1986) observed, "*any organization can do no better than the feedback it receives from its environment*" (p. 14). However, as Morgan (1982) cautioned, such assumptions are not always borne out in practice. The simplicity of explaining the theory belies the difficulties of dealing with turbulent situations, a problem that is compounded by multiple stakeholder interests. Often, the problem facing companies is not in the acquisition of information but in management's ability to use it to create policies in the mutual interest of all parties.

Instead of using issues management as a guidance and adjustive system, many organizations assume that it can protect them from change by blunting the opinions and power resource management of key stakeholders. Cybernetics lends partial explanation for how one system sets goals and corrects its actions based on feedback, but it does not provide means for defining the factors that affect relationships. Of particular importance is the need to account for negotiation and the debate over which criteria should be used to evaluate the distribution of resources that have public policy implications. In this sense, systems theory may be informative but less than useful, except to explain only in the most basic terms how firms adjust to and seek to have others adapt to them. Capturing the spirit of this limitation, Pearson (1990) reasoned that "an organization needs more *understanding* than is afforded by quantitative feedback" (p. 228).

Pearson (1990) forced us to realize that systems theory can lead to "a narrow functionalist perspective that ultimately will restrict the range of discussion on public issues because such discussion is seen to be dysfunctional." The options, which he framed as practicality or ethical necessity, force us to chose between a view "that emphasizes functionalism and one that emphasizes the ethical or humanistic implication of global interdependencies" (p. 227). Pearson was concerned that the desire to achieve control can become the heart and soul of systems theory.

Coupling systems theory and a rhetorical view of organizational response, Krippendorff and Eleey (1986) observed that "control implies the ability to manipulate some variables, and by applying knowledge of how these controllable variables affect features of the symbolic environment, to cause the symbolic environments to change in desired directions" (p. 17). Such control—even the attempts to achieve it—can be unethical and daunting. Nevertheless, control is not inherently dysfunctional, as Pearson (1990) concluded. Dysfunction occurs when people believe they can achieve control by using a cybernetic model based on interpretations of quantitative feedback only.

Rather than view control as one-way, one-sided, the message in this book is that savvy issues managers struggle to achieve the most favorable outcomes by fostering mutual interests with all stakeholders and stakeseekers through the distribution of public policy resources. This observation reminds us to avoid a single stakeholder bias—analysis that assumes that only one stakeholder affects the efforts of the entity to achieve or maintain interdependent harmony.

To avoid this narrowness, Bivins (1992) differentiated kinds of associations or linkages that exist between an organization and its constituents. Different kinds of linkage exist between an organization and its stakeholders: *normative* (linkages with organizations that face similar problems or share values), *enabling* (policy preferences expressed through governmental power or financial authority), *functional* (vital interdependencies without which the organization cannot survive: this type of linkage divides into input—such as relationships with employees or suppliers—and output—those with customers), and *diffused* (these result when individuals lack membership in identifiable groups). (Grunig & Hunt, 1984.)

Any group could have one or more of the four kinds of linkages with the focal organization. Environmentalists might routinely be thought to have a normative linkage, but they can be conceptualized as functional (customers) and as enabling (a powerful environmentalist might be governor, head of a governmental agency, or the fund manager for a financial institution). This view of linkages can address the kinds of stakes held by the relevant parties. Also, analysis of linkages should feature the holders' willingness and abilities to grant or withhold stakes as well as the seekers' needs for them and abilities to obtain them by alternative means.

Willingness to grant stakes can depend on degree of interdependence, reciprocity, alternatives (whether receiving or granting stakes), ease of exchange, need to grant or obtain stakes, and reward-cost decisions involved in the exchange. Ability could include the availability of other stakeseekers or factors such as time. If no other stakeseekers are available to receive the stakes, then a stakeholder may have to grant them. Some stakes deteriorate over time and may need to be granted or lost, for instance.

One way to integrate these concepts into a coherent rationale for issues management is to understand how people form opinions. Such opinions, along with awareness of norm behaviors and opinions held by significant others, prepare the individual to make decisions that are maximally rewarding. The extent to which opinions and decisions are rewarding or threatening to individuals predicts their willingness to seek and process information into useful opinions.

A powerful underpinning for issues management can be drawn from the theory of social exchange, which "involves the transference of resources" (Roloff, 1981, p. 25). If relationships cost more than they are worth, they are likely to be abandoned or reformed; if the cost is great and they cannot be terminated, sanctions and constraints are likely to be used to force change, thereby leading to new, and ostensibly more favorable, cost-benefit ratios.

This principle underpins issues management. It is rationale for executive strategic planning, whereby the threats posed to the strategic plan are mitigated and opportunities are exploited in responsible ways so that adverse consequences do not accrue later. Social exchange theory reasons that "an exchange can be thought of as a transference of something from one entity to another in return for something else" (Roloff, 1981, p. 14). As Prior-Miller (1989) observed,

> Organizational conflict will occur when inputs and outputs are not in balance and one organization or the other refuses to act to restore that balance. Organizational change will result from continually negotiating inputs and outputs. Organizational management will be both reactive and proactive in such negotiations. (p. 72)

Because of its stress on resource management, social exchange theory brings to mind the norms of reciprocity basic to each relationship. Considerations of security or safety are introduced into a community because of hazards associated with industrial processes. People expect fair and equal treatment. They seek to mitigate organizations' harmful impact on environmental quality. These norms are subject to debate. Standards of corporate responsibility are derived from norms at macrosocietal and microanalytic levels. Managements are well served by issues managers who know the costs that can result from strained relationships, whereby key stakeholders believe that the costs associated with the organization or industry outweigh the social and material benefits.

Based on these three lines of reasoning, this book advances from a definition and historical treatment of issues management to feature four central issues management challenges: (a) strategic planning, (b) constant issue surveillance, (c) aggressive efforts to ascertain and achieve corporate responsibility, and (d) willingness to openly, boldly, and collaboratively contest ideas relevant to the marketplace and public policy arena. This effort leads to the reasonable management of public policy resources. Issues management can help organizational leaderships to enact an organization that meets or exceeds the expectations of key publics and builds mutually beneficial relationships.

Several people lent their efforts to the completion of this book. A decade of students studying issues management forced refinements in my thinking, as have colleagues—including two reviewers of this manuscript. I have discussed and debated key points with corporate practitioners, academics, journalists, activists, and governmental officials. I remain committed to a rhetorical perspective, despite critics who believe it cannot be ethical or symmetrical. I believe that dialogue is sometimes shrill and sometimes quiet and patient. At times, people listen to one another and appreciate each other's ideas. At other times, they do not. But rhetoric—statement and counterstatement—forces people to think and reconsider their points. It assumes that good ideas prevail and bad ones fail. It believes that ethical standards result from the best thinking of many competing points of view.

A Foundation of Community

Issues Management as an Organizational and Academic Discipline

The term *issues management* is relatively new, but its practice and study are old. It is the product of turbulent criticism and change that angry publics seek to impose on business policies and practices. Recent interest in this topic began in the 1960s when activist groups, media reporters, and government pressed for myriad changes in business activities and policies.

Issues management emerged in the past century when executives of large corporations turned strategically to government to seek favorable public policy to define, defend, and champion their monopolistic practices. Conglomerates sprung up overnight and sought to dominate entire markets. Business enterprises, such as telephone and electric utilities, struggled to establish state-of-the-art operating standards, including the legitimacy of regulated monopoly.

For the first time in the history of U.S. business, bosses cloistered themselves in luxurious offices rather than work side by side with laborers. Boards of directors and shareholders had come to decide how workers' efforts were directed and corporate policy was formed and implemented. People's health and safety were dramatically harmed by manufacturing and marketing

1

practices. Eventually, executives were challenged to respond to outbursts of protest. Activists and reporters argued that business practices were corrupting the market enterprise system and society.

Eras of turbulence continued. The depression of the 1930s challenged government and private sector organizations to reformulate private sector practices and state or federal programs to protect the public interest. During World War II, corporations and government linked arms to produce a stunning global victory that served as the hallmark for a period of prosperity. The war effort changed the structure of labor and management relations and led to a new prosperity through research and development efforts that were fueled by the need for new products when Axis forces denied sources of raw materials vital to the Allied war effort. This industrial buildup created abundant new synthetic, chemical-based products and other goods that were affordable and available in ways that dramatically changed lifestyles for the population.

Entering the 1960s, the private sector felt smug. It had helped accomplish world peace and widespread prosperity. Confident executives were startled by outspoken criticism of all business activities. Sparked by antiwar and civil rights protests, key publics reexamined the principles of representative democracy and the relationships between companies and labor, consumers, and the environment. Authority was indicted as being irresponsible. Environmentalism, consumerism, and dozens of other "isms" emerged as vocal interests opposed prevailing principles of business and government. Activists became part of the political power base of this country.

New sociopolitical dynamics began in the 1960s to guide government and the private sector. Businesses lost much of their public policy clout as the result of four dramatic changes: (a) Natural resources, found to be limited and defined as the property of the citizens of the nation, were to be managed in the collective interest. (b) Society became sensitive to the increasing heterogeneity of values, attitudes, beliefs, interests, and cultures that destroyed the sense of policy consensus that prevailed at the start of the 1960s. (c) People lost confidence in large institutions, such as government, media, and business, and placed their confidence in activist groups to exert the collective power of individuals. (d) Standards of corporate responsibility changed (Pfeffer, 1981). This fertile ground fed the growth of issues management.

Today, advocacy groups are broad based as well as narrowly focused. One narrowly focused group, People Against Dangerous Delivery, based in Washington, D.C., applauded the civil court finding that Domino's Pizza was liable for encouraging its delivery personnel to drive unsafely to avoid having to discount pizzas that were delivered late. The point of the group's applause was a $79 million jury award in 1993 for a St. Louis woman who has suffered chronic headaches and back pain since being struck by a delivery person who ran a red light during a pizza delivery. When Wal-Mart, along with other large discount retailers, such as K-Mart, decided to stop selling handguns, activists applauded. Handgun Control Inc., a lobby group based in Washington, D.C., approved this move indicating that it would speed the progress toward a safer society. Corporate responsibility may have been less of a motive to discount chains than was the desire to lessen civil liability after several large chains had been sued by victims of gunshots by assailants who had purchased guns at those stores.

Blaming deep-pocketed businesses for the ills of the country, activists pressure the private sector to capitulate or undertake levels of aggressive self-defense unheard of three decades ago. This conflict was not merely the result of inadequate communication on the part of private sector organization. For that reason, issues management assumes that corporate philosophies and operating procedures may need to be overhauled to avoid the damaging constraints of public policy or to take advantage of business opportunities.

This brief review of the heritage of business and public policy will be expanded in Chapter 2. The glimpse provided here features the turbulent struggle between public and private interests that has fostered issues management. If businesses were free from criticism, they could act as they desire. They are often challenged to change how they operate to meet the expectations of many different groups. To participate in this process requires that issues managers learn the principles needed to guide the practice and become familiar with strategic prescriptions that can improve it.

Chapter 1 defines issues management by stressing how it supports strategic business planning. This chapter argues that issues management is the strategic use of issues analysis and strategic responses to help organizations make adaptations needed to achieve harmony and foster mutual interests with the communities in which they operate. It helps organizations grow and survive because it gives them another tool to maximize the opportunities and lessen the threats public policy trends have on their strategic business planning. This chapter and the remainder of the book address issues management from a corporate, private sector point of view, primarily because most research and commentary take that orientation. This has been the case because the primary focus of change has been on business practices. If companies are thought to be the problem, their role in the solution becomes a focal point of analysis. Despite attention to large companies, the principles of issues management can be applied to small business and nonprofit organizations as well as governmental agencies and activist groups. All organizations have a stake in public policy trends and outcomes. For instance, nonprofit hospitals were affected by policy changes raised by President Clinton's 1994 health plan proposals. Small businesses may not be able to engage in issue advertising, but they make rhetorical appeals in the appropriate forums for points of view on issues vital to their well-being.

Throughout this book runs the challenge Sethi (1977) called the *legiti-macy gap.* It results from the difference between what specific companies are thought to be doing and the expectations publics hold regarding those activities. The gap can result from differences of fact, value, and policy. The width of the gap, conceptualized in Figure 1.1, determines how strongly involved members of the public approve or disapprove of the company or other organization as being responsive to community interests (Kruckeberg & Starck, 1988).

This chapter reasons that large organizations cannot control issues and certainly should not be thought to dominate the public opinion process. By the time you have completed this chapter, you should be able to define issues management, see it as a vital part of the total management effort of organizations, and justify it as a process that fosters mutually beneficial relationships between organizations and involved publics.

What Is Issues Management?

Some people believe the answer to that question is the manipulation of issues to the advantage of large private sector organizations. A contrasting view recognizes that companies cannot manipulate issues to their interests for long, if at all. Savvy organizations use issues management to monitor issues, sharpen their strategic business plans, improve their operations, and communicate in ways intended to build and strengthen relationships with key publics.

This section keeps those activities central to a review of several definitions of issues management. The objective is to achieve the most accurate and embracing view of this organizational activity.

Is issues management a subfunction of public relations or an umbrella that encompasses it? How does issues management relate to strategic business planning? Is the function expected to reactively justify strategic planning, or is it vital to proactive strategic planning? In either case, the function cannot succeed without executive-level authority and budgetary support (Lukasik, 1981; Spitzer, 1979; Zraket, 1981).

Is issues management merely public relations revisited (Ehling & Hesse, 1983; Fox, 1983)? Is it a subfunction of public relations (Public Relations Society, 1987) or a program that companies use to improve their involvement in the public policy process (Public Affairs Council, 1978)? Is it an executive-level staff function *and* community-oriented sense of organizational culture that empower public relations by giving it greater involvement in corporate strategic business planning and management (Heath, 1988a; Heath & Nelson, 1986; Nelson & Heath, 1986)? Is it a new organizational discipline that

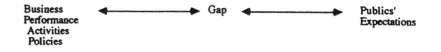

BASES OF GAP

Differences of fact
Differences of value
Differences of policy

Figure 1.1. Reconciling Business Performance and Publics' Expectations

features "public policy foresight and planning for an organization" (Ewing, 1987, p. 1)?

Is it "the organized activity of identifying emerging trends, concerns, or issues likely to affect an organization in the next few years and developing a wider and more positive range of organizational responses toward that future" (Coates, Coates, Jarratt, & Heinz, 1986, p. ix)? Or, as Hainsworth and Meng (1988) contended, does it give "senior management the means to intelligently participate in the public policy process" (p. 28)? No definition of issues management has achieved consensus nor has the discipline achieved its potential (Gaunt & Ollenburger, 1995).

How one defines issues management depends on preferences and prejudices. For instance, the Special Committee on Terminology of the Public Relations Society of America defined it as a public relations function: "systematic identification and action regarding public policy matters of concern to an organization" (Public Relations Society of America, 1987, p. 9). J. E. Grunig and Repper (1992) subordinated issues management to public relations, a function whereby practitioners respond to issues raised by key publics.

Definitions are most helpful when they specify the actions needed to engage in public policy activities (Hainsworth & Meng, 1988). Lauzen (1994) offered evidence that it is a management rather than a technician function. Processes typical of issues management take their rationale from the support they provide in defining and accomplishing the organization's strategic plan. This is not the activity of persons who are outside of the management cadre who otherwise support but do not guide the management function.

Efforts to define issues management must not lose sight of organizations' need to harmonize their interests with their stakeholders. As Ewing (1987) concluded, issues management "developed within the business community as an educational task aimed at preserving the proper balance between the legitimate goals and rights of the free enterprise system and those of society"

(p. 5). Issues management is a foresight discipline that can serve the needs of nonprofits, advocacy groups, and governmental agencies, all groups of people who assert their interests through public policy formation, mitigation, and adaptation. Thus, Ewing reasoned, "A corporation exists for the *optimization* of the satisfactions of its stakeholders" (p. 32).

Issues management is a means for linking the public relations function and the management function of the organization in ways that foster the organization's efforts to be outer directed and to have a participative organizational culture. Blending these functions is vital for organizations that seek harmonious relationships in an environment that is complex because of the number of publics and the variety of issues to be considered. Managing the response to these issues for decision making and strategic planning gives public relations personnel access to management (Lauzen & Dozier, 1994).

Public relations practitioners who fostered interest in issues management thought they could "expand the role of public relations beyond media relations and product publicity to a senior management problem-solving function critical to the survival of an organization" (Tucker, Broom, & Caywood, 1993, p. 38). In this way, it was designed as "the management process whose goals is to help preserve markets, reduce risk, create opportunities and manage image as an organization asset for the benefit of both an organization and its primary shareholders" (Tucker et al., 1993, p. 38). To this definition should be added "to the mutual benefit of its key stakeholders."

Issues management includes the identification, monitoring, and analysis of trends in key publics' opinions that can mature into public policy and regulatory or legislative constraint of the private sector. It involves the staff function that, along with technical and managerial personnel support, can develop a corporate or industry stance to be executed through strategic business plans and communication campaigns. No other corporate function more completely stresses the inseparability of ethical corporate behavior, public judgment, responsible production and delivery of goods and services, and internal and external attempts to inform and persuade targeted constituencies to gain their support. Issues management goes beyond communication with various constituencies. It can penetrate all operations. The underpinning principle of issues management is not to avoid legislation or regulation but to balance the interests of all segments of the community so that each enjoys the proper amount of reward or benefit in proportion to the cost of allowing industry free rein to impose its own operating standards.

The battle is not exclusively between companies and activists. Changed operating standards may result when one industry shifts the burden of solving a problem from itself to another, such as occurred when automobile insurance companies successfully lobbied for higher standards of car safety design. If cars are safer, people are less likely to suffer severe and costly injury, thereby reducing the cost to the insurance companies and shifting it to the automobile manufacturers. In addition to the concern for cost and profit, society is better if drivers and passengers are safer.

Regulatory and legislative intrusion may occur when an industry seeks to standardize and improve operating standards among its members. The rationale for this change is the desire to reduce the bad-apple effect of the worst performers being used by activists to characterize the operations of an entire industry. Although such efforts often have altruistic incentives, they also give competitive advantage to the businesses within the industry that are most prepared to meet the standards that they seek to impose on their competitors.

At times, public relations has featured the possibility of engineering consent (Bernays, 1955). Public relations was not expected to build relationships but to exploit them. It relied on publicity, press releases, and media relations and assumed that corporate image building depended on achieving maximum positive exposure in the press while avoiding negative attention. If critics opposed the way businesses operated, disagreement could be allayed if companies communicated their side effectively—more clearly and persuasively. This paradigm of public relations seemed committed to supporting the commercial activities through publicity efforts aimed at augmenting the impact of advertising. This view of public relations assumed that business problems were communication problems that would yield to communication solutions.

What replaced this model of public relations was a commitment to two-way communication, which J. E. Grunig (1989b, 1992a; J. E. Grunig & L. S. Grunig, 1989; J. E. Grunig & Hunt, 1984) refined into a normative two-way symmetrical model. Also, creation of the title "public affairs" led to the formation of the Public Affairs Council and the naming or renaming of corporate public relations departments to have a more powerful and authoritative, less puffery-oriented approach to external relationships. A third response was the formation of what some envisioned to be a new organizational and academic discipline: issues management.

All three efforts (normative two-way symmetrical public relations, public affairs, and issues management) were companion efforts to achieve similar ends but with different means. Depending on the preferences of each person discussing this issue, one of the three is likely to be featured as dominant. In each case, proponents of their version of the discipline realize that the end product must be an executive-level staff effort that can create harmony between the sponsoring entity and key stakeholder publics. That is the challenge, by whatever name.

Associating issues management with public affairs, the Public Affairs Council (1978) described it as "a program that a company uses to increase its knowledge of the public policy process and enhance the sophistication and effectiveness of its involvement in that process" (p. 1). The Council endorsed the now-standard issues management model that consists of (a) monitoring the public policy arena to determine what trends will demand a reorientation of corporate policy and communication process, (b) identifying those issues of greatest potential importance to the organization, (c) evaluating their operational and financial impacts through issues analysis, (d) prioritizing and establishing company policy positions by coordinating and assisting senior management decision making, (e) creating the company response from among a range of issue-change strategy options, and (f) implementing the plans through issue action programming.

Speaking as chairperson of the Issues Management Association, W. Howard Chase (1982) offered a widely quoted definition:

> Issues management is the capacity to understand, mobilize, coordinate, and direct all strategic and policy planning functions, and all public affairs/public relations skills, toward achievement of one objective: meaningful participation in creation of public policy that affects personal and institutional destiny. (p. 1)

Chase stressed the proactive aspect of issues management that "rejects the hypothesis that any institution must be the pawn of the public policy determined solely by others" (p. 2).

Maturing in his thinking, Chase (1984) defined issues management as issue identification, analysis, change strategy options, action programming, and evaluation of results.

> An issue change strategy option is a choice among carefully selected methods and plans for achieving long-term corporate goals in the face of public policy issues, a choice based on the expected effect of each method of employment, cost, sales, and profits. (p. 56)

Action programming entails the use of resources to gain the strategy option selected.

Stressing outcomes deliverable by issues management, Ewing (1987) defined it as "simply public policy research, foresight, and planning for an organization in the private sector impacted by decisions made by others in the public sector" (p. 18). It can help fill

> the policy hole in the center of corporate management, making it possible for the CEO and senior management to strategically manage their enterprise as a whole, as a complete entity capable of helping create the future and "grow" their company into it. (p. 18)

Its greatest contribution is gained by early and proactive efforts "to intervene consciously and effectively and participate early in the process, instead of waiting passively until the organization finds itself a victim at the tail end of the process" (p. 19).

Issues management entails efforts to achieve understanding and increase satisfaction between parties and to negotiate their exchange of stakes. It engages interlocking cultures that are in various states of compatibility and similarity. It fosters the interests of the stakeholders by helping an organization achieve its goals in a community of complementary and competing interests.

To achieve its potential, issues management must add value by allocating, defining, and distributing resources: human, financial, and material. It serves its sponsoring organization by engaging in a field in which each player seeks its own advantage. Although these competing and conflicting interests are such that all cannot be equally satisfied, issues management serves best when it assists in the planning, analysis, communication, and coalition-building efforts by which mutual interests are sought and appropriate resource allocation is achieved.

This section began by asking, what is issues management? The answer: It is the management of organizational and community resources through the public policy process to advance organizational interests and rights by striking a mutual balance with those of stakeholders. It supports strategic business planning and management by understanding public policy, by meeting standards of corporate responsibility expected by key stakeholders, and by using two-way communication to foster understanding and minimize conflict. It adapts products, services, or operations to policy or seeks to change policy to support products, services, or operations. It is not limited to media relations, customer relations, or government relations. It is engaged in strategic business planning options that may change operations, products, or services as well as communicate to establish mutual interests and achieve harmony with stakeholders. It is expected to keep the firm ethically attuned to its community and positioned to exploit, mitigate, and foster public policy changes as they relate to the corporate mission.

An Academic and Organizational Discipline: What Functions Does it Feature?

In response to pressures to constrain the prerogatives of companies, leading academics and practitioners seek to define the functions that are needed to correct this problem. Debates have refined the list of functions and the roles they play in the public policy process. Issues management does not occur in an organization that is not strategically planned to avoid unnecessary effects of public policy change or to use it to advantage its interests and those of its stakeholders (Heath, 1990). In addition to issue communication, issues management is part of organizational strategic planning, entails sophisticated issues monitoring and analysis, and needs to know how to strategically change to avoid being offensive to key publics.

Doubting that issues management was new, Ehling and Hesse (1983) surveyed Public Relations Society of America members. These researchers concluded that no new label or program beyond public relations or public affairs was necessary. According to Ehling and Hesse,

> Potential adopters saw "issue management" as a kind of everyday management that any or all managers could do, . . . construed as the relatively mundane business of being cognizant of "issues" that might have relevance to their organization or their office—and not much more. (p. 33)

Ehling and Hesse argued that issues management calls for nothing beyond the effective use of routine issues monitoring strategies (p. 33).

This survey relied on self-report responses from public relations personnel, and it focused narrowly on communication and issue monitoring. Thus, the data generated were flawed. First, public relations personnel have a strong incentive to report favorably on their activities. Second, issues management is not a function exclusive to public relations or public affairs personnel. A truer measure of the degree of innovation and adoption would be to ask department heads and key executives whether a comprehensive issues management program had been created and implemented, whether they had been trained to support it, and whether relevant planning efforts had been implemented at the department and executive levels.

Generating evidence that supported *and* contradicted Ehling and Hesse (1983), Buchholz (1982b) discovered that 91% of Fortune 500 companies had issues management programs. Leadership of these companies observed that such programs are extremely important (23.8%) or very important (50.0%). One indicator of executive support for the function was that the number of personnel assigned to it had increased by 47.1% during the 3 years prior to Buchholz's survey. Issues managers were responsible for identifying, tracking, analyzing, and prioritizing issues as well as formulating policy positions in response to them and implementing response strategies. A few respondents reported that issues management was vital to the long-range planning of their companies. Nearly 70% saw it as a function of growing importance. Approximately 40% believed that it would become part of corporate strategic planning. About 20% thought the future of issues management depended on whether the business-government climate continued to call for more regulation. Only 13% believed that issues management was a fad.

Post, Murray, Dickie, and Mahon (1983), in a survey of 1,001 large and medium-sized firms, discovered little evidence to confirm Ehling and Hesse's contention that practitioners routinely influence corporate planning. Part of this problem is that one half of all public affairs departments in major businesses were established in the 1970s. The influence public affairs exercised depended on four factors: (a) Advice is more influential when it focuses on the near-term rather than long-term issues. (b) The influence is greater in companies that are highly regulated and worry about their operating environments. (c) In companies that genuinely use long-term planning, public affairs is more vital than in companies that plan only for the short term. (d) Large companies rely more on public affairs than do small ones (Dickie, 1984). Among the many corporate communicators who complain that strategic planning often ignores public affairs is Bergner (1982), who blended the two functions, particularly for multinational businesses.

Internal politics related to each company's culture affected executives' willingness to redirect procedures and establish the matrix of key personnel necessary for an issues management program (Buchholz, 1982b). Failure by practitioners to be involved in corporate planning perpetuates their second-class status, particularly if they neglect environmental monitoring of potential issues and overly focus on media relations or legislative lobbying. Such individuals often fail to convert corporate officers to give more than lip service to issues management until a political threat or consumer controversy erupts. Capable professionals in finance, technical disciplines, and law often are called on to help prepare their firms to manage issues.

Rather than indicting the innovativeness of issues management, findings by Post et al. (1983) condemn executive recalcitrance and the role—or lack of one—played by many public affairs and public relations practitioners in the issues management process. Once issues management is associated with corporate strategic business planning and efforts to enhance corporate responsibility, it becomes distinguished from routine public affairs or public relations activities.

How issues management, public relations, and public affairs are viewed depends on two assumptions: (a) Organizations constantly struggle to adapt to their environment—both in terms of market and public policy forces. This adaptation requires that information be acquired and used along with wise evaluation of key publics' expectations to guide the organization's planning, management, and communication. (b) Public relations practitioners will be part of the dominant coalitions in organizations (J. E. Grunig & L. S. Grunig, 1989) only when they can influence strategic business planning and management in ways that enhance the bottom line (Ewing, 1987; Wartick & Rude, 1986). As we have seen during the wrenching period of downsizing, right sizing, and reengineering that characterized the 1980s and 1990s, any corporate function that could not contribute to the bottom line has been vulnerable.

This review suggests that issues management is not only public policy monitoring and analysis. Nor is it issues communication, such as issue advertising, community relations, or governmental relations. It requires that public policy issue discussions be incorporated into corporate strategic business planning and management. The lack of consensus regarding the term *issues management* is captured in Miller's (1987) observation: "Issue management isn't quite public relations. Neither is it government relations, nor public affairs, nor lobbying, nor crisis management, nor futurism, nor strategic planning. It embraces all of these disciplines, and maybe a few more" (p. 125). Issues management entails key, integrated functions that each organization needs to perform to profit through mutually beneficial stakeholder relations (*The corporate imperative,* 1982). Communication experts move into executive discussions as they help improve their organizations' ability to avoid criticism of their policies and actions and to take advantage of opportunities presented by public policy.

Perspectives such as these were made in response to critics of business policy and practices who gained influence during the tumultuous 1960s and 1970s by challenging the standards of business operations and creating the great era of reform. According to tradition, in 1977, W. Howard Chase coined the term *issue management,* which he designated as the new science. To recommend a new kind of corporate communication response to critics of business activities, Chase drew on his experience at American Can Company and on the lead of John E. O'Toole (1975a, 1975b) who may have coined the term *advocacy advertising.*

In accord with this trend, Bateman (1975) advised companies "to move from an information base to an advocacy position" in their responses to their critics and to build relationships with key publics (p. 5). This stance, he rationalized, was needed because "companies should not be the silent children of society" (p. 3). By 1976, terms such as *issue advertising* and *advocacy advertising* were being used in business publication discussions of the aggressive op-ed campaign made famous by Mobil Oil Corporation (Ross, 1976). At about this same time, the International Association of Advertising, in its global study of issues communication, urged adoption of the less contentious term *controversy advertising* (Barnet, 1975). Making the connection between advertising and issues, Dinsmore (1978) contended that "ideas could be sold like soap" (p. 16) but only if their presentation was complete and truthful.

Dozens of articles published in the late 1970s and early 1980s discussed the new role of corporate communication and the strategic responses companies needed to take to counter their critics. In September 1978, Kalman B. Druck, Chairman, Harshe-Rotman & Druck, Inc., told the Houston Chapter of Public Relations Society of America "that enormous opportunities await those who are willing to make the commitment, to apply professional management and public relations skills to the bitter confrontations industry is now facing" (p. 114).

In the 1970s, many advocates of issues management were communication specialists who worked for executives guided by the assumption that critics of business could be shouted down. This organizational function exhibited a business-is-sacred bias that featured issues advertising, a concept that produced a backlash (Ehrbar, 1978). In 1979, *Business Week* commented on this trend, featuring the political changes and the communication requirements: "The corporation is being politicized and has assumed another dimension in our society that it did not have as recently as 10 years ago." Consequently, "It is articulating its positions more clearly and urgently to government agencies, legislators, shareholders, employees, customers financial institutions, and critical audiences" ("The corporate image," 1979, p. 47). Critics such as Sethi (1976a, 1976b, 1977) strenuously argued that merely explaining the corporate point of view could never be efficacious. Companies that shout loudest often may deserve regulation most.

Sensitive to the limitations of a communication bias, some companies, such as Prudential Insurance Company of America (MacNaughton, 1976), institutionalized standards of corporate responsibility especially in their governmental relations programs (Bradt, 1972). Discussion of what companies do in the face of changing social issues increased managers' sensitivity to changing expectations that members of the public had regarding business practices (Heath, 1988a).

Although a communication paradigm dominated discussions of how companies could handle their critics, some executives advised early on that issues analysis needed to be incorporated into strategic business planning. William S. Sneath (1977), president of Union Carbide Corporation, said in 1977 that his company was using "scenario evaluation" as a means for projecting its business-planning efforts 20 years into the future. Public policy issues, such as environmentalism, were a vital part of the planning effort at Union Carbide. Sneath said that only time could judge

> our legacy not only in terms of the economic accuracy of our business planning but in the way we committed our best minds and our best intentions to meet the needs and aspirations of a free society in an increasingly interdependent world. (p. 199)

Although it overassumed the ability to predict long-range policy trends, his model of issues management recognized that slick issue advertising could not manipulate opinion and thereby manage issues.

Archie R. Boe (1979), CEO of Allstate Insurance Companies (1972-1982) and later president of Sears (1982-1984), created a Strategic Planning

Committee in 1977 and an Issues Management Committee in 1978. The two groups had interlocking memberships. The Issues Management Committee was chaired by a vice president who also was a member of the Strategic Planning Committee. As these examples demonstrate, issues management in its struggle for prominence does not rely exclusively on communication options; many leaders in the formation of the discipline recognized the need to integrate planning, public policy analysis, and business ethics along with advocacy communication.

In 1978, the Public Affairs Council advanced issues management in a pamphlet titled *The Fundamentals of Issue Management.* According to the council, "Issues management is a program which a company uses to increase its knowledge of the public policy process and enhance the sophistication and effectiveness of its involvement in that process" (p. 1). What were the functions required of issues management? The council listed these: "Identifying issues and trends, evaluating their impact and setting priorities, establishing a company position, designing company action and response to help achieve the position (e.g., communication, lobbying, lawsuits, and advertising, etc.), and implementing the plans" (p. 2). Communication was the heart of issues management, the Council thought. It proclaimed,

> Public affairs has increasingly come to mean not merely a response to change, but a positive role in the management of change itself—in the shaping of public policies and programs, and in the development of corporate activities to implement change constructively. (p. 2)

Sponsored by the Conference Board's Public Affairs Research Council, James K. Brown (1979) conducted a research project to determine how public affairs practitioners and corporate executives defined issues management. The study did not take the "good defense through communication" posture typical of Chase (1977) and O'Toole (1975a, 1975b). It offered its findings to help public affairs practitioners "and their colleagues in top management do a better job of planning" (Brown, 1979, p. ii). Rather than being limited to concerns regarding how issues mature into legislation or regulation, the study argued that issues management must be integrated and focused on the central task of helping the company—through its strategic management. What were its tasks, according to J. Brown (1979)? The answer: planning, monitoring, analyzing, and communicating.

What principle guides this activity? Strategic planning personnel need to spot, analyze, and know what can and cannot (should and should not) be done to communicate on public policy issues and how to adjust products and services to hostile environments as well as to take advantage of favorable ones. J. Brown (1979) reasoned that

> if management should accustom itself routinely to ask the full range of
> questions that ought to be asked about vital corporate decisions, taking into
> account all the relevant external environments as well as the internal environ-
> ment, this business of issues would become, properly, a non-issue. (p. 74)

No single issues management function can accomplish that goal. Many
functions are required, some of which require the expertise of public relations
practitioners, and the performance of which can strengthen the rationale for
including public relations in the dominant coalition of corporations.

The first calls for combining strategic business planning and issues
monitoring occurred in the mid-1970s. Strategic business planning and environmental scanning became partners—at least in the literature, if not in
practice. Typical of the state of strategic planning in the mid-1970s, Lorange
and Vancil (1976) did not include the public policy environment as vital to the
strategic planning process. In 1979, *Business Week* reported on the fledgling
trend by some companies to use environmental scanning to improve strategic
business plans and to alert line managers to changes in public sentiments
regarding operating procedures ("Capitalizing," 1979).

An early effort to identify the key functions of issues management
reasoned that it involved three activities: "issue identification, corporate
proaction, and the inclusion of public affairs issues in established decision-
making processes and managerial functions" (Fleming, 1980, p. 35). Business
professors, such as Fleming, led this innovation, and communication specialists and scholars joined later. Business faculty members, in particular Post
(1978, 1979) and Buchholz (1982b, 1985), produced seminal studies to
expose the need for companies to recognize the important role public policy
plays in their planning efforts and operations.

A recent milestone in this reasoning was the publication of *Issues Management and Strategic Planning* by Renfro (1993), a pioneer in the theory and
practice of issues management. His work centers on the factors that predict
how issues emerge and become worth considering. He stressed the need to
identify and monitor issues as preliminary to strategic planning. "The field of
issues management emerged as public relations or public affairs officers
included more and more forecasting and futures research in their planning and
analysis of policy" (p. 23). In this sense, "Issues management is an intelligence
function that does not get involved in the 'operations side' unless specifically
directed to do so" (p. 89). Despite its need to support business activities, this
function "is not closely connected to immediate operations and the bottom
line," and therefore, "It is difficult to determine the effectiveness and value of
an issues management capability" (p. 89).

As it has emerged, issues management is a reaction to activism and the
increasing intraindustry and interindustry pressures by corporations to define

and implement higher standards of corporate responsibility—as well as to debate in public what those standards should be. It encompasses *all* efforts corporations must make to create harmony with key players in their public policy arena—by sensing changing standards of the norms of business practice preferred by key publics, especially those that have become activists. Business leaders and faculty members have led the discussion of corporate responsibility. Early works by MacNaughton (1976) and Ackerman and Bauer (1976) considered the challenges of private sector adaptations to new operating standards. Efforts were made to understand the legislative, regulatory, and public opinion forces and to estimate what assumptions were preferred for early detection and proactive responses (Arcelus & Schaefer, 1982).

As this review demonstrates, issues management can be limited to a communication model or a commitment to high ethical standards, but leaders in the discipline have recognized the need to integrate strategic planning, public policy analysis, and communication (Marx, 1986). One of those leaders, Monsanto Corporation, has used issues management to determine which product lines are advisable in light of public policy trends (Fleming, 1980; Stroup, 1988). Describing Monsanto's contingency approach, Stroup (1988) observed: "Early knowledge of these trends would give the company more time to change negative attitudes toward business or to adapt business practices proactively if attitudes and expectations could not be swayed from the identified path" (p. 89). Thinking of this kind, demonstrating how issues management matured from a publicity activity to one involved in strategic business planning, is captured in Figure 1.2, which demonstrates the evolution of the discipline.

Proponents of issues management assert it is vital to strategic management in four key ways: (a) Systematic issues identification, scanning, monitoring, and analysis allows firms to intersect public opinion at formative stages. (b) Issues management helps organizations be proactive rather than reactive. (c) It supplies corporate executives with ample empirical and qualitative analysis to solve corporate planning problems. (d) Two-way communication can reach constituencies in a way that is collaborative and long range rather than short term. It is not limited to periodic press releases, media relations, and publicity strategies.

Issues management is a comprehensive and integrated program of planning, management, and communication. It may include public debate regarding what those standards should be. The program assumes that corporations must achieve harmony by influencing or accommodating to public policy stakeholders, although it never abandons the stewardship role organizations must play by asserting and defending their interests (Ackerman & Bauer, 1976; MacNaughton, 1976).

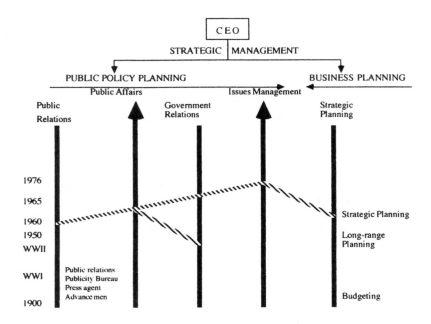

Figure 1.2. Evolution of Strategic Issues Management

Extending this viewpoint, Arrington and Sawaya (1984) claimed that the heart of issues management "is reconciliation of conflicting internal interests on public policy issues of strategic importance in order to make a coherent external advocacy" (p. 150). This activity requires analysis and planning of public affairs options that "should be viewed as analogous to corporate planning and research and development—as a strategic process to help realize the basic objectives of a company" (p. 158). Wartick and Rude (1986) claimed that issues management loses its identity and credibility when it is not positioned to implement comprehensive programs. It is most useful when it interlocks with strategic information management because corporate culture fosters the acquisition and use of information in strategic planning (Ansoff, 1980; Heath, 1991a).

A survey by Post, Murray, Dickie, and Mahon (1982) discovered that a critical phase in a company's effort to adjust to its environment is the decision to integrate a public affairs perspective into corporate planning and management. Of 400 public affairs personnel surveyed, 66% reported that they assisted in issues identification, monitoring, and analysis. The respondents provided information for the strategic business planning group and reviewed strategic plans to determine whether they were sensitive enough to social and political trends.

A workshop held in mid-1993 concluded that issues management has yet to reach its potential, for six reasons: (a) Executives worry that the effects of issues management programs are too long-term in a planning tradition in which management philosophy keeps executives focused on quarterly results and near-term solutions to long-term problems. (b) Much needs to be accomplished to refine the ability to quantify the impact of issues management on corporate bottom lines. (c) Communication is not the only function of issues management that often requires reactive and proactive corporate policy and practice changes to avoid collisions with public policy or to seize the opportunities it creates. (d) The discipline is not owned by public relations practitioners and can be thought of too narrowly as a means for achieving publicity or working with the media rather than concentrating on issues of law, corporate policy, strategic business planning, and technical operations changes as well. (e) It does not serve an organization adequately when it is not a corporate-level function that injects careful consideration of public policy planning options by seasoned senior corporate members involved in executive discussions. (f) Traditional public relations training and experience often leave practitioners too narrow in their visions of what they can offer to a company to think beyond communication solutions to problems that cannot yield to information exchange and messages designed for external publics (Tucker et al., 1993).

The issues management professional is faced with many challenges. At the moment, these experts wrestle with two imperatives: (a) Be sufficiently well educated in the interdisciplinary background that gives you the vision to see the public policy implications for an entire company, enterprise, or industry and (b) be persuasive based on a strong research foundation that convinces executive management of the hazards and opportunities that occur because of public policy and challenges to respond to community expectations (Ewing, 1987; Heath, 1988b; Tucker et al., 1993). Setting the goal of issues management, Robert L. Anderson (1982), former chairman and CEO of Atlantic Richfield Company, observed, "To command significant public support, business must do more than defend itself from attack. It must learn to reach out to society and to communicate and participate effectively with outside constituencies" (p. xv).

Does this call for organizations, primarily business, to work for mutual interests rather than narrow self-interest? Society regulates itself by two means, reasoned goodwill and law. Reasoned goodwill assumes that people who are committed to fostering trusting relationships can regulate their performance and judgments in ways that enhance rather than degrade the quality of the community. When reasoned goodwill fails, laws are passed and regulations are formed to control the behavior and shape the judgment of persons who cannot or will not conform to the reasonable expectations of the other members of the community. Issues management is an organizational tool that can be used to ascertain, alter, and adapt to the standards of reasoned goodwill and to form appropriate laws and regulation that achieve harmony within each community. It is not a means by which private sector entities can control society to their own narrow ends. Why? Because too many players have too much vested interest and are too sophisticated to allow that to happen. An array of players exerts influence through corporations, nonprofit organizations, governmental offices, and activist, advocacy groups—these are the policy rhetors of the present and future.

As Ewing (1987) concluded, "Issues management is about power" (p. 1). Organizations, as the collective expression of individual interests, engage in reward-loss analysis regarding the expediency of opposing or yielding to power pressures from stakeholders who can impose sanctions. The equation works like this: Assuming accuracy of understanding between the parties in contention with one another but suffering an unchangeable difference in evaluation, companies, regulators, or activist groups have the option of exerting influence or opposing the influence efforts of others. Issues management serves organizations when it assists executives to foster the bottom line by enhancing the quality of relationships with stakeholders in a power arena.

In an address to the Issues Management Association describing the consequences faced by Nestlé Corporation as a result of its controversial marketing of baby formula in developing nations, Rafael D. Pagan, Jr. (1983) reasoned, "For business, the cost of social awareness programs is great, but the cost of ignoring the outside world is greater." He proposed that "issues managers can help instill social awareness into a business" (p. 2). As executives realize the cost savings of monitoring and managing issues before they explode, issues management gains popularity. This is sage advice from the representative of a company that had blundered in its marketing efforts and thereby incurred international condemnation and product boycotts.

The key concern of issues management is policy. Although the opinions of various stakeholding publics are important, they can dramatically affect the company when they are translated into public policy. However, policy need not be created and implemented by one of the branches of government to be public policy. As Buchholz (1988) defined the concept, "Public policy is a specific course of action taken collectively by society or by a legitimate representative of society, addressing a specific problem of public concern, that reflects the interests of society or particular segments of society" (p. 53).

Not only is issues management interested in public policy but also the creation and implementation of policy internal to an organization. Internal policy should meet or exceed key public expectations if the organization is going to avoid suffering the consequences of a legitimacy gap. Based on the discussion reviewed in this section, issues management consists of four core functions: Engaging in smart business and public policy planning, playing tough defense and smart offense, getting the house in order, and scouting the terrain to gain early warning about troublesome issues (Heath & Cousino, 1990).

AMOCO and the EPA: Partners Instead of Foes

Can issues management ease the friction between businesses and their stakeholders? Issues management, as is true for all other functions related to public relations and public affairs, draws its rationale from the search for truth as the foundation for advancing community interests (Kruckeberg & Starck, 1988). It serves society best when it is used to discover facts and analyze premises and values regarding community expectations, to support strategic business planning. Issues management employs negotiation and collaborative decision making as key tools. Issues managers have learned that no corporate communication effort alone can protect business operations from unwanted intrusions by outside stakeholders seeking to impose their standards of community responsibility on businesses.

A central issue in our political economy is how to regulate private sector activities, not whether they should be regulated. Of related concern is the extent to which regulators and activists, or company managers for that matter, know the best ways to regulate business activities. The following case study demonstrates how organizational change, not communication alone, is needed to manage issues. The case stresses the importance of cooperative dialogue. It examines how AMOCO Oil Company engaged in a regulatory partnership with the Environmental Protection Agency (EPA) to decide the best way to operate a chemical plant so as to achieve environmental responsibility by lowering undesirable emissions without suffering excessive costs of misregulation. Although the project fell short of promise, it set a useful tone for cooperation.

The lesson learned: A joint, cooperative research effort could enhance the regulation of some parts of the plant that would have been underregulated and reduced the regulation of other aspects of the plant that would have been overregulated. This partnership between AMOCO and the EPA revealed that desired pollution reduction could be achieved for $11 million rather than the $41 million that would have been required if EPA guidelines had been followed without question. The benefits were even greater amounts of reduced emissions and cost savings.

How can petrochemical plants be regulated to reduce harmful emissions without adding undue cost to the final product? That question is at the heart of the controversy between petrochemical companies and state and federal environmental regulatory agencies. The question has profound implications for the political economy of our nation, especially as domestic companies confront competition from less strictly regulated competitors in the global economy. This question also underscores a point often ignored by key publics, such as knee-jerk activists who believe in the inherent good of regulation and members of the public who do not realize that they, as consumers, always pay for the cost of regulation as part of the price of consumer products.

The joint research effort began, reported Solomon (1993b), with a chance meeting of old acquaintances, one of whom worked for the EPA and the other for AMOCO. In conversation, they agreed that they would enjoy reevaluating the regulatory assumptions and guidelines used by EPA. The goal was to determine whether the guidelines achieved environmental protection in the most reasonable manner. The personal rapport and enthusiasm for the project were strained as the persons proposed a joint research project to their respective managements. Animosity, the product of years of wrangling between the industry and the EPA, led to distrust. Industry believed regulators lacked the expertise required to accomplish their job, and regulators assumed industry to be infinitely willing to stonewall to protect their operating procedures. AMOCO officials feared that if EPA officials were given free access to the plant operations, they would find many problems and areas of complaint, thereby leading to additional fines and increased regulation.

Finally, the project, focusing on AMOCO's Yorktown plant, began to come together. One of the first stages was the request by AMOCO that EPA stipulate that the study could not result in changed regulation, altered permits, or fines from violations due to oversights. EPA responded that it could offer no such shield. Tense discussions of regulatory practices and plant operations led to the profound realization that the two sides of the controversy did not speak the same language. Both sides had different terms for key pieces of equipment and operating processes. They realized that regulatory guidelines result from generalizations that may not achieve what they are intended to do when applied to a specific plant. Although regulations assume that all plants are the same, they are not. A final realization was that EPA does not measure plant performance based on emissions but on compliance with EPA standards, regardless of whether they achieve desired reductions and protect the environment. Regulatory inspection is conducted by individuals or teams who are trained to do nothing more than follow checklists. Surveillance of plant compliance focuses on the operations of parts of each plant and never views it holistically.

These realizations gave both parties an incentive to engage in the joint project. One motive each party had for engaging in the joint project was to prove itself right and its counterpart wrong. Another incentive, more wholesome, was to learn how to regulate plants properly. Thus, the project began and lasted for 4 years. One result was the discovery that a $41 million treatment process, routinely expected of all plants and installed in many, was ineffective; it was based on outdated data and regulatory assumptions. Soon, the EPA representatives realized that they did not know as much as they thought they did about regulating a petrochemical plant. Also discovered was the fact that a source of emissions had gone unnoticed and therefore unregulated. For an expenditure of $11 million, the joint research team agreed that toxic emissions could be properly reduced. The company could save $30 million, and the EPA enjoyed the success of having a more environmentally friendly plant. One other benefit was the potential rapport that could build between the research members: A spirit of teamwork displaced distrust and suspicion. The project never matured as designed, but it tantalizes us with possibility.

This case exemplifies the need for dialogue and collaborative decision making, the benefits of incorporating public policy issue analysis into strategic business planning, the importance of two-way communication, and the fact that the issue was one that required changes in the way organizations did business. These functions are the heart and soul of issues management.

 Strategic Business Planning and Issues Management

Issues management cannot have full impact if it is not part of the strategic business planning process. This section explains the strategic planning process and demonstrates how issues management can enhance that process by tailoring it to the public policy arena.

Describing planning trends, J. Brown (1979) observed,

> Ten years ago, a prominent consultant has stated, 80 percent of planning was concerned with what management wanted, 20 percent with how the world affected the company; now the figures are reversed—or at least ought to be. Hyperbole perhaps; but the trend is unmistakable, and doubtless irreversible. (p. 3)

Although 20 years old, this observation is not out of date. Its advice is relevant today because of the increased presence of regulation and legislation in private sector activities. As well as creating constraints, public policy promotes business revenue and generates initiatives as well. This section explains the value-added potential of issues management.

Strategic management entails the ability of an organization (whether profit making or nonprofit) to generate the revenue it needs to survive and grow. Management is the strategic acquisition and use of human and financial resources to create mutually beneficial relationships with stakeholders and stakeseekers. This planning process consists of delineating that complex series of independent and dependent variables that lead to the final planning objective of the organization, that dependent variable that is the product of all other variables, the acquisition and maintenance of resources. That planning model can guide the efforts of strategic business planning and management regardless of whether the organization is profit making or is not for profit. Each organization exists to the extent that it generates and wisely uses revenue.

As captured in Figure 1.3, corporate strategic planning is the complex and creative process of goal setting and strategy selection, whereby a business seeks to optimize profits or any other organization seeks to maximize its resource acquisition and use, including efforts to minimize the interference of stakeholders in the strategic use of those resources. Strategic planning consists of (a) defining an organization's mission, (b) setting the objectives that must be accomplished to achieve the mission, (c) engaging in tactical programming and budgeting to accomplish the objective, (d) managing resources during the period required to achieve the objectives, and (e) monitoring progress and making adjustments during the implementation of the strategic plan as required by situational analysis of the circumstances that impinge on it. Plans require different time frames; some are completed in 2 to 3 years, whereas others require 10 to 15 years. All matters flow from the corporate mission and strategic business plan, as organizations work to influence, adjust to, and take advantage of market competition and the public policy environment.

Strategic planning entails knowing short-term and predicting long-term trends and conditions. Such knowledge is achieved by conducting situational analysis, estimating strengths and weaknesses of the organization and the industry vis-à-vis marketplace and public policy forces, and engaging in creative decision making and resource allocation intended to accommodate to or exploit the situation. All of this involves developing, repairing, and strengthening stakeholder relations.

In conjunction with other staff and line positions, issues management—as does all of strategic planning—requires executive functions and decisions. Issues management needs to engage in decisions at the executive level, at the business strategy level, and at the functional level of operations. Each level has its unique issues management and strategic planning challenges (Hax & Majluf, 1991). Each level is subject to changes created by market and public

Figure 1.3. Integrating Strategic Planning and Issues Management

policy forces that pose constraints—and opportunities (Buchholz, 1988). How the mission is achieved depends on corporate and business planners' ability to formulate strategies. At the corporate level, these strategies are broad and conceptual. The strategies are more specific at the business and function levels. In conjunction with the formulation of a corporate mission and action plan, a corresponding plan is needed at each business and function level. Lower level plans are designed to support the upper level ones. Higher level plans provide guidance for lower level plans. Each set of plans is budgeted based on its cost in support of the total hierarchy of plans and objectives.

Stressing its role in planning, Arrington and Sawaya (1984) concluded that "issues management is a process to organize a company's expertise to enable it to participate effectively in the shaping and resolution of public issues that critically impinge upon its operations." They see this function as a complement to public affairs that is often "confined to reactive, 'fire-fighting' conduct." Because it is inseparable from basic business concerns, issues management "is simply never unrelated to bottom-line consequences" (p. 148). Therefore, Arrington and Sawaya proposed that issues management should consist of "three concurrent activities: foresight, policy development, and advocacy." Foresight involves identification, monitoring, analyzing, and prioritizing issues. But it "is neither futurism nor forecasting; it is pragmatic, recurring judgment about external factors critical to company success" (p. 149). Policy development, they believed, is "the routine 'heart' of issues management." It requires reconciling "conflicting internal interests on public policy issues of strategic importance in order to make a coherent external advocacy" (p. 150). The final function, advocacy, includes communication efforts used to reach targeted audiences and achieve campaign goals. In all of its facets, these authors reasoned, issues management supports strategic planning: "Strategic planning must ensure that various operating company plans are mutually consistent. Policy development in issues management must resolve differences among operating divisions on key public policy issues" (p. 153).

Strategic planning functions include "anticipating, researching and prioritizing issues; assessing the impact of issues on the organization; recommending policies and strategies to minimize risk and seize opportunities; participating and implementing strategy, and evaluating program impact" (Tucker et al., 1993, p. 38). One major professional challenge to issues managers is to "reposition issues management as a bridge between public relations and strategic planning with an eventual evolution to the planning function" (Tucker et al., 1993, p. 39).

The planning process is invigorated by functions that issues management performs: (a) Anticipate, analyze, and prioritize issues; (b) help develop an organizational position on each vital issue; (c) identify key publics and influential persons whose support are vital to the public policy issue; and (d) identify desired behaviors of publics and influential persons. These functions support each organization's mission (Tucker & Trumpfheller, 1993). Broadly applied, these functions can empower communication specialists. Narrowed only to communication functions, it falls short of being a management activity vital to strategic planning and operations. Again, those who want to be issues managers need to engage in smart planning, scout the terrain, get the house in order, and enact tough defense and smart offense.

Strategic business planning requires analysis and foresight of trends in the political economy that shape the business and public policy environments. The political economy expresses the value premises that comprise the ideology of each society and its microcosms. It reflects market trends and economic well-being of the members of society. It is an expression of policy guidelines regarding what corporate practices are acceptable and what are not. The political economy defines what players, whether in business trends or in policy formation, shape markets and public policy. The political economy defines the issues that confront each organization as a challenge or an opportunity.

Based on recent trends in this country, public and market policies tend to be based on one or more of the following issue motivators: security, equality, environmental quality, and fairness (Heath, 1988a). Security is a measure of the extent that business operations, products, and services are believed to pose intolerable risks for those who come into contact with them. Equality is a judgment of the extent to which persons are treated the same, for instance, as defined in terms of civil rights. Environmental quality is a value judgment on preferences regarding standards typically associated with environmental regulation. Fairness is an estimate of the value received for what is given in exchange; for instance, a service (such as the cost of electricity) can be thought to be too expensive. All people, according to this set of motivators, could be treated unfairly by the pricing of products or services even though each customer would be treated equally. Reducing issues to their essence helps persons engaged in issues monitoring and analysis. They become part of strategic planning and give a measure by which to estimate the basis of problem recognition.

Concerns connected to these motivators are the heart of the legitimacy gap (Sethi, 1977). The gap is the extent to which key publics and other stakeholders differ with corporate entities regarding what constitutes sufficient security, equality, fairness, or environmental sensitivity. Trouble or opportunity can result when key publics believe that a problem arises from the difference between what exists and what is expected. This gap can demand a corrective communication campaign or changes in business operations needed to mitigate or take advantage of the difference. These options are at the heart of the strategic business planning process that, if applied properly, obtains and uses information and judgment in ordinary and turbulent situations.

If planning is properly executed in normal times, it lays a foundation for unexpected events in turbulent times. As Renfro (1993) summarized,

> The prime tasks of strategic management are to understand the current and
> future operating environment, define organizational mission and goals, identify options, evaluate and implement strategies to achieve the mission and
> goals, and evaluate actual performance—to lead the organization with a vision
> of the future. (p. 57)

Mission and Vision Statements

Mission and vision statements express how each organization is positioned in its environment. Of special interest is its place among its competitors: its marketplace, its organizational character as an expression of its culture, and standards of corporate responsibility. "The corporate *mission* is the purpose or reason for the corporation's existence" (Hunger & Wheelen, 1993, p. 14). The statement is intended to differentiate each organization from all others. "A well-conceived mission statement defines the fundamental, unique purpose that sets a business apart from other firms of its type and identifies the scope of the business's operations in terms of products offered and markets served" (Hunger & Wheelen, 1993, p. 15). A corporate mission is a common thread or unifying theme; "those corporations with such a common thread are better able to direct and administer their many activities" (Hunger & Wheelen, 1993, p. 15). Mission statements translate into objectives by which results of the organization's activities are assessed. The statement is most serviceable when it allows for empirical measures of how well the mission and vision are accomplished. In the judgment of Bowman (1990), mission statements should reflect the "claims of relevant stakeholders" (p. 6) and express key company and community attitudes, such as those regarding growth, innovation, and quality. Issues managers are challenged to bring to bear on these discussions the sociopolitical and public policy factors.

Environmental-Situational
Position Assessment

Issues managers are expected to help assess the value assumptions and operant principles that shape the expectations of stakeholders who also influence standards of corporate responsibility and accountability that differentiate rewardable from punishable actions. Such analysis should be conducted by looking for the kinds of changes initiated through public policies that can increase a firm's cost of doing business. This approach to environmental scanning stresses the importance of being vigilant to forces, primarily those of the public policy arena, that can affect how firms do business. Situational analysis should search for threats and opportunities created by public policy forces. "Situational analysis requires that top management attempt to find a strategic fit between external opportunities and internal strengths while working around external threats and internal weaknesses" (Hunger & Wheelen, 1993, p. 157; Thomas, 1984).

Issues analysis must not only be sensitive to potential effects of public policy on the organization's policy and operations but it also needs to look for market advantage. The most important counseling that can be done by issues managers is to offer advice on community opinion and public policy trends. Of interest are trends that are likely to (a) constrain current organizational policy and thereby increase operating costs; (b) pose strategic advantage for organizations that can seize the opportunity to change policies and operations, thereby offering new products or services, reducing costs, and making other strategic business alterations; (c) offer options for improving relationships with key stakeholders; and (d) provide new means for fostering community interests.

Situational analysis needs to determine which stakeholders think the operations and policies of the organization are legitimate. Central to situational assessment is the image or reputation of the organization. In this sense, image is a group's attitude toward an organization (its officials, personnel, policies, operations, products, and services). This attitude is a composite of the beliefs (subjective probabilities) that the organization is associated with certain attributes and the evaluative valence (positive or negative) of those attributes. Such evaluations are basic to predictions that stakeholders will act favorably toward or against the organization in exchange for what is thought to be actions that reward or harm the stakeholder (Ajzen & Fishbein, 1980; Fishbein & Ajzen, 1975). Part of image is an assessment of how well it meets stakeholders' expectations; another consideration is the extent that it favorably differentiates the organization from others, especially those in competition for the same resources (Bowman, 1990). As Renfro (1993) observed, "The issues management system provides a forum for input throughout the organization into the policy and strategy development process" (p. 95).

Stakeholder Identification
(Allies-Supporters and Opponents)

Stakeholders are any persons or groups that hold something of value that can be used as rewards or constraints in exchange for goods, services, or organizational policies and operating standards. A *stake* is anything—tangible or intangible, material or immaterial—that one person or group has that is of value to another person or group. Issues managers are expected to identify key stakeholders, ascertain the quality of relationship between them and the organization, and determine what can be done to enhance that relationship. The quality of relationships predicts that stakes will be granted in support of the organization or used to punish it.

Activist publics: Collectivities that band together to increase stakeholder leverage

Intraindustry players: Other members of the industry

Interindustry players: Members of other industries

Potential activist publics: Persons, identifiable by demographics or opinions, who are likely to become activists if they recognize their self-interests are harmed or helped by actions of an organization

Customers: Persons and entities that exchange stakes for goods and services

Employees: Persons who exchange time, knowledge, and skills for financial reward

Legislators: Persons who create law or ordinance that prescribes which actions are rewardable or punishable

Regulators: Persons who implement law and ordinance by setting performance standards

Judiciary: Persons who interpret laws and ordinances

Investors (and other financial supporters, such as philanthropic donors to nonprofit operations): Individuals and entities that offer financial support for enterprises

Neighbors: Individuals who live in proximity to organizations and whose interests may be positively or negatively affected by operations in the vicinity

Media: Reporters, editors, and news directors who are expected to understand, report, and comment on issues and events

Stakeholder Analysis

Stakeholder analysis requires knowledge of the organization and its position in society. It requires mature judgment regarding the stakes various groups hold, their significance to the organization, the willingness of the groups to grant or withhold them, and the conditions under which the stakes will be given or withheld. As Freeman (1984) concluded, "One analysis of the stakeholder approach is that it spreads the traditional PR [public relations] role among every manager responsible for formulating strategic programs, where multiple stakeholders must be taken into account" (p. 221). Issues managers are expected to participate in these strategic management processes and "to scan the environment for new issues and new stakeholders and to bring these to the attention of the business unit managers responsible for unit performance" (p. 221). Stakeholder analysis demands the ability to determine where parties agree and disagree in terms of what they believe to be facts regarding an issue and the evaluation of it (whether negatively or positively as well as critical or trivial). To gain insights into the dynamics of stakeholder participation in public policy and market arenas, issues managers need to understand the trends that issues follow as well as the factors that affect those trends. This analysis requires the recognition that how stakeholders allot their financial and policy stakes has short-term and long-term consequences on the organization's ability to achieve its mission given its resources. One treatment of issues management in strategic planning recommends

> formally assigning people or groups within an organization the responsibility for the analysis of particular issues and the development of responsive strategies. Issues are specific trends and events within information-need areas that have a high level of immediacy and potential impact. (Aaker, 1992, p. 126)

Issues identification: Determining whether a problem or concern, a contestable point, exists that offers threats or opportunities for the organization's accomplishment of its strategic plan and mission

Issues scanning: Watching and searching for issues that can affect the organization

Issues monitoring-tracking: Observing the development of key issues by being sensitive to their duration, salience, and progress, as well as the fervor associated with them, and human and material resources that foster their continuation

Issues analysis: Diagnosing the argumentative structure of issues and under-standing that players are taking a position on the issue and why, knowing facts and premises they use to draw conclusions on the issue. Issues analysis entails estimating the probability of an issue's occurrence and impact on the organiza-tion.

Issues prioritization: Determining which issues have the greatest potential as opportunities or threats to the organization

Business-Economic Trends and Forces

Although other members of the executive cadre are likely to have equal or greater expertise to monitor and analyze business and economic trends and forces, issues managers must understand those forces. They need to examine how shifts in policy can affect the acquisition and allotment of human and financial resources as well as shape markets and competitive advantage. They should help formulate policy changes to support the acquisition and use of financial and human resources.

Public Policy Trends and Forces

In cooperation with executives, staff members, and operating personnel, issues managers monitor and analyze public policy trends to determine how shifts in norms, values, and legislative or regulatory codes offer market opportunities or threats. Focal points of this analysis are governmental bodies (legislative, regulatory, and judicial), industry policy bodies (typically trade associations), activist groups, academic and scholarly bodies and associations, and journalistic reporting and editorial agendas. As policy is refined by persons who are members of identifiable organizations, it goes through iterations that allow issues managers the opportunity to calculate the oppor-tunities and constraints that it poses. The change in policy can be pressed by the organization as well as by other groups—governmental, activist, or indus-try. Such options become addressed in the formation of the organization's public policy plan.

Strategy Formulation

The organization can enhance its economic gain and minimize its costs by looking for advantage, points of leverage, either by continuing operations and altering them. Strategy formulation should be based on objectives derived from mission and organizational self-assessment and be positioned through situation analysis. Mission statements are implemented by the formulation of objectives, the creation of strategies, and the use of programs to achieve the strategies (Hunger & Wheelen, 1993). One of the most important functions of issues management at this point in the strategic planning process is to comprehend and voice the standards of corporate responsibility that prevail in the community.

Market-Driven Decisions
in Strategic Planning

Some of each organization's planning is cast in response to market and other economic trends. (The following list is illustrative rather than complete.)

Undertake, abandon, or modify a product or service.

Target new markets for a product or service or abandon current ones.

Increase or downscale quality of a product or service.

Diversify or consolidate operations or holdings.

Change methods of acquiring financing to enhance economic advantage.

Change resource allocation or use.

Adapt to changing tastes (attitudes that have market impact).

Change vendors as a result of price or value.

Change labor practices as a result of market forces and employment trends.

Change operating procedures to become more profitable.

Public Policy-Driven Decisions
in Strategic Planning

Planning centers on strains and advantages created by the public policy environment. It may be a consequence of following or leading opinion or public policy trends or satisfying stakeholder expectations. (The following list is illustrative, not complete.)

Take a public communication stance on key policy issues.

Engage in actions to create, change, or defeat legislation or regulation.

Change operations and other market-driven decisions to adapt to public policy trends.

Change mission to adapt to or take a leadership role in public policy issues.

Change image to adapt to public policy trends.

Change operating standards (corporate responsibility) to adapt to public policy issues.

Alter employee performance criteria and procedures to adapt to public policy issues.

Change product or service lines to adapt to public policy issues and standards of liability or public expectations.

Change resource use in response to availability, cost, and prevailing attitudes of key publics or public policy.

Reassess and alter planning assumptions to conform to changes in priorities and definitions of premises fundamental to the political economy.

Change vendors as a result of public policy.

Change methods of acquiring financing as a result of public policy.

Change labor practices as a result of public policy trends.

Stakeholder Relationship Decisions in Strategic Planning

The desire and effort to build solid, long-term, and mutually beneficial relationships with stakeholders should drive the strategic planning process. This planning seeks to create, strengthen, repair, or build stakeholder relationships.

Ascertain and work to achieve mutual interests with stakeholders.

Engage in communication campaigns to redefine or to reassert company image to demonstrate conformance to stakeholder expectations.

Foster constituent relationships with stakeholders based on mutual interests.

Strategy Implementation Through Tactical Programming and Budgeting

A strategic plan has little meaning and no chance of success until tactics have been selected and budgeted. The *strategic business plan* comes to life through the allocation of resources to generate and wisely use revenue to benefit the organization and its stakeholders. Business plans are sensitive to standards of operations that are shaped in the public policy arena. Examples of these standards include liability, financing options, service quality, personnel requirements, and import-export procedures. Public policy changes are created by dramatic fluctuations in the economy as well as by legislative initiatives of key groups. Policies may occur due to actions at the federal, state, county, and municipal levels. These changes pose threats to current and planned activities as well as open opportunities.

A counterpart to the strategic business plan, the *strategic public policy plan,* entails the allocation of resources to create, change, take advantage of, mitigate, or defeat public policies through legislation, regulation, or litigation. This plan is a tactical option to engage in governmental relations to help create a climate favorable to the organization's strategic business plan while seeking to advance the interests of the stakeseekers and stakeholders of the organization.

A third plan, the *strategic communication plan,* becomes meaningful when resources are allocated to reach key publics with properly designed messages to meet these publics' needs to understand and formulate appropriate opinions and behaviors in the mutual interests of all parties. This plan is a tactical option to foster agreement and understanding of the facts, values, and policies vital to the organization's strategic business plan. The objective is to communicate openly and honestly with the intent of building harmony with interested parties in ways that lead them to cognitively and materially support the organization's efforts to achieve its business plan.

If one of the major strains in its environment is the legitimacy gap with its stakeholders, each organization needs a *strategic management of operations plan* that calls for an allocation of resources to lessen that gap. This plan requires allocations to accomplish several refinements. One requirement is to constantly refine standards of corporate responsibility. Organizations should consider in their strategic management the advantage to be gained by creating and maintaining long-term, mutually beneficial relationships. They are wise to use training and development programs to help employees achieve standards of social responsibility. As standards are ascertained, they need to be communicated to employees and other key publics. Operating units need to engage in issues management. To do this, they need to establish and implement controls to prevent other functions, such as marketing and advertising, from creating stakeholder relationship problems, such as over-promising the attributes of products or services in ways that cannot be met, making untrue product or service claims, adapting to market or policy forces in ways that offend the standards of corporate responsibility held by key publics.

Strains occur not only from what the entire organization does but also from actions by its operating units. For this reason, executives need *strategic development of unit missions and strategic plans.* What each unit does must support the corporate goals and mission (Hax & Majluf, 1991). To do this, each unit must create mission statements that specify the role it plays in the firm. Cognizant of the corporate strategic plan and in conjunction with strategic plans of other departments, staff and operating units need to develop their own strategic plans and determine how to achieve them through operations and policies. Based on how many resources each unit needs to support its strategic plan, budgets are developed and implemented. Without doubt, unit plans are enhanced by being integrated into the principles of the entire organization. Crucial to this planning effort is consideration of the advantages to be gained as well as the constraints to be avoided by assuring that unit plans conform to the organization's sense of corporate responsibility and support for its issues management effort. For instance, research and development efforts can be used to improve services to meet changing or solidifying standards of corporate responsibility. Or marketing plans need to be sensitive to how product or service claims meet or exceed expectations of stakeholders and do not offend the standards of corporate responsibility held by key publics.

The strategic public policy plan entails use of governmental relations to enhance the legislative and regulatory arenas for the organization and its stakeseekers and stakeholders. In the creation and implementation of this plan, the organization has several leverage points, times in events when changes can be affected in legislation and regulation. Efforts can be made to keep an issue from becoming a legislative matter by lessening friction with stakeholders through improving the organization's corporate responsibility performance; by becoming more open, honest, and competent in its communication; and by litigating issues. In a similar fashion, the organization can generate and foster legislative and regulatory change. A key strategic planning assumption is that if governmental policy can affect how the organization does business, then a plan needs to be created and implemented to foster governmental support for the organization's activities in ways that create or maintain harmony with its constituents.

Performing Strategic Adjustment and
Stakeholder Relationship Development

The adjustments and tactical shifts used by an organization need to be constantly adjusted to meet the changing needs and desires of the stakeholders as well as changes in the organization's mission and vision. Strategic management assures that operations and communication efforts are devoted to determining which stakeholder relationships are sound or need development, either by changed operations or enhanced communication. Stakeholder interests are likely to be at odds with one another, in varying degrees. One role of issues management is to open the organization to stakeholders so that their opinions can be ascertained and analyzed for implications regarding changes in operations, policies, or messages. Stakeholders are likely to have interests that are at odds with one another. For instance, investors like the organization to maximize its profits, an interest that may be at odds with environmental activists or consumer groups that oppose certain approaches to the generation of profit. Issues management is expected to reconcile these conflicts to the extent possible within current market and public policy forces.

Achieving Control by Evaluating the
Implementation of the Strategic Business Plan

Organizations set a vision and determine what objectives and tactics are
needed to achieve that vision. Constant monitoring centered on key measures
can determine whether tactics are achieving the plan. These measures need to
address the success of the total plan and its successful implementation by
levels and units: Applying a management-by-objectives model, tempered with
a commitment to the fostering of mutual interest, assessment entails the generation of empirical data to determine whether resources expended in the
implementation process were sufficient to achieve the goals and whether
the goals were met. Analysis also needs to be qualitative. It must assess the
quality of stakeholder relationships. Success is measured by the extent to
which stakeholders reward the organization's policies by granting them support or oppose those policies and work to constrain or redirect the organization
to alternative standards.

Issues managers can provide vital counseling at each point in the strategic
planning process. As Heath and Cousino (1990) have reasoned, the key is to
engage in smart strategic business planning, enact tough defense and smart
offense, get the house in order, and scout the terrain. These issues management
strategies can be charted across function and over a sequence of events (see
Table 1.1).

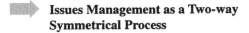 **Issues Management as a Two-way
Symmetrical Process**

This chapter is devoted to defining and exploring the functions required for
issues management. These functions are most useful to executive management
when they are brought into play as early as possible, while they can take
advantage of or correct the organization's position in relationship to its
stakeholders. In this effort,

> Public relations is most likely to contribute to effectiveness when the senior
> public relations manager is a member of the dominant coalition where he or
> she is able to shape the organization's goals and to help determine when
> external publics are most strategic. (L. E. Grunig, J. S. Grunig, & W. P. Ehling,
> 1992, p. 86)

TABLE 1.1 Integrating the Stages of the Monitoring, Planning, and Communication Functions

Monitoring Options	Planning Options	Communication Options
1. Identify stakeholders and stakes (mutual interests and points of conflict or disagreement).	1. Develop corporate and unit missions and goals.	1. Establish communication goals.
2. Scan or monitor public policy environment.	2. Integrate issues management into business planning and management.	2. Select target audiences, and engage in collaboration with key publics.
3. Analyze issues and determine issue priorities.	3. Select and structure issues personnel.	3. Select and refine message content and issue position.
4. Identify facts, premises, conclusions.	4. Budget for issues management.	4. Design messages.
5. Audit communication campaign.	5. Apply monitoring to revise code of social responsibility.	5. Select channels and communication venues— mediated, interpersonal, collaborative.
	6. Incorporate public policy issues into corporate planning.	6. Implement campaign and collaborative decision making.
	7. Form public policy stances, and create or implement public policy plan.	7. Reevaluate goals.
	8. Incorporate social responsibility into employee and unit review standards.	8. Reassess options.
		9. Reassess strategies.
	9. Reassess corporate stance on public policy and its fit with internal corporate policy and public policy plans.	10. Redesign campaign.
		11. Reimplement campaign.

This senior person needs to understand dynamic shifts in public policy issues and advise other members in the dominant coalition on the kinds of changes that are needed to build mutually beneficial relationships with key stakeholders (Dozier, Grunig, & Grunig, 1995).

Meeting this challenge, J. E. Grunig (1992a) reasoned, depends on executive management's support for human resource development, commitment to symmetrical communication, leadership through participative management, a participative culture, commitment to strategic planning, a sense of corporate responsibility, support for diversity, commitment to total quality management, support for excellence in management systems, and a culture that fosters collaboration. These criteria must be met by any organizational function seeking to be included in the dominant coalition. They are based on the ability of any function to add value to the bottom line.

One last concern in this regard is the extent to which issues management meets the challenge of two-way symmetrical communication. This model of public relations "is based on research and . . . uses communication to manage conflict and improve understanding with strategic publics" (J. E. Grunig, 1992a, p. 18; for a more comprehensive discussion, see J. E. Grunig, 1992b). The requirements for a two-way symmetrical relationship are these: interdependence between organization and interested parties, openness to the environment, dynamic adaptation to environment, equity, autonomy instead of control or dominance, innovation, decentralization of management, responsibility for consequences of actions and policies, conflict resolution, and the values typical of interest group liberalism (J. E. Grunig & L. S. Grunig, 1989).

Based on analysis started in this chapter, this book seeks to demonstrate how issues management can bring these criteria into play during strategic business planning. Planning options include adapting the firm to external policy or fostering an external policy favorable to the organization and carefully considering and integrating prevailing standards of corporate responsibility into planning, operations, organizational policy, and communication.

 Conclusion

Operating in mutual interest with stakeholders and with a commitment to achieve social responsibility is vital to maintaining or restoring management's authority to guide its organization's destiny with minimum external constraint. Society consists of the assertion of interests. Interests have marketplace importance as well as roles in the public policy arena. Policies are means by which personal and corporate interests are achieved. The key, whether for individuals or organizations, is to achieve harmony between internal policies and standards expressed by external groups. This fit is fundamental—the rationale for issues management.

What future lies before issues management? Its prospect is bright, concluded Wartick and Rude (1986), if it "can positively affect corporate performance by enhancing the firm's responsiveness to environmental change" (p. 125). Satisfactory outcomes require "the careful linkage of issue priorities to corporate objectives and the development of action plans to make the firm more competitive" (Littlejohn, 1986, p. 121). Issues managers are challenged to capture the critical changes in the public policy environment and to integrate that information into the strategic business plan and management strategies. This information can offer business opportunities, justify the curtailment or change of business activities, and guide the standards by which the organization operates.

A Search for Order

Arguments Over Public Policy

The evolution of issues management began at least 100 years ago. It continues to mature into a respected organizational function and academic discipline. Every time the corporate operating climate becomes turbulent, issues management's popularity soars. Business executives learn by trial and error that they must shape as well as respond to political conditions (Buchholz, 1982a; Divelbiss & Cullen, 1981; Weinstein, 1979). Such conditions are stormy, the more so when society seeks consensus.

"Public opinion" is a concept too general to be useful for issue monitoring and analysis, strategic business planning, issue communication, or ascertaining key publics' standards of corporate responsibility. Yet, in complex ways, decisions by corporate entities, courts, legislators, and regulators reflect a choice between opinions. As expressed in legislation, regulation, or legal interpretation, an opinion is the public's opinion; one view is better than others. The struggle between businesses, governmental agencies, and activists is a search for order, an effort to standardize public policy and related practices through informal agreement as well as legislative, regulatory, or judicial action (Wiebe, 1968). Summarizing this struggle for order at the turn of this century, Galambos and Pratt (1988) concluded,

The rise of the large corporation in J. P. Morgan's era marked a decisive shift in the nation's business system. In manufacturing, transportation, communications, and distribution, giant corporate combines were organized to bring order to their industries' markets and to exploit major technological innovations. (p. 2)

Cutlip (1995) captured the spirit and content of this shift by focusing on "the melee of the opposing forces in this period of the nation's rapid growth" (p. 187). The focus of Cutlip's history of public relations shifts noticeably from an interest in puffery and ebullient publicity to a serious tone when he addressed the clash of the robber barons and key members of the populist and progressive media. Activism rose to battle monopolistic capitalism. Capitalist titans fought one another. Carving corporate capitalism out of a small business and agrarian society was neither easy nor pleasant. Stressing this point, Cutlip (1994) reasoned that "only through the expertise of public relations can causes, industries, individuals, and institutions make their voice heard in the public forum where thousands of shrill, competing voices daily re-create the Tower of Babel" (p. ix). The origin of issues management was a battle for order.

The move toward order, industrialists realized, must be supported by governmental policy: "The government's role shifted decisively in three major areas in this century: single-industry regulation, cross-industry regulation that set rules under which all businesses operate, and government-directed activities that indirectly shaped the nation's business climate" (Galambos & Pratt, 1988, pp. 2-3). One residue of this effort, Tedlow (1979) observed, was that by the 1950s, public relations "had helped to alter permanently the public vocabulary of business" (p. 163).

Public policy advocates are faced with an array of options, including accepting policy changes wrought by others, mitigating the effects of those policies, analyzing the opportunities they offer, or creating policies favorable to their own interests. In such efforts, advocates seek wide acceptance of key premises that can influence how people think about the policies, products, and services of corporations and other large institutions. These premises provide the rationale for how companies plan and operate. Portending promise or peril for strategic resource management, those premises translate into strategic business plans (Sawaya & Arrington, 1988; Stroup, 1988).

This chapter will set a conceptual framework to explain the growth and change of public policy. Selected historical events will demonstrate the challenges and responses organizations have faced for over a century in the public policy arena, where one set of interests often meets strong opposition from another set. This chapter examines the origins of issues management before the turn of the century and progresses through the great depression to the post-World War II growth of goodwill toward business. This era ended abruptly during the 1960s. Activists continue to work to revise the premises of society. This chapter demonstrates that out of robust public debate emerge the public policies that guide business practices. This clash is the search for social order.

A Case in Point: One Company's Search for Order

One view of issues management is that it is a reactive approach organizations use to stop public policy. A recent example can be used to demonstrate how a company's issue position and strategic planning proactively sought advantages by adopting the proper image and adapting to key premises accepted by legislative and regulatory groups. This example highlights how strategic planning can advance a company's interests by building mutual interests with stakeholders and stakeseekers. The issue in this struggle has continued for three decades as companies, activists, and governmental officials work to balance the U.S. public's insatiable desire for petroleum and chemical products while protecting the environment. One premise that is fundamental to public policy and many corporations' strategic planning is this: That product or process that pollutes least, all other factors being equal, is preferred to its alternatives.

This premise was the foundation of a strategic planning and governmental affairs effort by Archer-Daniels-Midland Co. (ADM) which in the early stages dominated the federal policy debate over requirements that ethanol be included in all gasoline to reduce environmentally harmful automobile emissions. ADM is an agriculture giant that makes between 50% and 70% of the ethanol, a derivative of corn, that is manufactured in the U.S. The 1990 Clean Air Act requires service stations in the nation's nine environmentally dirtiest cities to reduce automobile pollutants by using either ethanol or methanol mixed with gasoline—or some other method. This struggle over public policy resources was part of ADM's strategic plan to create a huge market for its products.

ADM achieved a requirement that 30% of each gallon of gasoline must be ethanol. Reporting on ADM's campaign, Noah (1993) observed, "One reason ADM did no lobbying on this ethanol policy is that it didn't have to. Instead, its case was pressed by the Renewable Fuels Association, a trade group that lobbied the White House for months on the issue" (p. A10). This issue was one of President Clinton's campaign promises and is in the mutual interest of other producers of ethanol. The policy was advocated to reduce foreign oil imports and to please environmental groups. It is a case of public policy working for a company and an industry in the mutual interest of other vital segments of the nation, including farm belt interests (farmers, taxing authorities, farm equipment suppliers, financial institutions, and such).

Reasoning from the premise that that which has less negative impact on the environment is preferred, ADM needed to ascertain whether ethanol would have a positive impact on the environment and economy, without undesirable side effects. If the facts were there, the conclusion was evident. ADM's expedient policy grew from this argumentative stance, which was challenged by advocates, especially in the oil and gas refinery industry, who argued that ethanol in hot climates and at summer temperatures actually creates more pollution. They also argued that harvesting corn requires the use of substantial amounts of hydrocarbon fuels.

Because of the market stakes involved in this controversy, the oil and gas industry used an issue advertising campaign to stress the superiority of reformulated gasoline (RFG). This additive was designed to have less environmental impact than would competing products—including ethanol. This industry preferred to use a petroleum-based methanol derivative, MTBE. The industry also engaged in lobbying and filed suit over the requirement. In April 1995, a federal appeals court set aside the EPA rule that 30% of environmentally friendly gasoline would be ethanol. The decision was based on reasoning that although EPA can set performance guidelines, it cannot prescribe the recipe. In the summer of 1995, the EPA vowed to appeal this decision because it believed that its original decision was legally sound and technically defensible—it was also an embarrassment to a regulatory body to lose its authority to be regulatory. This case emphasizes how businesses and entire industries turn to the public policy arena to shape the marketplace in which they produce and sell products. This clash results from two industries' search for order.

Opinion, Key Premises, and Public Policy

One hundred years ago, astute business leaders realized that they could not function effectively based only on the belief that businesses have no other purpose than to provide goods and services. Managements make serious strategic planning and tactical errors when they base their decisions on economic assumptions and business strategies that many in the public neither understand nor appreciate (DiBacco, 1982). Critics of private sector policies have contributed to the quality of life by challenging business performance and demanding higher standards. Often, *big* is synonymous with *bad*. Technologies are a source of worry. Corporate leaders are thought to be motivated only by profit, uncaring about employees or the quality of their goods and services.

Participation in the management of issues has always reflected awareness that legislation and regulation extend into day-to-day production activities, marketing, and delivery of goods and services. With increasing sophistication, legislators, regulators, activists, and private sector leaders develop standards for acceptable corporate behavior, which they seek to apply with vigor and exactness. Failures by businesses to manage their affairs in ways that achieve public approval result in the creation of numerous governmental watchdog entities, such as the EPA, Occupational Safety and Health Administration, and Food and Drug Administration. In the past three decades, companies have been placed under more strict and insightful regulation than during the previous 80 years of their existence.

Norms used to evaluate business, activist, and government performance constantly change. Corporations, and other organizations, choose between complying with these norms or seeking to modify them. Companies have traditionally tried to maximize their options, whereas activist groups seek to limit those that they find offensive. Much as a driver with quick reaction time has a better chance of avoiding a traffic accident, successful issues monitoring affords organizations the chance to swerve rather than collide with some key public's opinion.

Discussion of such issues is not limited to a concern for business interests but is cast in terms of the effects policies have on society. For instance, the cost of reducing emissions and lessening risks of exposure to toxic materials will affect the U.S. economy. The National Petroleum Council, an industry advisory committee to the federal Energy Department, predicts that meeting new environmental regulations will cost $166 billion over 20 years. That is the cost of standing still rather than expanding plant operations, a sum that is twice the annual expenditures during the second half of the 1980s (Sullivan, 1993). That sum will factor into the price of products made from chemicals along with the cost of gasoline and other petroleum products. Parts or all of some plants will be closed rather than remodeled.

The marketplace, whether for goods, services, or ideas, is a potent force in our market-driven society. Corporations compete against one another for market advantage but will band together for protection against legislation or regulation they believe to be unwise. In self-defense, corporations and industries impose self-regulation. Activists groups have become part of the establishment, no longer fringe players. Sensitive to their image and public policy position, corporate leaders recognize the necessity of influencing public policy in their interests but also in the mutual interests of their stakeholders.

Argument Structure in Public Policy Debate

What assumptions should guide our approach to the public policy debates in this country? The structure of public policy communication is inherently dialogic, a process of give and take between interested parties (Heath, 1993). The ethical dimensions of this dialogue are captured by Pearson (1989):

> Dialogue is a precondition for any legitimate corporate conduct that affects a public of that organization. The prime concern of those departments is the constitution and maintenance of communication systems that link the corporate with its publics—those organizations and groups affected by corporate actions. The goal of public relations is to manage these communication systems such that they come as close as possible to the standards deduced from the idea of dialogue. This is the core ethical responsibility of public relations from which all other obligations follow. (p. 128)

Stressing the virtue of meliorism, L. Grunig (1992b) reasoned "that people do the best they know how for what they conceive themselves to be" (p. 86). Assertion of interests must culminate in an organization being at harmony with the key players of its environment.

Key messages used in policy debates voice relevant facts, reason from them by applying evaluative premises, and draw conclusions based on those facts and premises (Toulmin, 1964). To endure by satisfying the needs of society, public policy positions require a foundation in verifiable fact and evaluative premises that allows satisfying conclusions to be drawn.

This approach to the argumentative structure of policy analysis and debate is supported by the research and theory of Fishbein and Ajzen (1975; Ajzen & Fishbein, 1980). Their theory of information integration—expectancy value, reasoned action—argues that people hold attitudes of varying degrees of strength depending on how strongly they associate evaluative attributes with some object, situation, or action. The strength of these associations depends on the information (facts) the person holds and the evaluation (premise) associated with the premises.

Such analysis conforms with Kenneth Burke's approach to rhetoric. Meaning created and expressed through discourse constitutes what Burke (1951, 1966) called *terministic screens* which shape and limit people's interpretations of reality and prescribe what behaviors are normative. Terministic screens, especially those embedded in idioms, constitute zones of meaning once identifiable groups of people subscribe to them (Heath, 1991b, 1994). Viewed this way, all of the observations people make "*are but implications of the particular terminology in terms of which the observations are made*"

(Burke, 1966, p. 46). On this point, Burke reasoned that *"each of us shares with all other members of our kind . . . the fatal fact that, however the situation came to be, all members of our species conceive of reality somewhat round-about, through various media of symbolism"* (p. 52). Each idiom contains a unique view of economic, political, social, corporate, personal, and community interests.

This conclusion is fundamental to Parenti's (1986) charge that business discourse invents the opinion that members of society often enact without much critical judgment of it. Taking a less ideological stance, Andrews (1983) pointed out that "a prime function of rhetoric is to interpret and make meaningful what is in the process of happening" in society (p. 9).

Let's apply this theoretical framework to the structure of the policy argument of ADM to justify the use of ethanol as an additive. The fact: Ethanol added to gasoline (with the exception of high temperature months) reduces the emission of carbon monoxide, a key ingredient in automobile air pollution. The premise: The product or process that pollutes least, all other factors being equal, is preferred to other alternatives. The conclusion: Therefore, ethanol should be added to gasoline, a mandate in the Clean Air Act. As this terministic screen is shared by key public, it constitutes a zone of meaning.

By this approach to issue analysis and debate, we can understand the nature of a policy issue. Ehling and Hesse (1983) challenged persons who discuss issues management to precisely define what an issue is, especially a public policy issue. One answer to this challenge is that an issue is a contestable question of fact, value, or policy that affects how stakeholders grant or withhold support and seek changes through public policy.

Renfro (1993) reasoned that an issue is not the same as a concern; one or more issues will result from a concern. For an issue to exist, we need at least two parties with different points of view regarding how an issue should be resolved. Each point requires at least two possible resolutions. Over time, one choice will be accepted in favor of others. The importance of issues management is missed if we only think of an issue as being contestable. An issue is worthy of attention when it can have an impact on the organization (Dutton, 1993; Wartick & Mahon, 1994). The contest has implications for the distribution of resources, a conclusion that emphasizes the importance of thinking about issues management as strategic and ethical public policy formation.

These distinguishing characteristics surface, for example, when corporations become involved in disputes such as these: fact—whether oil companies control the supply of crude oil and therefore can create shortages to drive up prices; value—the standards of corporate responsibility (such as fair pricing) to apply in keeping with such power if it exists; and policy—whether electric utility (or telephone) corporations should be forced to compete.

Public policy issues are those with the potential of maturing into governmental legislation or regulation (international, federal, state, or local). A strategic issue

> is anything that may substantially impact your organization. Other ways to think of strategic issues are: all major questions needing answers; decisions needing to be made; things about the organization that need to be changed, corrected, or improved; or the primary challenges the organization faces. (Bandrowski, 1990, p. 18)

Issues management is a process for establishing a platform of fact, value, and policy to guide organizational performance while deciding on the content of messages used to communicate with targeted publics (including the company's senior managers). Issues communication can help establish platforms of fact, but facts alone are not enough (Stridsberg, 1977). Propositions of value often based on abstract ideals are used as rationale for deciding what regulatory or legislative measures are reasonable. The 1960s and 1970s produced many changes in value (Funkhouser, 1973). During the 1960s, environmental advocates made environmental quality a major value that led, for instance, to regulations of strip-mining activities.

Propositions of policy only come about after changes and analysis of platforms of fact and value. The logic, from the standpoint of an activist, is this: Companies are doing this (Y facts), which violates X values; therefore, they should be regulated in the following manner (Z policy). An effective issues analysis system focuses on where in this equation it is at the moment and what strategic response allows for greatest leverage. Whereas value issues are relevant to standards of corporate responsibility and the business plan, issues of policy are contestable in the public arena.

To move toward agreement on policy, people need to share a set of facts that accurately represent relevant circumstances and to establish causal or correlational links between actions, attributes, objects, or situations. How the facts are interpreted and policies are formulated depends on values and premises that are current in the minds of the policy decision makers. Public policy needs to be founded on the best available facts if it is to serve the public interest. For instance, a *Wall Street Journal* story reported a hot debate generated by the paper and chlorine trade groups regarding the health hazard of dioxin; reinterpretations by these groups asserted that dioxin is less hazardous than the EPA previously concluded (Bailey, 1992b).

In a similar effort, Exxon Corporation undertook a communication campaign to challenge the conclusion that long-term environmental damage had occurred in Prince William Sound. A key aspect of this campaign was to reinterpret the databases created by the government in its attempt to assess the damage done to the water, sediment, and marine life. Exxon wanted to be sure that the alleged facts were indeed accurate enough to be used for crucial interpretations and assessments of damage. One point of contention by Exxon was that some of the alleged samples of pollutants were actually diesel fuel that was mistaken for Exxon crude. A key analytic methodology being employed in the controversy between Exxon and governmental officials is called *fingerprinting*. This technique analyzes the levels of individual compounds in a substance. This methodology enables researchers to identify which pollutants came from each source. Once the fingerprint of the crude in the Exxon Valdez was identified, it was compared with all other samples to determine which ones came from the spill (Solomon, 1993a).

In this sense, we can approach the argumentative structure of opinions, however broadly held and by which identifiable groups, as consisting of facts, values, or premises, which lead to conclusions, including which policies (whether public or private) are preferred. This discussion also allows key publics to predict the liabilities and benefits of constraining or fostering admittedly complex corporate activities. It can be framed in terms of expedience, as interpreted by the political economy that is operating in each situation at a given time in history. This analysis explains why underregulation can result in socially irresponsible behavior on the part of individuals and organizations. Overregulation, on the other hand, can lead to a stifling operating environment that works against needed increases in productivity and job creation.

Businesses and other organizations can be viewed as rhetors who enact *personae* as well as affect meaning and identification (Cheney & Dionisopoulos, 1989) and as targets of external rhetoric between supporters and critics. Such analysis has been applied to the nuclear generating industry at Three Mile Island (Dionisopoulos & Crable, 1988), the Task Force on Food Assistance (Coombs, 1992), the key assumptions of industries trying for leadership in the information age (Gandy, 1992), and the rationale for conducting modern warfare (Hiebert, 1991). Olasky (1987) argued that industries define themselves and generate support for those definitions. For instance, in the early part of this century, the country preferred a free-market approach to public policy until American Telephone and Telegraph Company (AT&T) convinced key segments of the public and legislators that regulated monopolies were superior forms of business practice in key instances. In a similar way, the film industry, suffering criticism as having violated public standards of decency, developed a Motion Picture Code in the 1920s, a publicity shield to avoid governmental censorship.

The rationale that supports or challenges corporate policy and operations grows a bit at a time and is challenged and defeated at the same rate.

Considering this rhetorical process, Condit and Condit (1992) employed the concept of incremental erosion to analyze how antismoking activists chip away at the rationale of the tobacco industry, one premise at a time.

To understand the importance of the creation of such zones of meaning one might turn to P. Weaver's (1988) analysis of the problems U.S. corporations are having in adapting to the international marketplace. Despite their claims to the contrary, U.S. businesses gained a lot of favorable regulation and legislation that defined and fostered their domestic operations. By gaining this kind of control, they created their operating environment and adapted it to them. Tariffs, subsidies, official monopolies, tax breaks, wage controls, defense spending, and government-sponsored research—such policy lulled executives into lethargy and weakened their ability to adapt to the robust international marketplace.

For over a century, private sector organizations have engaged in the formation of policy that supports their self-interested policies and operations. In the contest to rationalize the role of large corporations in an open-market society, unfavorable media coverage and legislative intrusion often collide with a corporate desire to destroy critics, block change, or make regulation or legislation as favorable as possible. Out of this battle arises a common complaint that public policy intrudes into the well-being of private sector activities. Despite this common complaint, savvy managers know the advantages of favorable public policy and lobby for it. The history of this process is a struggle to define and negotiate conflicting interests, the search for order.

As the International Association of Advertising concluded,

> Business is subject to very careful scrutiny by several groups. Questions of factual error and omission are analyzed by the press and regulated by a wide variety of business and government bodies. Fallacious arguments are subject to a different kind of regulation: the ridicule of one's peers. The use of emotional persuasion is available to all. Such skills have served to render equal the Davids with the Goliaths. (Stridsberg, 1977, p. 94)

Stakeholders assert facts, seek to establish their priority of premises, and work to have others draw conclusions favorable to their interests.

This review suggests the nature of public policy dialogue, the impact language has on judgment, and the structure of argument: facts, evaluative premises, and conclusions. With this set of ideas in mind, the remainder of this chapter reviews the history of key efforts by private sector organizations, governmental agencies, activists, and professional associations. Each of these has worked to create and implement, through informal and public policy, key definitions of what they think is most favorable to their interests.

Origins of Issues Management

Near the end of the 19th century, regulation of business activities tended to be local. No national policy had been formed. Federal powers were limited. Nevertheless, the country was developing a national mentality made possible by improvements in transportation (such as rail systems) and communication (typified by the telegraph). Far-sighted business leaders could see that post-Reconstruction industrialization would lead to lucrative mass markets and would require business operations that would support the systematic operation of large organizations and a less distanced government.

The era was not without its models for corporate organization. The growth of U.S. firms was spurred following the American Revolution by protectionist "American System" reforms promulgated by Alexander Hamilton and his ideological successors. Most corporations operate under state charters pioneered by New York in 1811. As a legal person, corporations can conduct business, hold property, and incur debt. As ordinary citizens can, they, too, can be found guilty of committing crimes. Corporations have the constitutionally guaranteed power to act and speak as individuals.

At the close of the Civil War, the nation was fertile land for growing corporations. The war had cost the nation dearly in money and labor force. Corporations had provided needed war materiel. After the war, they underwrote financial development for expanded industrial production. Kingpins who could generate money—sometimes by bold stock fraud schemes—were destined to shape the last 30 years of the century and even the early years of this century.

Corporations evolved through trial and error rather than by calculated design. As a first step toward business concentrations, several manufacturing plants, small railroad companies, or oil refineries were brought together under committees that managed them in a trust. This system increased their efficiency and decreased competition. Through absorption and amalgamation, for instance, 138 companies were combined into United States Steel (Kolko, 1967).

Committees merged small companies into corporate giants, typified by Standard Oil. John D. Rockefeller, founder of Standard Oil, was a pioneer and master of the business practices and rationale needed to accomplish horizontal and vertical integration of business activities. Horizontal integration involved bringing several companies performing the same function, such as refining oil, into one corporate leadership. Vertical integration was accomplished by drawing to that structure a mix of functions that supported refining, such as crude oil production, transportation, wholesaling, and retailing (Galambos & Pratt, 1988). Even this master could not survive the scrutiny of ever more strident critics. In 1911, the Standard Oil Trust suffered the injunctive force of a federal judge and a federal antitrust lawsuit (Cutlip, 1995).

The nation's infrastructure began to burgeon as local markets were displaced with national ones. The slow metamorphosis from rural-agriculture to urban-industrial society demanded that farm produce reach the urban-industrial areas. This made farmers victims of the railroads that often charged them more for local shipment than it charged companies for long-distance freight.

Against roughshod industrialization arose the voices of farmer Populists and urban professional Progressives who believed corporations should be constrained by energetic governmental action. These two movements—made up of farmers, lawyers, small businessmen, ministers, and laborers—worked through legislative, judicial, and administrative channels to derail the robber barons who were creating an aristocracy of wealth. They revised state constitutions as a means for controlling the economic giants that appeared bent to destroy their livelihoods. As reform interests gained strength in legislatures, they demanded that corporations act according to a higher standard of corporate responsibility by changing their operating procedures to satisfy their critics and by communicating more openly and honestly with their publics.

The emerging corporate nation did not have established criteria by which to evaluate business performance. No ideological blueprint existed for the development of policies regarding corporate concentrations in manufacturing, railroads, and utilities. Standards had to be derived through public debate that featured activist protest. How large should a corporation be? Should the government regulate industry or was that task left solely to market forces? Could competition be maintained while small companies were being engulfed by larger ones or driven from the marketplace? To what extent should any corporation dominate a market by setting prices and establishing labor practices? The participants—corporate executives, labor leaders, government officials, and consumers—engaged in a tug of war of competing interests, values, and definitions.

The dominate philosophy of the era, Social Darwinism, championed unbridled tooth-and-fang capitalism. Face-to-face relationships that had characterized commerce were being replaced by distant corporate managements who knew little and cared less about the people who worked for the company, lived in its vicinity, bought its goods, and used its services. One characteristic of corporate policy in these robust years was that the less "outsiders" knew about corporate behavior and policy, the easier it was for business leaders to arbitrarily make decisions. Armed state militia and Pinkerton agents were means by which corporations communicated their policies to labor. Business-to-consumer communication often consisted in product and service advertising fraught with factual inaccuracy and hyperbole.

This information and policy vacuum presaged the need for pioneering issue communicators who, during the 1880s, called themselves publicists. Their influence should not be underestimated. Their sophistication was demonstrated in their ability to help forge new policies that limited the rampant price cutting by railroad lines that threatened the industry in the 1880s. Public relations-minded executives coupled with expert communicators forged an alliance between railroad industry leaders and politicians to bring order to the industry through the creation of the Interstate Commerce Commission in 1886 (Olasky, 1987).

Corporate spokespersons fought to maintain support for an ostensible laissez faire attitude against challenges by increasingly sophisticated lobby efforts of labor leaders and middle-class Progressives. Federal and state government officials learned that powerful corporate leaders did not want unlimited free competition, as evidenced by a variety of fundamental changes in the way they conducted business. One monumental effort to systematize business practices resulted in the standard 4'8" railroad gauge, making possible an efficient national transportation network.

Debates over the implications of corporate size and power resulted in the Sherman Antitrust Act in 1890. Whereas Progressive forces were successful in invoking federal and state regulation through a series of other important bills passed between 1890 and 1914, the agencies generally proved more cooperative than combative toward business. This cooperation demonstrates the widespread endorsement of premises favorable to corporate preferences. Kolko (1967) contended that shrewd industry barons quickly recognized the virtue of business concentration and used government to protect industries; they realized the reformist zeal of Progressivism could assist in these efforts. Part of the reason for this acceptance stems from the efforts of business publicists.

Although not immune to criticism, corporations have become a permanent part of the social, political, and economic fabric of the country. To examine the tension between public sentiment and corporate behavior, Galambos (1975) investigated the opinions several key occupational groups held toward corporate growth. He discovered that few individuals held rigid black-and-white views. Members of these groups were not always at war with corporations; indeed, often corporations were viewed as vital to prosperity. For instance, from 1879 to 1892, engineers saw their economic interest inseparable from the growth of corporations. One gripe by engineers, especially against railroads, was their miserable safety record. They argued that standards should be imposed to make rail travel and transportation safer for workers and passengers.

During this period, Protestant ministers applauded corporate growth as evidence of the realization of a divine mission. They broke out of their conservatism periodically to suggest a few social welfare programs. Southern farmers felt a sense of economic disparity created by corporate growth, but they appreciated the access to markets provided by large rail transportation networks. Midwestern farmers, too, appreciated this access but worried that railroads used government to shore up the industry. For this reason, farmers supported the Interstate Commerce Bill. Of these groups, laborers were the most concerned by growing business concentrations.

Passage of the Interstate Commerce Act (1887), Sherman Antitrust Act (1890), and Safety Appliance Acts (1893) were landmarks in consumer regulation. The first created the Interstate Commerce Commission to lessen the likelihood that railroad rates would be established by distant railroad czars. Wiebe (1967) observed that a few railroad "executives actually welcomed it as a protective cover" (p. 53). At the turn of the century, Progressive small businessmen and professionals lobbied for revisions in the Interstate Commerce bill that would take even more power from the railroads—by then, deeply in debt. Railroads tended to raise rates to offset these debts, a practice resisted by middle-class Progressives who did not want to shoulder new costs at the expense of their own businesses. The Interstate Commerce Act was important to railroad executives who were fighting deteriorating finances. This legislation allowed railroad executives to set rates, control competition, and revamp freight classifications in ways similar to what could be accomplished by the organizational tactic of pooling (Olasky, 1987).

Despite these trends, Galambos (1975) concluded that in 1892, "few signs indicated that the concentration movement would produce a major crisis in America's middle cultures" (p. 78). The depression of 1893 caused many to reconsider the liabilities associated with the unbridled pursuit of wealth by industrial combines. Farmers, especially, championed financial reform. In addition to their growing anger at the economic clout of bankers and other plutocrats, farmers had mixed feelings about the urban growth corporations were causing. Young people were being lured to the big cities far from their rural origins. "While the farmer was thus capable of conjuring up some highly abstract enemies, he lavished most of his animosity on those industries and firms with which he had direct economic relationships" (p. 96). Farm groups saw their influence erode. Their role as a counterbalance to corporations was being taken over by labor organizations. Lack of finances and leadership ended most of these economic-interest coalitions.

By 1901, farmers had become less angry toward trusts than other occupation groups, particularly engineers and laborers. Unskilled labor realized the battle lines had been drawn, particularly after the bloody rioting and harsh use of strikebreakers at Andrew Carnegie's Homestead steel mills near Pittsburgh in 1892. Homestead proved to labor that corporate giants, such as Carnegie, were determined to destroy labor unions and would kill to accomplish that end. Ensuing strikes were often violent. In contrast to the lower paid workers, skilled laborers looked on corporations positively because they offered promise of economic well-being, but they recognized corporations' power was not to be taken lightly. By the turn of the century, Galambos (1975) argued, the nation had begun to establish a coherent set of beliefs and attitudes toward the regulation of corporations. These opinions caused the regulatory measures of the later Progressive era to be more legally exact.

During the first decade of this century, corporate America lost one of its strongest supporters—the clergy. Doubts were raised whether corporations returned to the people as much as they took. Bremner (1956) observed that in contrast to other countries, ours has never accepted the assumption that some people must be in poverty. A dramatic change of opinion around the turn of this century was the discovery of poverty. The Social Darwinism of the previous century argued that poverty persisted only among the lazy and spendthrift. This was no longer accepted as fact, particularly by religious reformers who observed that low wages caused laborers to suffer despite their energy and frugality. Many social evils were laid at the doorsteps of business, as ministers became incensed at the poor health and living conditions typical in corporate towns. The clergymen believed that where morality and corporate growth had been positively related before, they were now at odds (Galambos, 1975).

Names such as J. P. Morgan and John D. Rockefeller, Sr., raised the ire of citizens who believed that the foundations of the society were being eroded because so few had so much power and wealth. The number of regulatory measures passed in the opening decades of this century indicated that the Progressive search for order was becoming more robust. Presidents of the United States joined the advocates for corporate reform, sometimes out of fear of losing a valuable portion of the electorate. As he did with other groups, Theodore Roosevelt encouraged farmers and other supporters of trust busting to renew their attacks on businesses. Passage of the Bureau of Corporations Bill in 1903 established the Department of Commerce and Labor; this marked for many Progressives the beginning of an important era of regulation. However, Kolko (1967) concluded, the measure was enacted with strong conservative support by industrialists who saw it as a way to lessen competition. Many battles were fought over wages and working conditions, at first, and later, over the quality of goods and services. Even though the debate was in its infancy, the public along with business was confronted with the need to formulate standards of responsible corporate behavior.

Companies did little to create a safe and comfortable working environment. With rare exception, wages were at a subsistence level that was achieved only by working long hours. Typically, entire families—including children as young as six or seven years old—had to work to survive. Some employers favored the labor of children who could work in small and cramped quarters, particularly important to save unnecessary excavations in coal mines. Railroad companies typically subjected employees to extremely dangerous working conditions. To oppose such conditions, workers could strike. Bosses worked to prevent this collective action. For instance, coal was often stockpiled by coal companies to prevent the possibility that a strike could be effective.

Abuse always sparks opposition. Muckraking journalists led by David Graham Phillips, Lincoln Steffens, and Ida Tarbell exposed the irresponsibility rampant in industry, particularly during the first two decades of this century. Books such as Frank Norris's (1903) *The Pit* and Upton Sinclair's (1906) *The Jungle* fostered discussion that helped lead to the Pure Food and Drug Act and the Federal Meat Inspection Act of 1906. This latter act was the culmination of an effort to reform the meat industry, which began as early as 1865 when Congress banned importation of diseased cattle and pigs. Meat reform was supported by some of the largest packers who, unlike their cut-rate competition, maintained sanitary plants and routinely inspected their product. The bigger firms wanted to extend government inspection to all packers to establish equity of quality—and expense. Similarly, the Pure Food and Drug Act was endorsed by the National Pure Food and Drug Congress, which included trade groups and industry representatives such as the Creamery Butter Makers' Association, Brewers Association, Confectioners' Association, Wholesale Grocers' Association, and the Retail Grocers' Association (Kolko, 1967).

Magazines were the major mass medium by which muckrakers reached their audience, the U.S. middle class, which was increasing in size and political importance. Steffens and Tarbell, in conjunction with Ray Stannard Baker, made *McClure's Magazine* the leading outlet for reformist material. Other key journals included *Everybody's Magazine, Collier's, Arena, Success Magazine,* and *Cosmopolitan.* All joined the reform battle out of conviction and the desire to increase circulation. Influential muckrakers found much to criticize about corporate behavior. Tarbell's (1904) *History of the Standard Oil Company,* first published in *McClure's,* was one of the first statements on corporate responsibility to find its way into middle-class living rooms. Steffens's (1904) *The Shame of the Cities* (also released that same year) provided another landmark exposé. In the face of the challenges by muckraking journalists, Cutlip and Center (1982) observed, "The corporations, the good ones along with the ruthless ones, had lost contact with their publics. For a while, they sat helplessly by, inarticulate and frustrated, waiting apprehensively for the next issue of *McClure's* magazine" (p. 76).

No public opinion change was necessary to condemn the consumption of tainted meat. When reformers alerted the public to unsanitary meat-packing conditions, it was ready to demand reform. An informed populace had well-established premises by which to evaluate such information and draw conclusions. Such dramatic changes in key publics' opinions underscore the reality that issues management can never ignore. The opinion battleground is the struggle between corporations who attempt to do business, for the most part, in ways that coincide with accepted standards of behavior and the public interest. This was a transitional era for business.

> The political economy of the United States was beginning to change in the Progressive Era in ways that gave business leaders pause, if not reason to fear for their future. As single-industry regulation became more prevalent, as cross-industry policies were implemented, as government-directed activities increased, executives sensed that they were losing contact with and control over their political and social environments. (Galambos & Pratt, 1988, p. 92)

The enemies were liberal reform critics of free-market economics. Public relations and trade associations were solutions.

Stridsberg (1977) approached this problem directly as he analyzed an advertisement titled "The Penalty of Leadership," used by Cadillac Motor Company in 1915. It advocated the need to maintain high standards of manufacturing quality. The ad masked the fact that the original "51" Model Cadillac was not very reliable. In this advertisement, the company proclaimed its commitment to quality by asserting, "In every field of human endeavor, he that is first must perpetually live in the white light of publicity." It continued,

> When a man's work becomes a standard for the whole world, it also becomes a target for the shafts of the envious few. If his work be merely mediocre, he will be left severely alone—if he achieves a masterpiece, it will set a million tongues a-wagging. (p. 41)

The theme, apparently, was that if people are critically discussing the quality of the Cadillac, their talk is motivated by envy, not justified criticism of inadequate engineering and manufacturing (p. 41).

By World War I, increasing numbers of corporations employed wordsmiths to explain to key publics the importance of business in underwriting modern abundance. Walter Lippmann (1961) noted in *Drift and Mastery* that effective execution of a series of such opinion campaigns by skilled practitioners Ivy Lee, Edward Bernays, and others led to growing recognition for the field and dramatically changed people's attitudes.

Because magazines and books were the primary media used by those seeking corporate reform, they were used by public relations practitioners. Instead of advocacy advertising, public relations specialists wrote articles extolling the virtues of a company or an industry while railing against pending regulation. Each case was presented as though it resulted from objective journalistic research. For instance, George Gunton was a popular economist who championed the free enterprise system in his capacity as editor of *Gunton's Magazine*. While in that position, he received a $15,000 annual retainer from Standard Oil (Kolko, 1967). As early as 1880, the railroad industry was being encouraged to recognize the value of public relations (Raucher, 1968).

Industry barons sometimes entered the fray as J. Ogden Armour did. He used *The Saturday Evening Post* (Armour, 1906) to defend some of the practices of the meat industry under attack, to invite public visits of his facilities, to describe sanitation efforts his company was taking to ensure high quality, and to support passage of inspection legislation. Several large packing concerns, including Swift & Co., published a series of advertisements to present a favorable image of themselves and proclaim their commitment to healthful meat-processing conditions.

In the new century, railroad company executives worried that the public did not appreciate the accomplishments and national importance of their industry. Indeed, farmers sought control, especially of the railroad rate structure. One of the earliest battlegrounds was Illinois where the Granger-controlled legislature passed a bill in 1873 that established the rates for grain storage in railroad warehouses. This act led to the landmark case, *Munn v. Illinois* (1877), in which the Supreme Court ruled that state legislatures can regulate private property in the public interest. The railroad industry hired the Publicity Bureau in 1906 to fight a move by President Theodore Roosevelt to impose regulatory legislation on them. The campaign failed when the Hepburn Act was passed, in large part because Roosevelt took his case to the people and won.

Now, the railroad industry reassessed its use of publicity. Many companies started their own public relations departments. More firms began to specialize in business communication, in what was proving a robust but difficult practice. For example, the Publicity Bureau was joined in this activity by a firm William Wolff Smith started in 1902 and an agency, Parker and Lee, which featured the talents of Ivy Lee. Lee was hired by a railway firm in 1906—the Pennsylvania Railroad—primarily to dispute the image that railroads were heartless. The campaign began with an article in *Moody's Magazine* in November 1907 that proclaimed the virtues of railroads, arguing that they had expanded the West, carried goods to markets, made travel possible, and employed hundreds of workers (Lee, 1907). Later, in 1916, a group of major railroads formed the Railway Executives' Advisory Committee to manage press releases and publish articles on the industry (Wiebe, 1967).

The growth of utilities was equally tumultuous. Promoters of the burgeoning electricity industry were among the first to use issue communication. The battle was not against regulation but between George Westinghouse and

Thomas Edison, who debated whether alternating or direct current should be the accepted technology. One of the first corporate public relations departments was established in 1889 by George Westinghouse who wanted to promote the electricity industry by championing alternating current. Edison soon joined in this contest of industry image and issues management. He sponsored a book titled *A Warning* to scare the public into favoring direct current. It argued that alternating current is too lethal. Its appendix listed persons who had been killed by electricity. Edison may have been instrumental in the state of New York's decision to use alternating current to administer capital punishment (Cutlip, 1995). In 1889, Westinghouse countered with a book, *Safety of the Alternating System of Electrical Distribution,* which extolled the virtues of that technology (Cutlip, 1995).

Through his secretary, Samuel Insull, Thomas Edison was able to obtain a 50-year electrical utility agreement with the Chicago City Council to operate as a regulated franchise. Insull brought his conviction in the regulated utility monopoly to his term as president of the National Electric Light Association. Although regulation might hold rates down from an optimal level, Insull argued successfully that it kept competition from entering a community and threatened the stability of a company (Olasky, 1987).

Another utility giant increased control over its industry in the last decade of the 19th century. Frederick P. Fish, who became president of the Bell Telephone System in 1900, recognized the need for his growing company to take its case to the public. The apprehension was that if the public did not understand the advantage of a monopoly, it would seek regulation or oppose monopolization. Either stance was contrary to the growth goals of the company. Raucher (1968) concluded "that by 1906 the American Telephone and Telegraph Company had a general policy designed to placate public hostility and had methods for broadcasting the news about that policy" (p. 49). That policy was aggressively continued by Theodore Newton Vail when he became AT&T president in May 1907. He sought to insulate the communication utility from public control by convincing Americans the phone company was operating in their interest. One of the first issue advertisements, put out by AT&T in 1908, emphasized the bond between the company and its customers:

> The Bell System's ideal is the same as that of the public it serves—the most telephone service and the best, at the least cost to the user. It accepts its responsibility for a nationwide telephone service as a public trust. (Garbett, 1981, p. 40)

By 1910, Vail had converted these ideas into a consistent long-term campaign stressing the advantages of a privately run, publicly minded system (Schultze,

1981). The rationale featured several key premises, one of which was that an integrated, regulated monopoly allowed people in different parts of town and in different cities to talk to one another (Olasky, 1987). To accomplish this end required public goodwill (Cutlip, 1995).

One of the first major tests of this opinion formation strategy came in 1913 when the Justice Department initiated an antitrust suit charging that AT&T had created an impermissible monopoly through its control of Western Union. To defend itself, a newspaper series was started under the name of Vail beginning in the *New York Times,* on September 4, 1913. The case collapsed. Part of AT&T's campaign was to avert governmental regulation, but another threat involved direct government ownership of utilities. By May 1928, AT&T Publicity Director Arthur Page could announce their educational efforts had successfully convinced the public that the phone industry was best handled as a monopoly. But he also prudently cautioned company executives over still-lingering concerns (Raucher, 1968). Thus, even though a victor in many battles over the years, AT&T never completely won the war for public confidence. This conclusion is best justified by the eventual breakup in the 1980s.

In the early years of this century, public relations practices by utilities and railroads gained popularity with manufacturing companies that feared anti-trust legislation. To protect International Harvester Company, George Perkins, at the direction of Cyrus H. McCormick, fought governmental action by the Bureau of Corporations in 1906. The publicity firm of Parker and Lee again joined the fray. The argument against antitrust legislation was couched in what had become the standard premise of "the benefits of largeness," an attempt to publicize the economics of mass production. The argument continued, corporations pay better wages than do smaller businesses. The campaign had some success because the Roosevelt administration dropped the case in 1908 (Raucher, 1968).

The Rockefellers drew heavily on public relations to protect Standard Oil against Ida Tarbell's claims that John D. Sr.'s philanthropy was "tainted money" and charges of violent strikebreaking in labor relations at their Colorado Fuel and Iron Company. Despite his efforts in behalf of the Rocke-fellers, Ivy Lee was soundly criticized for presenting one-sided, factually inaccurate material in his bulletin titled "Facts in Colorado's Struggle for Industrial Freedom" (Raucher, 1968, p. 27). Lee was of service to key industrial groups that sought to improve their image and challenge efforts to regulate them. He defended the Anthracite Coal Operators by reasoning that competitors should be excluded to ensure the production of high quality coal (Olasky, 1987). He assisted the Cotton Yarn Association who argued that constraints of trade prevented cotton producers from putting out low quality products, regardless of price (Olasky, 1987).

Advertising agencies, shortly after the turn of the century, offered their services to the beleaguered corporations. Following New York State's Armstrong Committee exposé of insurance industry corruption, the New York Mutual Life Insurance Company hired N. W. Ayer to conduct an advocacy campaign to restore confidence in the industry. Communication efforts were never separate from attempts by the Theodore Roosevelt, William Howard Taft, and Woodrow Wilson administrations to regulate industry. Public relations practitioners were brought into the fray to correct false information, champion traditional values, and argue that regulation was detrimental. During the first decades of the century, Raucher (1968) observed, increased corporate responsibility and ethical behavior became commonplace public relations themes.

Like many other aspects of the reform period, considerable discussion revolved around definitions of "good" and "bad" business concentrations, including the ways organizations advertised products and services. Discussion of the need for the Federal Trade Commission (FTC) began to surface in 1911. The National Civic Federation discovered the idea was broadly favored in an opinion poll conducted in 1911. The Progressive and Republican Parties endorsed it in 1912, and by 1914, the FTC was created to replace the Bureau of Corporations. As is true today, one of the hardest parts of achieving responsible corporate performance involves deciding what it is. The task is often assigned to the membership of regulatory bodies that often have representatives of the industries to be regulated serving on them.

Industries rightly have the information needed to assist the creation of such definitions. Soon after the creation of the Interstate Commerce Commission, the members realized that the data needed to ascertain the fairness of rates would have to be obtained from industry (Galambos & Pratt, 1988). In a similar fashion, the FTC was headed by the avowedly probusiness Edward N. Hurley. It was supported by and greatly influenced by the National Association of Manufacturers (Kolko, 1967). This association has engaged in extensive public relations battles that Cutlip (1995) believed have often failed and have not been cost effective.

The period from 1901 to 1939 was one of flux, as a corporate commonwealth was forged to replace the era of single corporate leaders, such as J. P. Morgan or John D. Rockefeller. The goals for national public policy were often blurred, and input came from an ever more diverse array of players. At issue was the laissez-faire approach, which "rested on the traditional American faith in the marketplace as an effective regulator" (Galambos & Pratt, 1988, p. 45).

World War I did not bring an end to reform and concern over corporate America. "The clergyman, the engineer, the farmer, the laborer—all found cause for distress in the immediate aftermath of the First World War"

(Galambos, 1975, p. 193). Labor's attitudes remained negative through the 1920s. With technological change making jobs obsolete, the greatest challenge facing the laborer was to protect his or her craft. A new twist in corporate issues management was the presence of Bolshevism; now, corporate representatives claimed criticism of corporate America was unpatriotic and communistic. Businessmen recognized that the flow of immigrants was bringing many people to this country who neither understood nor appreciated the economics of free enterprise. Business had no intention of letting competing economic systems gain a foothold.

This section has featured corporations as struggling—battling—to respond to pressures between themselves as well as those applied by activist groups. Despite the widely accepted view that large corporations dominated society at the turn of the century, activist groups played a major role in the first quarter of a century in the United States.

 The Great Depression and the Redemption of Capitalism

The era of the Great Depression demonstrated how improper business policies can lead to such damaging consequences that communication strategies are unable to rectify them. Only by making massive changes in the way business was done could society rebalance public and private interests. As a result of this loss in faith, new argumentative principles arose that have guided business practices and allowed for expanded governmental intrusion into those activities.

The financial collapse of the country during the Depression strained the relationship between the public and corporations. It raised anew questions as to whether large companies could function in the public interest. Because of the need to rebuild financial and industrial institutions, the public championed increased federal powers. Many in the clergy argued that one of the solutions to the Depression was to break up the corporations that had become too powerful. Rather than being totally at odds, government and business worked with surprising cooperation to return the nation to prosperity. The farmer, despite the impact on farm prices, emerged from the 1930s supporting large corporations that could buy produce and inexpensively sell equipment needed for future plantings and harvests (Galambos, 1975).

One telling result of this period was a loss of autonomy on the part of business executives. New legislation intruded into board room and executive decisions, at least on the assumption that companies had violated the national trust in their planning and operations. During the period, price stabilization was more important than fostering competition. One goal was to restore the ability of companies to meet payrolls and avoid massive layoffs that would in turn lead to fewer consumers, less revenue, and resultant layoffs—a downward spiral. Legislators were less interested in consistency of policy than in its effects; piecemeal regulation resulted. The incentive was not to stop industrial policy that generated profits but to ensure the wise use of that growth in the public interest.

> Although management of individual firms initially decried many of these changes in the economic functions of government, most would gradually adapt to them and discover that there were in fact many advantages to a corporate commonwealth that was more stable economically. (Galambos & Pratt, 1988, p. 126)

The 1930s and 1940s witnessed a series of issue ads stressing the virtues of capitalism to counteract prevailing doubt whether business could provide general prosperity. Business leaders feared the public no longer believed in the free enterprise system that had left them without work and dashed their hopes of prosperity, even survival. Galambos (1975) concluded,

> The values and attitudes of the new culture clearly emerged intact from the 1930s. By that time most Americans saw antitrust as a dead or dying issue. They were coming to accept—in varying degrees—a different outlook embodying modern, organizational norms and a new image of the large corporation. Gone was the deep hostility of the 1890s, the progressive era, and postwar crisis. By 1940 the corporate culture had largely supplanted the individualistic-egalitarian outlook of the nineteenth-century. The era of the organization man had begun. (p. 249)

To justify corporate influence in policy matters, some companies engaged in issue advertising. One campaign was devised by Warner & Swasey that in 1941 compared the lot of the French worker to his U.S. counterpart. "Wonder What a Frenchman Thinks About" exemplified how the company used the threat of Nazism to rekindle patriotic commitment to U.S. capitalism. It argued that the French laborer's greed led to the plight of working "53 hours a week for 30 hours' pay." Warner & Swasey voiced the regret of the typical French worker in these words,

> I wish I had been less greedy for myself and more anxious for my country; I wish I had realized you can't beat a determined invader by a quarreling, disunited people at home; I wish I had been willing to give in on some of my rights to other Frenchmen instead of giving up all of them to a foreigner; I

wish I had realized other Frenchmen had rights, too; I wish I had known that patriotism is work, not talk, giving not getting. (Stridsberg, 1977, p. 103)

This sad plight could be interpreted as directing the U.S. worker to support the interests of a united corporate America faced with an emerging fascist danger in the midst of the Depression.

Marshaled in the face of heated debate regarding the ability of U.S. capitalism to provide jobs and ensure the public economy, the theme of the importance of free enterprise has remained remarkably consistent over a nearly 50-year period (Garbett, 1981). Developed were Warner & Swasey ad themes, such as "Where do your wages come from?" (1944), "To cure a headache, you don't cut off your head" (1947), "If you own a hammer, you are a capitalist" (1948), and "They don't keep feeding you cheese after the trap is sprung" (1950). All of these ads discussed the problems of the welfare state. The campaign contrasted the dangers of large government and the virtues of U.S. free market enterprise exemplified in the 1970 advertisement, "What's right with America?" In one 1971 ad titled "Business men are like the bashful boy who sent his girl a valentine but didn't sign it," Warner & Swasey justified the use of issue advertising. Pointed out were facts on how business "taxes support America's schools 1½ days every week." Business contributes to charities and provides community support. Through its research, the nation is made better. Business is cleaning up the slums, training the unemployed and unemployable (Garbett, 1981, p. 47).

Other notable issue ads of this era included one used by the Chesapeake & Ohio Railway—Nickel Plate Road—to dramatize preferential treatment given transcontinental freight shipments, particularly agricultural produce. The headline made the point: "A Hog Can Cross the Country Without Changing Trains—But YOU Can't!" This ad ran in late 1945 and 1946 and was part of an internecine issue campaign waged within the railway industry.

The end of the Depression and new prosperity in the aftermath of World War II diverted attention from the problems of corporations. Moore (1982) concluded that business during the 1950s enjoyed a honeymoon with key publics. People were thankful to have work. The private sector again offered financial security for the average citizen. Beneficial changes in working conditions and an apparent new level of corporate ethics seemed to indicate that businesses had learned to be good community citizens. These changes combined with upbeat popular culture publicity surrounding wartime efforts (for instance, the "Riveter Annie" mystique) to help free corporations from the degree of regulatory scrutiny typical of previous decades.

In the Eisenhower years, little regulatory legislation was passed. The predictable economic recessions came and went without residual hostility or massive public interest activism. In general, this was a period of good feeling between the public and corporations that provided jobs and supplied goods and services to a people desiring to forget the difficulties of the 1930s and 1940s. Massive research and development efforts fostered by the war effort, and often funded by public taxes, led to the availability of new products that reshaped middle-class lifestyles. Secretary of State George Marshall tabbed political specialist George Kennan to create an Office of Policy and Planning in 1946. Its staffers advised Marshall on foreign policy developments and proved influential in providing support for the Marshall Relief Plan. The success of this program encouraged corporations to similarly review their planning and communication efforts (Nowlan, Shayon, & Contributing Editors, 1984).

The cold war with the Soviet Union helped blunt corporate criticism and led to prosperity in defense industries that were funded by public taxes. One harbinger of future nuclear regulation was the Atomic Energy Act of 1954. People's awareness of the danger of nuclear energy was born when they learned that devastating atomic weaponry had been used against Japan. Nuclear power as well as new industries, such as the space industry, grew out of the international struggles of this era, all of which led to new regulatory issues.

Old issues continued in perplexing ways. Corporations still directed issue communication against labor. For instance, Ohio Consolidated Telephone used an ad titled "The Case of the Amputated Telephone" in its efforts to discredit striking telephone workers by blaming them for damaging telephone lines: "Since July 15, [1956] when the strike against Ohio Consolidated began, more than 50 cables have been cut, slashed, burned, hacked in half—interfering with the phone service of more than SIX THOUSAND homes and businesses!" This ad could alienate the public against the strikers, who were compared with dedicated employees: "Supervisors manning local and long distance telephone boards—trying desperately to keep the lines open to you—have been harassed, threatened, intimidated, even shot at!" The ruthlessness of the vandalistic strikers was portrayed even more dramatically: "More than ten offices have had to be closed down for short or long periods—due to vandalism or because police protection was not adequate to handle the danger to operators and equipment!" (Stridsberg, 1977, pp. 106-107). Such advertising—a blatant labor-management power play—used scapegoating and blatant fear appeals.

Less combative, General Electric innovated in the 1950s and early 1960s by recognizing the value of keeping employees and other constituencies informed regarding corporate plans, management efforts to be responsible, and pending issues that could affect profits and employee interests. Timken Roller Bearing Company and Caterpillar Tractor demonstrated their citizenship by participating in issue discussion. For example, Caterpillar asked employees and surrounding communities to understand the need to "Hold the

Line on Wages" to remain competitive—especially in foreign countries and against foreign competitors. By anticipating union attacks on the company's contentions, Caterpillar muted labor's negative influence (Bateman, 1975).

Issue ads often addressed the self-interest of the company more than that of key publics. What was missing was a strong sense of what concerned key publics. Private sector management did not understand how little the public knew about operations and the requirements of finance, product development, liability, and pollution control. Feeling little pressure from the public, business leaders built new relationships with government. They believed government could be a source of revenue for products and services as well as research and development. They worked for government policies that brought new order to the free market playing field. Companies, such as those in the steel industry, used the war years to expand and modernize because they had a ready market for their products.

The questioning of private sector behavior, prompted in the post-World War II period primarily by the civil rights movement's analysis of all institutions, blossomed during the 1960s era of multifaceted agitation. The history of issues management parallels the tumultuous growth of corporations, marked by ongoing public policy contest between business critics and supporters. Supporters stressed the ability of corporations to create jobs and provide products and services. They opposed regulation, unless it stabilized the marketplace and boosted profits. Executives believed that if publics understood the plight of business, they would not champion restrictions.

Critics argued that companies must comply with ever-changing public expectations of responsible behavior. Under pressure, corporations began to reexamine themselves—but the road was not an easy one. Public policy revolutions always occur when massive reevaluation focuses on an era's underpinning premises. The euphoria of the late 1940s and 1950s misled corporations. Most were unprepared for the hostile outbursts of social reexamination that occurred during the 1960s and 1970s. That an uninformed public responded with such hostility is compelling evidence that business leaders had failed to keep in tune with public needs by listening to them. Companies had not fostered a platform of fact or affirmed key value premises. New premises arose with startling speed to reinterpret existing information about environmental quality, fairness of business practices, and equity in hiring and promotion. Firms usually believed the public was more gullible and unsophisticated than was the case. Rather than seeing the merits of involving critics in corporate planning, firms tried to keep them outside plant boundaries.

In the face of these challenges, some companies assumed the trouble would go away once the outrage burned itself out. They hoped the difficulties could be communicated out of existence. Many business leaders believed that stock claims about the damage of regulation and the destruction of the free enterprise system would heal the wounds of bleeding-heart agitators' criticism. Few if any industries realized that a new search for order was in the making.

 ### Dissent Flowers in the 1960s

During the Depression of the 1930s, the power of business was substantially blunted by a larger government that many citizens believed was preferable to irresponsible capitalism. Even so, people wanted to trust the inherent good of business ethics. By the 1960s, this value premise had changed; beneath the good feeling was a deep layer of skepticism about corporate performance. During the postwar era of "good times," growing dissent in the African American community and changing values publicized by the beat generation were signaling the most massive assault on business witnessed in this country. Many institutions—government, business, family life, organized religion, and education—were carefully scrutinized. The rift between critics and companies obtained full articulation when civil rights and antiwar protests became front-page news. The war in Vietnam became a forum for reexamining corporate behavior.

Addressing this dissent and dramatic change, this section examines the past three decades to explain why they witnessed the most dramatic constraint of business activities in this country's history. New premises emerged from these critics to revolutionize government and business.

The era of change began when new facts were laid before the U.S. public regarding the harm business was doing to the physical and human environment. Product safety and employment practices were two of the many corporate policies that changed as a consequence of new premises. A new definition of corporate responsibility altered business planning and management. New conclusions were drawn regarding the safe operations of nuclear generation, use of pesticides, harvesting of timber, production of oil and chemicals, financial institutions, automobile safety, and transportation. In these turbulent times, "government was more likely to be a partner or helpmate than an opponent of the modern corporation" (Galambos & Pratt, 1988, 154).

The past three decades witnessed a remarkable challenge to the privacy and authority that executives and business owners long assumed as their prerogatives. Coupled with the search for values that continued after the antiwar years, reform interests pushed for a broad reorientation in business ethics. *Corporate citizenship* became the major public affairs theme during these decades. Quality of life—and businesses' contribution to it—took on new meaning, once people who had not been politically and socially aware before the 1960s became aware that they could no longer take business policies and operations for granted. Labor unions demanded higher wages and benefits even if they eventually would outpace the ability of companies to compete with international businesses. Accelerating the breakdown of this social contract were record unemployment and bankruptcies, the uncertain government response to foreign sales in the country, deepening trade deficits, and a declining manufacturing base as America moved haltingly toward a postindustrial economy devastating to the future of many traditional industries.

In contrast to their "no-comment" counterparts, savvy executives and issue communicators realized that they no longer could withhold information or decline to comment. Damaging effects on images and sales resulted from public disclosures after company spokespersons tried to cover up embarrassing facts. Attempting to restore credibility, a number of CEOs stepped forward to personally represent their companies and be visible on matters of public interest, even though image masters sought to (re)present companies as image rather than substance (Cheney, 1992). The private sector became interested in applying sophisticated social science techniques not only for product sales but to market ideas. Companies undertook campaigns to politically educate and foster participation by employees, shareholders, customers, and other allies. They became involved in grassroots programs and sought to build constituencies to marshal support for issues relevant to the needs of their firms. Trade associations and political action committees (PACs) became valuable means for expressing the corporate position without individual businesses having to be visible. The result has been vigorous efforts to influence legislative activities at the local, state, federal, and international levels in ways quite different from previous decades.

Until 1971, corporations were expressly forbidden from contributing to federal candidates and their party organizations. The Federal Election Campaign Act of 1971 and its amendments in 1974 and 1976 allowed corporations, unions, and industry special-interest groups to form PACs and use them to funnel dollars into political campaigns. PACs have become an ancillary part of most major corporations, even though they are more likely to increase access to elected officials rather than to dominate them (Alexander, 1988). Public interest groups, such as Common Cause, were troubled by corporate and special-interest PAC contributions to political campaigns. Some employees felt obligated to contribute to the company or union PAC despite a desire not to. Some companies supplied key employees with "raises" with the express intent that that money would find its way to their PAC.

Uncertainty regarding the appropriate standards of conduct is difficult for a firm to tolerate, just as it is for an individual. During prior wars, businesses that supplied materiel and armaments had been played up as making a heroic contribution to the country's security. Activists against the Vietnam War reversed that equation. Dow Chemical, for instance, was singled out for attack because it produced napalm. Napalm is a gasoline-based military weapon that incinerates what it touches—including innocent men, women, and children. Before Vietnam, Dow had been viewed as a good company for which to work. College graduates had lined up for job interviews, but antiwar sentiment changed this. By the 1970s, Dow's favorable image was replaced by that of a warmonger, indiscriminately destroying nonmilitary targets. Students scorned job interviewers and made the purchase of Saran Wrap synonymous with incinerating innocent men, women, and children.

In addition to corporate activities related to the Vietnam War, a series of challenges broadened the range of business practices and values that felt the sting of this new criticism. In 1962, Rachel Carson stunned the nation with a series of articles in the *New Yorker* titled "Silent Spring," later published in book form. She alleged that insecticides and herbicides have serious side effects as silent killers. For the first time, the public learned how heavy metals, such as mercury and lead, seep into the water systems, where they are picked up by the simplest forms of life. As each higher level of life eats each lower one, the poisonous metals are stored in fat tissues; these poisons are ingested in ever more concentrated amounts when little fish, which eat plankton, are devoured by larger fish. Eventually, the poison concentrates in humans who eat the larger fish.

A new level of concern for the quality of life spread throughout society; the public became aware that local concerns multiplied into problems of global proportion. Ecologists argued for a "spaceship Earth" concept in caring for our planet. Pollution was characterized as a form of global suicide. Biologists and allied groups pronounced rivers and lakes dead and held national rallies to protest the destruction of the environment which the agitators argued was a common legacy. Popular musicians and singers participated in this effort, lending visibility to the problem and building a popular culture that rejected corporations.

The positive contributions made by chemistry were obscured by the discovery of the impact of toxic waste and related issues. Events such as the Cuyahoga River catching fire in Cleveland dramatized the seriousness of chemical pollution. Ecologists mobilized to conduct memorial services dedicated to the past beauty of the countryside. Once, DDT had been hailed as the victory of chemistry over pests. In the 1960s, it came to symbolize the destruction of wildlife populations. Even the national symbol, the bald eagle, was likely to become extinct if remedies were not put into place. The legacy of the land, so deeply ingrained in the American people, had nearly been lost because of indifference, wanton waste, and corporate profits.

How the private sector responded to these new facts, premises, and policy conclusions determined whether it could avoid more stringent regulation and win back public trust. When even soft drink containers became a political issue, the question shifted back to corporations. One of the most famous Advertising Council public service campaigns was the "people start pollution, people can stop it" effort financed by Keep America Beautiful, Inc. It featured a Native American shedding a tear for the fouled landscape. By drawing attention to the need for individual (as compared to collective) responsibility in combating litter, the series adroitly sought to reposition the pollution issue by downplaying its industrial origins and deflecting efforts to punish business. This theme is not surprising, because the volunteer coordinator of the Ad Council campaign was W. Howard Chase, then with American Can Company. Board members of Keep America Beautiful also included representatives of soft drink companies, brewers, glass bottlers, and aluminum can manufacturers (Barnouw, 1978).

Ralph Nader helped spawn this consumer concern in 1965 when he proclaimed that General Motors' Corvair compact was "unsafe at any speed." New standards of automobile safety were imposed on the car industry, in part by consumer interest groups but even more resoundingly by the massive insurance industry. This group wanted car manufacturers to implement automobile designs that would lessen the costs of injury, death, reconstructive survey, and rehabilitation. Elements of the public, educated by advertising to desire high quality products at low prices, angrily gave birth to consumer interest groups. Many critics demanded that corporations deliver all that they promised in their product and service advertisements.

Rebuffed consumers formed organizations presenting a potent counterbalance to corporate interests. Consumer concern and environmental protection continued into the 1990s. Large consumer coalitions, such as the Consumer Federation of America, drew their financial support and membership from across the nation. Opposing sophisticated corporate lobbying efforts, consumers borrowed strategies refined by other activists who had learned to use government to reshape corporate performance. Tactics have included media blitzes, class action suits, boycotts, defiant rallies, injunctions, and grassroots lobbying of government agencies. Since the 1960s, the consumer movement has turned its attention to virtually every aspect of human life touched by business.

Of the 35 major health, safety, and environmental laws that had been passed by 1982, starting with the Dangerous Cargo Act in 1877, 26 came into being in the 1960s and 1970s (Renfro, 1982). These cover tobacco and alcohol abuse, flammable fabrics, poison prevention packaging, mine and railroad protection, water pollution control, clean air, noise control, lead-based paint restrictions, food quality control, and myriad other issues that introduced a new vocabulary and an accompanying set of values. The National Environmental Policy Act of 1969 required environmental impact statements. In slightly more than a decade, environmental acts were passed regarding endangered species (1973), safe drinking water (1974), transportation of hazardous materials (1975), toxic substances (1976), solid waste disposal and resource conservation (1976), surface mining (1977), hazardous liquid pipeline safety (1979), and environmental compensation and liability (1980). Recent additions to this list include the Hazardous and Solid Waste Amendments (1984), Superfund Reauthorization Act and Emergency Planning and Community Right-to-Know Act (1986), Water Quality Act (1987), Lead Contamination Control Act (1988), Ocean Dumping Ban Act (1988), offshore production and transportation legislation of 1990, and the Clean Air Act (1990). Many aspects of corporations' and citizens' lives are affected by a deluge of legislative acts: Highway Safety Amendments (1984), Age Discrimination in Employment Act Amendments (1986), Americans with Disabilities Act (1990), Asbestos Hazard Emergency Response Act (1986), Civil Rights Restoration Act (1987), Commercial Motor Vehicle Safety Act (1986), Comprehensive Smokeless Tobacco Health Education Act (1986), Drug-Free Workplace Act (1988), Education of the Handicapped Act Amendments (1986, 1990), Fair Housing Act Amendments (1988), Cash Management Improvement Act (1990), Older Workers Benefit Protection Act (1990), and Social Security Amendments (1983, 1991). These pieces of legislation require that billions of dollars be spent to reengineer society. An array of governmental agencies, state and federal, was created to formulate and implement regulations aimed at achieving new levels of corporate responsibility.

The terms *biodegradable, returnable,* and *recyclable* became hallmarks of responsible "green" product marketing. Housewives learned that plastic containers, which seemed so convenient, would last in unsightly landfills long after they themselves had died. Nuclear generation and nuclear waste disposal became issues made more salient by the Three Mile Island nuclear generating facility incident. Legislative acts made executives personally liable for ensuring that their companies complied with standards relating to toxicity and clean air and water. Acts went so far as to state that executives did not have to have direct information regarding noncompliance; they would be liable for creating an organizational culture that allowed noncompliance by subordinates.

The relationship between employer and employee became more regulated. The Occupational Safety and Health Act established an administrative agency charged with ensuring that workers not be subjected to unsafe or unhealthy working conditions. Asbestos became a major corporate political issue, particularly when it was learned that companies involved in mining and processing asbestos had covered up evidence linking it with cancer.

Revolutionary changes in employment, hiring, salary, and promotion practices dramatically redefined the standards of corporate responsibility. Resulting from efforts by the civil rights and women's movements, firms were required by federal law to become "equal opportunity employers." Employees' rights to speak out publicly on controversial issues were protected, as was the right to disclose illegal actions by their employers.

The love-hate relationship between corporations and their employees took a dramatic turn in the 1980s. Employees in the steel industry saw their skills become obsolete and their jobs lost, as steel production in the United States declined to World War I levels. At the same time, a new assembly line of "information highway" operators was born. Workers were voting to do away with their unions. Employees were buying their companies to keep them from relocating or going out of business. In several instances, such as at Rath Packing Company, new worker-managers quickly learned that one of the first changes must be a reduction in wages and size of workforce. Another dramatic occurrence in the 1980s was a reduction in the number of oil companies through mergers. Little criticism was launched against this trend despite the fact that only a decade earlier, attempts were made to break up oil companies in hopes of increasing competition and lowering gasoline prices. At the same time oil companies were allowed to merge, the AT&T Bell System was forcibly divided into interconnected but independent operating components.

Privacy emerged as a major employee and consumer policy issue. Frustration with massive, impersonal databases, computerized mailing lists, electronic banking, and computerized telemarketing and children's access to adult material have played a part in the consumer push for government oversight of information industry practices. A landmark piece of legislation pertaining to potential government abuse was the Freedom of Information Act of 1966, amended in 1974, which gives public access to many federal records. This act also made public certain information that corporations have on individuals. The Privacy Act of 1974 balanced this by specifying that documents regarding employee performance must be guarded from scrutiny by unauthorized individuals. Later, the Foreign Corrupt Practices Act (1977) reflected congressional concern that information and guidelines were needed for corporate behavior overseas. The act specifies that companies operating abroad must implement adequate internal measures to prevent illegal payments to obtain business.

Many governmental agencies have the power to demand information from corporations and make it public. These agencies include the Securities and Exchange Commission, Federal Trade Commission, Federal Communications Commission, U.S. Postal Service, Occupational Health and Safety Administration, Office of Economic Opportunity, Nuclear Regulatory Commission, Consumer Products Safety Commission, Organization for Economic Cooperation and Development, and the EPA.

Acquisition of information is only part of the policy effort. In regulatory efforts, debate always centers on which criteria should be used in determining what constitutes responsible business behavior. Corporations have much of the technical expertise and information necessary to discover the best methods for solving problems, but until pressured, they are often reluctant to use this knowledge.

Executives ruefully discovered that changes in attitudes, beliefs, or norms of behavior led to public condemnation of corporate behavior that had been tolerated, and even applauded, by a previous generation. The earliest interpretations of the criticism launched against the private sector in the 1970s focused on what company issue analysts thought was anticapitalism. They believed that reporters misunderstood what companies were trying to accomplish and did not appreciate established business principles and methods. Instead of recognizing that the controversy resulted from differences of opinion regarding the standards of acceptable business practices, private sector issue analysts diagnosed the problem as resulting from misunderstanding. Thus, they prescribed increased communication without acknowledging that business had implemented standards that did not meet expectations of critical publics.

Political pressures were brought to bear by activists. They selected the issues, provided information needed to ascertain whether problems existed, established the agenda for debate, preempted "moral" arguments by convincingly couching their case in public interest rather than self-serving commercial terms, and engaged in relentlessly well-organized and tactically intelligent campaigns attractive to media reporters. Environmental groups, for instance, matured from ragtag operations to boast memberships in the millions. They acquired money to engage in research, to establish wildlife preserves, and to create partnerships to protect the environment.

Developing a platform of understanding, using or establishing premises, and earning trust have become the heart of issues management and collaborative decision making. Having a false view of a corporation is worse than having an uninformed one. Shrewd companies attempt to cooperate with leaders of activist groups rather than destroy them and demean their efforts. One interesting case of cooperate-consumer coalition is the Food Safety Council, which was formed out of the mutual interest of companies and consumers to bring order to the chaos of safety standards for food ingredients (Steckmest, 1982).

Because of uncertainties surrounding nature and toxicology, the American Industrial Health Council was formed in 1977. Approximately 200 companies and trade associations provided support for the shared interest in monitoring toxic waste and materials issues. The council represented an array of industrial concerns, including pharmaceutical and petrochemical companies. The council drew together those interested in metals, textiles, and other consumer goods that could be toxic or that produce toxic wastes. The members shared the commitment to better understand the nature and control of toxic materials.

Another example of collaborative decision making: To counterbalance the drive for regulation of disposable aluminum cans, industry companies and municipalities have sponsored recycling programs. Not only did this campaign help abate the move to outlaw throwaway containers and impose returnables in their place, it also supplied aluminum companies with a cheaper resource that requires less electricity to process than does the refining of raw materials.

Environmental standards for business have been hotly contested. Debates regarding levels of ozone, noise, light, sulfur oxides, nitrous oxide, and heavy metals have yielded a clearer picture regarding what fixed and mobile sources contribute to the total amount of air pollution and ozone damage. Typical of sudden radical challenges to business operations, E. I. Du Pont de Nemours & Company was one of many companies caught in the chlofluorocarbon (CFC) controversy that grew from a scientific paper published in 1974. It charged that the CFCs in refrigeration, aerosol propellants, and foam-blowing agents rise into the atmosphere where they damage the ozone layer, which in turn increases exposure to ultraviolet wavelengths and leads to other serious problems.

Du Pont's campaign was managed through a steering committee chaired by the division manager of the Freon Products Division of the Organic Chemicals Department. This committee consisted of members from marketing, research, legal, advertising, and public affairs departments. Issue advertising was handled by the N. W. Ayer agency, assisted by Hill & Knowlton, Inc. A matrix arrangement resulted in a complex, interlocking approval process. The campaign discussed facts and reasoning involved in the fluorocarbon controversy. The initial ad, under the signature of Chairman of the Board Irving S. Shapiro, ran in major daily newspapers and two trade publications, *Aerosol Age* and *Editor & Publisher*. Du Pont expressed its willingness to fund research into the potential damage of its product to the complex chemistry of the atmosphere. Survey results indicated the campaign helped open the discussion. As data were acquired and research and development efforts progressed, manufacturers of CFCs and the industries that used them, such as computer component manufacturers, implemented alternative processes and moved to eliminate CFCs from production and industrial use.

The Alaskan pipeline and controversies over offshore drilling and access to the Alaskan National Wildlife Animal Refuge denied energy industry boardrooms the freedom to disregard the environment. A visit to oil fields in this country allows anyone to witness environmental devastation that is more than 70 years old. A similar visit to contemporary oil drilling and production sites offers tangible evidence of the marked improvement in corporate responsibility, albeit forced by regulation. Industry spokespersons have not been reluctant to point to these accomplishments in an attempt to refurbish their tattered corporate images.

At times, companies look bad because of inept explanations of their situation to the press and other publics, but they often deserve the criticism they receive. For example, *The Wall Street Journal* presented a story about Walter Peeples, Jr., whose "tiny company, Gulf Nuclear Inc., is," he claimed, "the victim of onerous, nitpicking regulations made by regulators of 'questionable competency.' " One of the worst errors occurred when a lathe operator accidentally cut in half a capsule containing Americium-241, a radioactive isotope. The contents splattered around the workshop and nearby lunchroom. The firm failed to file the state-mandated report of the accident, and employees were told not to mention the accident (Burrough, 1983, p. 17). This is one of a legion of incidents where failure to comply with standards of responsible behavior resulted in reinforced doubts about companies' willingness to be ethical and responsive to the public trust.

Three decades of energetic criticism and robust development in issue communication, plus the prospect for future challenges, provide the context for the study and practice of issues management. Those who manage, design, or critique issue campaigns have learned that they cannot assume that these tactics will establish mutual interests with all stakeholders. They have come to see the virtue in negotiation and collaborative decision making. They have learned the lesson that issue communication cannot solve problems and abate criticism that require improved business operations. "Government officials who had tolerated business's foot-dragging for several decades responded to mounting public pressures by demanding immediate solutions to a series of difficult problems" (Galambos & Pratt, 1988, p. 213).

Issues management's history reminds us of the options needed to bring or restore harmony between corporations, employees, consumers, and key publics. Discovery of new facts about nutrition or the impact of products on health, for instance, can affect changes in how companies are viewed. Premises used to evaluate this information change over time and become widely accepted, as was the case for one of the underpinning premises of the foreseeable future: That which is environmentally sound is preferred to that which is not. Out of the blend of information and premises reflecting values of society, conclusions are drawn and public policy is forged.

One victim of the turbulent past three decades is the assumption, promoted by public relations pioneer Edward Bernays (1955), that consent can be engineered. Business historians, Galambos and Pratt (1988) reflected on the dislocating transition for business in the 1970s: "Just as the Vietnam War forced the nation to reassess its military and political power in international affairs, however, so the energy and environmental crises forced difficult reassessments in the nation's business system" (p. 202). Regardless of the interest of any person or organization in this drama, the long-term goal of society and the organizations that conduct or regulate business is to achieve sufficient order so they can strategically plan and systematically achieve those plans. If companies cannot always manage issues, they can implement effective strategic business plans, engage in useful communication, and manage their public policy plans.

Pendulums swing. The off-year 1994 elections witnessed a landslide of conservative candidates entering office or maintaining their seats—what was billed by some as a "Contract with America." One of the key players in that contract was Representative Tom DeLay (R. Texas), House of Representatives Majority Whip, who is resolved to ferret out and end unnecessary regulations. Whereas one bias in government is that if any regulation is good, lots more is better, DeLay believed that most regulation is a waste or imposes incorrect assumptions and unnecessary restrictions (Noah, 1995). As the public policy arena nears the end of the century, the move toward conservatism and lessened regulation swings back toward the position of an earlier era.

The annual price tag of regulation is frequently placed at $450 billion, which government imposes on business and consumers. In the current governmental climate, legislators such as DeLay are revisiting assumptions about legislation and regulation. Congress is exploring this change by (a) assuming the need for a regulatory moratorium, (b) limiting unfunded mandates, and (c) examining the costs of regulation as part of each piece of legislation. The challenge facing this Congress is to

> demonstrate that it stands not only for less regulation, but more prudent regulation that is based on sound economics. The regulatory resolution will not be complete until Congress moves from procedural reforms to substantive reforms based on a principled revision of the statutes. (Hahn, 1995, p. A12)

The movement of the pendulum is dialectical, a search for order.

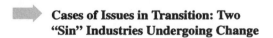

Cases of Issues in Transition: Two "Sin" Industries Undergoing Change

The search continues. Two dramatic cases shed insight into trends of attack by critics and responses by industries. This section seeks instructive understanding by examining the pressures on and responses by the tobacco and alcohol beverage industry. These industries produce products that are enormously popular, a vital part of U.S. culture and economy. Both industries manufacture and sell products that have been associated with addiction and health problems. Both industries have worked to balance their traditional marketing approaches to build on the lifestyle advantages to be derived from using their products and claims by critics that the products have serious negative health, social, and economic consequences.

The Tobacco Industry: From Chic to Sick?

The tobacco industry is under significant pressure from scientists, legislators, regulators, and activists who continue to fight for increased restrictions
on smoking. Representative Waxman (D. California) brought the senior executives of the tobacco industry under the spotlight of committee hearings in
1994. Grilled for days before the House Energy and Commerce Committee's
Subcommittee on Health and Environment, executives denied any connection
between their products and health problems. Although many businesses have
been able to counteract or prevent regulation by changing their policies and
operations, the tobacco industry has few change options. Despite the ban on
electronic advertising, cigarette makers have maintained markets by redirect-
ing their advertising efforts to more clearly defined reader segments and have
engaged in a massive publicity effort, such as sponsoring sporting events that
allow the industry access to televiewing audiences—without advertising.
Smoking is characterized as fun, such as the high lifestyle portrayal in the Joe
Camel ads. Typical messages insinuate that smoking is part of adult lifestyles,
even though manufacturers realize that appeals that seem to encourage smoking by youngsters will incite public interest wrath.

The marketing communication strategy used by the industry includes
sophisticated public affairs lobbying and heavy use of print and outdoor
product reminder ads combined with an adult-oriented information program
spearheaded by the Tobacco Institute. As the backbone of its legislative
campaign, the industry stresses tobacco's economic importance, marshals
farmers to engage in grassroots lobbying, maintains liaison with powerful
congressional figures, defends its products in court, and challenges every
health-related claim launched against the product.

One goal of the Tobacco Institute has been to keep open the debate on
medical findings linking smoking with a variety of health ailments. In one
advertisement the Institute circulated in October 1983, several "answers"
were provided to the "most asked questions about cigarettes." Typical of the
content was the conclusion, "A nonsmoker might have to spend 100 hours
straight in a smoky bar to inhale the equivalent of a single filter cigarette."

Whereas the Institute spearheaded advocacy communication for the industry, R. J. Reynolds Tobacco Company undertook its own print advertising
campaign to (a) bolster its corporate image, (b) help differentiate R. J.
Reynolds from its competitors, and (c) display social responsibility by demonstrating concern over the smoking controversy. Reynolds offered what it
believed to be factual and unbiased information to "separate fact from friction" in a proactive attempt to open communication between smoker and
nonsmoker. Because the ads complement industry efforts, however, a strong
case can be made that their primary motivation is to forestall or prevent
regulation.

Public interest groups have targeted an outright ban on all tobacco advertising as one major way to lessen young people's desire to smoke. Cigarette advertisements constitute nearly $900 million in revenue for magazines, newspapers, and billboards. The allegation is that advertising lures impressionable kids via sexually appealing and attractive role models such as the Marlboro Man or Virginia Slim Woman and the cartoon representations of Joe Camel. Scholars' research findings link cigarette advertising with children's and adolescents' reactions to cigarettes and the onset of smoking behavior (Botvin, Goldberger, Botvin, & Dusenbury, 1993; Goldstein, Fischer, Richards, & Cretan, 1987; Pierce et al., 1991).

Reynolds met this issue head on in 1984 by acknowledging the apprehension of parents who see the plethora of cigarette advertisements placed where they can be seen by children. The company announced, "We don't want young people to smoke. And we're running ads aimed specifically at young people advising them that we think smoking is strictly for adults." Reynolds reported that cigarette advertising is designed not to get people to start smoking but to switch from one brand to another. "That's why we don't [product] advertise to young people." The Reynolds message to teenage readers was, "If you take up smoking just to prove you're an adult, you're really proving just the opposite." The advertisement concluded, "After all, you may not be old enough to smoke. But you're old enough to think." Critics of smoking point to the allure that advertising has when it tells children that they are not old enough to do adult actions.

Another paid message in the 1984 series disputed whether environmental tobacco smoke (ETS) is harmful to nonsmoking persons who happen to be in the vicinity of smokers. One point made is that "there is little evidence—and certainly nothing that proves scientifically—that cigarette smoke causes disease in non-smokers." Cited was testimony from a 1983 ETS conference on lung cancer that " 'An overall evaluation based upon available scientific data leads to the conclusion that an increased risk for non-smokers from ETS exposure has not been established.' " The ad quoted chief statistician of the American Cancer Society, Lawrence Garfinkel, who said, "Passive smoking may be a political matter, but it is not a main issue in terms of health policy."

With statements such as these, R. J. Reynolds sought to weaken the criticism of ETS. Restaurants, retail stores, government offices, businesses, and airlines have realized the popularity (to say nothing of lower maintenance) associated with no-smoking restrictions. Airlines, either on a voluntary basis or due to federal restrictions, created a no-smoking policy. Through a series of ads in 1994, Reynolds argued that the issue must be settled by individuals through "respect" and "accommodation," not "confrontation," "segregation," or "legislation." Smoking "annoyance is neither a governmental problem nor a medical problem. It's a people problem." The solution is "talk." Reynolds advised, "Smokers can help by being more considerate and responsible.

Non-smokers can help by being more tolerant. And both groups can help by showing more respect for each other's rights and feelings." The issue, from Reynolds's point of view, is for nonsmokers to stop hassling smokers.

Reynolds's attempt to build public understanding by offering information smokers can use to defend themselves against personal attack is innovative but may not be very effective. The proposal for more civility certainly will not convince either the Surgeon General or hard-core antismoking agitators to stop in their tracks. It might blunt support for such groups if enough people were convinced that regulation is not the best way to solve this problem. Many people who do not smoke prefer not to have the air they breathe fouled by the behavior of others. In one sense, there is no incentive for nonsmokers to breathe that air; the incentive is on the other side: persons who want to smoke and the industry that wants to peddle cigarettes. Where is the accommodation and compromise, with nonsmokers having nothing to gain and only something to lose?

As well as seeking to reduce tension between smokers and nonsmokers, the industry resorted to libel action. The concern of the industry has been the reporting of information and the drawing of conclusions that it alleges are not true. A libel suit was initiated in 1995 by Philip Morris against Capital Cities/ABC Inc. regarding claims made in a newsmagazine show, "Day One," that the company spiked its cigarettes with nicotine—added extraneous or extra nicotine to raise it to an unnatural level. Issues of operating philosophy and manufacturing procedure are central to the public scrutiny of this industry, the objective being to establish whether it is engaging in activities that violate public standards of appropriate operations. This suit was dropped in August of 1995 in exchange for a public apology, which Philip Morris aired on Monday Night Football and ran in major daily newspapers around the country. ABC acknowledged that the two parties disagreed on major facts in this news report but admitted, "We should not have reported that Philip Morris adds significant amounts of nicotine from outside sources."

In self-defense, tobacco companies opted for a two-pronged approach, image and issue. In 1995, Philip Morris engaged in a print advertising campaign to demonstrate its corporate responsibility. The theme of the ad was the effort Philip Morris was exerting to limit minors' access to cigarettes, framed with this statement: "At Philip Morris we have always believed that minors should not smoke, nor should they have access to cigarettes." To demonstrate its commitment, it listed 10 actions it was implementing. (a) Place on each pack and carton the statement, "Underage sale prohibited." (b) Discontinue giving free samples of cigarettes. (c) Discontinue sending free samples of cigarettes through the mails. (d) Deny merchandising benefits to retailers who are convicted of selling cigarettes to minors. (e) Join legislative efforts to prevent minors' access to cigarettes through vending machines. (f)

Intensify efforts to prevent use of the logos on products marketed to minors. (g) Vigorously support posting of signs in retail outlets indicating the illegality of selling cigarettes to minors. (h) Assist vendors in prohibiting sales to minors by circulating "Ask first—It's the law" literature and conducting education programs. (i) Assist legislative actions to require that cigarette sales be under direct control of retail sales personnel. (j) Join in legislative efforts to license retail sales outlets.

Due to the multiple stakeholder character in issues management, this position was viewed as a victory by antismoking groups, although some activists viewed it with skepticism and would not accept any measure short of a total cessation of cigarette sales. In addition, the propositions in the ad caused the retailers to bristle because they reasoned that they were being portrayed as the bad guys in the ad. They did not believe that they were responsible for children smoking.

Issue ads sponsored by the National Smokers Alliance, supported by tobacco companies, argued against intrusion of big government into people's lives. The theme, explained in text and reinforced in clever graphics, was that the preferences of a few—antismoking fanatics—were imposed on the many who want to exercise freedom of choice, including smoking. In a second print ad in 1995, the Alliance asked, "Who will they target next?" Rather than portraying efforts to lessen people's exposure to smoke as a positive health measure, the industry cast this battle as an issue of personal freedom. How far could that go? In a third ad, the Alliance warned that the "lifestyle police" will progress beyond cigarettes to "rub out leather," "ban coffee," "no free thinking," and "no red meat." The graphic was a person tied down and staked with all of these restrictions.

Philip Morris Company has emphasized the right—the freedom—of smokers to use its products. Such value associations are important as key stakeholders debate standards of corporate responsibility and contest the facts that relate to how well companies meet them. Few industries have been under siege longer and by such powerful foes than has the tobacco industry. The companies remain resolute, most recently during the 1994 hearings before the House Committee.

Antismoking groups continue their efforts to chip away at the public support for smoking as well as at the favorable governmental treatment of tobacco products. In July 1996, the Federal Drug Administration concluded for the first time that nicotine is a drug and therefore must be more closely regulated. Related to that decision was the recommendation that tobacco products not be sold through vending machines and that sanctions be placed on cigarette advertising, especially the use of Joe Camel by R. J. Reynolds.

By 1996, thousands of articles and research reports had claimed that tobacco products increase the likelihood of cancer, heart disease, and respiratory problems. Representatives of the federal government had become convinced that nicotine is addictive and should be regulated as such. Critics, including state attorneys general, have begun to argue in court that the impact of these products on the health-of-society costs are greater than the benefits. State governments are asking the tobacco industry to pay for their medical cost damage. Antismoking critics are quick to point out that tobacco product advertising does not make persons fully aware of the hazards of the products.

The tobacco industry responds to each of these claims arguing that they are not based on sound scientific research and reasoning. Since the 1960s, cigarettes and other tobacco products have been required to carry warning labels. For this reason, the tobacco industry emphasizes that smoking is a voluntary action by adults. Industry spokespersons believe that people have been warned of the potential harm of using tobacco products and are capable of deciding for themselves whether to purchase and use them.

The defense the industry has created asserts that it has spent millions to improve the quality and safety of its products. The industry has denied scientific allegations about the health impacts of its products and asserts that it acts responsibly. In 1996, President Clinton increased pressure on the industry by seeking to have various contents of tobacco listed as controlled substances because of their addictive effect. He launched a campaign to restrict children's exposure to cigarette advertising and to the sale of tobacco products. Taking voluntary action, large store chains, such as Target, decided not to sell tobacco products despite the fact that they are typically quite profitable. The future will test the industry's ability to maintain its sense of denial against such great odds.

The Alcohol Beverage Industry: Images of
Youth, Health, or Uncontrolled Binge?

Building on growing concern about alcohol abuse, public interest groups politicized drinking. Some colleges fear student performance on tests and course work is harmed by the high profile of beer distributors on campus. The legal drinking age has been raised in most states. Bartenders, restaurant owners, and hosts of private parties have been held responsible for the sobriety of guests and the actions of guests who injure other parties due to alcohol. Groups such as Mothers Against Drunk Driving continue to seek stiffer offender penalties.

Critics of alcohol advertising attempt to imprint the same product stigma that has been effective in the battle against tobacco. Out front is the Washington-based Center for Science in the Public Interest, which includes the National Council on Alcoholism, United Methodist Church, and the 5.5 million-member National Parent-Teacher Association. Much like the early anticigarette campaign, these groups are focusing their protest on television messages that play up themes of fun and irresponsibility. Like tobacco interests, industry spokesmen argue that no correlation exists between beverage advertising and product abuse and that alcoholism was a problem long before TV commercials. Under pressure, networks have tightened their standards for alcohol ad copy.

One advertising and marketing response by the industry is to deemphasize the "virtues" of excessive consumption. Anheuser-Busch, in 1984, spent over $6 million on educational programs to combat alcohol abuse. The brewery employed baseball celebrities to caution against product overuse. The industry sponsors Advertising Council print and broadcast public service announcements stressing that "friends don't let friends drive drunk." Responsible members of the industry will provide on request videos and other materials to assist parents and teenagers in their discussion of the responsible use of alcohol. Ads have been employed to demonstrate how motor skills deteriorate under the influence of alcohol. Besides advertising, industry communicators offer booklets, films, speakers, and other materials to enlist educator and parent support for responsible use of alcohol. For example, The Licensed Beverage Information Council, in conjunction with the U.S. Department of Treasury, alerted pregnant women to the effects of alcohol on unborn babies. Such campaigns helped increase awareness through information, but they also have had the additional persuasive potential of "proving" the industry does indeed care about how its products are used and about the people who use them.

A 1991 *Wall Street Journal* news story summed up the problems facing the industry: "Despite years of image-burnishing by the alcohol industry, the vast majority of Americans still believe the booze business is irresponsible and unethical and that its ads encourage teen-agers to drink, a new study shows" (Lipman, 1991a, p. B4). The study was commissioned by the industry. Why does such suspicion and outrage exist?

 ## Conclusion

This chapter described how key publics' and organizations' contest for order is a debate. Interested participants seek to provide facts, shape premises used to judge those facts, and draw conclusions from that combination. Individual statements blend into collective opinions. If chaos reigned, companies and other key segments of society could not conduct their activities. For this reason, a primary rationale for issues management, the dialogue in society is a search for order.

Scouting the Terrain

Strategic Planning Based on
Scanning, Monitoring, and Analysis

Recall those movie scenes, especially in westerns, where a hero or heroine studies the landscape to find safe shelter or to watch for friends or villains coming over the horizon or around the corner? Likewise, no executive who intends to plan and manage effectively likes surprises, especially unwelcome ones. Persons responsible for the management of organizations need a means by which they can obtain and use public policy relevant opinion. It can be used to determine what standards of organizational performance are likely to suffer the least amount of conflict that can waste valuable human and financial resources.

Opinion landscapes shape market forces and affect operating costs. Change happens. A competitor presses for new product or manufacturing process guidelines. A market changes dramatically. A regulator alters ground rules, which can add to the cost of doing business. An activist group challenges established assumptions by reasoning from different principles than a business or governmental agency does. Some nut tampers with a product. Workers are hurt when an operating process fails because the standards on which it is based are inadequate. A reporter writes an accurate and embarrassing feature story. Activists or members of another industry call for public policy changes that affect an organization's business plan. Even for companies that employ situational analysis, misstatements, misrepresentations, and disagreements may require immediate response. A crisis may require issues analysis.

The person who wants to be a vital part of the executive team needs to understand his or her industry well enough to know what changes can add costs to how business is done or where business advantages can be obtained (Reeves, 1993). Viewed this way, "An issue becomes strategic when top management believes that it has relevance for organizational performance" (Dutton & Ashford, 1993, p. 397). Often, one or more members of the organization recognize the nature and seriousness of an issue and sell it to management. As management comes to share the sense of opportunity or harm that can result from the issue, they move to name it, collect information about it, discuss it, and assign key individuals to the issue. Managements are more likely to find subordinates willing to watch for an issue and bring it to executives' attention when the management cadre is open to and rewards such initiatives (Dutton & Ashford, 1993).

Surprise can upset the execution of a strategic business plan and require a new or altered public policy or communication plan. Strategic business planning requires effort to bring turbulence under control (Dutton & Duncan, 1987). Surveillance can increase the likelihood that they can accomplish their strategic plan (Markley, 1988; Sawaya & Arrington, 1988; Stroup, 1988).

This chapter establishes a rationale and tactics for issue identification, scanning, monitoring, analysis, and priority setting. It sheds light on how issue analysis should look for conflict and mutual interests between a firm and its stakeholders. Of importance is the ability to ascertain as early as possible what issues need attention and determine how they can be used in a company's strategic guidance system. One concern is estimating which issues may yield to communication and which ones require new procedure or policy to repair, maintain, or strengthen relationships with stakeholders. The goal is to identify and understand incompatibilities between cultures—zones of meaning—to seek ethical and harmonious resolution of frictions that arise from opinion differences.

 Things Go Bump in the Dark

Effective issues managers engage in environmental-situational position assessment. To develop and execute their plans, executives must know the opinions surrounding their organization. They should be committed to situational analysis that can help them avoid the unexpected. To define that process, this section lays out a rationale and structure for integrating strategic business planning and issues monitoring.

Issues monitoring and analysis shed insight into beliefs and attitudes held by stakeholding publics that can affect the destiny of an organization by the way stakes are granted or withheld. Issues monitoring and analysis seeks to know what facts, premises, and values key publics use and what conclusions they draw from them. Much of the general public knows or cares little about issues that can affect the destiny of an organization, but the opinions of key publics can be crucial to its success. Opinions may be unfounded, incoherent, ill-defined, unproven, and inconsistent; they nevertheless may be vital to the future of the organization.

Opinions of key publics can affect corporate decisions related to marketing, product development, operating standards, options for financing business activities, consumer protection, transportation and manufacturing safety standards, and environmental protection. If planners and strategists make incorrect assumptions about this landscape, as they did in the early 1960s, they are likely to steer their companies on a collision course with the expectations of key publics. Strategic business planning cannot be successfully executed by managers who have little idea of, and inaccurately understand, the market forces, technical innovations, vested opinions, public policy, and fiscal opportunities or threats that lie ahead of their firms. As a firm might be on a collision course with market factors, it can also be positioned in a strategically indefensible way on matters of public policy that can affect its ability to achieve its strategic business plan.

Issues monitoring and analysis need to be strategic. No organization can identify, track, and respond to every issue. It cannot afford to bog down in issues identification, scanning, monitoring, and analysis so that it defaults in the public policy process because it tries to do too much with every issue and accomplishes too little with the ones that truly make a difference to the success of the organization. Some issues are easy to track. Once they enter legislative, regulatory, or litigation processes, they can be traced through formal channels. Issues often seem to have more of a life than they deserve; they are like a nuisance dog—constantly under foot. Issues managers reveal that much of what concerns them today worried them a decade ago, with subtle change.

Some issues become so technical that they leave the realm of public discussion and are debated or negotiated in legislative, regulatory, or judicial chambers by experts for companies, governmental agencies, and activist groups. Rather than dramatic issue shifts, their concerns revolve around subtle technical changes such as measures of toxicity, levels of pollution, or the entry of new players in the public policy marketplace.

Issues management entails the skilled balance of four functions: (a) Strategic business planning with a vigilant eye to public policy trends; (b) scanning, monitoring, and analyzing issues to understand the terrain; (c) communicating in ways that create a good offense and tough defense; and (d) being sensitive to changing expectations of corporate responsibility and adapting to those standards. Strategic planning creates business plans and determines how to achieve them, including the option of employing public policy and communication plans. Planning must consider circumstances—internal and external—that will affect how and whether the business plan is accomplished.

To assist strategic planning, issues managers—in coordination with key persons throughout an organization—must scan the environment to (a) ascertain what public policy issues are arising and progressing, (b) know their substance, (c) identify why they are staying alive and what players are sustaining them, and (d) learn from the analysis. Scanning, monitoring, and analysis may give companies time to change business policies, undertake a communication program, negotiate differences, collaboratively make decisions, create a platform of fact, propose the best values by which to judge the issue, or counter unwise policies. Scanning and monitoring can give technical experts and managers time to develop a stance to take advantage or lessen the impact of emerging or changing issues (Krippendorff & Eleey, 1986).

Situational analysis is the foundation for developing and implementing business strategy, which, according to Hax and Majluf (1991),

is a coherent, unifying, and integrative pattern of decisions;

establishes the firm's objectives, action programs, and resource allocation priorities;

selects the businesses the firm is in or should be in;

attempts to achieve a sustainable advantage in each of its businesses by responding properly to opportunities or threats in the environment, given the firm's strengths and weaknesses;

engages all levels of the business (corporate, business, functional); and

defines the economic and noneconomic exchanges it intends to make with its stakeholders and stakeseekers.

Public policy change options demand environmental-situational position assessment:

Obtaining input from all levels (executive, staff, and operations) regarding the implications of public policy changes on business plans and operations

Scanning and monitoring the issue environment to determine internal and external stakeholder groups' standards of corporate social responsibility (expectations of how businesses should operate in the public interest)

Identifying, analyzing, forecasting, and prioritizing issues based on their potential impact on the organization

Scanning and issue analysis can be proactive or reactive. Reactive scanning focuses on the search for obstacles. Proactive scanning looks for issue opportunities, those shifts in opinions that the organization can use strategically to foster mutual interests between it and its stakeholders.

▶ Rationale of Issues Identification, Scanning, Monitoring, Analysis, and Priority Setting

The term *issues management* is often used as though it entailed nothing more than issues monitoring and analysis. That view of issues management is limited, because it does not include a rationale and strategies for responding proactively to what is learned during the monitoring process. This section justifies the need for proactive attention to emerging and ongoing issues.

In his seminal work, Chase (1984) reasoned that "an issue is an unsettled matter which is ready for decision. Trends, on the other hand, are detectable changes which precede issues" (p. 38). In similar fashion, Moore (1979) defined an emerging issue "as a trend or condition, internal or external, that, if continued, would have a significant effect on how a company is operated over the period of its business plan" (p. 43). Reflecting on such definitions, Crable and Vibbert (1985) stressed the importance of treating trends, issues, and policies as quite discrete concepts.

An *issue* is a contestable point, a difference of opinion regarding fact, value, or policy the resolution of which has consequences for the organization's strategic plan. It is a matter of concern that results from what is thought to be true (factual), of value, or wise policy. A *trend* is the trajectory an issue takes because of the discussion it receives and the sociopolitical forces that impinge on it. A *policy* results when an issue is resolved through governmental action or voluntary actions by a company or industry, a negotiated agreement between combatants, or social convention.

Trends and issues are more likely to be interactive than linear. Trends result from relatively small to significantly large shifts in beliefs and attitudes that can redefine corporate performance standards or result from the awareness that such standards are being violated. Trends probably do not yield to corporate communication and may not involve specific issues that a company needs to consider in its business, public policy, or communication plans. An issue is more focused. It has the potential, once key groups begin to promote it, to require resolution—the expression of one set of standards in contrast to others or one solution in competition with others. An issue is defined by those public advocates who have an interest in it.

Issues exist in a hierarchy of abstraction. For instance, the environmental issue embraces thousands of narrow issues of fact, value, and policy. Each large issue is divided by categories; for instance, the environmental issue is divided by chemicals, plants, animals, and agricultural practices. Chemicals can be divided into categories, such as toxic and carcinogenic. Plants can cover an array from giant redwoods and firs to swamp and marshland growth. Animals are divided by types—for instance, water turtles and wolves. Even in that regard, the issues related to them are different. Turtles, for instance, are an issue when their ability to survive as a species is threatened by shrimp-harvesting measures. In contrast, wolves are not threatened by otherwise routine agricultural events but by farmers and ranchers taking overt actions against them, ostensibly to protect livestock. Viewed in this complex hierarchy of generality and interest, the status of each issue is derived by its place in each key public's issue agenda and society's issue agenda. Even in that regard, we confront related issues, such as the need for wood for houses and paper or the use of endangered plants for needed medicines.

Issues may be *universal,* affecting much of society and requiring the intervention of government or massive changes in industrial policies or procedures. Environmental issues tend to be universal, for instance. Some are *advocacy* issues, those identified by and promoted by activists. These may entail shifts in values or the adoption of new perspectives favored by the advocacy group. If such issues are quite narrow or local, they are *selective.* They can grow or fade, depending on their seriousness and the rhetorical competence of the group. They either fade, are dealt with by the stakeseeking group, or grow into advocacy issues. *Technical* issues are those that often are identified, analyzed, and solved by specialists with special training or expertise. Depending on its nature, an issue may change types (Reeves, 1993).

An issue may affect the way a firm defines itself, generates its revenue, and sets its goals. As a contestable point of fact, value, or policy, it arises when one or more key stakeholder groups concludes that a problem results from the difference between what a firm is doing and what the group expects it to do, a standard of corporate responsibility. If the gap is serious enough, it can mature into changes in public policy (legislation, regulation, or litigation). As J. Grunig (1989a, 1992a; J. Grunig & Hunt, 1984) has argued, issues managers should be interested in what key publics recognize to be a problem, believe to affect their self-interests, and feel constrained to take actions about. Of central importance is the fact that persons work hard to obtain information, talk about, and form opinions on issues related to their self-interests (Petty & Cacioppo, 1986). Issues are not just trends or unsettled matters but contestable points that concern the self-interests (even altruism) of key stakeholders that lead them to support or oppose corporate actions and public policies (Heath & Douglas, 1990, 1991). For this reason, issues monitors should define key publics, not based on demographics but on opinion positions people hold, their issue involvement, and their communication patterns (Berkowitz & Turnmire, 1994; Vasquez, 1994).

As well as understanding factors crucial to situational analysis, issues managers need to know the components of such analysis. In this regard, Renfro (1993) highlighted four intelligence activities: "(1) scanning for emerging issues, (2) researching, analyzing, and forecasting the issues, (3) prioritizing the many issues identified by the scanning and research stages, and (4) developing strategic and issue operation (or action) plans" (p. 64). A lot has been made of the matter of observing and predicting emerging issues.

A widely adopted model, presented by Chase (1984), features issue identification, analysis, change options, and action program. Acknowledging the influence of Chase, J. Johnson (1983) offered a model that Hainsworth and Meng (1988) used to feature scanning-monitoring, identification-prioritization, analysis, (strategy) decision, implementation, and evaluation. Johnson (1983) said that strategy-decision is "the pivotal stage." What are the options? Management "might decide to 'hold the fort' and take no action, or it might decide to implement a full-blown action plan in an attempt to 'kill' or mute an issue before it 'takes off' " (p. 26). Taking this stance, Johnson's model is communication oriented, featuring messages as the answer to public policy problems. This model depends on early intervention using communication to blunt issues before they do harm.

The Public Affairs Council offered a version of issues management functions that consists of five building blocks: (a) identification, (b) evaluation, (c) priority setting, (d) corporate response, and (e) implementation. This model does not integrate these issue activities into strategic business planning and management or the creation of standards of corporate responsibility (Armstrong, 1981).

By connecting corporate business strategy and public affairs planning, Fleming (1980) proposed a matrix: On the X axis of this process are identification of issues, communication, introduction of issues into planning, preparation of corporate plan, review, and approval. This sequence is complemented by Y axis functions: establishing corporate and division issues, analyzing planning premises, and preparing issue reports.

One contingency model, provided by Wartick and Rude (1986), features identification, evaluation, and response development. Even though this model is broad and assumes that these functions are continual, not linear, it does not capture the breadth of functions needed for issues management. It omits the key function of creating and implementing standards of corporate responsibility. A contingency model encourages issues managers to not think defensively about how to protect the company from public policy changes but to look for opportunities and to use public policy to create them.

Supporting this view, Arrington and Sawaya (1984) claimed that the heart of issues management "is reconciliation of conflicting internal interests on public policy issues of strategic importance in order to make a coherent external advocacy" (p. 150). This activity is proactive if public affairs is "viewed as analogous to corporate planning and research and development— as a strategic process to help realize the basic objectives of a company" (p. 158). According to survey data gathered by Wartick and Rude (1986), when issues management becomes a function of public affairs or public relations, it often loses its identity and credibility because these departments do not implement comprehensive issues management programs.

Emphasizing the contingency approach, Stroup (1988) observed, "Early knowledge of these trends would give the company more time to change negative attitudes toward business or to adapt business practices proactively if attitudes and expectations could not be swayed from the identified path" (p. 89). This view makes issues management vital to corporate planning and management. Ewing (1987) reasoned that strategic information management should be part of the systemic processes and culture needed to acquire and use information in planning. Various scholars agree (Ansoff, 1980; Dutton & Duncan, 1987; Dutton & Ottensmeyer, 1987; Lauzen, 1994, 1995).

Rather that a model based on steps of issues monitoring, this process is best conceptualized as four interlocked functions that operate simultaneously and contingently: (a) strategic planning and management; (b) development and implementation of standards of corporate responsibility; (c) issue identification, scanning, monitoring, and analysis; and (d) issue communication. Without all four functions, issues management is unlikely to achieve its potential to empower personnel to exert influence on behalf of their organizations.

Underpinning assumptions needed to guide issues identification, monitoring, and analysis are provided by coorientation. One coorientation model features three dimensions of a relationship: understanding or agreement, congruence, and accuracy (McLeod & Chafee, 1973). Broom (1977) proposed that the image or issue position preferred by a corporation be compared against that held by key publics. He suggested that

> a public relations problem exists if there is a discrepancy between the corporate definition of an issue and the views held by members of an important public. Reducing or eliminating this discrepancy then becomes the motivation for the informational and persuasive messages directed to the public. (p. 111, see also the legitimacy gap, Sethi, 1977)

Coorientation assumes that no absolute standard for issue truth, corporate image, or ethical behavior exists because such standards are formed by the dialogue between an organization and each of its stakeholder groups. The extent to which these opinions diverge can result in magnitudes of dissatisfaction on the part of the corporation and its publics. If their positions converge, both parties should be satisfied. By applying this analysis, issues managers can estimate degrees of satisfaction and accuracy as the basis for calculating whether harmony or friction exists and for formulating options to increase harmony and reduce friction.

Accuracy is an expression of the extent to which the leaders of an organization and members of stakeholder groups hold the same opinions on key points and know what each other believes. For instance, if both sides wrote down what they thought the other side believed on key issues, what was written would be the same if they understood one another. Satisfaction is a measure of the degree to which both sides evaluate (positively or negatively) what they know in the same way. For instance, a timber company and an environmental group might agree (know accurately) that the company engages in clear cutting, a means for harvesting timber. The two parties might not be equally satisfied that the practice is environmentally sound (Heath, 1990).

Issues identification, scanning, monitoring, analysis, and proactive response are vital aspects of issues management. These functions assist responsible managers in spotting issues and determining appropriate responses to reduce friction between their organization and their stakeholders. Organizations are wise to build long-term, mutually beneficial relationships and to observe and respond to potentially harmful conditions as soon as possible to avoid those issues from becoming more difficult to resolve to the mutual interest of all parties.

 Tactics of Issues Identification, Scanning, Monitoring, Analysis, and Priority Setting

Issue monitoring and communication draw on an evolving body of experience and research to make planning systematic. Advancing from the rationale established above, this section offers advice on how issues managers, along with other key members of the organization, can conduct a comprehensive effort to become alert to and stay abreast of emerging issues.

Communication practitioners and scholars have for two decades advocated the use of social scientific systems to observe and monitor issues at stages when firms still have adaptation options (Bevk, 1979; Coates et al., 1986; Coyle & Stephens, 1979; Franzen, 1977; Goldman & Auh, 1979; Grass, 1977; J. Grunig, 1977a, 1977b; Jones, 1975; Lerbinger, 1977; Marker, 1977; Stamm, 1977; Strenski, 1978, 1984; Tichenor, Donohue, & Olien, 1977; Tirone, 1977; Van Riper, 1976; Zentner, 1978). Over a decade ago, Renfro (1982) reported that at least 200 Fortune 500 corporations had established management-level groups to monitor and formulate corporate responses to public policy issues. A more recent study, consisting of 101 responses from

Fortune 500 companies, found that 60% of the sample used year-round issue-scanning systems. Firms that use scanning achieve higher growth and greater profitability than their counterparts (Subramanian, Fernandes, & Harper, 1993; see also Daft, Sormunen, & Parks, 1988).

To refine strategic management information systems (Ansoff, 1980; Dutton & Duncan, 1987; Dutton & Ottensmeyer, 1987), discussion focuses on organizational structures and the ambiguity of information and the resultant uncertainty (Huber & Daft, 1987). Key elements of uncertainty are doubts and predictions about what will happen (state), what the effect will be, and what response will occur, either on the part of the key public or the organization (Gerloff, Muir,& Bodensteiner, 1991). As well as looking outside of the organization, issue managers must understand its culture, organizational and political structures, and strategies of public policy issue analysis. Thousands of issues emerge but do not mature into concerns that require much, if any, response by the company. Even without comprehensive issue identification and response techniques (see Figure 3.1), an organization tracks changes in key issues and attempts to ascertain how their resolution can affect its business, public policy, or communication plan.

The ostensible value of identifying and acting quickly on emerging issues assumes that such issues mature from a felt concern on the part of many people. The opposite can be true. It is difficult to find and respond to the concerns of widely scattered and unorganized segments of the population. Issues may or may not be influenceable at the legislative or regulative stages. At those stages, highly skilled and perhaps well-funded opponents and supportive coalitions enter the fray. Instead of having to influence the opinions of large numbers of persons who are difficult to reach with a communication campaign, organizations may collaboratively resolve issues during hearings, through lobbying, and even at the point of litigation. Whereas environmental groups cannot win everyone or even a majority of persons in a community to share their concerns, they can use litigation to stop what they believe to be offensive corporate practices. The point: Too much can be made of the concept that issues become less influenceable as they progress through the system, as a rationale for early intervention. Later intervention—once an issue begins to solidify—may be advisable because organizations can have a better sense of their influence options at that point.

The difficulty regarding emerging issues is knowing which ones will become the mission of key and powerful groups or reporters and achieve sufficient vitality to deserve an organization's serious attention. Many issues die a natural death and never amount to anything. Few issues mature. Telling the difference is vital because no organization has the resources to scan, monitor, and respond to all issues. Casting reality into this process, Renfro (1993) concluded, "Anticipating emerging issues may be—and usually is—

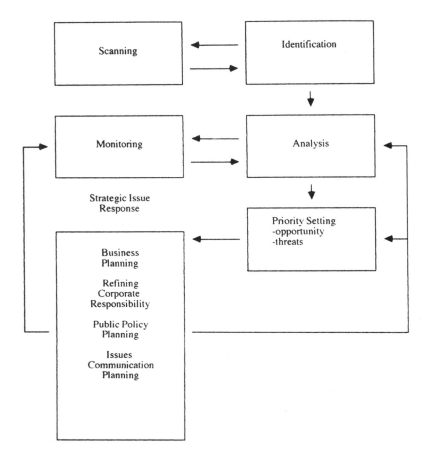

Figure 3.1. Issue Alert and Response Process

both inadequate *and* better than ignorance of them" (p. 8). Thus, Renfro asked, "What is good information about future emerging issues? Simply put, it is information that helps decision makers to improve their performance so they can achieve a better future than they believe would otherwise occur" (p. 8). Is missing the issue at its emergence crucial? "Social trend may take decades to gain prominence. In each case it is the dynamics of the system within which the issue moved that determines the time dimension" (pp. 10-11). Indeed,

> Most issues become credibly foreseeable only when they have become so stable as to be impervious to outside forces, including those generated by a

corporation's issue action program. In other words, by the time an executive has enough confidence in a forecast to justify expending his or her limited resources, it is often too late to have any real impact. (p. 12).

Although issue scanning, monitoring, and analysis occur constantly, they need to be phased into the normal planning patterns of the organization if they are going to have their maximum effects. Drawing on years of work with sophisticated issues management systems and senior executive discussions, Renfro (1993) observed, "Usually, successful issues management systems are built to run on the strategic management cycle, often an annual process" (p. 103).

Thus, Renfro (1993) reasoned, processes relevant to issues management, as part of strategic planning and management, should begin with a "recognition of the need for faster, clearer, earlier intelligence on emerging issues," no matter how "minimal, unarticulated, disjointed, confused, and tardy it may be for getting information about the changing environment into the organization" (pp. 104-105). The ability to scout the terrain means getting the best available information as quickly as possible and making the most of it to understand the opportunities and threats the public policy environment poses for corporate plans, policies, and operations.

Issues Identification

Issues identification involves determining whether a problem or concern (a contestable point, difference of opinion, legitimacy gap) exists that could affect an organization's ability to achieve its strategic business plan. Issues arise because of concerns that surround a company's product, service, operations, policies, location, or personnel. An issue may result from changes in evaluative criteria—a new sense of corporate responsibility. Another source of an issue is the discovery that a company or industry is doing something offensive, in violation of current expectations by key publics.

The only issues that are likely to affect public policy are those promoted by stakeholders who have power and rhetorical sophistication. Thus, issue identification entails not only recognizing concerns but also determining whether that concern is likely to manifest itself in legislative or regulatory outcomes. For this reason, many issues can be handled by attentiveness to stakeholders' interests without engaging them in the public policy arena.

During issues research, Renfro (1993) advised the use of issue briefs that (a) define and explain the issue; (b) explore its various positions, sides, and options as well as the parties that have an interest in it; (c) determine the nature, timing, and mechanisms of the potential impact of the issue; and (d) guide attention to additional sources of analysis regarding the issue. These briefs are thinking documents that precede the formulation of issue position papers, which, based on the data captured by the briefs, assert the position and tactics executives are going to take on the issue.

Identifying issues is difficult because of *complexity,* the number of variables that affect the emergence and growth of an issue. *Turbulence* increases as the issue environment becomes more unstable, less predictable, and more uncertain. Issues are more difficult to identify when the *information load* increases requiring that more data must be obtained and analyzed than an organization may have resources to accomplish. Analysis is more demanding when issue positions are *ambiguous* and *complex,* when the *number* of participants and issue positions are high, and when participants have *many opinion options* because the issue has not become well defined. *Interdependence* can be a stabilizing or destablishing factor in issue identification. The destabilizing aspect of interdependence results when individual players or issue positions do not respond in thematic or predictable ways, thereby making issue extrapolation difficult or impossible (Huber & Daft, 1987). One activist tactic is to be unpredictable and constantly changing, to keep the company guessing. Critics often make incremental changes that slowly erode the acceptance that once existed regarding a company or industry's operations, policies, products, or services, a rhetorical strategy that has been called *incremental erosion* (Condit & Condit, 1992).

Identification may result in the awareness that a new issue is emerging, a concern exists that may mature into an issue for several reasons, or an issue has existed for some time but has avoided detection or taken a new turn. The issue may find the organization rather than it finding the issue. For that reason, a firm should constantly scan for issues.

Issues Scanning

Issues scanning can be compared with the process of watching a radar screen, perhaps as we do on televised weather reports where storm formations are identified by each sweep of radar. This strategy entails constantly watching for issues to emerge and become salient. Scanning involves looking for credible discussions, scientific discoveries, or concerns that could be important to the organization's planning and operations. At this stage, the issues manager is more interested in spotting figures when they appear on the horizon than in determining whether they are friends or foes and deciding whether they will last only a moment or stay for a while. Issues tracking and evaluation calls for sustained efforts to use benchmark data as starting points to extrapolate formation and change of opinions by key publics. Indicators of issue shifts can include the number of people who are aware of an issue, whether it is serious enough to warrant corrective action, and the strength and variety of opinions that agree or disagree with issue positions of the company.

Where do we look for issues? They often emerge in obscure publications and outlets. One safe generalization is that by the time an issue has reached the point of being discussed in mainstream daily newspapers or national news magazines or appears on local or national news, it has emerged. Issues can first appear in scholarly research: masters' theses, dissertations, convention papers, scholarly journals, quasi-scholarly publications, opinion publications, underground press, underground internet discussions, specialized narrow-viewpoint journals and papers, cause journals, special-interest newsletters and other publications, conferences, voiced concerns of non-mainstream political candidates, and ungeneralized comments in a community. The next layer of publication outlets includes books, industry journals, trade publications, larger circulation scientific or social scientific journals, call-in talk shows, letters to the editors, and bellwether newspapers or other mainstream media outlets. Issues often emerge in publications that are read by members of the company other than issues managers, such as lawyers, human resource personnel, or chemical plant technicians. Thus, the issues management team needs to be a matrix of individuals who are trained and given incentives to scan for issues that are reported into a "watch" mode that can lead to monitoring.

Issues arise from diverse sources: special interest advocates, media commentators, governmental agencies, industry leaders or bad apple companies, technical experts, community leaders, and other industries. Companies that have a lot of contact with customers, such as utilities or retail outlets, may find it useful to arm telephone service representatives or salespersons with cards that allow them to record and report customer concerns and complaints. Pipeline operators (whether intrastate or interstate) may provide cards for personnel who monitor the lines and have contact with persons who live and work near them. Similarly, cards could be sent to persons whose property is crossed by these lines. The value of having people fill out such cards, ones that ask relevant questions to assess whether concern exists or is growing, is that it allows for a broad range of responses to surface—even though the survey is nonprobabilistic. It allows for members of a community to voice their concerns into an early warning system.

An issue should be placed into the company issues monitoring system only after it meets three criteria: (a) It is listed in standard indexes, suggesting that journalists have come to believe that it is legitimate and worth general public discussion. (b) A case can be made that the issue will threaten company operations or offer opportunity for market advantage. (c) The issue is associated with at least one identifiable group (whether business, government, or activist) that has the track record, or the potential, of bringing it to the legislative agenda.

Shifts in values, expressed concern, research findings, calls for solutions to problems—which people did not think of as problems before: These begin on the fringe of thought in a society. To visualize this process, think of the opinion of the public—on any issue—as constituting a bell curve of opinion both in terms of extremes of issue positions and degrees of awareness of each issue. The ends of this curve constitute cognitively involved proponents and scoffers regarding an issue (J. E. Grunig, 1989a; Heath & Douglas, 1990, 1991). The middle population knows less about the issue, has fewer thoughts and opinions about it, and takes it less seriously. The mainstream may shift to where the fringe once was.

By the time much of the population becomes aware of an issue, the vanguard has explored new facets of it. For this reason, companies implement systems whereby key personnel are asked (perhaps as regularly as each week) to indicate one issue that they believe deserves attention. Such reports, made to a central person such as the manager of public affairs, keep key persons alert to the emergency of issues and serves as an early warning system.

Issues Monitoring

Issues monitoring assumes that some issues pose threats or opportunities and therefore should be watched to see how they develop, which advocate takes a particular position, and the extent to which the issue achieves public and opinion leader visibility and credibility. Issues are monitored or tracked to ascertain whether and when they become associated with established and powerful advocates who have the potential to sustain the discussion and press an issue to its logical outcome, such as change in regulation or legislation. Issues do not sustain themselves. Part of strategic monitoring is knowing the factors that sustain each issue and observing whether they are working for its development or demise.

Issues monitoring includes issues forecasting. One problematic aspect of issues monitoring and analysis is foretelling the future of an issue—whether it will increase or decrease in salience and whether its consequences for the organization are likely to be more or less serious. Forecasting entails making extrapolations as to whether (a) the trend will continue, stabilize, increase, or decrease in momentum; (b) change will occur in the breadth and depth of coverage and discussion by the media, governmental agencies, activists, and others in business (intraindustry and interindustry), (c) a rise or decline will take place in terms of the number of people (segmenting into key publics) who favor or disfavor a particular issue position, who adhere to key premises and values, and who know and believe crucial facts; (d) change will be seen in the number, degree of conviction, composition, and role played by opinion leaders; and (e) trends of these kinds will lead to or away from legislative action.

Issues may be watched at two levels of abstraction. One level is the shift in basic principles or premises that results from extensive discussion, typically requiring much or all of a decade or more to reshape taken-for-granted assumptions about the "way things are." Two powerful examples quickly come to mind. One is the shift that has occurred whereby individuals feel less responsibility for their own actions and blame negative consequences on someone else; for instance, four decades ago, if a person was hurt using a power tool, he or she would feel foolish for not being careful or well prepared to use it. Now, the lawsuit begins before the blood is stanched because the fault is assumed or alleged not to lie with the user—who may have been careless or drunk—but with the manufacturer who should have designed the tool so that even a drunk, incompetent fool could not be hurt using it. The second powerful shift in basic premises is the result of environmentalists arguing that progress does not give governments, individuals, or companies license to take actions harmful to the environment.

This last point underscores the second level of analysis on which a monitor should focus. As large principles or assumptions change, new frames of mind become important for the particular application of those general principles to individual cases and decisions. For instance, changes in environmentalism may have quite different implications for the food industry, bringing implications for packaging or agricultural methods to the forefront of debate. In contrast, actions of the chemical industry, although scrutinized by environmental principles, may be affected in quite different ways and therefore it needs to monitor issues differently.

Values translate into the premises by which people draw conclusions based on the data with which they are familiar. For instance, previous to the 1960s and 1970s, consumers were usually considered to be "unsafe" or "foolish" if they were harmed while using a product. Now the tables have turned, and public value systems hold corporations responsible. When values change, the probability of regulation increases.

Monitoring issues is easier if the players stay on the same trajectory. But that is not always the situation. An interesting case occurred when after years of pressing the petrochemical industry to abandon the production of CFCs, the EPA reversed itself and asked Du Pont, one of the largest producers, to abandon its concerted effort to phase out production. The 1990 Clean Air Act called for manufacturers to cease all production by the year 2000 in an effort to relieve the environmental damage of the ozone layer. Du Pont, after years of opposing this restriction, agreed to curtail production and made rapid strides toward that end. This effort was derailed by EPA, which wanted to ease the pressures on the related industries that needed to create alternatives for CFCs, which are used as part of refrigeration systems and to clean high-tech industrial products such as silicon chips. The cost of changing, retrofitting, or buying alternative air conditioners, EPA feared, was likely to lead to a consumer backlash. The action by EPA baffled Du Pont and infuriated environmental groups (Noah & Carey, 1993).

Monitoring can be divided into distinct but interrelated phases. The first assesses the situational environment of the organization, the second monitors issue trends, and the third determines whether the organization's efforts (strategic business planning, communication, or public policy positioning) make a difference in the direction and outcome of the issue. Many organizations fail to conduct pretest and posttest analysis to determine the success of their communication or other adjustive efforts (Stridsberg, 1977, p. 81). However, Chevron links issues, image, and product advertising and monitors measurable changes in relevant opinions (Winters, 1988). Cost, of course, is a factor, but tracking an issues communication campaign has the same advantages as does tracking operating costs, production figures, profits, or employee satisfaction. Some researchers doubt that campaign impact can be accurately assessed because so many variables are involved. Determining the company's or industry's image or polling for public sentiment on certain issues may not enable an issues management team to determine what a campaign contributed.

Of substantial value to any issues monitoring team is Renfro's (1993) contention that issues progress through six stages: (a) *birth* (the result of key changes), (b) *definition* (some persons or groups characterize the issue), (c) *name* (attach it to a few terms that give it identity), (d) *champion* (key players become identified with and advocate the issue), (e) *group* (interested parties become definable as a demographic or interest group), and (f) *media recognition* (editors, reporters, and news or program directors believe the issue is worth reporting because it has or deserves status of news). A crucial stage is naming: "Those who define the issue win the debate," which can lead to the complementary advice: "Redefine the issue to win a new debate" (p. 40). This truism is one long-standing reason for analyzing and publicly discussing an issue early, in a proactive manner, rather than allowing reactive strategies to limit a group's response options.

Discussing the focal points in the monitoring process, Ewing (1980) advised issues managers to conduct private discussions with leaders who are sensitive to public opinion trends, particularly those below the surface of mass media visibility. In addition, the issues manager should monitor newsletters, books, and reports of special interest groups, foundations, and governmental agencies. Monitoring should include analysis of popular entertainment sources, such as plays, movies, novels, and television programs. Themes expressed through entertainment, especially television programming, follow the formation of opinion and constitute a period where it seems to be becoming firmly established. For instance, in 1994, the mother in the cartoon strip "Sally Forth" spent a week of anguish over whether her daughter would become a smoker as the result of selecting the controversial marketing icon Joe Camel as the subject of her art project. Another comic strip that has contained antismoking comments is "Doonesbury," which periodically features Mr. Butts as a prosmoking advocate, lobbyist, and beleaguered smoker who suffers because of corporate or governmental policies regarding smoking.

Needed information can be extracted from existing research studies, syndicated studies, industry sources, and customer studies. Research methods include watching for information and opinion, printed or broadcast, that relates to the company or industry. Methods can range from discussions with experts and the use of focus groups to content analysis and opinion surveys.

One feature of the information superhighway is the availability of electronic databases that can be used to scan, monitor, and track issues. Electronic databases can be used internally so that key issues personnel can communicate with one another through alerts to indicate changes in issues and in the company's response to them. These internal databases can be used by members of the issues monitoring and analysis team to keep up to date with the status of each issue. Forms such as that shown in Table 3.1 can be entered into company databases and shared among individuals, who update the information in the form on a routine basis. This form is designed to capture all aspects of an issue. It assumes that issues are promoted by key stakeholding publics and can take a trajectory that leads to new laws and regulations. The form can indicate who has been assigned responsibility for each issue. It focuses on mistakes the company or other organization has made that may have caused the emergence of the issue. It addresses response options and focuses on the cost impact of the issue.

External electronic database searches can be conducted through any of several vendors who sell access to their databases. Such services offer possibilities for monitoring in ways never before possible. In recent years, several large database companies have begun to provide access to hundreds of daily, weekly, and monthly news and opinion publications. By using databases, one can acquire a great deal of on-line information via a computer with a modem. Some database vendors are CompuServe, Inc., Data-Star, Dialog Information Services, Inc., The H. W. Wilson Company, Mead Data Central, OCLC Online Computer Library Center, Inc., Orbit Search Service, STN International, DataTimes Corporation, Dow Jones News/Retrieval, and ETST—Human Resources Information Network. These vendors routinely supply catalog listings of the database offerings they provide. One standard resource useful for locating desired databases and the vendors that supply them is *Gale Directory of Databases,* which is a standard holding at reference desks of college and university libraries as well as larger municipality and county libraries.

Thomsen (1995) interviewed 17 issues monitors at 12 companies. The respondents believed on-line databases allowed them to intercept issues earlier, thereby allowing them to understand and develop positions on issues earlier than otherwise would be the case. Thomsen concluded that the practitioners appreciated "the breadth of information available on line and the speed at which it can be delivered" (p. 119.) With this information, issues managers were more likely to be included in the strategic planning efforts of their companies.

If an issue were developing, a person who subscribed to one or more of these databases could do a daily, weekly, monthly, quarterly, or annual search for all news stories and other reference items that address that topic. This process is similar to going to a regular library and using a reference system to locate journal articles or newspaper stories before going to the magazine, journal, or newspaper to locate the story to be read. Some databases provide access to news stories and company press releases. Some contain vital scientific or social scientific data.

On-line electronic database research can be done by downloading the texts of articles, news stories, and abstracts of research conducted on the issue. Once the data are downloaded, they can be stored on the issue monitor's computer. It can be printed. Once it is on a computer file, it can be transmitted to other persons via computer systems (such as e-mail) or it can be entered into a monitoring system, such as that described in Table 3.1.

This research tool cuts down on the difficulty of obtaining and managing information, an issue that is widely debated as a matter of cost-effectiveness. Renfro (1993) discussed the cost-effectiveness of using computerized scanning processes: If people have to keystroke data into the computer, it is not cost-effective.

> The experience of many has been that the benefits of computerization do not yet offset the high costs of having every word and letter pass through a keyboard and having every idea summarized and resummarized. When an organization has the computer technology to enter scanning information by key word and date into a computer file via a simple copier, then the cost benefits change rapidly and favor computerized scanning systems. Without this technology, experience suggests that computerization is a distraction from the purpose of scanning. Even with advanced input technology, computerization will not be cheap, but the costs of large storage systems are declining rapidly. (p. 76)

Access to Dialog and other database services allows issues managers to get data on-line and store, retrieve, and share it with others without the data ever seeing the light of day.

TABLE 3.1 Issue Monitoring and Analysis Form

1. Name of issue
2. Cognizant person who is primarily responsible for monitoring and analyzing the issue
3. Internal liaisons (personnel who support the effort of the cognizant person)
4. External liaisons (external individuals and groups who support the effort of the cognizant person)
5. Relationship between this issue and other issues
6. Influential persons, special-interest groups, companies who are taking a stand on the issue
7. Stage of development
    Priority 1: Legal-administrative litigation
    Priority 2: Legislative watch
    Priority 3: Pre-legislative
    Priority 4: Potential legislative
    Priority 5: Emerging issue
8. Implications of this issue for the company mission (with cost estimate)
9. Implications of this issue for the company corporate responsibility standards (with cost estimate)
10. Alternative operating procedures (with cost estimate)
11. Stress points or threats associated with the issue
12. Opportunities associated with the issue
13. Public policy plan
14. Communication plan
15. Measurable outcomes for assessing the management of this issue
16. References and attached supporting documents

Some practitioners are keen on the use of electronic databases, whereas others are reluctant to use them. Weiner (1994) cautioned against overreliance on electronic databases because they do not include as many original sources as competent clipping services do. Databases do not include many widely read publications as well as publications and newsletters of organizations. They do not include all parts of the publications they do contain. Database services do not include pictures and sidebars.

One reservation is cost (Weiner, 1994). Some vendors of clipping services argue that they are cost-effective, whereas the use of databases is not. Forward-thinking clipping services are undertaking database searches as part of their vending efforts. As Weisendanger (1994) observed about database searches,

> Almost anything can be done faster, more easily, and more accurately by flicking a modem switch or pressing a fax machine button. Some even say these new tools are as cheap or cheaper than the older mailing, clipping and monitoring methods, especially if savings in staff time is factored into the equation. (pp. 20-21)

AP Alert, for instance, gives access to 10,000 stories each day in nine industry categories, all at the speed of electronic transmission and in a form that is readily incorporated into corporate e-mail and database services. No longer does a news story or a scientific study need to be obtained through the mail, photocopied, and put back into the mail. All of that can be done electronically—a future that seems more promising than dark.

Technology is not the total answer. Data are only as good as the insights of people who analyze them. Issues forecasting is difficult because many factors affect the trajectory of an issue or the outrage associated with it. Some potentially explosive issues never take on the momentum experts predict. Some crucial issues go unnoticed. In Kahn's 1967 futuristic study, which extrapolated the major issues of the latter half of this century, he made no mention of the energy crisis that occurred in the 1970s (Kahn & Weiner, 1967). But after the OPEC embargo, he didn't need a crystal ball to feature it in his 1976 study (Kahn, Brown, & Martel, 1976).

To improve projections, futurists continue to refine monitoring and forecasting strategies. Nearly two decades ago, Ewing (1979) discovered 150 forecasting techniques, although only a few were widely used then or are employed today. Coates et al. (1986) shortened the list to 25 means for getting and making sense of data: networking, precursor (bellwether) analysis, media analysis, polls and surveys, juries of executive opinion, expert panels, scanning and monitoring, content analysis, legislative tracking, Delphi, conversational Delphi, consensor, cross-impact analysis, decision-support systems, computer-assisted techniques, small-group process, scenario building, trend extrapolation, technological forecasting, decision analysis, factor analysis, sensitivity analysis, trigger event identification, key-player analysis, and correlation-regression. Some of these are methods for obtaining information; others feature statistical analysis. All can be expensive; some are very expensive. All have their problems, limitations, and strengths. Some overlap and complement one another, but the following ones deserve special consideration.

News hole analysis employs content analysis of newspapers, magazines, and electronic media and works on the principle that the dominant public opinion issues and topics are those that command proportionately larger amounts of space or time. Naisbitt (1982) made a splash in *Megatrends* where he projected public opinion changes occurring in the 1980s that would dominate attention for the foreseeable future, based on the proportion of news coverage devoted to each issue. This analysis assumed that what is discussed predicts what key publics will be thinking. It reasons that coverage in news outlets leads in the formation of issue awareness and position formation.

Doing analysis by actually reading a sample of newspapers and news magazines is quite time-consuming. One variation on this content analysis is to use one of the newspaper and news magazine electronic databases discussed above. Using a key-word search, an issue monitor can obtain a listing of the news stories that contain the key word. Once this list of references has been acquired, the issue monitor can count the number of stories and can even determine whether the interest is local, regional, or national. By tallying and monitoring the trends—more or fewer stories—over a period of time, an issue monitor can estimate whether interest in the story is growing, remaining stable, or declining. This rough estimate can be refined by other news hole techniques if such analysis is deemed to be cost-effective.

Trend extrapolation assumes that media agendas change slowly, as do issue trends. Current issues can be projected a few years into the future with a reasonable degree of reliability. Such projections are often adequate because most issues never reach the point of being formed into legislation. Those that do are subjected to long and tedious discussion that becomes more narrow and focused as the issue enters the legislative arena. In contrast to this slow, orderly development, some major events, especially disasters, can have a dramatic effect on public policy formation. Predicting disasters is difficult.

Trend impact analysis takes advantage of the ability of computers to store and analyze vast amounts of data that are used to project the short-term future. Monitoring consists of collecting brief summaries of issues created by specialists who read specialized and general publications to sense trends and estimate the intensity of issue discussion.

The Delphi technique draws on experts' opinions to sense important developing issues. Once this information is gathered, it is submitted to the people who were surveyed to determine whether they agree with individual estimates of issue trends. Related to the Delphi method is the snowball interviewing technique, whereby people are asked to name influential people on an issue. Those people are contacted and asked the same question. Through repeated inquiry, the network of key players becomes evident. That group is used to generate data.

Forced rankings are used to allow the members of the survey to place the issues into priority, based on their learned judgment of their importance.

Cross-impact analysis assumes that a trend will come true. The purpose of this technique is to estimate the ripple effect that would result if it did.

Computer simulations have been used to combine data gathering and trend projection. With increasing sophistication, computers can help answer "what-if" kinds of questions based on extrapolations of historical information that is placed into a matrix of weighted variables. For instance, a computer projection can compare technological development, trends in public sentiment, economic-condition projections, and issue extrapolations. "What-if" questions can be answered by examining the impact on the other variables that would result if one issue changed.

Focus groups consist of specially or randomly selected groups of demographically important citizens or issue specialists who engage in topical discussions led by facilitators. One advantage of focus groups is that the conversation of one or more members can spark thoughts and comments in other members. Unlike surveys that reveal only opinions they are designed to disclose, focus groups can elicit candid and unpredictable responses. They can estimate the outrage factor in issues, as the American Bankers Association used them to discover the anger persons felt toward the 10% withholding-tax provision proposed by the Reagan administration (Elmendorf, 1988). Focus groups can obtain opinions from key stakeholders regarding what they find acceptable or offensive regarding corporate policy (Heath, 1987-1988).

Standard survey techniques are useful. Lindenmann (1977, 1983) instructed monitors to know what the study is supposed to discover, what populations are to be included, and how to develop and execute the instrument and report data. In addition to identifying where issues are arising, monitoring may discover whether key segments of the public believe an issue constitutes a problem. The issues manager needs to know whether stakeholders hold inaccurate beliefs. Smith (1980) demonstrated the ability of poll data to be used to track and profile shifts in certain public policy topics from 1946 to 1976: foreign affairs, economics, civil rights, social control, and effects of government. Some issues were relatively stable, whereas others changed dramatically.

Archival research—whether manual or through electronic databases— can be conducted to determine whether articles discussing an issue are based on information that can be refuted or is accurate and whether the basis for arguments is legitimate. The issues team should compare the facts as it understands them against those believed by key publics and asserted by critics. Such research may include candid diagnostic studies of the organization's strengths and weaknesses.

At a given time, any company or industry will have hundreds of pieces of federal, state, and local legislation—to say nothing of regulations by agencies—that will (or at least could) affect operations or mission. For each issue, two dimensions are vital: *likelihood* (probability that an issue can grow to affect the organization) and its *impact* on the organization. (See Figure 3.2.) For each issue, a company needs to develop means for creating likelihood and impact estimates. What is the likelihood that an issue will mature into legislation or regulation? The impact statement addresses the effect an issue could have if it is brought into legislation or regulations. Out of both kinds of monitoring, a firm can develop its strategic response when, based on likelihood and impact estimates, cost-effectiveness statements are prepared.

Even though a department such as issues management or public relations-affairs has the primary responsibility for issues monitoring, some issues are

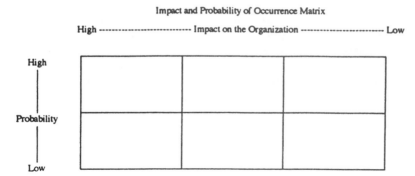

Figure 3.2. Impact and Probability of Occurrence Matrix

best monitored by members of other organizational units. Each department should understand its role and responsibility in the monitoring process and should create issues impact analyses. For example, the finance department has to be sensitive to issues of fairness and security in regard to how the organization generates money. The operating section of a company can monitor three broad types of issues that concern input—the source and quality of materials. Materials must be safe; obtained in a way that does not offend standards of environmental quality; and fairly and with equality, without damaging others' interests.

Monitors should identify the players—opponents and supporters of an issue, how cognitively or behaviorally involved they are, how they define the issue as a problem— the solutions they advocate, if any, and the likelihood that opinion will lead to activism (J. E. Grunig, 1989). Monitors should ascertain what sources of information and opinion stakeholders are relying on, keeping in mind that as issues mature, concerned people turn to more specialized communication vehicles, including interpersonal conversation and using general media to scan for issue developments (J. E. Grunig, 1979, 1983; Heath, Liao, & Douglas, 1995; Rubin & Sachs, 1973).

Of importance in the monitoring process is the discovery of the facts various stakeholders know, find believable, and use in their discussion and analysis. Of related interest are the premises they use in their analysis, conclusions, and advocated policy changes—whether public or as voluntary change by the company or industry. Monitoring can ascertain the effect issue discussion is having on the image of the company (attitude toward it), its product or services, or the industry.

Monitoring can use tracking efforts of other groups, especially those of critics. Such analysis can refine the monitoring system and analytic conclusions it is likely to make to either confirm or disconfirm the company's views. This analysis is a kind of mirror into which the company can look to see how others view the same issues. Activist publications, such as *National Wildlife,* provide an annual review of the status of key issues such as air quality, wildlife, water quality, forests, soil, and quality of life. Firms interested in environmental concerns can use such publications to monitor issues because how others evaluate the status of an issue is a focal point against which one's own opinions can be compared. Issues monitoring and analysis blend.

Issues Analysis

Scanning helps discover issues, whereas monitoring and analysis estimate their intensity and intellectual or sociopolitical viability. Issues analysis examines facts, premises, conclusions, and policy recommendations that are employed by discussants of the topic. What facts are central to the discussion? Are they accurate? Are the premises that are being used to interpret the information widely held, newly forming, or under attack? Which values are basic to the issue discussions, as determined by whom? Are these values the appropriate ones to draw correct conclusions and then create the best policy changes?

Of importance to the analysis of issues is an understanding of the argumentative content of the macroissues, the changing premises and principles of society. Macrosocial shifts in principles such as environmentalism may have dramatically different implications for different industries, such as bottle laws' impacts on the alcohol beverage or soft drink industry and forest protection efforts' effects on the timber industry.

Issue analysis requires an understanding of (a) the public policy process; (b) anticipated social, economic, technological, and political changes; and (c) each issue advocate's objectives. Important analytical focal points are the trajectory and salience (immediacy and prominence) of each issue (Chase, 1984; Jones & Chase, 1979). Renfro (1993) featured several dimensions of issues: Objective-subjective, external-internal, and location of the interest (national-regional-local). Whether an issue is external or internal is a matter of how the information comes to issue monitors, whether by internal persons or external sources such as scanning services.

Rather than treating opinion as mere response items on a survey, one preferred approach is to understand how response items cluster into arguments. Researchers may create survey response items so that they dissect the content of arguments that constitute public opinion. To understand opinion, issues managers should comprehend the depth and breadth of the opinion positions as sustainable arguments (Davison, 1972; Dillman & Christenson, 1974).

Issues analysis entails careful consideration of whether the facts underpinning an issue are accurate, given the best available analysis. Analysis may weigh the appropriate methodology to use in making the judgment. It evaluates the premises central to the positions taken on the issue, the facts on which it is based, the kinds and quality of reasoning, and the conclusions that are being drawn based on existing or advocated principles and premises. Premises may be well established (taken for granted), in the process of being formed, under pressure to change, or held narrowly by serious issue advocates or fringe groups lacking and unlikely to attract a following.

Issues analysis is often difficult because the data needed to understand the issue may be incomplete or conflicting and the evaluative premises may be contestable. The asbestos industry was aware of connections between their product and damage to lung tissue. This awareness led management to commission scientific research regarding the health effects of its product. Based on that research, executives concluded that asbestos posed little or no harm to persons' health who were exposed to it (Brodeur, 1985). In recent years, scientific debate has addressed links between electromagnetic fields and health problems—with few if any conclusive results.

Not only should analysis examine the arguments in the issue debate, but it should also investigate the players engaged in the dialogue. Issues managers should consider experts' and key publics' experience with the issue. Because they play instrumental roles in how issues form and how information about them is disseminated, opinion leaders and media gatekeepers should be located in the process. It can concentrate on elected and appointed government officials. The major concern is to locate people who are friendly and unfriendly to the issue position.

Along with concern over who is saying what about which issues, issues analysts should consider the pathways of influence. Which spokespersons have access to media reporters and editorialists? Which players are likely to or actually have influence over legislators or regulators? Which members of the dialogue are mute or lack a voice because others are ignoring their statements or drowning them out? Which players are credible? Who considers them to be credible or doubts their credibility? What voices can be trusted? This analysis acknowledges that information and influence diffuse throughout a community through a communication infrastructure.

Renfro (1993) saw issues analysis as playing a major role at the corporate level where senior management uses it for proprietary strategic management. At lower corporate levels, issue discussion keeps other executives involved in the input, processing, and output of issue positions and strategic planning options. Analysis involves dialogue with customers, clients, and other key stakeholders.

> A corporation does not stand alone but in an environment composed of its customers, clients, and suppliers. Where emerging issues are forcing change in the immediate environment, it is essential that the corporation include input from its customers, clients, and suppliers in both its scanning and its issue detection system, as well as communicate its issue concerns and research to them. (p. 95)

This communication often occurs through issue newsletters, issue-relevant activism, and trade associations.

Analysis needs to examine trends. Ewing (1980) explained the five-step issue trend analysis system adopted by Allstate Insurance: (a) The first stage is problem recognition, the belief that some problem exists—a gap between what is found or thought to be the case and what is expected. (b) The second stage occurs when dissatisfaction gets a name and becomes topical. (c) During the third stage, media pick up the issue. Often, the second and third stages are inseparable. Critics give the issue a name, form it into a slogan, and make it visible, especially by gaining attention of the media. Analysts can scan research guides, such as the *Reader's Guide to Periodic Literature,* including those that are included in on-line databases, to note when an issue becomes so well established that it is used as a key word to index articles. The outrage factor can be estimated by noting the number of articles on a topic and the kinds of publication in which they are printed. (d) The fourth stage Ewing identified occurs when pressure groups take note of the topic and add it to their list of grievances. In some instances, pressure groups raise issues and give them visibility; in other instances, these topics become developed by one or more persons and may be adopted by larger or allied pressure groups. (e) Issues have matured to the fifth stage when legislators or regulators discuss them and formulate policies about them. Although this model focuses on activists, they are not alone in moving issues through their evolutionary trends. Many other organizations, including other companies within an industry or other industries, create the impetus for issues sustaining themselves to the point of public policy changes.

Issues analysis can be used to determine the origin of the issue, including the political, social, and economic forces relevant to its formation. Analysis attempts to isolate the forces that impinge on change. The issues manager is encouraged to consider the past and present issue situation—its history and current status. To understand this process, Jones and Chase (1979) advised the issues manager to discover the source and intent of each issue-relevant statement, its target and message, and the tactic of which it is a part. Issues change strategy options (priority setting) involve deciding what issues the organization will commit to and in what manner. Concerns in this stage are (a) the risks involved in undertaking a communication campaign, (b) confidence in the information, (c) accuracy of forecasts, (d) likelihood the situation will correct itself, (e) timing, and (f) the direction the situation is likely to take. Reactive, adaptive, and dynamic (proactive) options exist.

As individuals work to bring their analyses of issues to the attention of executives, they are likely to meet greater success when they can demonstrate the payoff or harm that can result from skillful or inattentive responses. Of related interest is the recommendation for actions in regard to the issue that can be taken, proactively or reactively (Dutton & Ashford, 1993). Managements that are capable of high levels of information use are more likely to strategically achieve positive outcomes and control the organization's reaction to the issue (Thomas, Clark, & Giola, 1993).

Issues Priority Setting

Issues priority setting entails monitoring and analysis to determine what issues constitute opportunities or threats to the sustained implementation of the strategic business plan. Based on this priority, additional resources may be allotted to create and enact an issue response program that features the threats or opportunities involved in the issue. As that decision is made, the response is effected by changes in the strategic business plan, the standards and implementation of corporate responsibility, the public policy plan, and the communication plan.

An *issues response action program* involves elements of strategic business planning, communication initiatives, public policy planning, and refinements of corporate responsibility designed to correct the situation. It begins with setting or refining goals and discussing what strategies can effect the desired change. That matrix comes into full effect because a variety of disciplines is needed to determine the best issue response (Buchholz, 1982a). Response analysis may determine the targeted audiences, message design, and channels needed to reach the audience. Responses may include negotiation and collaborative decision making.

Issues are traditionally divided into five levels of priority that can be called a legislative cycle:

Priority 1: Legal-administrative litigation

Priority 2: Legislative watch

Priority 3: Pre-legislative

Priority 4: Potential legislative

Priority 5: Emerging issue

Issues in the first four priorities are relatively easy to monitor because they have emerged and are being discussed in established, traditional public forums and governmental arenas. Because determining what issues are emerging is so difficult, many companies rely on the fact that after an issue emerges, it takes 10 to 15 years to reach final legislative stages.

Note that the strategies of monitoring depend on the status of the issue. For instance, once an issue has made its way into the legislative process (legislative watch), monitoring centers on knowing the preferences and influence of key legislators, key lobbyists, administrative executives, and the major influence brokers. Under those circumstances, monitoring may entail little more than maintaining contact with legislators, legislative aides, conference committee members, and key watchers of the political process, such as legislative-beat reporters. The monitoring process during the administrative period shifts from legislators to regulators. During litigation, the watch shifts to court dockets and trial proceedings.

Courts can be overlooked as a locus of issue response, simply because so much goes on in the media and in regulatory and legislative arenas. Court decisions can either create, define (redefine), or resolve issues. In 1995, the Supreme Court became the focal point of a discussion regarding the limits of governmental intrusion into environmental issues. At issue was legislation related to endangered species, especially the habitat protection rule. On one side of the issue were groups such as Sweet Home Chapter of Communities for a Great Oregon, U.S. Chamber of Commerce, National Association of Realtors, National Association of Home Builders, Cargill, Inc., Defenders of Property Rights, and four Native American Groups, including Navajos and Jicarilla Apaches. Supporting strong restriction were the Interior Department, National Wildlife Federation, Sierra Club, Western Ancient Forest Campaign, Defenders of Wildlife, and prominent scientists. The key issue related to the power of government and the wise use of that power (Barrett, 1995).

Issues-impact analysis must include decisions that focus on what procedures, processes, and cultures need to be changed inside and outside the firm. Opinions are difficult to change; issues analysis should estimate how difficult a key opinion will be to change, whether actions and policies on the part of the company or industry need to be improved, whether all parties are basing their judgments on the same information, whether the information is correct (or at least best), and whether interpretative frames used to evaluate it are similar or dramatically different. This analysis can be placed into a tracking model to estimate the opinion strength of key stakeholders as the issue moves through the legislative cycle. This line of analysis should estimate the extent to which the issue proponents are sophisticated in their efforts, funded for a campaign, and dedicated to see the resolution of the differences. Because of the kinds of tasks involved, costs are easier to estimate for changes in operations than they are for an effective communication campaign. This realization should not preclude a communication campaign or organization procedure improvements.

 Creating an Issues Monitoring and Analysis Team

Issues are too complex and difficult to spot and monitor for any individual or group to perform this task properly. A serious problem facing persons engaged in issues management for a company, trade association, activist organization, government agency, university, or nonprofit group is the limitation of time, knowledge, and analytic insights. Issues management requires that issues be observed as soon as possible so they can be monitored to ascertain whether they offer threats or opportunities for the organization. For an organization, this task is daunting. The issues manager needs to know how to create a monitoring and analysis team, the topic of this section.

One grave mistake issues managers make is to assume that they, individually or in conjunction with key staff members and executives, can identify and analyze public policy issues early enough to take appropriate proaction to exploit opportunities and avoid collisions with criticism and unfavorable policy. Issues monitoring and analysis ought to be systematically diffused throughout an organization rather than be the responsibility of a single concentrated group. Organizations characterized by participative management cultures prefer to use issue teams, persons drawn from various parts of the organization. The team may exist informally and be quite fluid (Lauzen, 1995).

An organization has many people in positions where they can watch for issues, monitor their growth, and analyze potential impacts on the unit or the entire organization. A systems approach to this task assumes the presence of input (what goes into a system), processing (how the input is handled), and output (the result of processing). For instance, organizations take in issue-relevant information. Once this information is considered, planning can lead to a change in corporate policy or a decision to undertake a communication campaign. In the latter option, information is output to be received as input by targeted audiences who process the information and decide whether to accept it or reject it. If targeted audiences accept the information, the corporate side of the issue may prevail and the issue dies. Collaborative decisions may result.

Planning and issues analysis does less good when it remains local to the unit engaged in them. Issues managers often serve as the links between persons who discover and interpret issues and the executives who engage in issues response (MacElreath, 1980). However, it does not take long for many issues to rise and move horizontally as units share their issues monitoring, analysis, and planning efforts with other staff or operating units as well as executive management. Figure 3.3 indicates the vertical levels needed to be integrated into an issue monitoring team. It requires input from those responsible for strategic business planning and needs to draw on experts from each of the organization's key operating units. The input from that team needs to be integrated into and coordinated with the public policy team and issues communication team efforts.

To do the best job it can for the organization it serves, issues management needs to be a staff function with carefully selected and designed matrix interfaces between units and programs. As Renfro (1993) advised, "The executives who participate in the issues management process need to reflect the range of interests of the corporation" (p. 122).

> For this reason, members of the issues management group are often drawn
> from across the organization in all major dimensions—organizationally,
> geographically, divisionally—in the style of the matrix management concept.
> This assures the richest flow of emerging issues information. (p. 123)

Issues management can reside in one department or be diffused throughout an organization and embedded into its planning, operating, and communication decisions. If a company has a highly pyramidal structure, the primary responsibility for issues management is likely to be assigned to one major officer who works with a matrix of experts to monitor the trends in public policy, advise the corporate planning process, and communicate with constituencies. If the company has a diffused managerial system, many people may be simultaneously responsible for aspects of issues monitoring. In both situations, a matrix management system seems to be typical, whether the activity is concentrated or dispersed.

This process confronts management, issues specialists, and unit members with key challenges. Successful implementation requires training and coordination as well as a participative culture that fosters discussion of issues rather than stifles such concern. This process offsets a common complaint about the training and performance of persons in organizations—that they only understand and concentrate on the operations or market side of matters. Issues management requires that internal partnerships be created so that many eyes and minds are engaged in the process. Such efforts demonstrate two valuable points to members of organizations. One, issues management is everyone's responsibility. Two, solutions to potential public policy issues reside in how the organization meets or corrects stakeholder expectations and works in conjunction with the disciplines vital to its operations.

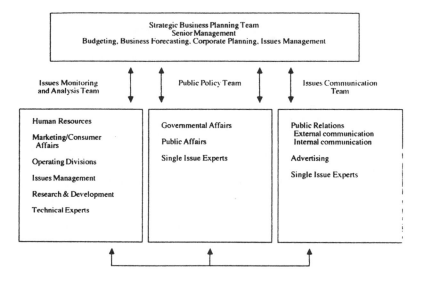

Figure 3.3. Issues Monitoring, Analysis, and Priority Planning Matrix

As issues move through the planning process, they become visible to individuals who would otherwise be less likely to observe them as quickly, if at all. Persons at the unit level are probably better prepared to identify and analyze the issue, interpret its implications for stakeholder relations, and engage in the kind of analysis needed to estimate the potential of the issue for or against the organization. The ability of people at the unit level to make their issues visible depends on their training—their understanding of issues, their analysis of the impact they could have on the organization, and their recommendations for correcting or exploiting the issue. This is a rhetorical process, whereby personnel need to present their issue analysis in ways that call attention to it.

One step is to imagine how individual units in the company should be informed of the process as well as trained and empowered to participate in it. Training begins with helping key members of these units, perhaps through their strategic planning efforts, to understand the importance of this issues management task and to understand how they can contribute to it. One issues manager for a utility company held brown-bag sessions once a month; during these sessions, she explained the process and collected names of persons who volunteered to support the project.

How people are trained to be part of this process and how their information is used determines the impact that issues management can have on the organization. J. E. Grunig (1978) discovered that people who have constant contact with the public may have a distorted view of the public's attitudes toward the company. He argued that unless extraordinary effort is exerted, little accurate information flows from management to employee or employee to management. The individuals with the most accurate information about the public's attitudes toward the company are those who are minimally involved with the public and who have to exert extra effort to find such information. These individuals are ones least likely to serve as liaisons with the public.

Key questions to be addressed when units prepare their strategic plans are these: Are issues emerging or maturing that can affect how we in this department, and ultimately the organization, conduct business and achieve objectives? Such issues need to be incorporated into the plan for discussion and strategic resolution. Once they are identified, they need to be analyzed for their implications. What impact can the maturing of these issues have on our business, and what plans can be undertaken to maximize opportunities and minimize threats from the issues if they develop?

Another place to look for issues is in the disciplines basic to the unit's planning and operation. Disciplines are data driven. They change as new information is discovered and analyzed. Disciplines either change from within, what is discovered by leading members. Or they change in response to claims made by critics. Such changes may be minor in the beginning but can amplify if early action is not taken to change in ways that mediate or take advantage of the issue. The key elements of analysis are (a) definition of the issue, (b) estimation of its potential for impact on the unit or entire organization, (c) analysis of the power of the persons and groups involved with the issue to keep it alive and promote it to its public policy maturity, and (d) suggestions for avoiding the threat of the issue or exploiting it to the advantage of the organization.

Strategic issues management programs are evaluated by the quality of their output: timely, efficient, and accurate issues identification; timely and accurate issue transmission to decision makers; and strategic issue response. Done properly, the result is legitimacy of decision making, perceived decision-maker control, and an image of responsiveness. In this sense, as issues increase in complexity, responsive organizations accomplish higher levels of information richness—ability of a system to handle needed information. A combination of increased uncertainty and need for accountability predicts the amount of resources an organization will allot to its strategic information management system (Dutton & Ottensmeyer, 1987; Lauzen, 1995).

Several factors affect how organizations accomplish strategic issues diagnosis. The strongest triggering criterion is the awareness that an issue can affect the organization's ability to accomplish its strategic plan. Once recognized, an issue's urgency is assessed—the perceived need to respond. One indicator of urgency is the extent to which powerful external publics recognize the importance of the issue for their agendas. Another indictor is the sense of responsibility the company has regarding the status of the issue. A fourth factor in the diagnosis process is the perceived feasibility of making an appropriate response to the issue, which is likely to result from how well the organization believes it understands an issue and its perception of its capacity to respond. When organizations understand an issue and have the capacity to respond, change is more likely to occur and more quickly. Other factors affecting the rate of a company's response are the beliefs (degree of consensus), perception of need for change, and amount of resources to resolve an issue (Dutton & Duncan, 1987; Lauzen, 1995). Organizations are stronger when they invest in intelligence resources and view change constructively.

This section has provided research and guidance to help make the monitoring process more effective by creating a team composed of the appropriate people. This group needs issues expertise and the support from management.

 Issue Content: Basis for Issues Analysis

Issues take on content as a result of the opinions, facts, evaluations, and conclusions advocated by the parties engaged in dialogue. This section examines the content of issues and sheds insight into how they can be interpreted.

Underpinning issues analysis are at least five constructs: the need persons have to reduce uncertainty (obtain and understand information) about factors that affect them, evaluation (judgment), power influence, cognitive involvement (attentiveness to issues related to self-interest), and balance between rewards or benefits and costs. At heart, this social exchange model assumes that key publics weigh the benefits they receive from their interaction with an organization against the costs of that relationship (Heath, 1990; Prior-Miller, 1989).

Issues can be analyzed rhetorically by featuring their argumentative content and structure. Rhetorical analysis features propositions of fact, value, and policy. Facts are verifiable and objective; value judgments center on what is right and wrong. Propositions of policy result as persons and groups interpret issues and ponder ways of solving problems. Each proposition is instrumental in building understanding and satisfaction, the basis of relationships between publics and organizations.

People filter, distort, and ignore information that does not confirm their attitudes, including those toward businesses, a premise of social judgment theory (Sherif, Sherif, & Nebergall, 1965). People who champion corporations will likely excuse most instances of corporate misbehavior because "you can't make an omelet without breaking an egg," or they will ignore the information as tales told by a biased media.

People who question the performance of private sector organizations willingly accept facts that confirm their predispositions. Those who have negative attitudes toward businesses are ripe for information on issues that can lead to regulatory constraints. In addition to the facts these individuals hold, they and their supporters have a complex of values regarding the wisdom of regulating corporations. Values change over time bringing about new standards of what publics will accept or reject. Although persons may reject information they do not find agreeable to their opinions, that does not mean that they are unwilling to know that information or to be aware of related opinions and arguments (Petty & Cacioppo, 1986).

Fishbein and Ajzen (1975; Ajzen & Fishbein, 1980) demonstrated that individuals process information into attitudes that consist of evaluations and beliefs. Each proposition is a belief, measured by the extent to which it is thought to be true. To each belief is attached an evaluation. This approach to cognition assumes that individuals (or groups targeted by issue campaigns) may believe many propositions about companies, activist groups, products, services, industries, or issues. They will have many accompanying attitudes. This approach helps issues managers decompose complex issues or images (Denbow & Culbertson, 1985).

We can explore this line of reasoning by imagining a company about which we hold four beliefs: It sells a safe product, exploits its laborers, damages the environment, and supports athletic events through its community relations. The first question we would ask is how firmly any individual believes each of those attributes to be associated with the company (0-100%). The extremes of this scale indicate that the individual does not believe the attribute is associated with the company or the attribute might be absolutely associated with the company (100%). The next question is whether a positive (+), neutral (o), or negative (-) valence is associated with the attribute. We might assume that safe product and support for athletics are associated with positives, whereas exploitation of labor and damaged environment are likely to have negative valences. On one hand, the stakeholder may support this company in the marketplace by purchasing the product or may oppose the company and buy from its competitors. The person in question might want the company to be prevented by public policy from polluting or exploiting labor. The person might not feel these attributes are a problem needing correction and want to see solutions negotiated or collaboratively decided.

Issues analysis can determine whether all publics operate from the same platform of fact and whether it is accurate. A review suggests the diversity of issues of fact that provide insight into firms' operations and requirements:

Cost of production, including research and development

Harmful effect of products

Impact of regulation on costs of products or services

Impact of industry on environment

In addition to facts, analysts must address values, the premises publics use to interpret facts.

Virtues of regulation-deregulation

Virtues of achievement and incentive

Virtues of working together to solve problems

Value of large companies solving large problems

Analysis reveals what companies stress as being essential to their productivity, profitability, and progress. It identifies points of departure between companies and their critics.

Based on the interaction of fact and value, advocates argue for or against policies. The logic is this: If certain facts are true and if specific values prevail, a policy is thought to be reasonable or unreasonable, as evidenced in the following examples:

Cutback on government spending

Support for air quality legislation

Regulation that gives unfair competitive advantage

Changes of policy regarding federal land

Unleashing an industry to produce products to serve the nation's needs

Such policy positions are subject to contest by opponents and supply discussants and collaborative decision makers with information about the advantages and disadvantages of specific regulation.

Issues managers can isolate beliefs that need to be strengthened, weakened, or changed. Communicators can attempt to change the evaluations (positive or negative) attached to the beliefs or alter the weight that belief-attitude statements have in people's judgments. Collaborative decision making may be needed to solve problems if challengers' arguments are beyond refutation.

The public's desire for legislation or regulation can be understood by realizing that people seek to maximize their gains or minimize their losses. For these reasons, segments of the public may favor or oppose governmental intervention and constraint. The most powerful incentive for regulation occurs when individuals attempt to minimize their losses. Such incentives have come in the form of protection against asbestos, acid rain, visual or air pollution, noise, dangerous toys, flammable garments, or cars that are unsafe. Looking at an entire community, one is likely to find a curvilinear relationship between cognitively involved supporters and cognitively involved opponents. In a case concerning a controversial plastics plant in Texas, 67% of the community voiced support of the plant because of its financial benefits, whereas 17% opposed it on economic or environmental grounds (Heath, Liao, et al., 1995).

Issue content is the meaning each issue takes on as it is discussed in the public forum. The views of people grow from the self-interest and altruistic interests they feel about the issue. The savvy issues manager listens to the issues positions espoused and looks to see how his or her organization needs to adapt to the issue, to collaboratively resolve conflict, or to take advantage of the issue's trends and implications. Analyzing an issue is the prelude to forming a response to it.

 **Response Planning: Stakeholders
and Target Audiences**

One place to look for issues is in any difference of opinion between an organization and its stakeholders. A stake is something of value that a stakeholder can grant or withhold. Persons and groups prefer to award each stake in ways that maximize the return for it. Stakeholders can present the stake either by bestowing rewards or issuing punishment. For example, environmentalists buy gasoline from Chevron because of its reputation for management based on the environmentally oriented "People Do" campaign (Winters, 1988). Issues managers resolve issues that create conflict and engage in collaborative decision making to strengthen or repair relationships with key stakeholders.

Persons in operating and staff units should think in terms of stakeholder relationships. The matrix in Table 3.2 can be used to reduce public policy issues to manageable terms. Issues impact analysis requires three tasks: (a) isolate key stakeholders; (b) determine what kind of value underpins each issue, and (c) identify the motivator that will trigger involvement on the part of the stakeholder.

TABLE 3.2 Issues Matrix

Stakeholders	Issue Type[a]	Dominant Motivator[b]	Consequences
Employees			
Consumers			
Neighbors			
Investors			
Intraindustry			
Interindustry			
Regulators			
Legislators			
Activists			

a. Issue types: fact, value, policy
b. Dominant motivators: equality, security, environmental quality, fairness

Violations of stakeholder expectations will lead to public policy initiatives. An axiom of stakeholder exchange is that parties turn to government to force firms to meet expectations of how they should perform in exchange for stakes. Stakeholder problems can lead to public policy constraints that can be avoided by proactive planning and improved operations.

Planning should give conscientious attention to the nature of the stakes, their importance, the basis on which they would be withheld or granted, and exchange ratios—what is expected for what is received. Of related interest is the willingness of stakeholders to grant or withhold their stakes. How willing are they to exchange them? What can be done to increase the chances they will be granted rather than withheld? What operations or policies increase favorable exchange?

An issues campaign can target people who have a vested interest. During the 1983 campaign against the 10% withholding tax on savings accounts, sponsors of the campaign realized that anyone with a savings account was a stakeholder. The campaign was successful because it spoke to the self-interest of its targeted audiences. People did not want the IRS intruding into their savings accounts and stock profits (Elmendorf, 1988).

One response option is reputation management. Media follow the predictable path of reporting business mistakes and dramatizing weaknesses rather than championing virtues. In this regard, the three commercial networks were similar in their coverage, although Nimmo and Combs (1981) concluded that they differed in the degrees of sensationalism, precision, and objectivity in reporting on earlier disasters such as the Three Mile Island incident. Trust is increased when publics learn that they can depend on an organization to reward rather than harm them. The public is reluctant to accept claims made by sources perceived to be untrustworthy and acting out of narrow self-interest. The solution is to achieve mutual interests with stakeholders.

 **Conclusion**

Issues management functions must be performed strategically to achieve corporate public policy and strategic business planning goals. They require surveillance to observe issues that have potential impact on the business plan—as threats and opportunities. To do the best planning requires that issues managers obtain data about trends and analyze issues to determine their potential impact on the business plan, public policy plan, and communication plan. A variety of response options are available to issues managers. The best feature positive options needed to resolve conflict in the mutual interest of all relevant parties.

Corporate Responsibility

Getting the House in Order

Any organization that operates in a manner that is indifferent to or flaunts the performance expectations held by key publics can eventually suffer substantial legislative or regulatory penalty. No corporation or other stake-dependent organization can operate—create and implement a successful business plan—if it loses control to one or more external constituents. For that reason, issues managers of businesses and other organizations constantly work to put their houses in order. Chapter 3 emphasized the importance of issues monitoring to learn what concerns and opportunities could affect strategic planning and management. This chapter demonstrates how the information acquired from surveillance can be put to wise use. The objective of issues management is not merely to prepare for guests when they are arriving but also to act in ways that would lead unexpected guests to be pleased by what they find.

This is a power resource issue. Stakeholders prefer giving their stakes to stakeseekers who do most to achieve a balance of mutual interests. That vital principle reminds us that issues managers are in the business of power resource management, not merely seeking to change opinions. To manage issues requires that an organization needs to diminish the difference between what it does and what its stakeholders expect it to do. When firms' operations

119

offend stakeholder expectations, legitimacy gaps foster the desire by stake-holders to correct those operations (Frederick & Weber, 1990; Sethi, 1977). Policy issues arise when stakeholders express standards of performance that are new or applied differently than does the organization under consideration. Issues managers work to know the preferred standards of corporate responsi-bility and conform to those they cannot change, a search for order.

Caught in these circumstances, issues managers can negotiate and reduce major differences with stakeholders. The private sector is learning from its experiences. As Paluszek (1995) championed,

> Business is increasingly in society not only in its traditional role of improving the standard of living—by generating jobs, offering products and services and paying taxes—but also via an overlay of sensitivity that supports employees, empowers customers and investors, and relates to the needs of local, national and international communities. (p. 49)

Although this observation may overstate the achievement of new corporate personae, it captures the trajectory of change that has occurred in the past three decades.

This chapter shows how corporate responsibility can be achieved through carefully formulated management policies and operating procedures that are refined and maintained by constantly reviewing plans, operations, and person-nel who are trained to assure they help achieve corporate responsibility. Central to this discussion is an analysis of the rhetorical rationale for corporate responsibility, the means by which an organization senses shifting standards, which it uses to refine its culture and management philosophy and which it communicates to attract stakes. This analysis begins by examining how the effort to achieve mutually satisfying interests with stakeholders begins with a search to know the appropriate standards of corporate responsibility.

  Mutual Interests: The Basis of Corporate Responsibility

What standards of performance—corporate responsibility—must be met? How does the enterprise know those standards? Change results when activists and other stakeholders demand new standards. Industry groups seek higher or better defined operating performance of their members; they work to impose them on another industry. Glacial shifts in the ideology of society reshape the standards by which companies must eventually learn to operate (McGuire, 1990).

Enhanced standards of corporate responsibility strengthen the design and implementation of the strategic business plan. If preferred standards of corporate responsibility exist but are not widely accepted or implemented, a public policy plan can seek to have them translated into legislation or regulation. One way to respond positively to stakeholder expectations is to stop doing that which is offensive. Such improvement may require increased performance within an industry—fostering standardized operations. Businesses may propose legislation and regulation collectively to achieve superior operating standards and to foster mutually beneficial relationships with their stakeholders.

Polishing the ethical performance of an organization or industry requires many interrelated activities: monitoring key publics' opinions to assess changing standards, integrating issues management into corporate strategic planning, updating codes of conduct, and informing key stakeholders regarding the standards the organization has achieved. Savvy management prefers to draw favorable rather than unfavorable attention. For this reason, organizations' efforts to establish and implement appropriate corporate responsibility should not be static.

Who are these key players? They can include executives, key employees (such as whistle blowers and persons sensitive to shifting standards of acceptable performance), independent experts, industry bellwethers, trade associations, reporters, activists, regulators, legislators, panels constituted to include critics, and legal experts. Issues managers should be concerned with the opinions of key publics, not the public as a whole. They should monitor the opinions of stakeholding publics—even though they are likely to be inconsistent with one another.

Successful issues management programs avoid a defensive stance in regard to changing expectations of stakeholders and prefer to look proactively for competitive, bottom-line advantage by meeting or exceeding stakeholder expectations. This approach to corporate responsibility takes us beyond typical feel-good community-relations programs. Innovative issues managers seek advantages by establishing harmony with stakeholders in ways that lessen unwanted intrusion into strategic business planning and management of the organization while fostering mutual interests.

Four points demonstrate the difficulty of defining and implementing proper standards of corporate responsibility. First, a multiple-stakeholder approach to issues management recognizes that each stakeholder may have different expectations of how the organization should operate. For instance, individuals who invest in a company (investment dollars as stakes) may have less concern than activists (regulatory stakes) for its ability or willingness to meet high standards of air or water quality. Environmental issues demonstrate the complex balance of stakes and definitions of what is legitimate and acceptable. In the timber controversy of the Pacific Northwest, myriad interests exhibit varying degrees of compatibility and conflict: timber companies, loggers, communities dependent on wages and revenue produced by the industry, conservationists, animals, and persons desiring to purchase lumber or housing at the lowest cost.

Second, no absolute standards of corporate responsibility exist; they are defined by each generation and may differ for each stakeholder. For instance, standards of product safety have become more demanding during this century. Some seemingly obvious standards—such as the principle that companies are best when they provide information openly and candidly—may not be universally appropriate. For example, companies are allowed to protect proprietary processes and are required by law to protect the privacy of employee records (Simms, 1994).

Third, executives are outraged by accusations that they prefer unethical business practices. Whether insensitive or truly noble, they are not easily persuaded that their business judgment is legitimately subject to what they may see as carping comments by persons who have no knowledge of business processes and no right to voice preferred standards. Executives are more likely to see the wisdom of achieving a higher level of ethical performance when they realize that their operations could be more successful by doing so; they rely on utilitarian ethical standards when making their business decisions (Premeaux & Mondy, 1993).

Fourth, public policy standards are contestable. Contests focus on questions such as, "Does a problem exist?" "How serious is it?" and "What needs to be done to solve it?" Priorities of operating standards require the definition and ranking of standards of performance.

A "public interest first" strategy is complicated when executives are reluctant to respond proactively to external, nonmarket forces. Many operations personnel fear that issues managers will interfere with the orderly performance of their jobs. Because of these internal political problems, issues management programs need the commitment and participation of executives. The growth of activism in the past three decades has forced companies and other large organizations to realize that they cannot think narrowly and self-interestedly—to the detriment of others' interests.

Control of a firm's destiny can only be achieved by taking high moral ground as the rationale for strategic planning and operations. Astute assessment of the macrosocial standards of corporate responsibility can be used to tailor the operating standards of each organization in ways that achieve mutual interests with key stakeholders. Focus groups can be used to determine the outrage factor that people may experience if they learn of offensive policies and activities of an organization (Elmendorf, 1988; Heath, 1987-1988).

This process should exhibit a bold commitment by each organization to be a constructive part of its community (Kruckeberg & Starck, 1988). To do so requires an understanding of relational variables to ascertain whether each organization has achieved harmony with members of its community or is moving in that direction. But publics may be cynical. One study found that 42% of shareholders do not expect a high level of ethical behavior on the part of companies. Although 72% want disclosure of ethical performance, only 32% believe such reports would be better if audited by independent review (Epstein, McEwen, & Spindle, 1994).

To define and implement standards of corporate responsibility, issues managers can follow several steps. Improved standards of corporate responsibility can be used to increase harmony with stakeholders and increase the organization's strategic business advantage.

Ascertain the standards of corporate responsibility held by key stakeholders.

Compare those standards to those preferred and used by the organization.

Determine whether differences exist and, if so, whether they strain the relationship.

Ascertain whether differences in facts account for the disparity in expectations.

Decide whether value differences constitute the disparity between the organization and its key stakeholders.

Budget for change options, whether communication strategies, public policy efforts, or redefined strategic business strategies to respond to stakeholder expectations.

Alter performance or operating standards to lessen the legitimacy gap.

Take a communication or public policy stance based on correct facts or preferred values when the community interest would be better served.

Eliminate misunderstanding and disagreement by supplying facts or redefining standards vital to the community interest.

Incorporate preferred standards of corporate responsibility in strategic business planning, and communicate with key external stakeholders.

Integrate standards into individual, unit, and corporate performance review, including efforts to achieve total quality management.

Use improved standards of corporate responsibility to achieve competitive advantage.

Integrate these standards into product, service, and organizational reputation messages.

Achieving mutually beneficial interests is not easy in a multiple-stakeholder environment. Not all stakeholders see the world in the same way. Interests often conflict. Priorities differ. By achieving high standards of corporate responsibility through fostered mutual relationships, issues managers can attract stakes and avoid costly conflict. Good performance is a bottom-line issue.

Nestlé: A Case of Failed Corporate Responsibility

Many case studies demonstrate the strains that can plague an organization that offends stakeholder sensibilities and fails to make proper corrections. A classic case is Nestlé Corporation's infant formula marketing controversy (Post, 1985). This case reveals how activists persist until they are satisfied that an organization has learned it lesson—put its house in order.

October of 1984 marked a turning point in a hotly contested battle that centered around Nestlé Corporation's marketing plan to increase its sale of infant formula in less developed nations. In that month, the International Nestle Boycott Committee announced the end to a struggle that originated in 1977. By 1984, observers of this legendary case had reason to conclude that its resolution exemplified the true meaning of issues management. The case brought several key publics into one arena: activists, industry members, media, federal authorities, foreign governments, medical experts, and World Health Organization (WHO) officials. Little did those who applauded the ostensible resolution of that controversy know that it would continue for at least another decade, despite Nestlé's promises to improve its standards of corporate responsibility.

The case extends back to the 1930s when medical experts recognized the health risk of bottle-feeding babies in impoverished regions around the world that lacked sanitary water. Marketing campaigns in such countries encouraged mothers to use milk substitutes, mixed with water, to feed their infants. The problem arose because without sanitation and clean water, bottle-feeding introduced children to health and nutrition problems that breast-feeding does not. Mothers may overdilute the bottle milk, leaving the infant without proper nourishment. Once the mother stops nursing, she soon loses her ability to produce milk, thereby depriving her infant of that nourishment. Up through the 1960s, milk substitutes became increasingly popular in less developed nations. Industrywide marketing became extensive. Advertising, which showed healthy, robust children, was complemented with marketing programs conducted by local nurses on company payrolls.

Critical of this business practice, Dr. Derrick Jelliffe persuaded the United Nations Protein-Calorie Advisory Group to investigate. The public learned about the problem in 1974 when Mike Muller published a series of articles in *The New Internationalist* and a pamphlet titled *The Baby Killer.* In Switzerland, home of Nestlé, the title was changed to *Nestlé Kills Babies.* A trial in 1975 engendered substantial publicity and spurred the formation of numerous pressure groups.

A crucial moment of the controversy occurred in mid-1977 when the Infant Formula Action Coalition (INFACT) began its boycott of Nestlé products. Organizers allied with the National Council of Churches' Interfaith

Center on Corporate Responsibility. INFACT began to work with staff members of Edward Kennedy, Chairman of the Senate Subcommittee on Health and Human Resources. Eventually, the coalition included the highly respected WHO by pushing for comprehensive ethical standards in infant formula marketing. The Carter administration supported the boycott but the Reagan administration did not. Opposition Congressional leaders pictured President Reagan as insensitive and renewed their mobilization efforts. Hearings conducted by the Senate Subcommittee on Health and Human Resources focused attention on Nestlé.

The coalition boycott targeted Nestlé's U.S. operations. The prolonged challenge had an impact: Nestlé executives began to develop a siege mentality. The company tried conventional media relations and press agency responses to neutralize a pervasive, morale-wrecking attack. Management recognized that the cost in morale and public image was high. By 1981, Nestlé had retained and dismissed two of America's largest public relations agencies that had been unable to restore the company's image and divert attention from its questionable marketing strategies.

Rafael D. Pagan, Jr. (1983), then serving as president of the Nestlé Coordination Center for Nutrition, recalled,

> The essential first step in resolving the infant feeding dilemma was for Nestlé to recognize that it was a political, as well as a nutritional, issue and therefore to recognize the legitimacy of some of our critics' concerns and to listen to them carefully. (p. 4)

One of the most difficult tasks of issues managers is convincing executives that policies must be changed when they are at odds with stakeholder opinion. As Pagan concluded, "A primary task of issues management, then, must be to reach beyond our profession and work with senior executives to instill attitudes of awareness and openness in our business firms" (p. 8).

To solve its problems, Nestlé formed five policies: (a) It would improve its corporate performance rather than combating claims made by its critics. (b) Full authority of top management was directed to solving the problem. (c) The issues management team and corporate management decided that corporate policy change was needed before a communication campaign could succeed. (d) All levels of management were instructed to support the campaign. (e) Issues managers relied on advice and information from managers of operations and several key units.

Born from the fire of public criticism and activist pressure, a code of business ethics was produced by Nestlé in conjunction with the WHO. An industrywide group, the International Council of Infant Food Industries, was created to develop a code to regulate the industry. The code banned commission payments to milk nurses. The company agreed to reduce mass media advertising and to adopt a low marketing profile.

Assisted by its critics, Nestlé drafted a "Recommended UN Code for Marketing Infant Formula" in 1981. Once the code was adopted, the company worked for 2 years to translate it into company policies and procedures. During this stage, the Nestlé Infant Formula Audit Commission (NIFAC), created with the assistance of Senator Edmund Muskie, played a vital role. On several points, the Nestlé code differed from the one created by the WHO. To remedy problems of vagueness and inconsistency, NIFAC scientists, clergy, and ethicists reviewed specific instances where the Nestlé and WHO codes differed from one another. Through this mechanism, Nestlé attempted to ensure that it complied with the spirit of the WHO code and translated its own code into specified employee performance standards.

By 1981, the industry seemed to be moving vigorously to put its house in order. The code helped the interested parties clarify the standards of acceptable behavior. Having lost profits and suffering a collapse in employee morale during this protracted contest, Nestlé seemed to stand as a model of business ethics and allowed its operations to be audited. The auditing agency, NIFAC, seemed to serve as testament to what could be done once a firm decides that the temper of the times demands a higher standard of ethics.

Once Nestlé convinced others of its sincerity, the boycott eased. After considering Nestlé's code, a United Methodist Church Task Force voted not to boycott its products. At least for a while, the company stood as a model of corporate responsibility. The industry began to work with Third World physicians and foreign government representatives. Industry sales rebounded. Nestlé's struggle to reform itself coincided with the task of formulating *The OECD Guidelines for Multinational Enterprises,* a workable set of corporate ethics for operations abroad.

This case demonstrates the difficulty of achieving compatibility between the long-term commitment necessary to change operations and short-term management desire for return on investment. Management seemed to acknowledge that it could not operate in a public policy vacuum and finally awoke to the full meanings of activism and corporate responsibility that were sensitive to key community interests.

The Nestlé case seemed to be a "happily ever after" story, with the NIFAC serving as an industry model of how to implement community-sensitive standards of corporate responsibility (Muskie & Greenwald, 1986). The performance of the company should have moved closer to the standards expected by its critical publics. Such was not the case. Protests were renewed in 1989, when, in the judgment of its critics, the company was perceived to have reneged on its commitment to a higher sense of business ethics (Johnson, 1989; C. Salmon, 1989).

Even in 1993, child-health advocates were demanding that Nestlé meet the ethical standards it had helped to create. Groups such as Infant Formula Action were using electronic mail bulletin boards as well as more conventional communication channels to disseminate criticism of the company. The International Baby Food Action Network argued that company practices violated the WHO-NIFAC agreement and reasserted the position that substitutes should not be widely marketed without great caution and that mothers' milk was preferred. An international network of activist and scientific groups monitored the performance on the milk supplement issue. Outraged by what it believed to be deception and recalcitrance by Nestlé, Action for Corporate Accountability (ACA) maintained its boycott of Nestlé products and called on the company to comply with the agreement it had signed. ACA claimed that Nestlé was continuing the practices that had caused the furor in the 1970s.

This case study starkly demonstrates the extraordinary efforts critics of business practices will undertake for their causes. If a problem exists, it will be corrected. Correction may be voluntary or coerced. If the interests become unbalanced, activists will work to put them right.

 ## Standards of Corporate Responsibility: A Rhetorical Rationale

Standards of corporate responsibility are the product of advocacy, a debate that addresses the standards by which key organizations are judged. To appreciate this struggle, this section delves into the rhetorical structures that form the content and appeals for new and improved standards of corporate responsibility. As opinions are formed by and yield to rhetorical challenges, society forges new performance standards.

Each firm's or industry's standards of corporate responsibility are affected by macrosocial principles as well as by opinions key stakeholders hold. The same can be said for the actions of governmental agencies, activist groups, and nonprofit organizations. Each set of premises is subject to rhetorical contest. Key premises are used to evaluate the practices of public-sector and private-sector organizations. These premises are used to interpret information. They drive the assumptions used to create public policy (Pearson, 1990). They underpin efforts to negotiate differences and collaboratively solve mutually interesting problems.

Broad principles of organizational performance change slowly. Once they become widely accepted, they provide the framework that all mutually interested parties use to judge corporate responsibility. For instance, during the last three decades, the locus of responsibility for safely operating power equipment or electrical appliances has shifted from the person using them to the companies that design, manufacture, and sell them. Another example is the requirement that all companies be accountable for their environmental impact; how that premise translates into strategic planning and public policy is different for a real estate development project than for operators of a chemical plant. One last illustration focuses on the premise of freedom to use products that are not illegal; the tobacco industry challenges legislative control of its product, such as prohibiting smoking in company or public buildings.

A powerful rhetorical force behind the development and implementation of standards of corporate responsibility is the expression of self-control. Although ostensibly self-imposed, control is prompted by forces outside. Many people—for example, those confronted with risks associated with chemical companies—do not believe that such businesses would voluntarily implement standards of self-control that would meet community expectations (Nathan, Heath, & Douglas, 1992). Technical experts who work in the industry believe chemical companies voluntarily exert high standards of control over hazardous processes, whereas technical experts who do not work for the chemical industry have less faith in its sense of corporate responsibility (Gay & Heath, 1995).

Such skepticism may be warranted by how corporate personnel respond to accusations that they engage in unethical business practices. Responses to such charges are likely to exhibit a desire to manage impressions—to engage in reputation management. One study found the following responses routinely made to such accusations: (a) denying that the event occurred (12.5%), (b) offering the excuse that the organization was not responsible for the event (10.6%), (c) justifying why the event happened after acknowledging that it had, and arguing that the criteria applied to the event were incorrect, and (d) conceding or agreeing that the event happened as alleged and acknowledging that the company was responsible (Garrett, Bradford, Meyers, & Becker, 1989). One responsibility of issues communicators is to obtain and share the facts surrounding an event; another is to make honest and candid attributions for its cause.

Such findings explain why the public's confidence in regard to corporate management has tumbled. This outcome is the product of discoveries that corporate managements flaunt community expectations and the resultant gap between what management expects of itself and the standards critics have forged through rhetorical contest. Three decades ago, in 1966, 55% of the public had "a great deal of confidence" in the capability and moral qualities of corporate leaders. By 1976, the confidence level had fallen to 16% (Kelly, 1982). In 1983, Gallup research placed the figure at 18% for those who gave business executives "very high" and "high" ratings for honesty and ethics. In the battle of trustworthiness during the 1980s, corporate leaders trailed TV commentators (33%), journalists (28%), and newspaper reporters (26%) ("Honesty and Ethical Standards," 1983). A decade later, some figures remained relatively the same, but others showed dramatic change: business executives (20%), newspaper reporters (22%), television commentators/ reporters (28%), U.S. senators (18%), and members of Congress (14%) ("Honesty and Ethical Standards," 1993).

The public can't decide whether it distrusts government or big business more. Schellhardt (1975) reported two decades ago that whereas 56% of the public favored increased government regulation of companies, 35% favored less. A March 1981 Harris survey reported that even though 53% of the public felt big government was a problem, approximately 80% believed its protection was needed against corporations. One reason that activist groups have become popular and powerful is the need for individual citizens to band to gather aggregate sufficient power resources to force changes in business practices and governmental policies.

One likely explanation for the loss in confidence of corporate performance is the fact that expectations forged through public debate are higher today than they were three decades ago. Through investigative reports, violations of public confidence become widely known. Firms participate as citizens in a changing political environment. Championing this spirit, Chase (1982) wrote,

> The noblest aspect of freedom is that human beings and their institutions have the right to help determine their own destinies. Issue management is the systems process that maximizes self-expression and action programming for most effective participation in public policy formation. (p. 2)

Companies and other organizations address the standards of corporate performance, working to change those that are unwise and adopting those that foster the community interest.

Two decades ago, Sethi (1974, 1977) believed many corporations fell short of prevailing standards of corporate responsibility. He worried that the media would be unable to manage the space and time available so the public would have adequate access to all viewpoints. He wondered whether people would have the time and patience to wade through the flood of information to become well informed. Of related interest, however, is the loss of public confidence on the part of media reports, perhaps the product of unethical journalistic practices such as falsifying reports and engaging in hyperbole.

One response by activist publics is to turn to special publications, those by activist groups. For instance, environmentalists prefer to get detailed information on those issues from environmental magazines (J. E. Grunig, 1980). Persons who are concerned about the economic benefits and harms that result from the operations of a chemical plant in a small community tend to monitor the local media for information on that issue. But they also demonstrate a strong interest in obtaining information from interpersonal contact, government publications, and the company executives (Heath, Liao, et al., 1995). In this way, highly involved publics exert special effort to obtain the quality information they need to form opinions that satisfy and protect their interests.

The public cannot count on reporters, editorialists, and news directors to be critical of private-sector marketing and advertising practices. Ability of marketers and advertisers to wield the club of advertising dollars has muted some critics, so discovered the Center for the Study of Commercialism (Zachary, 1992). Despite reporters' and editors' claims to the contrary, Zachary concluded, "in interviews, both happy advertisers and concerned journalists say several converging forces have meant softer coverage of advertisers" (p. A1).

One focal point in this battle for confidence is the interpretative frameworks reporters use when evaluating business activities. Media leaders help form what the public holds as its standards of acceptable corporate behavior. Therefore, issues communicators provide information through media relations backgrounders and public forums to help reporters understand and appreciate a corporation's point of view regarding its operations. Attempts to inform media leaders and reinforce their commitment to accurate and knowledgeable reportage have been made by corporate representatives such as Tom P. McAdams (1981), speaking as Chairman of the Board, Independent Petroleum Association of America, and Herbert Schmertz (1983), formerly vice president of public affairs at Mobil.

Executives address key publics in an attempt to build or restore confidence concerning their responsiveness to community needs and expectations. T. M. Ford (1984), CEO of Emhart, spoke as he received the 1984 Leadership Award for excellence in communication from the International Association of Business Communicators. His theme centered on the challenge and cooperation that can exist between corporations and professional communicators to increase the quality of communication. Such messages may build a more supportive climate for corporations.

Robert W. Lundeen (1983), Chairman of the Board, The Dow Chemical Company, examined this theme as the keynote speaker at the annual Business Journalism Awards banquet of the Interstate National Gas Association at the University of Missouri, Columbia. He embraced the words of Thomas Jefferson: "Nothing can now be believed which is seen in a newspaper." The relevance of this observation was the gap between the "media elite" and the "business elite." He observed, "A very wide cultural gap lies between working journalists in newspapers, television and radio and most, if not all, industrial executives and professionals." The problem is that "Neither side quite understands what the other is up to. Neither side quite trusts the other. So there is hostility." The gap translated into divergent perceptions—competing and conflicting zones of meaning. Dow executives saw themselves as savvy, competent, and responsible. When they read about themselves, they saw themselves portrayed as "arrogant polluters, insensitive to the health of their own workers, of consumers of their products and of plant neighbors." Such conclusions by journalists and external critics may assume that business problems have simple solutions. Lundeen begged the press to double-check facts by seeking them from several sources. He implored writers to realize that companies are not inherently evil and should not automatically be approached with suspicion. He favored dialogue and encouraged writers "to get it right and then tell it right so that 235 million Americans can judge it right."

Words alone will not convince the public of the standards of corporate responsibility that strengthen the community. Actions are required, as was demonstrated by Archie Boe (1972), CEO of Allstate Insurance Companies:

> Allstate is—as are most insurance companies—in a unique position to function as a "public interest" corporation since we literally stand in our customer's place in matters of financial loss. Very simply, their loss is our loss: What is good for them is good for us. (p. 2)

He continued,

> When feasible, we serve as advocates or counselors for our customers, speaking and acting in their name as they would do, if they had our collective knowledge, training, experience and expertise in public matters affecting their interests. Our sense of corporate responsibility has moved us into an active role as a public interest corporation, which has a "guidance system" concerned with human values and customer's needs. I think we've demonstrated from our efforts in securing drunk driver legislation, improved bumpers and related auto design, and modernization of the automobile insurance system, that Allstate has both the will and skill to meet its responsibilities and, at the same time, balance its public and self-interests for the benefit of all concerned. (p. 2)

These ideas Boe credited to General Wood of Sears, who

> had a sign over the front door and it's still there. It says, "Business must account for its stewardship, not only on the balance sheet, but also in matters of social responsibility." We have incorporated this philosophy in our advertising efforts. (Boe, 1972, p. 3)

Businesses are not alone in their efforts to debate public policy, especially in regard to the standards of corporate responsibility expected within a community of interest. Nonprofit organizations take stands on issues in the regulatory marketplace (Bates, 1982; Booth, 1978). They may even advocate issue positions that challenge companies' policies.

One principle that has become increasingly central to business planning in the past three decades is that if companies want to minimize externally imposed standards, they must self-regulate by ascertaining and implementing appropriate standards of ethics. Writers became aware of this need in the 1960s; this concern led to seminal work by Anshen (1974) and Sethi (1974, 1977). Market forces alone do not shape the fate of corporations; public policy change plays its role (Buchholz, 1982b, 1985). For this reason, corporate planning should couple with the formulation of business ethics (Post, 1979). Reflecting on the learning curve of public affairs, Post and Kelley (1988) concluded,

> The public affairs management field has undergone tremendous change over the past five years. Change will continue as the field moves toward professionalization and legitimization within the corporate world. This trend should help organizations move from coping with external demands to anticipating how demands can best be met within the technical and economic context of the organization. This is the essence of being a responsive corporation in the modern world. For the central institution of our age, that is neither too much nor too little to ask. (p. 365)

Under pressure by critics, private-sector organizations evolved three lines of reasoning to justify spending corporate funds to advance their side of contested issues (Stridsberg, 1977). One, each company is an aggregate of the persons who own it. Because shareholders have a common stake in what happens to the firm, they should be willing to defend it and its industry. Two, employees deserve a collective voice in the outcome of issues and are allies for corporate efforts. Three, commitment to customers and other external stakeholders requires that businesses shoulder the stewardship of participating in the creation of operating standards that respond to the mutual interests of all stakeholders.

Through their comments—as well as actions that reveal their commitment to mutual interests—companies help shape the standards by which they are judged. For this reason, Cheney and Dionisopoulos (1989) observed that

> corporate communication (in practice and in theory) must be self-conscious about its role in the organizational process (which is fundamentally rhetorical and symbolic) in responding to and in exercising power (in public discourse), and in shaping various identities (corporate and individual). (p. 140)

The challenge to management, Smircich (1983) wrote, is to mediate "the relationship between environment and organization toward a fit; that is, managers align organizational and environmental forces to a desired state of congruence" (p. 227).

Organizational discourse affirms or disaffirms and employs premises that have become part of people's thinking and behavior.

> Such hegemony does not refer to simple or outright domination but rather to control over the (value) premises that shape basic and applied policy decisions. In essence, corporate discourse seeks to establish public frames of reference for interpreting information concerning issues deemed important by Corporate America. (Cheney & Dionisopoulos, 1989, p. 144)

Carried to the extreme, Sproule (1989) reasoned, "Organizations try to privatize public space by privatizing public opinions; that is, skillfully (one-sidedly) turning opinion in directions favorable to the corporation" (p. 264).

One way to study standards of corporate responsibility is to view them as themes that run throughout a story, a narrative. In this sense, life—personal and corporate—is envisioned as exhibiting narrative form and content. The assumption: All of what people and organizations do must fit into a narrative, where characters enact themes that motivate their actions and serve as the rationale for what they do. In this sense, discourse is inherently narrative, exhibiting two traits: narrative fidelity (a story should conform to known or assumed facts) and probability (a story should be internally consistent and coherent) (Fisher, 1985, 1987).

This view of the standards of corporate responsibility assumes that all of what a firm is perceived to do communicates to audiences powerful statements about the organization. Actions speak as loudly as words (or more so). Enactment is the performance of narrative form and content, a means by which a company—for instance—becomes to its key publics as an actor presents its persona to an audience. Such performance becomes the experiential data audiences use to determine whether the organization exhibits values that the stakeholders favor or reject (Heath, 1988a, 1994). Through public dialogue, standards are forged that are used to evaluate the performance of the organizations that play major roles in society. Standards change. So must organizations' strategic management principles.

 Changing Organizational Policies: Getting the House in Order

Expectations of how organizations—public and private—should perform changes over time. The simplest standard of corporate responsibility is captured in that timeless bit of advice: Don't do anything that you do not want reported on the front page of the newspaper or the top-of-the-hour news report. This section addresses that challenge looking to the strategies that organizations can use to put themselves in order—to meet or exceed stakeholder expectations.

For many years, as Chapter 2 demonstrated, large companies dominated this debate and created a definitional hegemony that biased decisions in their favor. The past 100 years have demonstrated that standards of corporate responsibility are not absolute; they change as the product of complex rhetorical enterprises engaging scholars, activists, corporate executives, reporters, and government officials. The product forged from this discourse operates as a macrosocietal level—broadly generalized abstract ideals—that are used in specific cases—the microsocietal level—unique to each company, industry, nonprofit entity, or government agency. These entities are expected to ascertain and implement standards of corporate responsibility, which otherwise will be imposed through legislation or litigation.

Issues management begins by getting its house in order, a point driven home vigorously during the 1960s and 1970s. Corporate leaders began to bring outsiders into the discussion to obtain a more objective view of the issues and strategies involved. In this spirit, Paul Garrett, who had served as Vice President of Public Relations at General Motors, endowed a professorship at Columbia University to foster the belief that businesses need to do more than resist change. Business leaders "have the knowledge and skill required" to aid in accomplishing social goals. "They owe it to society as well as to the business system to make these contributions in a creative and forthright manner" (Anshen, 1974, p. ix).

In response to the turmoil surrounding corporate ethics in the 1970s, the Business Roundtable commissioned a study of corporate ethics that culminated in *Corporate Performance: The Key to Public Trust* (Steckmest, 1982). This book was developed "to provide a forum for the examination of economic issues facing the nation, to develop reasoned positions on those issues, and thereby to contribute to the formation of public policy" (p. ix). The project evidenced a willingness by corporate leaders to debate such issues as corporate performance and governance, consumer and employee rights, and the difference between legal and ethical requirements.

Through hard experience, firms discovered the subtle but profound distinction between legal and ethical behavior. For too long, corporations attempted to hide behind the veil of legality without realizing that the public makes a real distinction between the two. Insensitive managements could claim an action, procedure, or policy was legal, even though it markedly violated public expectations of trust and morality. Issues managers learned the harsh reality that key publics are the final judges of corporate behavior.

Violation of publicly held standards can only lead to public condemnation and public policy constraints if such results are discovered by nonindustry researchers. Scandals associated with such research result because instead of obtaining and using information to guide ethical business policy, some companies deny the findings, destroy them, or suppress them as well as fire the researchers. Some executives are frustrated by the prospect that others can "dictate" how they will operate their companies. Unwillingness to acknowledge the presence of critics ignores the reality that some of them have legitimate beefs that can be persuasively disseminated to publics as the first step toward increased legislation or regulation.

Where do savvy issues managers focus their attention in their effort to identify, monitor, and define ethical concerns? Four categories of concerns stand out: Political economy, management concerns, stakeholder motivators, and issues of corporate responsibility (see Table 4.1).

The broadest set of ethical concerns arise from the organization's economic, social, and political interests (Wartick & Cochran, 1985). Each political economy defines these interests. In this regard, dramatic shifts occur in a society. As N. Smith (1995) observed, "Marketing strategies are increasingly subject to public scrutiny and are being held to higher standards. Caveat emptor is not longer acceptable as a basis for justifying marketing practices" (p. 85).

Based on their definitions of these concerns, managers are responsible for implementing several considerations: ethical, conceptual, technical, functional, and operational. Operational management refers to the means to satisfy customers, improve products or services, and husband assets wisely. Functional management involves maximizing revenue, minimizing costs, and optimizing returns. Technical management requires the involvement of all relevant people in decisions, the wise use of information, and the application of technology. Conceptual management is accomplished by setting objectives, gaining advantages, and building competencies. Ethical management assumes the ability to gain commitment, expand cooperation, and create community. Done singly, any of these management challenges would fall short. Combined, they provide a substantial statement about corporate responsibility (Hosmer, 1991).

Definitions and implementation of standards of corporate responsibility must embrace the spectrum of issues: economic, legal, ethical, and philanthropic (Carroll, 1991). Legal concerns become the foundation for legal argument and judicial decisions. Economic issues are inseparable from considerations of corporate responsibility—whether carefully scrutinized or not; companies do not operate in an economic market without making decisions on how to balance profits and the interests of the marketplace. Philanthropy can become a show rather than an honest expression of the company's

TABLE 4.1 Focal Points for Ascertaining Stakeholder Expectations of
Ethical Performance

Political Economy	Management Concerns	Stakeholder Motivators	Corporate Responsibility Concerns
Economic	Ethical	Security	Economic
Social	Technical	Fairness	Legal
Political	Functional	Equality	Ethical
	Conceptual	Environmental	Philanthropic
	Operational		

commitment to the community in which it operates; philanthropy is more profound when it benefits the community and the sponsor. Independent of situation assessment are dominant themes of moral consideration. Taken together, these factors translate into axioms that Carroll argued serve the good of the company and community: Do good for the community, be ethical, obey the law in spirit as well as principle, and make a profit. These bits of sage advice need to be considered in combination with stakeholders' interests.

Policy analysis and ethical considerations need to be based on key motivators that seem to be universal to stakeholder concerns and public outbursts on matters of corporate responsibility: security, equality, environmental concern, and fairness (Heath 1988a). People want to be secure from risks—at least those they believe to be intolerable. No longer will key segments of society tolerate unequal treatment, although achieving full equality seems to be an endless battle. Groups such as environmentalists demand that companies have a positive rather than negative effect on the environment. People want to be treated fairly. Standards such as these are pivotal points when looking for issues that will prompt activism and governmental intervention.

The focal points featured in Table 4.1 need to be central to planning and operations while making every effort to meet bottom-line requirements through strategic planning decisions. The desire is to seek to add value to each organization's operations by fostering mutual interests with key stakeholders. For instance, one cost benefit for seeking higher ethical standards is to avoid the expense of dealing with regulatory agencies. Although reactionary mitigation can be used to demonstrate savings, making a cost-effect case for proactivity may be more difficult. Despite the belief by Weissman (1984) and Chrisman and Carroll (1984) that corporate responsibility pays for itself, Cochran and Wood (1984) found a low correlation between corporate responsibility and financial performance. The degree of corporate responsibility exhibited by companies corresponds to the age of their manufacturing facilities. For instance, factories built before 1960 are more likely to pollute and cost more to bring within federal and state standards.

Recent findings are worth the attention of executives engaged in strategic planning. Corporate responsibility can affect people's willingness to engage in business transactions and stakeholder loyalty (Owen & Scherer, 1993). Makeover (1994) claimed that corporate responsibility is good for business. Herremans, Akathaporn, and McInnes (1993) found that business reputations correlate positively with financial performance. Examining the trend toward sustainable resources, Elkington (1994) concluded that companies are integrating environmental values and competitive strategizing. Three phases of analysis are used. Life cycle analysis is employed to find out the history of a product from manufacturing through its use by consumers to a safe return to the environment. Integration of business activities and total quality management helps organizations to use resources wisely—environmentally and financially. Auditing assesses whether management tactics are achieving stated objectives. The good business news is that the buying public tends to use corporate responsibility standards to guide its purchases.

Another reason for increased sophistication in monitoring public standards is the growing number of court awards against companies. Thirty-five years ago, a $1-million settlement was news. In 1980, 130 multimillion dollar awards were routinely given; this jumped to 235 in 1981 (Foote, 1984). In 1994, the jury in the Exxon Valdez case trial ruled that the company should pay $5 billion dollars in punitive damages. The plethora of attorneys and the widespread sense that companies have infinitely deep pockets and should be the only entity responsible for the safe use of products lead to the prospect that issues managers are going to need increased sensitivity to the pressures for refined standards of business ethics that arise through court decisions.

Cooperative expressions of self-interest, however, may be on their way into the thinking of executives and issues managers. Environmental groups have achieved impressive compromises in what key industries will agree to do to protect the environment, including wildlife species. Rather than fight environmental issues in court, one leading member of the timber industry— Georgia-Pacific—agreed to set aside large regions of forest and to employ environmentally sensitive harvesting measures to protect the red-cockaded woodpeckers that are living on its land. The agreement calls for Georgia-Pacific to protect 113 red-cockaded woodpecker colonies that need old trees for a suitable habitat. These colonies dot 4 million acres of forest. The company will maintain a 200-foot buffer zone around each colony; an additional 100 acres will be protected adjacent to each colony for the birds to feed. A total of 56,000 acres was committed to the project. The company will be allowed to selectively cut trees in those areas. This action on the part of a company affects many stakeholder interests, which are as likely to be in conflict as in harmony. The company wants to minimize environmental intrusion into its operations and to avoid the stifling wrangle that has occurred between environmentalists, loggers, and logging company executives in the Pacific Northwest regarding the northern spotted owl (Olgeirson, 1993).

The ethical quandaries suggested in the case of logging should not catch issues managers and executives off guard. Advocating making planning skills systematic, McGinnis (1984) observed, "Intelligence is the firm's ability to simultaneously scan and interpret its external environments, monitor itself, and communicate effectively with itself" (p. 46). To achieve balance, a company should "be centralized and decentralized simultaneously" (p. 46). Issues management can help departments concentrate on the internal and external policy implications of their activities. A common set of operating standards and an awareness of public policy implications offers managers in diverse parts of a company a collective sense of their operating environment constraints.

Corporate planning requires that each major department develop an issues analysis and response plan. This effort begins by reviewing highlights of the previous year and identifying the key challenges it expects to face in the coming 12 months. The next step is to specify how these challenges will be met in conjunction with all other departments. Putting this plan together requires internal discussion and coordination. At the end of the effort, a master plan summarizes how each department will perform and how it can count on specific actions from other departments.

By sharing information in this manner, issues managers can have proactive input into operating activities early enough to matter. Communication support can be realistically budgeted, and operations and financial managers have a ground floor opportunity to consider and authorize the funding of the issues communication. One of several benefits that arise from this planning process is the increased awareness of external scrutiny of their efforts—a means for making them conscious of operating expectations others have of them. Operating units become more sensitive to and willing to self-impose publicly acceptable standards of ethical behavior once they are forced to consider such eventuality in the planning process.

So far, so good. But theory and reality do not always mesh. One theme comes up time and again: Too often, corporate planning does not carefully consider public affairs advice on policy issues unless the company is involved in a controversy (Post et al., 1983). Based on data that are a decade old, we can wonder whether half of all companies still fail to use public affairs expertise in defining issues or prioritizing their importance. Do more than one quarter of public affairs departments provide long-term sociopolitical forecasts and planning scenarios? These figures are heartening if they demonstrate a trend toward more use of public affairs expertise, but if not, they are bleak. Case studies suggest that the impact of public affairs departments on planning is low in utility companies and banks, high in computer companies, and moderate in the chemical industry. Differences in the extent to which issues management is used in corporate planning seem to coincide with the personalities of the CEOs more than any other factor.

As the Post et al. (1983) survey revealed, public affairs has greatest influence on short-term problems faced by corporations rather than long-range planning. In fact, "The influence wanes unless great care is taken to interpret the long term to line managers so that it has immediate relevance." This limitation seems predictable, given companies' quarterly planning mentality. The survey also disclosed that public affairs is more likely to be influential on corporate strategic planning in highly centralized companies. The authors concluded, "Companies using long-range, strategic planning of a qualitative nature are far more likely to have influential public affairs offices." This seems "intuitively logical because strategic planning tends to examine the environment more broadly and systematically than do operationally focused and/or less formal planning systems" (p. 147).

Such planning makes operations people aware of the public policy consequences of their business decisions and alerts communication experts to possible dangers of business policies and procedures. In this way, issues management is infused into corporate planning and evaluation. By continuing careful coordination, line and staff executives have the opportunity to make adjustments during the year by monitoring how well the plan is working and whether it continues to coincide with management thought, business opportunities, and public expectations. Issues management fits comfortably with management by objectives.

Planning can include estimates of the kinds of groups that will make a positive or negative reaction to company and industry policies and actions. Such estimates can be made issue by issue and group by group. Each group can be placed on a pro-con continuum. Some groups are valuable because they are willing to buy products or services. Other groups are important because they are willing to take sides on public policy debates. Sometimes, sizable groups of individuals fall into both categories. After identifying each issue by group, the company can determine what information each has and the attitudinal impact of the information.

Corporate decision making, Schwenk (1984) argued, follows three stages: goal formulation-problem identification, strategic alternatives generation, and evaluation and selection. Issues management has its strategic corporate planning role at each of these three stages. At the first stage, issues managers can help corporate planners determine the public policy implications related to corporate goals by isolating and weighting input-output variables that impinge on operations. Issues management seeks to clarify the effect of key publics' expectations on specific corporate practices. The third stage requires that the cost-benefit analysis of the first and second stages be resolved so that strategies can be selected to foster corporate profit and image goals. Planners estimate the complex of variables that includes marketplace competition, production costs and schedules, transportation, acquisition of materials, capital improvement, labor conditions, and financing costs. The standard worst-case scenario equation goes like this: What reaction will occur if chemical plant operators allow periodic discharges of noxious fumes? What outcries will be heard if a manufacturing procedure failure kills dozens of people?

Issues managers must recognize that the more their recommendations are complex and risky, the less likely they are to be successfully implemented (Fidler & Johnson, 1984). As Brodwin and Bourgeois (1984) demonstrated, few executives get beyond their short-range problems to articulate long-term projections. Compromise is an essential to success, even if it means abandoning optimal plans. Corporate culture contains value judgments, such as ethics in marketing, product design, employee relations, quality of work, and competition; they are vital to matters regarding how each company treats its customers, neighbors, and employees (Drake & Drake, 1988). Unwilling "cooperation" by managers coerced into supporting projects they do not really believe in generally leads to failure, even when the proposal has merit.

Diagnostic studies determine the opinion environment and how to use it to reconsider the corporation's performance strengths and weaknesses. Rowe and Schlacter (1978) claimed that unless corporate responsibility is integrated into organizational structure, its issues campaigns will flounder once investigative reporters or shrewd activists discover that message claims are narrowly self-interested or mask unethical corporate performance. To avoid such gaps, they proposed the use of a social audit to "identify those social responsibilities that a company thinks it ought to be discharging." It may be used "to examine what the company is doing in these areas and to determine how satisfactory is the performance." If a performance gap is discovered, the audit can effectively "determine how far the company should go in filling it" and "whether a company is vulnerable to potential criticism or attack." The ultimate goal of the audit is to bring together "the thinking of managers at all levels of a social point of view" (p. 10).

How does a company become sensitive to the opinions of stakeholders? Post et al. (1983) discovered that companies have hired issues managers and created organizational arrangements such as public policy committees, public issue task forces, and formalized public affairs-corporate planning coordination. These arrangements can integrate staff activities and business operations to achieve corporate objectives. To prevent being unduly myopic, issues monitoring, J. Brown (1979) concluded, "must include external validation" (p. 34).

If two heads are better than one, then many heads can be even better when attempting to refine and use standards of responsible performance. Many companies have experimented with matrix management to bring together operating managers and other specialists for planning and executing issues campaigns (Buchholz, 1982a; Thompson, 1981). In its effort, Monsanto used an Issue Identification Committee and an Emerging Issues Committee to look for opportunities and threats in key operating areas. The objective was to isolate critical issues. Gulf Oil Company created a Public Issues Committee to draw together key thinkers whose views were critical to planning options of the organization (Littlejohn, 1986). Groups foster discussion of current and emerging standards of corporate responsibility and reflect on the implications of those trends for business planning and other opportunities to implement standards of ethical performance.

In addition to having a close working relationship with executive management, the matrix must bring together experts that draw on a vital range of expertise: (a) managerial—finance, economic forecasting, marketing, product liability, and personnel aspects of the company, (b) technical—production and handling of company products and services, including engineering (or its technical equivalent, such as pharmaceutics or medicine), (c) public policy—formation of issues, (d) governmental affairs—ways public sentiment becomes legislation, and (e) corporate ethical behavior—strategies for auditing corporate social performance. Every effort should be made to involve people whose collective understanding of the company represents all of the major decision points and departmental-product-plant operating activities.

Getting the house in order requires that sensitive individuals need to be challenged to ascertain those changing expectations that are likely to be imposed on an organization or industry if they are not self-imposed. Because of the complexity of modern organizations, a matrix-planning arrangement is needed. Codes of performance need to be created and implemented in ways that attach them to the performance review of personnel, operating units, and the entire organization. Despite their ostensibly heightened awareness of what such codes should contain, public relations practitioners seem to be less involved in the development and implementation of standards of corporate responsibility than they should be (Heath & Ryan, 1989). This is the case, even though public relations practitioners have good standards of business ethics that can support this effort (Ryan, 1986; Ryan & Martinson, 1983, 1984, 1985).

Corporate ethics are more complex than the public realizes. One difficult but fundamental step is deciding the content of the code. Like all regulations, principles embodied into codes are ambiguous and subject to distortion. This fact does not excuse executives from attempting to codify business ethics. Boilerplated lists are unsatisfactory answers to complicated issues. One corporate response is to become more "transparent." For this reason, Shell Oil Company proclaimed a commitment to divulge all information on request that did not violate the law, compromise the integrity of employees or customers, reveal proprietary secrets, or disrupt secret negotiations (Steckmest, 1982).

Even if vague, principles espoused in codes set the tone for organizational policies and employee behavior. At least one study found that the presence of codes of conduct did not correlate with fewer corporate violations of laws and regulations. The type of industry and size of company are stronger predictors that violations will occur than is the presence or absence of a code of conduct (Mathews, 1990). The degree to which a company's values disagree with those of its stakeholders is likely to reflect the profitability of the firm (profitable firms are more ethical than those that are desperate to survive), its size (larger firms may differ more from stakeholder expectations), the amount of product diversification (the more products supplied by the company, the greater its chances for differing with key publics), and the speed of growth (a slower growing company may exhibit fewer differences) (Cochran & Nigh, 1990). The challenge facing issues managers is to avoid allowing the physical nature of the organization to dominate efforts to satisfy public expectations.

Codes—whether formally created or merely a product of corporate culture—provide answers that individuals, departments, and the entire organization need to guide strategic planning and operations. As Arrington and Sawaya (1984) observed, corporate planning is most interested in the business environment, whereas issues management people concentrate on public policy events that impinge on the business. One place these disciplines join is when ethical concerns are used to refine strategic planning. Wise companies think in terms of the mutual interests it has with its stakeholders. Wise executives link profit maximization with an incentive to serve the community. They plan to foster or at least not hinder the public policy interests of its stakeholders. Exhibiting stewardship, they use profit-making ability for the social needs of the community. To help refine long-range corporate planning scenarios, issues management foresight is challenged to define ethical concerns and key stakeholder expectations so that they can be translated into strategic plans and operating standards.

One hotly contested issue among public relations, marketing, and advertising practitioners and scholars is whether these three disciplines should be integrated or remain separate. One key issue is whether public relations, or all of a firm's efforts to maintain corporate responsibility, would be harmed if public relations or other relevant disciplines were less likely to serve as a watchdog over the choices made by personnel responsible for marketing and advertising. Because they have to deal with crises that result from failure to meet publics' expectations regarding how a company should behave, public relations personnel may indeed have superior sensitivity to which corporate choices and actions are potentially offensive to key publics. In any event, issues managers fail to do their full job if they fail to help the company put or keep its house in order.

Several examples of marketing efforts that suffered substantially from outbursts of consumer advocates include marketing Dakota cigarettes to an ostensibly gullible female market who associated smoking with a rugged lifestyle. Another example is the battle waged over the marketing of malt liquors in the early 1990s. G. Heileman Brewing Company wanted to name its brand of malt liquor, PowerMaster. Foes of excessive drinking, along with Black leaders, charged the company with corporate irresponsibility. One problem was the high alcohol content of the drink. Another was the fact that Heileman, along with other malt liquor marketers, targeted low-income, inner-city Black consumers, who suffer a high incidence of alcohol-related illnesses. Instead of em*power*ing its consumers, it stood a good chance of doing the opposite.

In the early 1990s, the beer and liquor industry targeted the female market (which then consumed 20% of the beer on the market) with tailored products such as fruit-flavored alcohol drinks. The most explosive problem was fetal alcohol syndrome, a birth defect. The National Council on Alcoholism and Drug Dependence charged that the industry was targeting women in their childbearing years. Beer manufacturers used ads portraying women in professional working attire consuming beers and women consuming them while engaged in intimate conversation. The advertising made no effort to stress the perils associated with drinking while pregnant. Although alcohol can lead to health problems, ads avoid such topics, preferring to associate the product with pleasant outcomes rather than unpleasant ones. Health activists pointed out that young women, the target market, seem less aware of the health hazards of drinking and noted that the industry did nothing to sufficiently warn women of those hazards.

Infomercials hawk a variety of products, such as those to remove cellulite or to restore hair. They provide hyperbolic glosses about how various persons earned quick fortunes by following the real estate advice of a spokesman who recounts the millions he has stored in the bank by lolling in a resort setting. Complaints about the misleading, deceptive, and unsubstantiated content and claims in these presentations prompted the Federal Trade Commission, in 1990, to impose regulatory sanctions over the content. One industry response was the formation of the National Infomercial Marketing Association, which sought to establish guidelines for responsible performance by its members as well as other producers whose advertisements could bring further and harsher regulatory sanctions (Lipman, 1991b).

One marketing campaign, by Revlon, raised the ire of members of the African American community. The campaign used commercials containing footage of Nat King Cole singing, "Unforgettable." The fragrance commercial featured only White models, until a Black model was added to it as an afterthought. This kind of clumsiness has led 60% of the African American community to think that advertising, whether electronic or print, is designed primarily for White consumers. They believe it is insensitive to their needs, interests, and images (Bird, 1993).

One function of trade associations is to help establish industrywide performance standards and to monitor member organizations' compliance with them. One agency that polices advertising claims for accuracy is the National Advertising Review Board. In 1994, it ruled that Wal-Mart could no longer use the advertising claim, "Always the low price. Always." The statement was not true—so said representatives of the Better Business Bureau and competitors such as Dayton Hudson Corporation's Target Stores, Meijer Inc., and Vision World Inc.

Self-regulation begins with an honest, objective, and candid assessment of the behavior of the industry as a whole and of its component companies. Industries establish groups to monitor issues and attempt to regulate behavior industrywide. The Chemical Industry Institute of Toxicology receives contributions from its constituent companies to study and commission studies regarding toxicity. Organizations such as the Energy Production Research Institute are designed to help sponsoring companies increase their performance, including the ability to understand and respond intelligently to technical, social, political, and economic issues.

Few if any industries have suffered more dramatic changes in standards of business ethics than have the tobacco and alcohol industries. The quickest way to demonstrate this dramatic change is to compare the rampant social drinking and smoking in vintage black-and-white movies to policy positions today that condemn social drinking as part of business practices and relegate smokers to a location outside primary business areas. Because of growing concern about alcohol abuse and health effects of tobacco, groups are politicizing these once-fashionable products. Some colleges are acting on their concern about the harm alcohol abuse has on student performance on tests and course work. Other groups have made drunk driving a political issue leading to stiffer penalties for offenders.

Publics' concern has put pressure on the alcohol industry to create and implement higher standards of ethical performance. Central to this controversy is the Washington-based Center for Science in the Public Interest, which includes the 5.5-million-member National Parent-Teacher Association, the United Methodist Church, and the National Council on Alcoholism. These groups are protesting televised advertisements of alcoholic beverages that play up themes of fun and irresponsibility. Under pressure, the three major networks have tightened their standards on advertisement copy. Critics of alcohol advertising have attempted to place the same product stigma on alcohol that was placed on cigarettes.

The beer and wine industry is adapting to a changing climate of corporate responsibility. One advertising and marketing response by the industry is to deemphasize excessive consumption—"Know when to say 'when.' " In 1984, Anheuser-Busch brewery began to spend $6 to $7 million on educational programs to combat alcohol abuse. Gavaghan (1983) reported that the Licensed Beverage Information Council, in conjunction with the U.S. Department of Treasury, decided on a campaign to alert pregnant women to the effects of alcohol on fetuses.

Public criticism should prompt corporate leaders and operations managers to determine whether the charges are true. One primary motive for activism is a widely held and deeply felt belief that companies and other organizations are irresponsible in their stewardship of the public trust. "What if" considerations are vital to the discovery of gaps between the organization and its key stakeholders (Shim & McGlade, 1984). One answer to this problem is monitoring to increase the organization's and each operating unit's self-control. As Camillus (1986) reasoned,

> Control is a behavioral process that involves measurement and evaluation of the performance of organizational units, the identification of deviations from planned performance, the initiation of appropriate responses to the deviations, and the monitoring of remedial actions, all done with the intent of ensuring that managers' decisions and action are consistent with planned organizational objectives. (p. 11)

As is emphasized in Chapters 9 and 10 regarding crisis and risk prevention, management, and communication, the incentive of each relevant organization and its publics is to responsibly control those activities that pose a threat to others.

Although many companies have alleged an increase in their commitment to issues management, Goodman (1983) concluded that the marriage of standards of corporate performance with employee appraisal systems has been slow. Such is the case because executives have a hard time narrowing the number of issues into a manageable package. Issues are not easily defined. Their vagueness and number, Goodman argued, can paralyze many companies from taking specific response strategies or making firm corporate-level commitment to change. This indictment becomes more profound when companies attempt to join standards of ethical responsibility to performance standards by which to assess executives, managers, and personnel. The bottom-line consideration for managements is that if they do not respond to such pressures proactively, they are likely to be faced with activists pressing those issues to an extreme that is unreasonable.

One mark of maturing professions and industries is the formulation of codes of ethics. Many industries have learned the market and image advantages of establishing codes that guide and regulate business activities. Another mark of ethical maturity is the realization that an organization is not a moral agency and that personal ethical responsibility cannot be ignored by anyone who becomes part of an organization. Ethical responsibility is the burden of individuals, no matter how many are joined into a single enterprise, a point that society has demonstrated by requiring criminal penalties for managers who willfully violate statutes (Dunn, 1991).

Although his statement is fraught with the irony surrounding the tobacco industry, George Weissman (1984), former Chairman and Chief Executive Officer of Philip Morris, Inc., set corporate responsibility into its sociopolitical context: "Like property, the corporation is a creation of the state. It gets its charter from the government. To survive, the corporation subjects itself to regulation by government, and to serving the needs of government and the commonwealth." The heart of the relationship is interdependence between business and society. This point "is fundamental to understanding the concept of corporate responsibility in its current context; to understanding that we are not dealing with a fad; and to understanding that we are dealing with the fundamental existence and survival of the corporation" (p. 67). Businesses are expected to have more involvement in community affairs, formerly the responsibility of government (Chrisman & Carroll, 1984).

Platitudes are likely to foster as well as frustrate efforts by organizations to discover that standards of corporate responsibility truly make a difference in their relationships with key stakeholders. One goal is to achieve the common good (Mahon & McGowan, 1991), to achieve community (Heerema & Giannini, 1991). The challenge is to know how the interests of the organization merge with those of its stakeholders. To achieve corporate responsibility requires a constant search for ways to maximize mutual interests, the ability "to act with rectitude, to refer their policies and plans to a culture of ethics that embraces the most fundamental moral principles of humankind" (Frederick, 1986, p. 136).

Think positive and be proactive. Those guidelines are more than platitudes. They suggest, according to cognitive categorization theory, that if managers think negatively—a threat—about an issue, that perspective will persist, perhaps leading to a downward spiral of ever more dire predictions and hostile, reactive responses to the proponents of the issue or the cause of the threat. In contrast, a positive, opportunity-seeking stance fosters individuals' efforts to be proactive, looking and consequently finding positive responses (Dutton & Jackson, 1987). When issue managers adopt a positive view of the concerns that arise in their environment, they are more likely to adopt ethical, community-oriented responses than is predicted if they see only threat, which motivates defensive responses.

Where should some of the focal points issues managers and corporate responsibility monitors look for potential strains on the legitimacy between their organization and key publics?

* Quality of products and customer service
* Fair pricing policies and practices
* Ethical and responsible advertising
* Timely and proper equipment and facility maintenance and repair
* Timely and appropriate resolution of customer complaints
* Responsiveness to the community in which the organization does business
* Demonstrable commitment to society
* Increased access to society and its benefits, especially through schools and community services
* Provision of jobs and economic advantages in excess of harms to the community
* Enhancement of the environment through reduction of energy consumption, proper disposal of wastes, recycling, the use of recycled goods and materials, and contracting with environmentally conscious suppliers
* Demonstration of concern by performing periodic social audits

Does doing good enhance marketing? Gildea (1994-1995) reported a national survey conducted in 1994 regarding how a business's social performance affects decisions by customers, employees, and investors. Based on ranking data, the following list was compiled, ranging from most important to least important factors in making decisions relevant to a specific company: business practices, community support, employee treatment, quality, environment, service, price, convenience, and stability. Purchasing behavior includes, but is not limited to, considerations of behavioral intention. Analysis revealed that 34% of the respondents would avoid buying a product or service from a company they perceived as unethical. Sixteen percent seek information to consider a company's business practices and ethics as part of their decision making. Of substantial importance, 50% intended not to purchase a product or service from a company they considered not to be socially responsible. Put those data before management, and see whether issues management can help businesses with strategic planning and bottom line performance.

What then should companies do? Gildea (1994-1995) drew four suggestions from the report, all of which have profound issues management implications.

1. Study the scope of your corporate responsibility.
2. Closely analyze your reputation and those of your competitors.
3. Measure and manage what "drives" the perceptions of those reputations.
4. Put the findings to work for you in the marketplace. (p. 21)

Ascertaining changing standards of corporate responsibility is daunting. Some organizations fail to try. Others do not change based on what they learn. This section has demonstrated that effort is required. People must be assigned to look for changing standards and bring what they learn to bear on the organization's planning and management options. Efforts to change can have positive outcomes for the organizations that do most to meet key stakeholder expectations. Conflict, the cost of friction and dissent, is the cost of not learning to change.

 **Corporate Responsibility Partnerships:
Communicating Ethical Performance**

An organization needs to make its changes known as they happen. This section addresses the communication of ethical performance. At this nexus occurs public relations' major contribution, defined as

> the management process whose goal is to attain and maintain accord and positive behaviors among social groupings on which an organization depends in order to achieve its mission. Its fundamental responsibility is to build and maintain a hospitable environment for an organization. (Broom, Lauzen, & Tucker, 1991, p. 223)

The goal is to do this not with *the* public but with many publics, each of which may have slightly or profoundly divergent expectations of what the organization should be doing and how.

Rather than fear the comments of activists, working with them gives them less incentive to go to the press when they experience concern or outrage regarding some aspect of a firm's activities. Their greatest power comes through inflamed statements carried by the media. Such statements demonstrate that something is so wrong with a company that it deserves attention. Effective media relations can use reporters as issues watchers. When someone in the media calls, his or her questions signal the presence of an opinion or issue that could grow in consequence. The company's side of the story may kill the news item because once the reporter understands what a company is doing, the story may die.

Companies can weaken their ability to present themselves as honest and ethical either by dismissing their critics' concerns or by making inadequate although ostensibly positive responses. Sims (1992) offered the following sage bits of advice: (a) Be realistic—do not promise what the organization or industry cannot delivery, (b) encourage organization or industrywide input into the standards and the best means for accomplishing them (as well as the stumbling blocks), (c) allow diversity, (d) allow whistle blowing, (e) provide ethics training, (f) recognize the ambiguity that is inherent in ethical standards and their implementation, and (g) integrate ethical decision making into employee and operating unit appraisal.

Several companies have resorted to communication campaigns that provide information valuable to key publics; such tactics have the potential of demonstrating to those publics that companies are willing to use their expertise to promote the good of the community. In this fashion, Pfizer Pharmaceutical Company has run a series of advertisements that discuss symptoms of major diseases. This advertising may help interested parties to understand certain major diseases and be better informed regarding symptoms and cures. Perhaps the most successful service to a key public campaign was that which featured the "Shell Answer Man." Shell Oil Company discovered that many people did not understand even simple facts about automobile maintenance, repair, and safety. Phillips Oil Company tried to show how its diverse range of products served humanity in ways beyond the typical automobile fuel and service station market. Philips also provides an annual environmental statement and announces its availability through ads in general publications, such as the *Wall Street Journal* and specialized outlets such as *Audubon Magazine.*

Issues communication is best when it fosters mutual understanding that can foster trust. This communication must be two-way and collaborative. Companies need to address issues of concern felt by key publics and report accurate information about their operating problems and conditions. The more that organizations meet key publics' need for information, the more likely they are to be praised rather than criticized. Taking a position such as this challenges corporations to open the "windows of vulnerability" whereby they can increase public understanding instead of blind compliance.

Communication alone usually cannot solve problems where corporate behavior differs significantly from key publics' standards. One mistake companies have made is to develop codes of responsible behavior and tout them to key stakeholders before they were fully incorporated into operations. Failure to achieve and maintain the standards so publicized can embarrass the company when someone—a vigilant activist, a reporter, or a disgruntled employee—reports that the code was never translated into action and employees knew they could not be penalized or might even be rewarded for failing to comply with the code.

One response to unfavorable or inaccurate reporting begins with good media relationships. If media relations personnel foster good relationships with reporters, they can call on that rapport for a payback. The reward of doing business properly and being candid and responsive with reporters is the legitimate expectation that a favorable story will be written to feature some significant change in how the firm operates in an attempt to set or meet appropriate standards of responsibility. This response strategy is more than just doing community relations, although that can count for something and always demonstrates the news value of human interests. It results from changes in the way business is conducted in the name of meeting higher levels of ethics to meet or exceed community stakeholder expectations.

A second means for getting the point across is to use paid image advertising. Chevron Oil Company's "People Do" campaign has won the favor of environmentalists (Winters, 1988). It, along with other oil companies' advertising, has demonstrated the measures firms will and are taking to be more responsive to public expectations beyond merely turning a profit and paying taxes and wages. Likewise, issue ads of the U.S. Council for Energy Awareness demonstrated a high level of responsibility by the nuclear power industry to operate safely, to reduce dependence on foreign oil sources, and to reduce air pollution often associated with other energy sources, particularly coal used to generate electricity. Such discussions, actual claims about company performance, have increased impact if they demonstrate the connection between increased operating standards and the actions that result from those standards.

A third opportunity for communicating new standards of corporate responsibility is through financial documents, such as the annual report. Financial stakeholders appreciate companies' ability to generate profits in ways that demonstrate preferred standards of responsibility. Such claims are strengthened when they demonstrate how improved ethical standards increase profits, especially by avoiding increased amounts of regulatory constraint, limiting legal liability, increasing market share, or operating efficiently. Sometimes, companies realize that by improving their engineering standards, for instance, they can use more of the feedstock materials they purchase while reducing environmentally damaging wastes and emissions, thereby avoiding unnecessary regulatory constraints. Companies can tout the reduction in raw materials used, the improvement of processes to lessen environmental impact, lowered accident rates, and other practices that mark financial and ethical improvements (Cowen & Segal, 1981).

Another means for communicating increased standards of corporate responsibility lies in the array of vehicles used to reach employees. Organizational culture is vital to the way employees conduct themselves and perform their work. If standards are being implemented that meet or exceed key public expectations, such information is useful for employees who use it to achieve a sense of empowerment and organizational identification that results from thinking about how well they are doing their jobs and achieving organizational success. In this sense, employee empowerment is a post hoc kind of analysis, whereby they look back on their efforts with a sense of achievement (Albrecht,

1988). This achievement is fostered and reinforced when the organization demonstrates that employees' efforts achieve new performance standards. For instance, one chemical plant in the Texas Gulf Coast region undertook an aggressive employee empowerment effort to stress to its personnel, as well as report to the public, how well empowered engineering and operating personnel do in abating environmental discharges. Personnel benefit from improving the performance of their plant. When engineering techniques are proven and patented, the relevant personnel receive monetary reward when proprietary processes are used by other plants. The result: Although this is the largest plant in the region, its environmental emission levels are among the lowest. This favorable outcome results from a culture that empowers employees to improve plant operations.

Despite the obvious advantages to be gained by building employees into the advocacy team, many companies take the stance that employees must be mute regarding corporate mistakes. Otten (1984) concluded, "Slowly but steadily, states are beginning to protect employees who blow the whistle on dangerous or improper business behavior" (p. 11). Even Mobil, which has been one of the most strident advocates for open corporate communication, settled out of court with Agnes L. Connolly, who had been fired for being incompetent. She had reported two toxic chemical accidents that had occurred at Mobil's Environmental Health and Sciences Laboratory. Such incidents demonstrate the inconsistency between corporate policy and behavior and counteract efforts to involve employees in achieving corporate responsibility. Provisions in the Mine Safety and Health Act, the Toxic Substances Control Act, the Occupational Safety and Health Act, and the Water Pollution Control Act protect workers who report violations. Some companies, such as IBM, Bank of America, and Prudential Insurance Company, have established programs to protect employees who report corporate mistakes.

A final means for communicating corporate responsibility is to integrate such claims into product and service advertising. Products that do more to meet customers' expectations, resulting in purchasing value, attract consumer attention. If enhanced processes are used, one of the truest tests is that they result in enhanced products. Such claims are worth making. If a better product is manufactured, that is news worth communicating in detail to customers.

As Post et al. (1983) pointed out, the central thrust of public affairs offices is "to narrow the gap between corporate practice and public expectations" by functioning "as a 'window out' through which management can comprehend the social and political environment and a 'window in' through which relevant external constituencies can understand the organization" (p. 139). Organizations face the difficult task of providing information about their activities and their executives so that key publics and audiences are fully and accurately informed. The standards of corporate responsibility that activists hold are inseparable from their willingness to champion, allow, or discourage legislation and regulation. Activism suggests that external force must be brought into the power dynamics to force responsible behavior on individuals who otherwise would not act in the public interest.

If executives are going to establish and implement meaningful standards, they must create a climate and culture that supports that goal. Nowlan et al. (1984) advised against the pitfalls of (a) not appropriately rewarding those involved, (b) permitting value systems to obstruct the process, (c) having ill-defined committee priorities, (d) allowing information-gathering systems to be poorly organized, and (e) overloading the people so that they cannot be systematic. One of the first steps in forming an issues committee is to examine the "corporation's culture—the methods, attitudes, and practices of its corporate and division managements . . . Those companies whose cultures have provided the most hospitable environment for the group process in the past will also be successful in their efforts to create consensus-building and awareness-building committees on a wide range of corporate problems" (p. 13). Executives need to create a mutually beneficial dialogue with employees, customers, media leaders, investors, and other constituents (Nagelschmidt, 1982). When the food group companies were found to be providing products that lacked nutritional value or actually provided food content that was harmful (such as fat content), they formed nutrition focus groups and advisory panels of concerned housewives.

Issues communicators engage in dialogue and collaborative decision making to ascertain what standards lead to best organizational practices, those that create mutually beneficial relationships. Standards of corporate responsibility are of vital interest to society. Thus, rhetorical challenges and definitions are aimed toward creating and refining them. Once they are in place, that fact is worth communicating to key external and internal audiences.

 Conclusion

Issues management entails executive commitment to ascertain and comply with appropriate expectations of corporate responsibility. Confronted with these conditions, issues managers can lessen the legitimacy gap by changing the organization's behavior rather than altering public expectations. Proactive change takes its value referent from "the body of sometimes dimly or poorly expressed but deeply held moral convictions that comprise the culture of ethics" (Frederick, 1986, p. 135). Organizational leaders incorporate issues monitoring into the organization's structure, scan issues development and public interest group activity, and work to achieve communication goals that blend corporate goals and the concerns of various audiences and key publics. All of this is easier said than done.

Special Interest Activists
as Foes or Allies

The United States has a tradition of activism. Two hundred years after the Declaration of Independence, the nation still reveres a form of government that fashions policy through debate and activist politics. This form of government is not without problems. While helping frame the U.S. Constitution and the Bill of Rights, James Madison worried that factions would destroy the new republic. Nevertheless, he and other political geniuses established the First Amendment to foster expressions of controversial views as well as citizens' right to obtain information and opinion as precursors to changing their circumstances. Agitation, even revolution, is as American as cherry pie; at least, that was a rallying cry of the antiestablishment 1960s.

At times discordant, public policy contests between key groups are fundamental to our sociopolitical power system; interest groups speak to reveal problems and inject values into dialogues by which issues are judged and solutions are weighed. Activist groups arise, mature, and fade. They help people exert power collectively that they lack individually. Through refined insights, pooled information, shared values, and common goals, cooperative actions can benefit all parties. Strategic issues managers realize that this contest is for power resources.

Chapter 2 described how activists join together to restrain the prerogatives and actions of organizations with aloof, insensitive executives. As

L. Grunig (1992a) observed, "The activist group's intent is to improve the functioning of the organization from outside" (p. 504). She noted that the groups intend "to influence and change a condition through means that range from education to violence" (p. 504). Each group works to make itself useful to its followers. It positions itself as speaking in the public interest. Either through issues communication or collaborative decision making, issues managers can prove to key publics that they do not need to rely on activist demands to achieve improved performance by the firm, governmental organization, or other activist targets.

Against this background, the purposes of this chapter are fourfold: (a) to justify the contention that activism entails public policy resource management, (b) to describe the life cycles of activism, (c) to explain the rhetorical processes of incremental erosion, and (d) to suggest strategies that issues managers can employ to work constructively with interest groups. This discussion demonstrates that activists voice issues and empower individuals who otherwise would never be able to change key aspects of society. Influence exerted in the public policy arena results from the power resources activists acquire and use efficiently (Blalock, 1989). Activist groups work to acquire and use stakes as a means for encouraging or forcing change. Viewed this way, issues management often entails balancing relationships with multiple stakeholders and stakeseekers, each of which has unique opinions and interests.

Dealing with several activist groups and other stakeholders can be difficult. For instance, in 1995, Shell Oil Company created an advisory panel consisting of industry specialists, governmental officials, and leaders of prominent environmental groups to determine the fate of a massive oil production platform that needed to be retired from service. This panel decided that the platform should be taken into deep Atlantic Ocean waters and sunk. Greenpeace protested, and the decision and decision process came apart. This case reminds issues managers that "activist groups vary in size, range of issue involvement, tactics, and effectiveness—but all (especially the smallest, most active ones) are potentially damaging to the target organization" (L. Grunig, 1992a, p. 513).

Although this chapter focuses on the nature and role of activists in the public policy arena and the issues management process, it does not ignore the fact that a substantial amount of legislative and regulative change occurs for reasons that may have little to do with activism. Public policy change also results from pressures between companies within an industry and between companies in different industries. Policy changes result from politicians' agendas and judicial decisions. Without ignoring these forces, this chapter focuses on activism, citizens banding to express their interests. The wise issue manager realizes that in a multiple-stakeholder environment, the concerns that must be addressed are not likely to be narrowed to the relationship between one company and one group of activists. That model is too simplistic to capture the dynamics of the public policy planning and action process. Bridging differences and achieving mutual interests can be challenging, requiring the marshaling of a variety of resources through a business plan, a public policy plan, and a communication plan.

 ## Power Resources and Moral Outrage

How we view special interest advocacy and agitation depends on who we believe activists are and how we define their political role. Two early writers, Tarde (1922), in *L'Opinion et la Foule,* and LeBon (1925), in *The Crowd: A Study of the Popular Mind,* viewed activists as disrupting a systematic and well-managed society. This elitist notion arose from the belief that the best class deserved to rule without challenge. Activists were called rabble-rousers. That view was challenged by Saul Alinsky (1971) who wrote *Rules for radicals* to empower the poor, disadvantaged, and concerned by giving them practical strategies by which to advance their cause.

The pejorative word "rabble" may not accurately describe activists on environmental issues or religious champions of decency on television. Activist groups, especially in recent years, routinely draw members from every economic and educational strata of society. Membership can be fashionable. Members, as well as leaders, represent professions. Housewives protesting unsanitary food-processing conditions can hardly be characterized as rabble. The *Wall Street Journal* gave front-page attention to the struggle of one woman, Mary Sinclair, victorious after 15 years of battle against Consumers Power Company. Construction of its Midland, Michigan, nuclear plant was abandoned despite $4 billion costs. Not a stereotypical radical agitator, Sinclair was a 65-year old mother of five, married to a lawyer, and former Republican county chairwoman (Winslow, 1984).

Small-business persons and neighbors who do not want their small communities to be changed by outsider, large corporations became protesters in the early 1990s to resist efforts to open Wal-Mart stores in an ever growing number of small communities. Local residents, some of whom had moved to the country to avoid crowds, resisted Walt Disney's efforts to locate a theme park near the hallowed Civil War battlefield in Manasas, Virginia, in 1994. The National Wildlife Federation issues a MasterCard to qualifying members in conjunction with MBNA America, a national bank. Such financial status demonstrates that this activist group is not a ragtag operation. The American Association of Retired Persons was founded in 1958 to advocate social service support for the elderly. By 1995, it had acquired 33 million members, a $400-million budget, and the ire of conservative congress persons who resented the lobbying efforts of this group in behalf of Medicare, Medicaid, and Social Security. This group's membership draws from the powerful voting-age population between 45 to 65 years, which has not only increased in size but also developed sophistication in its dealings with Congress. Major environmental groups raise money, buy land, commission research, and have extensive grassroots lobbying efforts. Some pretty pricey pieces of Washington, D.C., property are owned by activists. Activism has become institutionalized; activists cannot accurately be described as rabble.

Any issues manager who thinks of the opposition as rabble is likely to be at a disadvantage. Such stereotypical responses may swing the power balance to members of an interest group who understand how to use the media or position themselves as a voting bloc to pressure regulative or legislative bodies to act in what activists define as the public interest (Murphy, 1992). They may stall the granting or implementing of permits a plant needs to operate; such measures were used by a handful of community activists near Galveston, Texas, in opposition to strategic planning efforts of Mitsubishi Corporation, one of the largest companies in the world. Residents and fishermen (recreational and professional) feared the proposed copper plant would be a health hazard, due to emissions of lead, and a threat to property values (Heath, 1995).

When people become dissatisfied with their conditions, they join together to change them and thereby become an activist group. Successful groups are skilled at obtaining and wielding economic, political, or social resources (Blalock, 1989; Gamson 1968, 1975; Oberschall, 1973, 1978; Simons, 1970, 1972, 1976). Social conflict entails "the intentional mutual exchange of negative sanctions, or punitive behaviors, by two or more parties" (Blalock, 1989, p. 7). Activists and their targets have a mutual stakeholding and stakeseeking relationship. Activists not only work to create and use stakes against the organization but they also seek stakes it holds.

A view of issues management that ignores the public policy power and rhetorical influence of activists is naive. And we must avoid limiting issues management to the negotiation of contested positions between *one* organization (a company or industry, for instance) and *one* activist group. Many issues management problems arise because multiple stakeholders and stakeseekers press an organization for specific concessions. Also, an issue can arise rhetorically—such as a concern over safety in living near a chemical plant—even when no group exists for the organization to negotiate with as a representative of a community of concern.

We are wise to think of this process not as one-way but as dialogue—two-way interaction. Issues communication, including issue advertising, is used not only by private-sector organizations but also by activists. Special interests rhetorically press government to intervene on issues that they help publicize in the media. Activists introduce issues into political campaigns. They use political contributions, voting blocs, and endorsements to encourage or coerce candidates to take stands on key issues. They supply volunteers to assist in political campaigns. They make issues visible, sometimes by dramatic protest or by pressing them through referenda.

Accustomed to doing business in relative tranquillity prior to the robust growth of activism in the 1960s, corporate and governmental leaders tended to view such groups as threatening. Too often, a negative, reactive attitude toward such groups led business people to the knee-jerk desire to defeat, even destroy, the "enemy." Shants (1978) described the combative attitude of members of the nuclear generating industry who wanted to fight antinuclear "activists not with facts but with closed factory gates, empty schools, cold and dark homes and sad children" (p. 10). This rhetorical stance implies the company is correct, protesters are wrong, and through punishment, the public can be bludgeoned to understand and accept the difference.

A combative stance is ironic because many activists like nothing more than to punish private-sector and governmental organizations. This adversarial, or win-loss, posture occurs when the sides presume to have an exclusive grasp of the truth and want to silence their opponents or bait them into making statements that key segments of the public will find offensive. Combativeness increases the likelihood of hostile polarization that can mature into confrontation. Visible issue combat can do little to improve some stakeholders' attitudes toward companies. When a company battles a group that seems to be acting in the interest of the "people," they appear to flaunt their contempt for the public interest. For this reason, some firms, such as large food companies, have wisely used activists to help establish the criteria of responsible performance, such as standards of wholesome food. Savvy firms harmonize their goals and policies with activist positions.

Activists use legislation, regulation, and litigation to limit business options. Early-warning, issue-scanning systems can alert corporations to emerging issues and identify highly motivated individuals who are attempting to focus public attention on them. Many issues arise as the product of the effort of a few individuals who are troubled by some aspect of society or corporate behavior. By articulating the issue and demonstrating the extent to which it affects the interests of others, activists attract followers, make the issue visible, assert their own premises that they believe should guide public policy discussions and decision making, and employ power resources.

What resources are employed in this effort? Resources are stakes, something of value that a group has that is sought by other groups, whether corporate, governmental, or activist. Stakes can include the purchase of goods and services, the ability to engage in litigation, the casting of votes, and lobbying the legislative and regulatory process. Other stakes are community support or opposition for permits a company needs to expand or to continue operations. Favorable comments to reporters are stakes, as are critical comments and complaints. Some power resources may be extreme, even violent, such as those used by antilogging activists who drove large spikes into trees to prevent them from being cut for timber (or at least threatened to do so). Once the spikes were driven into trees, they could not be sawed into boards without putting crews of sawmill employees into danger due to the likelihood that the large saws would explode into shrapnel if they struck the nails.

Activist groups are often portrayed as liberals who oppose practices of key businesses, among others. Indeed, activist groups, such as the National Rifle Association, may take issue positions that support rather than oppose companies, in this case, DuPont and firearms manufacturers. Activists may oppose one another: Common Cause versus Fair Government Foundation, Children's Defense Fund versus Center for Effective Compassion, Sierra Club versus Frontiers of Freedom, National Organization of Women versus Independent Women's Forum, and Public Citizen versus Project Relief. Other mainstream activist groups include Consumer Federation of America and Consumer Union. Pro-life groups battle pro-choice advocates.

As Wallack, Dorfman, Jernigan, and Themba (1993) pointed out, activists use media advocacy. They combine "community advocacy approaches with the strategic and innovative use of media to better pressure decision makers to change policy" (p. xi). The media continue to look for community interest stories. Outraged charges and demonstrations of problems by activist groups have media appeal and cost activists nothing in terms of publicity for their ideas. "Advocacy is a catch-all word for the set of skills used to create a shift in public opinion and mobilize the necessary resources and forces to support an issue, policy, or constituency" (p. 27).

Each activist group develops its unique view of what ought to be; these expectations can have implications for how private-sector organizations operate. Such groups form a culture that views the world and evaluates business activities in terms that may be at odds with preferences of company executives. This struggle can take at least two directions. One focuses on constraints that groups can impose on companies to limit what they can do and how they can do it. The second struggle is to alter the culture of society in ways that lead to some corporate actions being prohibited that once were allowed. Managed poorly, cultures of the enterprise and the group collide. Managed effectively, these cultures can lead to positive outcomes for both groups.

The concept of *culture* can be used as a focal point for comparing the decision-making processes and expectations of companies and of activists. This analysis becomes clearer if we define culture as a way of thinking about ourselves—our identity and our actions—and the world around us. This line of analysis reasons that culture is a defining variable that accounts for why different groups think of the world in unique ways, in ways that can be at odds with one another.

Morgan (1986) defined culture as "a process of reality construction that allows people to see and understand particular events, actions, objects, utterances, or situations in distinctive ways" (p. 128). If a culture is a way of thinking, persons who share that culture constitute a zone of meaning—a shared sense of reality. If zones differ sufficiently, conflict and negotiated settlements may be required (Heath, 1994). Central to activist efforts is the presentation of key premises that, if adopted in public policy decision making and dialogue, lead to conclusions different than before. Antismoking activists assert the premise that cigarette smoking is harmful to health, to challenge tobacco companies' contrary view. Environmentalists assert the premise that industrial processes that degrade air or water quality should be curtailed. If that premise becomes accepted by key publics, companies or other types of targeted organizations are expected or mandated to implement new operating standards. Thus, activism arises from moral outrage and leads to attempts to create and exploit power resources to change the offending practices and policies.

 ### Activism and Strategic Business Management: Power Resource Management

Issues managers should understand the cultures that surround their firms so they can determine how each one can affect executives' efforts to create and implement their strategic business plans. A constructive solution to this problem is to plan for outcomes and employ management options that are compatible with the cultures and thereby satisfy mutual interests. Compatibility is a reasonable outcome, perhaps the product of collaborative decision making. Issues managers may help change their firm's culture (its standards of corporate responsibility) so that it is more compatible with stakeholder expectations. Issues communicators may undertake campaigns to change external cultures to increase harmony. This section explores the proposition that successful management of this friction requires working to keep differences from manifesting themselves in public policy changes that lead to destructive solutions to problems.

This outcome requires that issues managers monitor for differences and mount appropriate planning, communication, or operational change offenses or defenses to seek mutually satisfying outcomes with key groups. Settlement of differences can prevent a concern from becoming an issue so compelling that the company is forced to accede to changes that are not constructive to the mutual interests of relevant parties.

Groups seek to affect the missions that companies set for themselves and the management options they prefer to use to achieve those ends. Strategic planning results from interpretations of the situations in which executives find themselves and the ways they believe resources can be used to accomplish their ends. Two aspects are crucial: (a) the markets by which the organization acquires the resources it needs to survive and grow, and (b) the public policy environment, in which constraints are imposed or opportunities are created by legislative, regulatory, or judicial bodies. Activist groups can affect any of these.

Strategic business planning considers constraints and opportunities facing the organization. Hunger and Wheelen (1993) differentiated types of environments. The external environment consists of conditions that could affect a firm's ability to achieve its desired outcomes, as expressed in its mission, given the compatibility or conflict between its interests and those of persons outside of it. This environment, in turn, can be divided into two parts. The task environment "includes those elements or groups that directly affect and are affected by an organization's major operations. Some of these are stockholders, governments. suppliers, local communities, competitors, customers, creditors, labor unions, special interest groups, and trade associations" (p. 12). The societal environment "includes more general forces—ones that do not directly touch the short-run activities of the organization but that can, and often do, influence its long-run decisions," for instance, "economic, sociocultural, technological, and political-legal forces" (p. 12).

Issues arise from the societal environment (cultural, economic, political, and technological) and from the marketplace environment. This realization led Hunger and Wheelen (1993) to propose a planning acronym—SWOT: external environment (O = opportunities, T = threats) and internal environment (S = strengths, W = weaknesses). Planning assumes the ability to exert control over resources needed to achieve desirable outcomes.

Power resource management entails the ability to employ economic, political, and social sanctions and rewards through means such as boycotts, strikes, embargoes, layoffs, lockouts, legislation, regulation, executive orders, police action, and judicial review. Power resource management assumes the ability of a group, a company, or a governmental agency to give or withhold rewards—stakes. At the extreme, coercion entails granting or withholding punishment or rewards. Coercive persuasion draws its potency from the fear on the part of a group, company, or agency that punishment will be given or rewards withheld (Simons, 1972).

During early stages of activism, agents of change must acquire power. Mere outbursts are unlikely to foster issue development beyond the point of outrage. Activist power consists of the number of people who support the movement, alliances and other third-party assistance, media attention, and favorable responses by key people in power institutions, such as the judiciary, members of Congress, administrative officers, leading educators, or religious leaders. Persuasion is necessary to help obtain, maintain, and marshal power resources and to develop allies and opinion favorable to goals and strategies of the activists.

A dominant theory of power is that it is the ability X has to affect how Y achieves its goals. Barnes (1988) argued that this definition does not actually define power but merely indicates when it is present. The telling point is captured in the question: What characteristics of X or the nature of the situation give X the ability to affect Y? The answer to that question addresses what power is in each circumstance. As a starting point, Barnes directed our attention to the focal point:

> Whether we talk of rights and obligations, or of roles and institutions, or of patterned social relationships, the import is much the same: we are talking of a presumed structure and orderliness in social activity, and a need to understand the nature and the basis of such structure and orderliness is implied. (p. 20)

Power results from value premises and social norms—expected and accepted patterns of thinking and acting: "The normative order must reflect not internal pressures within the psyche but the pressures people exert upon each other" (Barnes, 1988, p. 42).

Meaning—a shared sense of social reality—is the basis of society and social order. Stressing this point, Barnes (1988) concluded, "Every society possesses a shared body of technical, manipulation-related knowledge, knowledge of nature, and a shared body of social knowledge, knowledge of a normative order" (p. 55). Power, therefore, results from shared knowledge— the norms and expectations that are captured in this collective view of selves, social relationships, privileges and obligations. As interest groups and private-sector organizations contest assumptions and norms, they define and redefine power, "the structure of discretion" (p. 62). Power, in this sense, is the "capacity for action and the possession of power [is] the possession of discretion in the use of capacity for action" (p. 67). Issues managers need to sense the ebb and flow of social meaning (and its sense of preferred expectations) and the application of that meaning as means for obtaining and distributing stakes, the management of power resources.

Activists participate in formation and re-formation of macrosocial opinions, premises, or principles and in their application to specific companies or industries. Sophisticated activists are aware that key global opinions of society need to be changed. They understand that how opinions are adapted and applied to specific companies, industries, products, and services is crucial to accomplishing their activist missions.

Each power player seeks to privilege itself with the ability to address issues in ways that are self-interested or altruistic. Message strategies concentrate on types of evidence and propositions of fact, value, and policy. Despite their ostensible objectivity, media are prime players in these controversies. They may be little more than channels through which combatants communicate. At other times, they help wage the controversy. An underlying realization is that issues conflict is not only a matter of agreement; it entails power resource management. Activist rhetoric entails efforts to obtain and marshal power resources that can be used to correct problems and make dramatic improvements by forcing change in the way a company or governmental agency does business.

When critics are dissatisfied by corporate performance, they attempt to convince key publics that government must protect their interests by intervening against business. Activists appeal to these publics out of the need to develop a power base of sufficient magnitude to restrain and regulate industry. Under pressure, governmental officials may act in the name of the will of the people to correct corporate behavior or to buffer corporations from their critics. Depending on the dynamics between these factions, issues communication can be used to convince key publics that regulation is unnecessary or if it is necessary, that it should foster the mutual interests of all relevant stakeholding groups.

One important, although widely criticized, power resource is the PAC. PACs got a boost in 1974 when the Federal Election Campaign Act outlawed large individual or corporate donors from giving money to candidates' campaigns. For this reason, corporations, unions, trade associations, and interest groups started PACs to channel money to candidates as a means for participating in the power game of established politics. PACs are sponsored by a variety of business interests, such as realtors, physicians, and defense contractors. The Realtor PAC and the PAC of the American Medical Association are two of the richest (Jackson, 1984b).

Contributors use PACs to gain access to legislators to explain their views on an issue and detail its public policy consequences. In that sense, PACs do not ensure direct influence over legislators but increase access to them (Alexander, 1988, 1989). Corporate PACs can keep employees—and other constituents—politically educated and give them opportunities to contact legislators. Corporate PACs can develop and circulate issues books that employees can use for their own public policy education and to share with others, including legislators—on both sides of issues (Jackson, 1984a, 1984b).

Mapes (1984) provided evidence that PAC funds given to one side of a controversy encourage a counterattack of spending. As evidence of this point, she noted the large amounts of money spent by those who support weapons systems were countered by groups that support arms control and nuclear freeze. She concluded,

> Contrary to the hue and cry raised about the corruption of the political process by PAC money, the record shows that some members of Congress can accept money from PACs, even a great deal or money, and still cast votes that defeat utterly the interests of their benefactors. (p. 28)

She observed how defense spenders pushed tons of money into the campaign of Joseph Addabbo (D, New York). As Chairman of the House Appropriations Subcommittee on Defense, he received large sums from arms-control PACs. He had a nearly perfect voting record on arms control but still was in a position to be fair and understanding to the interests of armament. Military contractors interested in the MX missile and President Reagan's space defense system contributed more than $900,000 to Senate candidates in 1984. Targeted candidates were members of the Senate Armed Services Committee and the Defense Subcommittee of the Senate Appropriations Committee ("Arms concerns," 1985).

Some PACs promote ideology and candidates who adhere to it, for instance, the National Committee for an Effective Congress, Fund for a Democratic Majority, the Committee for the Future of America, Independent Action, Democrats for the '80s, and Progressive Political Action Committee. Donors to the right-wing PACs are typically businessmen or people with agricultural interests. The left-wing contributor profile is a young professional educated in the humanities and social sciences (Green & Guth, 1984). PACs offer issues managers an opportunity to help shape the political agenda and build constituencies.

Constituency building is a key to public policy resource management. J. Grunig and Repper (1992) reasoned that "public relations makes organizations more effective by developing relations with stakeholders in the internal and external environment that constrain or enhance the ability of an organization to accomplish its mission" (p. 118). To support corporate strategic planning, Grunig and Repper argued that expertise is needed at three stages: (a) the stakeholder stage—when groups exist that have stakes needed or wanted by the organization to achieve its mission, (b) the public stage—when groups realize that they can use their stakes to lever changes in the performance of the target organization or industry and when these groups form to exert their influence, (c) the issue stage—when publics raise and force issues that they believe need to be resolved in their interest.

If their interests are affected, people become strategic in the search for information and useful opinions. As they do so, they can be treated as a public that can either create or join an activist group, or they can merely be an audience sympathetic to its messages, issue positions, and public policy or market-side stance. This section has stressed the notion that as issues become more focused and people see reason to agree with some and oppose others, they are likely to be strategic stakeholders—issue constituents who withhold stakes as a means for gaining individual *and* collective advantage. Once this occurs, it has become a reality that issues managers need to use in their recommendations for strategic business planning.

 Stages of Activism

Writers have proposed various models to depict activist movement life cycles. For instance, L. Griffin (1952) identified three stages (inception, rhetorical crisis, and consummation), whereas Oberschall (1973) argued that movements progress from commitment formation, through mobilization, to confrontation. Stewart, Smith, and Denton (1984) proposed a five-stage model: genesis, social unrest, enthusiastic mobilization, maintenance, and termination. Any list may be misleading because movements vary; without some sense of how activism develops, issue monitoring and responses to activists are likely to be unfocused. This section features five stages that embrace the effort of activism: strain (problem recognition), mobilization, confrontation, negotiation, and resolution.

Such analysis can become the basis for designing a monitoring and strategic issue response plan. For instance, the model used by a major Southwestern utility company is based on the belief that issues develop through five stages. (a) Vague discontent: A few members of the public and a few experts-agitators begin to discuss some topic that eventually receives media attention. (b) Politicization: Groups begin to form and agitate collectively to increase the visibility of an issue, to propagate discussion and concern, and to attract followers and money. (c) Legislative awareness: Legislators promote topics and generate bills. (d) Regulatory guidelines: The campaign to control a company or industry reaches a crucial stage when an existing or newly created agency is assigned the responsibility for executing regulatory guidelines. (e) Judicial debate: Corporations seek a court ruling against the regulation or law. To keep on top of developments in each stage, the company (a) monitors issues, (b) discovers allies, (c) communicates with constituencies to lay a foundation of key public and employee opinion, (d) establishes coalitions with other groups, and (e) implements a lobbying campaign.

Issues managers need to understand that conflicting premises are a vital part of activism. In their rhetorical positioning, activists assert premises that express concerns about problems they find and solutions they prefer. These premises often focus the clash between them and the organization, industry, or institution they are challenging. Activists work to put key facts, values, and policy preferences into the public dialogue. They believe that as others learn the facts, values, and policy preferences, a new set of expectations will emerge and demand improved corporate and government policy. Recently developed premises have centered on issues such as health hazards of smoking, environmental damage of industrial or governmental practices, failure of institutions to achieve equality on race or gender, and liability to persons who use products and services.

Issues monitoring can track the evolution of individuals and unorganized publics into organized activist groups or can address the development of issues as each group argues for or against specific points of view. Monitoring can assume that groups and the issues they promote progress through five interdependent stages: strain, mobilization, confrontation, negotiation, and issue resolution. Not all issues groups progress through every stage. Some groups mistakenly try to get to one of the later stages before the requisite foundation has been established; later stages may collapse because they lack the necessary support. Likewise, activists can fail if they are unable to progress beyond the first stages. Because of favorable circumstances, some activists succeed without going through all stages.

The value of any model is its ability to provide insight into how and where organizations can constructively intervene to reduce the strain that motivates activism. Regulation and legislation are created and imposed during confrontation, negotiation, and resolution. If an activist group never progresses that far, the corporate monitoring system may be credited with doing its job so that strategic planning could adapt to and mitigate emerging issues or that issues communication strategies appropriately responded to activist concerns.

Strain

On a given day, hundreds of people—a potential constituent audience and public—feel discomfort about various aspects of their lives. Isolated instances may occur when families suffer the tragedy of children losing their lives or being seriously harmed, perhaps due to improperly constructed toys or flammable clothing. People may have difficulties concerning automobile warranties. Rashes may appear on some people who live near petrochemical plants. Children may develop cancer in patterns that seem to correlate that ailment with exposure to electromagnetic fields. CFCs damage the atmosphere, or chemicals lead to declining predatory bird populations.

Awareness of such conditions can lead people to believe that problems exist. This sense of strain results from a comparison of what is versus what should be, a perceived impairment (Smelser, 1963). Recognizing problems (J. Grunig, 1989a; J. Grunig & Hunt, 1984), activists work to persuade others that their self-interest is being damaged, that norms have been violated, or that new values need to be applied to evaluate corporate behavior. In this way, they insert facts, values, and public policy solutions into the public dialogue.

Activists desire to change conditions that cause discomfort or prevent people from obtaining or enjoying advantages they believe they deserve. "A social movement represents an effort by a large number of people to solve collectively a problem that they feel they have in common" (Toch, 1965, p. 5). The feeding ground of activism is "the ranks of persons who have encountered problems" (p. 9). Activists seek to convince potential supporters that strain is serious enough to warrant collective action to change it and thereby move toward equilibrium or comfort. One example of such tactics is the rhetorical stance by the Humane Farming Association, which challenges what it believes to be inhumane farming techniques. Using a picture of a pig confined in a iron cage, the Association used a issue ad in 1994 to demonstrate the horrors of pig husbandry as well as allege that the industry puts consumers' health at risk because of its "routine use of sulfamethazine, antibiotics, and other drugs that can be passed on to consumers." How is the typical pig treated? "Day after day, she rubs her nose across the front of her crate. In sheer desperation, she bites the metal bars."

Strain does not only occur during economic hard times. For example, outbursts during the mid-1960s followed two decades of strong corporate growth and prosperity (J. Brown, 1979). As the International Association of Advertising (IAA) observed, "The historical view of controversy advertising suggests that it is a product of periods of economic expansion. The spread of affluence in such periods encourages new publics to expect or demand a voice in social and economic decision making" (Stridsberg, 1977, p. 96). Strain is most persuasive when established social, economic, or political norms are violated and expectations go unmet.

Smelser (1963) viewed social change as the result of concerns that range from a relatively undefined interest, such as fads, to norm-oriented or value-oriented issues. Fads (crazes or panics) have little permanent impact on the social, political, or economic character of a society. In contrast, major movements result in dramatic change. For instance, the civil rights movement has struggled to implement the norms based on freedom, equality, and pursuit of happiness. The environmental movement has revolutionized lifestyles and notions of safety. Environmentalism changed values as a precursor to altering personal and corporate behavior and policy.

Value-oriented movements work to reform social, economic, or political values prior to changing norms. Around the turn of this century, the value of unrestrained corporate free enterprise was repudiated by Populists and Progressives who feared it would lead to corporate monarchy. Product safety and environmental protection are two values that have dramatically altered corporate operating environments. As values are redefined, issues monitors must estimate which changes are fads and which will alter business or government operating environments. Issues monitors are wise to be alert to opinion shifts marked by a change in intensity of opinion, a measure of how deeply activists feel about some issue. Intensity can be empirically measured by the strength of beliefs or attitudes that are often expressed in highly evaluative terms.

The extensiveness of support is another measure of the intensity of an issue. Strain can be measured by the number and kind of people who belong to a group or support the issues it promotes. Because activist leaders need large numbers of supporters as a power base, extensive and enduring support is crucial. Coincidental to this measure of effectiveness is the ability of the group to attract third-party support and form coalitions with other activist groups and legitimate members of a power bloc—a governor, mayor, president, religious leader, or celebrity.

Beyond ideas, activism may test the willingness of combatants to risk their lives, property, position, or economic stability (Heath, 1979). Corporations have an advantage in communities where people are unwilling to risk losing income. But if the risk of loss, such as the danger of radiation or toxic waste, begins to outweigh the economic loss, agitators may confront the company with a new set of dynamics. In these ways, persons calculate the constraints against their activism (J. E. Grunig & Hunt, 1984).

Strain is strongest when it expresses the self-interest of members, actual and potential. Groups create a sense of strain by showing how business actions violate the self-interest of segments of the population. Sometimes the problem is readily perceived, such as when companies improperly dispose of toxic waste. The public is likely to assume the waste was being processed in compliance with acceptable procedures. When it discovers such is not the case, it is primed to support regulatory or legal action against the offenders. Activists "often are characterized by their motivation, fervor, and enthusiasm; they will persevere until they achieve their goal" (L. Grunig, 1992a, p. 504).

Issues monitoring can ascertain the extent to which a group has achieved legitimacy—public acceptance as a reputable commentator on an issue. A group has become more legitimate when it is called on to express its opinion in the media and addresses a point of view that is accepted by key publics and community leaders. Unless activists become legitimate representatives of some issue position, they are unlikely to forge legislative or regulatory change needed to pressure an industry. Whether media treat these voices of change as legitimate or aberrant is crucial. Another measure of increasing strain is the extent to which people identify with the group and its themes.

Strain is expressed in rhetorical statements that blend emotional terms, the marshaling of evidence, and careful reasoning. Emotion gains attention; evidence and reasoning give an issue permanence. Out of conditions of strain, the group builds "a fire under its members by stressing the intolerability of their fate." "The result is to reinforce the member's conviction that he (*sic*) must take action" (Toch, 1965, p. 83). A "sufficient condition for the outbreak of collective behavior is communication" when united with "a shared culture and a common orientation among the discontented group." Activism focuses "attention on the same incidents and the shared culture ensures that a similar interpretation of those events will be made" (Oberschall, 1973, pp. 310-311).

In the development of strain, atrocities can be explosive. The civil rights movement of the 1960s gained impetus when the nation learned the horrors of racism when some people bombed a church, killing children in a Sunday school class. Labor atrocities, employment inequities, rivers catching on fire, chemically produced birth defects, and cancer resulting from asbestos production—these are a few dramatic instances that changed corporate policy. Businesses or governmental agencies may call such instances "crises." To activists, they are "atrocities."

A challenge facing corporate communicators and activists is to reach key publics with simplified versions of often complicated issues. During pollution battles, even the regulators and scientists may not understand and agree on the components of pollution, a safe level of chemicals emitted into the air, or the best technology to stop the emissions. Because issues may be complex, activists attempt to simplify and freeze attention on a few defensible statements, perhaps key examples, which followers believe to be true and can easily remember. An atrocity is vivid and easy to understand, it can be difficult to explain away, and the burden of proof has shifted to the corporations or to governmental agencies. Activist rhetoric is often most effective when it is expressed in hyperbole.

After awhile, the dramatic effect of hyperbole wears off, but the residual redefinition creates new perspectives that linger in key publics' minds. Activists use redefinition to place a new interpretation on a situation, a product (such as cigarettes) or service, a corporation or industry, or a governmental agency. If the reinterpretation catches on, especially with reporters and followers, the company, industry, or agency has become vulnerable to change. Under business as usual, Dow Chemical, during the Vietnam years, would have been seen positively as the manufacturer of napalm. With napalm, U.S. troops could be more effective against the enemy. After negative characterization of napalm by the antiwar activists, it became known by many as an indiscriminate and horrifying weapon that destroyed innocent victims as well as the enemy.

An activist group takes a vital step toward the establishment of strain once it creates a perspective that, like a new pair of glasses, allows a key public to see its world in a different way. This new perspective does not constitute the movement, but it is a vital step toward developing the power resources needed to force legislative or regulatory change. To develop and maintain follower commitment, activists rest their case on righteous purpose. Activism is presented as a solution to a problem. Its rhetoric is like a morality play; it symbolizes good, whereas the adversary epitomizes evil. Activists try to become an extension of each follower's identity. They symbolize followers' aspirations for a better life, goals to be gained by supporting the group. Their rhetorical stance challenges routinely accepted facts, values, and public policy positions.

Companies, industries, and governmental bodies can redirect or refute claims that strain exists by managing certain issues, symbols, and rewards. Edelman (1964) suggested that "restiveness occurs when the state is not symbolically aligned with those who feel threatened" (p. 167). This requires that government either take the side of business or those who seek change. Activists often perceive the state to be an enemy to change. Throughout such battles, government must maintain the symbolic value of its presence. Individuals cherish "the images of society, of right and wrong, justice, and injustice, success, and other moral components of their view of the world and where they themselves are situated in it" (Oberschall, 1973, pp. 83-84).

Activists, environmental groups for instance, use prosocial rhetorical strategies to get audiences to comply with recommended actions. Such groups claim that rewards will be achieved if followers hold environmentally responsible opinions and take individual and collective actions recommended by environmentalists. They draw on their expertise regarding environmental issues to recommend opinions and actions. They also moralize environmental issues. In addition to positive appeals, environmental groups forecast negative outcomes that will result from irresponsible environmental behavior (Baglan, Lalumia, & Bayless, 1986). This tactic is intended to persuade followers and other targeted audiences to trust the advice and comply with the environmentalists who seek positive answers to questions and concerns in the public interest.

Strain results from facts and premises basic to argumentative conclusions, such as the harmfulness of cigarette smoking, the need for companies and other institutions to not harm and even protect the environment, and to protect the safety and welfare of workers and customers. The power of the activists' rhetorical stance is the likelihood that their claims will become new ways of thinking by influential members of society, leading to new actions and solutions to problems.

Mobilization

Strain—a product of problem recognition and outrage—is activists' energy source. If it is sufficiently strong, people will join a group or at least support it with their approval and even with membership dues. However, activist groups do not exist long on fire and brimstone alone. If they are to be potent forces of change, they must achieve structure, conduct routine tasks, and maintain or increase membership. Activist groups require a division of labor, motivated supporters, and monetary resources—the resources of mobilization.

Mobilization occurs when activists begin to gather and marshal their public policy power resources. Activists seek followers who sacrifice time, money, reputation, and, in extreme instances, personal security. Persuasion supplies ideals, emphasizes self-interest, and fosters identification sufficient to sustain the activist group. In this battle of wills, corporations and governmental agencies often have the advantage of being able to outlast the activists. Companies and agencies can simply ignore activists on the assumption that they will run out of the fuels of ideology and outrage. Defined in terms of the acquisition and use of power resources, power is the product of three variables: resources, the degree to which they are mobilized, and the efficiency of that mobilization (Blalock, 1989). The incentive for creating and employing power resources entails the desire for subjective expected utilities—gains through collective efforts. In such efforts, strategic issues managers realize that although the entity they represent may have some goals that differ from those of activists, the likelihood is great that both entities share goals that can be the basis for reconciling differences (Blalock, 1989).

To build commitment, activists must win victories that evidence their ability to solve their followers' problems. Sage activist leaders may pick easy battles they know they can win, to symbolize power. They call on followers to participate in ways that do not go outside their experience or willingness to act. They minimize the perceived level of risk to be encountered by supporters and convince them the rewards of participation are justified (Alinsky, 1971). Activist leaders realize that "to be effective, they must show evidence of widespread support—hence, they frequently resort to mass rallies, demonstrations, petitions, and other forms of visible aggregation of the discontented groups and their sympathizers" (Oberschall, 1973, p. 308). Idle threats are the death knell of activist groups. Corporations and governmental agencies are barraged with so many complaints and appeals to change that they are willing to resist or ignore all but those that seem capable of ending business as usual.

During mobilization, activists seek media attention (Wallack et al., 1993). Achieving favorable attention is sometimes difficult because activist voices often compete with one another for reporters' attention. Typical reportage consists of a quotation from an activist, a corporate spokesperson, and a governmental agency representative. The goal is to be prominently and favorably featured on front pages, editorial sections, and top-of-the-hour news reports. As well as using their own media to disseminate messages, activists work to appear favorably in the standard media and to at least seem to have broad and enthusiastic support.

This movement requirement is important for issues monitors. Prior to becoming visible in the media, an activist group may have a following, however broad or committed. If issues monitors are alert, activists can be discovered before they become visible to large numbers of people. Outreach efforts by the company or industry may solve problems and reconcile differences between it and activists before they become entrenched into routine news stories on the issue.

During mobilization, many activist groups develop their own communication systems that typically include a variety of newsletters, magazines, newspapers, videos, and speakers bureaus. Typical of the sophisticated, slick magazines activists develop are *Audubon* and *National Wildlife*. Both are products of wildlife groups that engage in environmental lobbying. The Audubon Society has obtained corporate sponsorship for hour-long television programs that are periodically aired on cable channels. Environmental groups circulate stories and articles that reinforce their followers' love of nature and wildlife. Both discuss and monitor ecology issues. Typical of this discussion, the February-March 1995 issue of *National Wildlife* summarized the results of data gained from monitoring legislative and executive commitment to environmental policy. The Editorial Board (1995) used this opportunity to chide those in government who were less supportive of environmental issues that *National Wildlife* editors believed was wise. The review concluded, "By almost any measure, 1994 was a disappointing year for those Americans who looked to federal lawmakers for strong leadership on environmental and conservation matters" (p. 34). The Editorial Board worried that the gridlock between the Congress and President Clinton would harm initiatives such as cabinet status for the EPA and the effort to create a Biological Survey in the Interior Department. The blame for these failures was largely focused on the property rights movement, which is supported by big industry and large agricultural concerns. The goal of this coalition is "to weaken laws designed to protect natural resources, the environment and public health" (p. 34). Such resistance was maintained in the face of survey data that indicated that 76% of Americans wanted stronger water quality regulation, 51% wanted a stronger Endangered Species Act, and 82% supported reform in the federal Mining Act.

That same issue of *National Wildlife* included the "27th Environmental Quality Review," which characterized 1994 as the year of gridlock and provided issue updates on seven topics: wildlife, air, energy, water, soil, forests, and quality of life. Each topic is headlined with an abstract; for instance, the quality of life abstract stated, "Research uncovers potential new threats to human health from an ominous class of toxic pollutants" (Editorial Board, 1995, p. 41). Such updates serve the interest of followers of the National Wildlife Foundation, and they help issues monitors track the progress of issues by viewing them through the lens of key activist groups.

During mobilization, activists must resist the dangerous tendency to factionalize, to fragment as leaders vie for followings. They challenge one another's' resolve, boldness, and issue positions. They destroy one another in what they think to be the best interest of the total movement. A test of power is the debate over slogans and symbols that foster identification and simplify the movement ideology. "To be a part of an organization viewed as potent is evidently to derive some feelings of effectiveness" (Edelman, 1964, p. 109).

During mobilization, an activist group is strengthened by its ability to achieve coalitions that add to its legitimacy. If judges, legislators, government executives, and regulators are unwilling to support the group's position, it is unlikely to mobilize appreciable power resources. For this reason, a power strategy is to threaten legitimate leaders of society with the prospect that they must support the movement or lose their own authority and position. Activists seek celebrities who identify with their cause and lend their names to make it visible and legitimate. Petition drives give an activist group a sense of legitimacy; they suggest that its cause has popular support. Activists often buy ads to proclaim their endorsements. They also seek alliances with other groups that have a similar interest and take compatible stands on the relevant issues.

Corporations have used many tactics to resist special interest mobilization. They have worked to disrupt the sources of funds. Legitimate figures in society can be discouraged from endorsing the group. Corporations may increase laypeople's risk of supporting the group by threatening layoffs or shortages or by showing the costs that will result if the group's efforts are successful. Businesses or governmental agencies may argue that support of the group is not needed because it cannot solve the problems and activists' efforts are likely to be unproductive.

Such tactics can lead to additional outrage and increased opposition. The best long-term solution to difficulties with activists is to employ strategies that allow for both sides to win.

Confrontation

Activists are ready to confront their enemy once they can marshal the requisite power resources. Confrontation occurs when a group attempts to force a corporation or governmental agency to recognize its legitimacy and acknowledge its demands. They use confrontation to polarize society to choose between their position and that of their corporate or governmental adversaries. "Radical confrontation reflects a dramatic sense of division" (Scott & Smith, 1969, p. 2). Confrontation tests whether the group can be ignored. By the time confrontation occurs, the situation may have gone so far that the company or agency must work hard to mend fences and build bridges.

Jackson (1982) observed, "Issues can't be 'managed'; confrontation can" (p. 212). Companies should avoid confrontation because conflict can legitimize activists and help them obtain or maintain momentum and enhance their fund-raising and membership drives. Issues managers should recognize when its opposition is strong because its point of view is legitimate, but they should not fear conflict when facts and solutions deserve analysis. Indeed, periods of conflict can be used to get the corporation's message across to key publics and put issues into the public policy agenda. Conflict can prove that activists are ill-informed or are employing shallow reasoning.

Rather than unwisely allowing an issue to mature to confrontation, Jackson (1982) advised corporations to identify and minimize their vulnerabilities. Once conflict begins, he observed, companies have several options: (a) "Stick to the issue at hand." (b) "Be able to admit you're wrong, or could be." (c) "Don't be afraid to alter your position." (d) "Find good things to say about others and their viewpoints." (e) "Present your views forthrightly and do not apologize for your self-interest." Flagrant use of legal authority or money can be counterproductive. Veterans of activist battles from whom Jackson drew advice cautioned companies to avoid counterattacking the credibility or personality of the activists; rather, they should focus on providing valuable information to help interested parties understand the corporate side of the issues. Companies may be hurt more than helped if they escalate controversy. Throughout Jackson's advice ran this theme: Maintain a win-win attitude (pp. 216-220).

During confrontation, each side fights for legitimacy and to be recognized as the preferred spokesperson on the issue. Activists struggle to be recognized as the bargaining agents for change by associating their power and issue position with the public interest and commonly held principles. Companies attempt to keep key publics' opinions on their side; they try to portray confrontation as likely to result in negative consequences. In contrast, activists work to keep their followers committed to the cause and attempt to maintain support by characterizing corporations in negative terms. They show their followers the virtues and necessity of confrontation. Activists argue that change can come only through their efforts.

In the battle over the use of nuclear fuel to generate electricity, for instance, antinuclear advocates portrayed utilities as being unwilling to change from a dangerous fuel to more inexpensive and safer energy sources. Managements of these facilities were portrayed as being reluctant to admit defeat. Ratepayers were told they would pay a great deal more for electricity because of the faulty judgment of industry leaders. Activists stressed the risk factor and characterized the technology as unsafe and unnecessary. They used sit-ins and picket lines to prevent the construction of generating facilities and resisted the loading of nuclear fuel into the facilities. They justified these measures because they, as they say, stood between the public interest and corporate misjudgment and avarice. In this manner, confrontation can divide opinion and interfere with "business as usual."

Activists attempt to become part of the established governmental system by creating agencies that oversee their interests. One such agency, the Center for Auto Safety, survived even during the Reagan administration, which was unfriendly to business critics. One report suggested that as many as 100 public interest groups operating in the federal government continued to be influential because of the tenacity of their leaders. The Natural Resources Defense Council, which had been active in controlling hazardous waste, saw its budget increase from $400,000 in 1970 to $5 million annually. Activist groups stay in business because they provide government officials with valuable information and help draft legislation (Schorr & Conte, 1984). Activists conduct research, offer advice, contribute position statements for governmental officials, and even receive federal and state funds to advance their causes (Bennett & DiLorenzo, 1985).

Activists may use referenda and initiatives to require legislators to deal with issues they might otherwise avoid. Battles over propositions give them free and favorable press, but such contests can place them at a disadvantage. Once an issue is placed on a ballot, companies use advertorial advertising in all media. Activists gain power if they wage a successful proposition battle, but corporations often prove formidable. On one proposition battle in California, despite favorable public opinion, corporate interests defeated an attempt to ban handguns. Corporations typically outspend interest groups. In a November 1982 proposition battle in California, corporate interests spent approximately $1.50 per vote to defeat a container law that would have required recycling beverage bottles and cans. Nearly 60% of the companies' approximately $3.5 million budget, managed through Californians for Sensible Laws, was spent on radio and television advertising (Waz, 1983).

Activists use shareholder meetings as forums to criticize actions of targeted companies (Ingersoll, 1985). With sufficient numbers of shares of stock, they can gain the floor to address issues regarding corporate policy. Shareholder protest can attract media attention; reporters look for drama. Religious groups or state or city pension funds, which hold sizable amounts of stock and can acquire proxies, use this strategy to bring attention to their issues. One of the strongest groups, the Interfaith Center on Corporate Responsibility, represents approximately 100 religious orders with a combined stock investment of $10 billion. Taking military armament as an issue, five church groups once demanded Burlington Northern reveal its contracts for transporting nuclear warheads and nuclear fuels for atomic submarines. Other groups challenged Eastman Kodak's participation in the "star wars" defense planning. Many multinational companies were challenged to withdraw from South Africa. Such action against Wells Fargo led it to withdraw loans from South Africa to prevent a resolution from going to the shareholders. Other issues included unfair labor practices in Latin America and South Korea (Coca-Cola and Control Data), discrimination against Catholics in Northern Ireland (TRW, General Motors, United Technologies), international lending practices (Bank of America, Chemical Bank, Bankers Trust), infant formula marketing (American Home Products), economic minorities (Sears, Roebuck and K-Mart), and acid rain (American Electric Power) (Moskowitz, 1985).

In the aftermath of the Exxon Valdez oil spill, environmental activists used the Exxon shares owned by the New York City Employees Retirement System to introduce into a shareholder meeting what came to be called the Valdez Principles. Developed by the Coalition for Environmentally Responsible Economies, the list called for protection of the biosphere, sustainable use of natural resources, reduction and safe treatment of waste, wise use of energy, risk reduction, marketing of safe products and services, redress for environmental and personal damage, commitment to inform employees and the public, appointment of environmentalists to serve at the board and executive levels, and annual reporting and independent auditing of environmental performance. These principles became a standard list introduced at other companies' shareholder meetings and proposed during negotiations with petrochemical companies. The principles increased pressure for more environmental responsibility even if they were defeated by shareholder votes.

Davis and Thompson (1994) advised corporate managements to take a social movement, as well as an efficient market, approach to their dealings with shareholders. Increasingly, for instance, large pension funds and certain fund managers use corporate responsibility standards to assess whether to maintain a business's management team and whether to include the organization's stock shares in its portfolio.

During confrontation, issues are framed into propositions. Both sides contest issue development by producing information and facts to support their positions and oppose the other's. The contest centers on the interpretation of these facts and their implications in light of various value perspectives. Confrontation is likely to center on the wisdom of the policy changes advocated by the activists, who argue that specific regulatory policies should be implemented in the public interest.

Schwartz (1982) reported that businesses are improving in their ability to communicate with legislators and other Washington, D.C., thought leaders to explain their side of controversies. Corporate spokespersons are increasingly adopting a win-win perspective that represents business and activist interests fairly and seeks a mutual, balanced, and legitimate outcome. Schwartz's survey characterized effective communication as being well-informed, knowledgeable, accurate, accessible, candid, open, and without high-pressure, hard-sell tactics. Executives learned they cannot withhold information or hide facts that will eventually surface through the efforts of reporters and activist critics. For this reason and the good sense of being open and honest, more companies have adopted a candid effort to bring the best information to bear on each issue.

One strategic advantage activists have is time, which to companies is money. For this reason, court and public hearings allow them a power resource. Injunctive intervention can be a powerful confrontational strategy. Activists can sue to have legal review of the wisdom of allowing companies to act as they prefer. For instance, activists prevented construction of a copper plant in Texas City, Texas, because they forced legal review of the operating permits the plant was required to obtain either from the State of Texas or the federal government. Eventually the proponents of the plant abandoned their efforts to bring it into being (Heath, 1995).

During confrontation, power resources of the combatants are tested. Persuasion supports the resources needed to achieve confrontation by maintaining and marshaling resources, by intensifying commitment, and by drawing and contesting issues.

Negotiation

Conflict results from a clash over valued and scarce resources or positions as well as the opinions related to the value and distribution of those resources. It is heightened in proportion to the importance each combatant places on the outcome, the winning of the resources or positions. If strain is the foundation of activism, then change is aimed at achieving harmony. Corporations may be smart to accede to the demands of activists without waging open battle. Outcomes can be dire if corporations fight to defend unpopular policies and premises or to adhere to operating procedures that are no longer popular. If businesses adopt those stances, they can be made to look like the villain in a political melodrama. The crowd is sure to hiss and boo.

One dramatic change in the role of activism in our society has been the increased use of negotiation and collaborative decision making. It centers on what interpretation of a problem or what solution is preferred. To answer those questions entails the uses of facts, values, and preferred policy positions that have been contested at previous stages in the activism process. Issues, such as those involving smoking or environmentalism, have become narrowed to the point that much of the dialogue transpires in courts and regulatory hearings rather than in the open press. Issues relating to dose response or parts per million (or billion or trillion)—concepts vital to discussing technical risks— are often not easily understood by lay publics and lack the kind of glamour that attracts journalists. For this reason, issue participants often express opinions and negotiate solutions out of the light of public attention, not because of a desire for secrecy but due to the failure of most reporters to be interested in arcane discussions. Much negotiation is unspectacular. It takes place in the halls of legislation and offices of administrators and regulators. Some negotiation transpires in courts and judges' chambers.

During negotiation, each side seeks to gain as many advantages or minimize as many losses as its power and argumentative ability allow. One of the frustrations at this stage is the unwillingness of either side to agree to specific points on which to stand firm. Companies complain that activists often are unwilling to settle on a specific solution or standard for drawing conclusions. Activists may lose advantage once they have struck an agreement. One of their tactics is to constantly battle for increased standards. To settle on a standard would end their appeals for increasingly higher standards. Such tactics frustrate the negotiation process. They can mask a win-lose attitude. Key publics' opinions and their ability to grant stakes continue to be important during negotiation. The advantage each side in the controversy is capable of exacting depends, at least to an extent, on what key publics come to believe is fair.

Even in the announcement of the outcome of the negotiation, corporations or interest groups can characterize the situation to their advantage (or disadvantage if they intend to continue the fight). They may describe the constructive role they played in the development of effective legislation. Announcements of change, made in the public interest, can go a long way toward building a positive, supportive environment for future operations. At the end of negotiation, advocates need to persuade interested publics that solutions achieved will eliminate the problems that fueled the controversy.

What can be negotiated? The list is long, but several items are particularly relevant: facts and conclusions from those facts, the rules and premises that are used to make decisions, the value priorities that are applied to solve the problem, policies, time frames for making the corrections and implementing the policies, and the persons who are relevant to formulating the solution as well as implementing it. Collaborative decision making leads to constructive outcomes for all interested parties. For instance, after several years of opposing the intrusion of Wal-Mart into their state, Vermont residents allowed the retailing giant access to Bennington on the stipulation that it could not create a massive shopping center on the outskirts of town but rather, had to locate its operations in a 50,000 square-foot space once occupied by Woolworth. The measure was intended to protect downtown shopping from what the residents had called "sprawl-mart."

Research by Murphy and Dee (1996) underscored the reality that negotiation and compromise are not easily achieved. Examining the relationship between companies and extremely polarized activist groups, they discovered that each of these groups espouses an ideological position that actually differs from their behavior. For instance, one side might espouse a particular environmental position but act in ways that do not correspond to that ideology. Of even more importance is the finding that the ideological positions espoused by the companies and the activists were very similar. Nevertheless, neither group wanted to accept that similarity and use it as the basis for negotiating solutions. The differences between activist groups and the targets of that activism often seem to reach a point where the issues are personalized and compromise is a matter of losing face, not a pretty prospect for resolving public policy differences.

Conflict needs to be resolved. One side can capitulate. Typically, however, negotiation results in a decision that is satisfactory to all stakeholders. A dramatic instance of that occurred in 1996 when Maxxam Corporation—a logging company often vilified by activist groups—reached a negotiated settlement with various wilderness advocates, the state of California, and the federal government. Those governments paid $380 million (cash and other logging lands) to create a reserve from Maxxam lands that preserved 7,500 acres that had scenic, historical, scientific, and ecological value. This negotiated agreement was the result of years of contentious struggle. It ended with perpetual preservation of ancient, virgin redwood forests that Maxxam had threatened to cut. "We wanted to see a lot more," said Julia A. Levin, the senior attorney for the Natural Heritage Institute in San Francisco (Woodyard, 1996, p. 24A). The group wanted more forest land in the settlement. Maxxam wanted millions more in pay.

Immediately after this settlement had been reached, the four parties held a joint press conference to announce the results of this debate that had waged in the media for years. At the press conference, the parties began the process of resolution, bringing the dispute to a close by gaining its acceptance on the part of their stakeholders.

Resolution

If skillfully managed, issues communication by all parties can help resolve controversy and create or reestablish harmony. This phase in a controversy is vital, especially in a multiple-public, multiple-stakeholder model where competing interests must be satisfied and reconciled. The major requirement of this stage is to determine how society and the interests of key players can be adjusted to accommodate the results of the settlement. If trade-outs and decisions favor business most, activists have a hard time agreeing to them. The opposite is also true. If the negotiation is fair and open, conflict can end or be reduced, and the parties can gain support for the agreement.

One problem in the resolution of conflict is the selection of the people who will administer regulatory programs. Isaac and Isaac (1984) found that as activists become a part of established governmental systems, they often take their political agenda with them and attempt to implement it. Many issue battles consist of a dialogue between technical specialists, particularly natural or behavioral scientists or engineers. Some researchers are unwilling to take stands on issues, whereas others join their sciences to issue politics. Interest groups have their own scientists, as do the companies. The government will have its cadre of specialists who give opinions. Science is often not definitive; new research findings may lead key players to reopen controversies once thought to be settled.

Even when prevailing opinion is for or against some issue position, the weight of scientific evidence and efforts of politicians will be key factors in how the regulatory battle will be played out. Politicians, whether representing a specific constituency on an issue or not, have their own agendas. Some will favor the interest-group side of the issue on a technical question, and other politicians will take the corporate side. As in poker, how the regulatory battle plays itself out depends on the relative power and skill of the players. It may be settled or redirected by election outcomes. One dramatic instance of that occurred in 1994 following the Republican landslide that gave it control of both houses of Congress. During much of 1994, Representative Waxman (D. California) used his chair on a major subcommittee to grill tobacco executives about the health effects of tobacco on smokers and the manufacturing procedures that may include increasing the addictive components of cigarettes. Following the 1994 legislative election, the new chair of that committee, a Republican from Virginia, claimed that the tobacco industry had satisfactorily answered all questions and deserved no more restrictions over its operations.

From this review of activist theory, four conclusions are justified. (a) Without effective issue communication, power resources cannot be obtained or maintained. (b) Tactics of inducement and constraint lose their effectiveness when they are not sanctioned by public opinion. (c) Political pressure is likely to result once activists gain enough power. (d) Negotiation, collaborative decision making, and other forms of issue communication are needed along with new and improved policies to restore or achieve harmony among the interested parties.

▶ Incremental Erosion

Throughout this discussion of activism—especially the previous section that outlined its stages—two themes are central: Groups work to obtain and use public policy power resources and they rhetorically challenge their opponents' positions and justify their own. Organizations that lack power must draw on, or change, the assumptions and principles of society to empower themselves; those that have power must work to maintain it, in part by justifying the rationale for their power. "Established groups," Gamson (1975) observed, "must maintain the loyalty and commitment of those from whom they draw their resources; challenging groups must create this loyalty" (p. 140).

Whereas the previous section of this chapter stressed the efforts activists employ to obtain and marshal power resources, this section features the rhetorical components of that process. Of special interest is the rhetorical effort to privilege the policies and actions of some groups while undercutting the rationale for other groups' policies and actions. The best approach to issues management is to seek maximum harmony and agreement among the participants. Managing responses to and generating policies from a multiple-stakeholder environment is daunting. Through what they say and do, private-sector companies, government organizations, and activist groups work to justify themselves by adopting or creating assumptions that serve to rationalize their discretion.

Activists may chip away at the foundations of their enemies, one premise at a time. These assumptions may become generally accepted—part of the macrosocial opinions—or they may be narrower, localized to a specific interest. Persuasion is vital to social movements; it "is not so much an alternative to the power of constraints and inducements as it is an instrument of that power, an accompaniment to that power, or a consequence of that power" (Simons, 1974, p. 177). Power and persuasion support one another. Persuasion keeps people committed to the belief that groups that have power deserve to keep it and, therefore, their policies and actions are correct.

Successful critics make small demands and introduce a bit of information into the public commentary at a time. Using incremental erosion, activists chip away at their adversaries. Incremental erosion, as defined by Condit and Condit (1992), is the use of rhetoric by activists to slowly and steadily challenge and deny the assumptions on which their opponents build their case, justify their actions, and generate support. Activists create points of view to which targeted companies must continually respond; issues are slowly—incrementally—redefined to the advantage of the attacker. The Condits concluded,

> Working on different target audiences at different times, the activist group
> attempts to chip away at the various supports underlying its opponent's

position. It makes a series of gradual and small moves designed to maneuver opponents into a position where they have no more rhetorical options. This is done by establishing rhetorical exigencies—needs, conditions, or demands to which the opposition must respond—while simultaneously establishing rhetorical constraints that limit the strategies available for response. (p. 242)

Each activist statement can attack specific principles that provide rationales for company policies and procedures.

One target of incremental erosion is the tobacco industry. For years, it claimed that smoking made people attractive. Critics featured the health and cosmetic hazards of smoking. The industry used ads to tell youths that smoking was adult behavior that they should not engage in until they were old enough. Critics claimed that instead of being expressions of corporate responsibility, such ads gave young people incentives to smoke as a means for demonstrating that they were adults. Antismoking activists, in conjunction with key legislators and regulators, realized that an outright ban of cigarettes and other tobacco products would not work. So they chipped away at the industry. They ridiculed advertising claims that associated smoking with fun, recreation, and health. They worked to prove that nicotine was addictive. If it is addictive, they reasoned, it should be treated as a drug and banned or carefully controlled. Without nicotine, cigarettes would become far less popular. They wanted severe restrictions on the sale of cigarettes, decreasing their availability—such as banning cigarette machines—for children. Such bans would also make it more difficult for adult smokers to purchase cigarettes. Constant litigation and regulatory discussions have addressed the health effects of tobacco products. Incremental chipping rather than direct and total frontal assault seems to give advantage to the critics of the industry.

The entertainment industry has suffered its share of criticism. One recent target of what key publics, especially parents, believe to be irresponsible behavior is the electronic-game industry. Set in an opinion environment that has become extremely sensitive to acts that ostensibly lead to or sustain violence, congressional review has sought to protect children from being motivated or reinforced to be violent—or perhaps just desensitized to violence. Targets of such criticism include stores that sell computer games and companies that create, manufacture, and market them. One game called "Night Trap" required that players defend a group of scantily clad sorority sisters who are being attacked by zombies who were intent on sucking the blood of victims by using a giant syringe. Another game, "Mortal Combat," allows players to rip out opponents' hearts or spines or bash their brains. Under activist assault, companies rationalized the design of such games by employing the principle of free speech, First Amendment premises. They defended their games as being harmless. But the issue is tightening because of the increasing effort to combat youth violence in this country (Pereira, 1993).

Companies ask for trouble when they ignore criticism of potentially powerful groups that can use formal informational means for exerting power resource management. Rather than waiting for protests to occur over real-looking guns, for instance, two giant toy store chains pulled them from their shelves and destroyed their inventory. Although they had sold guns that had markings that police officers, for instance, could use to distinguish whether they were toys or real, children sometimes altered their guns to look more real. Public concern arose over accounts that police officers had killed children holding such guns, increasing the likelihood that police associations and angry parents would work in concert to seek to ban such toys.

Whereas a win-loss attitude may be the lifeblood of activism, it is the death knell of a corporation. Viewed this way, activism does not arise from misunderstanding but from attacks on some premises and the substitution of others. In this vein, Tichenor et al. (1977) argued that "community conflicts to an increasing degree involve a contest over information and its interpretation" (p. 107). The interpretation of fact and the contest over information may be part of activist use of incremental erosion.

Incremental change occurs because issue positions emerge and grow slowly. "Usually, issues are born, or make their debuts, in some highly specialized, limited-circulation publication or within some small group of those most interested and involved" (Renfro, 1993, p. 71). From narrow discussions (those of interest to a highly involved, but relatively small group), they can (but do not necessarily) grow in interest and are reported and discussed by the general media, such as news magazines or television feature programs, such as *60 Minutes.* These discussions, Renfro (1993) observed, ripple outward in increasingly broadcast outlets. They often start in professional or academic publications and progress to special-interest publications. People have favorite sources of information and opinion. The more cognitively involved people are, the more effort they are willing to expend to obtain important, issue-relevant information. They turn from easily accessible stories in the general media to conversations with persons whose opinions they value. Increased involvement is likely to lead people to prefer companies, government agencies, and activists as sources of information (Heath, Liao, et al., 1995).

The involved publics need to know companies' sides on controversial issues, just as they should know the positions held by their critics (Gwyn, 1970). The heart of much controversy, Finn (1981) believed, is that organizations, critics, and the media are "frustrated about the problem of getting the facts out to the public" (p. 6). Against this effort to bring issues to light and give them play in the pubic arena, politicians often protect the established system. As Nimmo (1974) concluded, they mobilize images in support of the political community, its regime, and its leaders by clever manipulation of the symbols that people respond to with meaning. Preservation of social order depends upon political elites who can accurately gauge and guide public sentiment through symbolic appeals. (p. 146)

One defense against the erosion of confidence in corporations is to portray them as great providers. Addressing this point in one of its ads, "Why Elephants Can't Live on Peanuts" (1979), Mobil Oil Company argued that big corporations are needed to solve big problems. Addressing the big task of finding, processing, and distributing petroleum products, Mobil characterized itself as the large elephant that cannot live on peanuts—inadequate revenue— alone. It portrayed activists as parrots and monkeys that complained unsympathetically about the elephant's needs. One day, the other animals needed an animal of sufficient size and strength to do a vital task and called on the elephant, which came to the rescue. Mixing image and issue, this ad concluded, If a big company is needed to do big tasks (image), then corporations should not be forcibly made smaller through government regulation (issue).

Power is defined by the ideology—central premises—of society. The rationale underpinning the power of business features its ability to deliver goods and services, provide jobs and pay taxes, and otherwise promote the welfare of society. Macrosocial opinion grants companies the power to hire and fire employees. They can produce goods and services as well as charge a fair market price for them. Within limits set by the macrosocial opinions of society, companies have the power to determine the quality and quantity of products and services. To the extent that they are restrained in these choices, other power forces have come into play.

Persuasion, including the rhetoric of identification and redefinition, involves the use of words and other symbols to create and change opinion and to motivate people to act as a group. Followers of an activist group become identified with one another through new labels, such as "environmentalists," or "animal rights advocates." Words create divisions between group members and those opposed by the group (Burke, 1969b). Activists appeal for support and motivate resistance against the "enemy." Language of agitation develops a climate of opinion that justifies the tactics of power resource management.

As Ellul (1971) observed, "Although revolt invariably centers on what is concrete, immediate, and palpable, once revolution is rooted in the hearts of men (*sic*) it cannot fail to support elements of myth and ideology." What companies and governmental agencies must watch for is the creation of new beliefs that support new norms of behavior. A major change can lead to the implementation of these norms through governmental regulation, in the effort to create a perfect society. Stressing that point, Ellul concluded, "Revolution is bound to embody a journey to the absolute in the hearts of those who take part of it" (p. 47).

Activists are strongest, McLaughlin (1969) concluded, when their "ideology is in accord with the Zeitgeist of the era" (p. 349). Activist groups survive by associating the interests of their followers with dominant political and moral symbols (Edelman, 1964, 1977). Values such as fairness, equality, aesthetics, and security underpin issue contests. From a corporate point of view, freedom is central—free enterprise is a cultural archetype. In contrast, activists use it to argue for antitrust legislation; the people should be free from the tyranny of monopolies—because restraint of trade is unfair. Labor rights were championed in the name of freedom: labor should be free from unfair labor practice. Aesthetics, a world of beauty, has been called on to combat pollution. Equality, fairness, and safety underpin social-movement persuasion because they are central to the U.S. ideology.

Under attack, institutions struggle to stop the erosion of their authority that is defined by the ideology of society. Basic documents give principles from which control agents draw their authority.

> The constitution thereby becomes the concise and hallowed expression of man's (*sic*) complex and ambivalent attitude toward others: his wish to aggrandize his goods and powers at the expense of others: his fears that he may suffer from powerful positions of others and from their predations. (Edelman, 1964, p. 19)

Activists help shift opinions. Typically, such shifts occur slowly, incrementally, during which the principles justifying the corporate view erode and are replaced by principles advocated by activists. For example, child labor was once accepted practice. Through arguments, a power constituency began to believe that children were better off in school than in coal mines or sweat shops. In similar fashion, Louis Brandeis argued that women should not be required to work long, hard hours because of their weaker constitution. This view, argued in *Muller v. Oregon* (1908), which seemed enlightened nearly 90 years ago, has in the past two decades been opposed by women who argue that many jobs should be open to them because they have the strength to perform the same tasks as males. Each position reflects a different set of beliefs and values. As this section has demonstrated, change occurs incrementally through rhetorical pressures and counterpressures between private and public-sector organizations and activist groups.

▶ Corporate Responses: Fostering Mutual Interests Instead of Antagonism

When we think about issues management, we often focus on antagonistic relationships. One alternative to seeing activists as foes is to view them as allies. They can help companies define product quality, as occurred when the food industry quit fighting mothers who doubted that the food they bought and prepared for their families were sufficiently nutritious. Food group companies created consumer advisory panels to learn what the mothers wanted to serve their families and would buy for them to eat. Combat gave way to a win-win outcome.

One innovation increasingly used by petrochemical companies and electric utilities is community advisory committees (CACs). Such committees are sponsored by companies that seek to maximize concerned citizen participation as a means for increasing understanding—perhaps of technical issues—while lessening unconstructive criticism. Companies often hire facilitators who organize a CAC, create its bylaws, set its agendas in cooperation with its members, and conduct its business. CACs serve as sounding boards for companies who strive to create harmony with adjacent communities and solve mutual problems. One example is the use of such groups by Tampa Electric; through the advice of a CAC, a different site was established for the construction of a much needed electricity generating plant. The site was selected because it solved a problem and resulted in the least harm to the community. In the chemical industry, CACs increase understanding of technical issues and operating procedures and help the sponsoring company to adopt emergency response messages that increase understanding while avoiding a sense of condescension (Heath, 1994).

Activists can become stumbling blocks to corporate efforts to execute their business plan on the assumption that lost time is lost dollars. Pressure to increase the cost of doing business is used as an incentive for the company to agree to operate in a manner preferred by the pressure group. Issues managers may ask themselves whether their industry or organization has goals in common with the pressure group, whether their goals can only be accomplished at the expense of that party, or whether their immediate goals are not in conflict but the difference of opinion arises from some other conflict over scarce resources (Blalock, 1989). A basic question for issues managers to address, as the precursor to forming meaningful relationships with critics, is the following: What goals do the entities want to achieve that foster their mutual interests and lay the foundation for collaborative decision making?

Corporate types, for that reason, accustomed to command and control mentalities are frustrated when they cannot direct the opinions and actions of persons who criticize their business and governmental activities. This kind of mentality can lead to unfortunate and counterproductive strategies and outcomes. One of the most sage advisers for the corporate set is Philip Lesly (1983, 1984, 1992) who has refined a series of lists of do's and don'ts. Some of them require basic issue monitoring to become informed and able to formulate strong and constructive responses to critics: Know the situation and the climate, know your people, know your adversaries, know what to do, and know how to do it. Although Lesly's approach is firmly committed toward maintaining the self-confidence of management, he acknowledged that the outsiders, the critics, could make valuable and constructive contributions to an improved organization. Thus, he advised, "Listen—they may have something to offer," and he continued, "If a group has legitimate arguments and shows it has a sound approach, enlist its leaders" (Lesly, 1992, p. 330). In other words, Lesly offered advice on how to deal with the unreasonable and unwise critics, but he squarely directed managers to listen, learn, and be able to know what valid criticism was being made. Isn't this the essence of issues management?

Sometimes, company or industry personnel are alarmed at how well activists understand and how firmly and insightfully they disapprove of certain policies and actions. Corporate leaders also feel deep frustration over the ignorance concerning their industry by those who advocate new regulations. A complex problem may not yield to a simple answer. During the energy crisis of the 1970s, for instance, Atlantic Richfield invited public comment on the transportation problem; company officials encouraged viewers and readers to propose alternative transportation solutions. The best suggestions were publicized by ARCO. Advertisements ran on television, daily newspapers, national newspapers, and Sunday newspaper supplements in what ARCO believed were its major production, refining, retail marketing, plus influence areas. Surveys revealed a high degree of awareness and approval of the campaign theme (Stridsberg, 1977).

Fraser (1982) pointed out two advantages of forming coalitions: Numbers count, and coalitions save money. By using coalitions, which may include the critics of corporate behavior, issues managers minimize adversarial relationships. To build coalitions, Fraser recommended that issues managers define issue-related problems and select ones on which to focus. Subsequent steps should identify allies and opponents and decide how participants can be attracted to the coalition and involved in the issues management process. The coalition effort must have budget support. The coalition should monitor its progress and communicate its efforts to constituencies through many channels. Members of a coalition become channels of communication. A coalition must evaluate its results and communicate them to its constituents. "A coalition is effective only when its issue has merit and the coalition members are organized, informed, and conscientious enough to communicate the worthiness of the effort" (p. 194).

Groups that are potential coalition partners come in many kinds. Each kind offers unique opportunities and challenges to the organization seeking to build the coalition. Types include (a) leaders of groups that are tired of expensive confrontation and need to seek consensus; (b) leaders of groups that share the same side of an issue, especially its solution; (c) leaders of groups that have similar self-interests in the issue and its resolution; and (d) leaders of groups that are naturally drawn together because of widespread acceptance of preferred issue outcomes (Tucker & McNerney, 1992).

Pires (1988) advised issues managers to follow key steps when attempting to create coalitions: (a) define objectives, (b) know the issue, (c) build an alliance, (d) maintain flexibility, (e) treat people decently, and (f) maintain contacts. To decrease the likelihood of confrontation or weaken its impact, companies can create a coalition with interest groups. Pires (1983) developed these guidelines through her efforts as Planning and Constituency Relations Manager with Texaco. The impetus for this cooperative effort was a move by civil rights groups in 1982 to scrutinize credit policies in the petroleum industry. The NAACP, combined with related constituency groups, had a membership of 16 million people, a sizable power bloc. Texaco's coalition effort grew out of a 1979 audit of Texaco's image that disclosed that Texaco had an opportunity to work with key stakeholders. By working to understand the constituencies, relationships strengthened; lines of communication opened (Pires, 1983).

As well as dealing with external publics, employee constituencies can be informed and mobilized in issue campaigns. Employees are most likely to participate in a corporate grassroots effort when they experience high cognitive involvement, are committed to the organization, have experienced success in being active on noncompany issues, and recognize that the issue facing their employer concerns their interests (Heath, Douglas, & Russell, 1995).

An issue campaign can create a coalition with stakeholders whose interests complement those of the company or industry. One example is a well-orchestrated grassroots campaign that resulted in repeal of part of President Reagan's 1982 tax-reform measure (Elmendorf, 1988). The provision would have required banks and other savings institutions to withhold federal income taxes on the first 10% of the interest earned by depositors. Then Treasury Secretary Donald Regan estimated that $20 billion of interest and dividend income was not reported. Sponsors hoped to (a) increase the likelihood of reporting and (b) get monies to the government sooner than if they were paid only as April 15 approached. From the industry standpoint, if the money were sent to the IRS, it would be unavailable for loans and other investments. Individual savers would lose income on the money sent to the IRS.

To pressure Congress to overrule itself and prevent the measure from becoming effective in July 1983, a savings industry coalition was formed, spearheaded by the American Bankers Association (ABA). Surveys found that most taxpayers were uninformed about the new law, but nearly 70% of heads of household opposed it once the ramifications were explained to them. Some 15,000 "how-to" campaign kits, costing nearly $100,000, were assembled and distributed to member banks, savings associations, and credit unions. Grass-roots appeals to customers earning interest or receiving dividends to write their senators and representatives were first made beginning in January 1983, designed to peak in March as the new session of Congress began work.

A record-setting 22 million responses soon had at least half of the House members and a third of the Senate cosponsoring repeal legislation. Regan, Senate Finance Chairman Robert Dole, and House Ways and Means Chairman Dan Rostenkowski were not used to such a popular uprising. So skillful was the campaign that bankers were able to maintain their position even though they also drew the wrath of President Reagan who labeled them "a selfish special interest."

Not all banks or savings associations participated (some opted for a low profile), but those that did waged a masterpiece campaign linked to pocket-book issues (Salamon, 1983). The outraged Dole and Regan threatened to retaliate with even stronger measures as punishment—but the constituent folks back home had spoken. Withholding was stayed. The lobby "had humbled some of the nation's most powerful leaders" (O'Shea, 1983, p. 4C).

An advertisement prepared in 1983 by the ABA cogently represented the types of arguments and appeals used in the campaign. Entitled, "Next, the Federal Government Is Going to Withhold Taxes from Your Savings and Interest," it was printed under the signature of ABA President William H. Kennedy, Jr., Chairman of the Board, National Bank of Commerce, Pine Bluff, Arkansas. The ad's central point was this: "Savers and investors will lose the use of billions of dollars each year" unless the act was repealed. It was unnecessary, the ABA argued, because the taxpayer compliance rate for interest and dividends was between 85% and 90%. The law would impose new reporting measures on banks and savings associations that would be likely to increase compliance to nearly 100% by making them virtual collection arms of the government. This intrusion, the ABA contended, "represents yet another attempt by the federal government to force its way into your everyday life." Set against these arguments was the observation that the new regulation would create "a mountain of unproductive paperwork and an inconvenience to you—so that it will have the use of your money as an interest-free loan."

The IRS proposal was unfair, reasoned the ABA, because more than three fourths of individual tax returns result in a refund. If a taxpayer earned $200 dollars in interest and had $20 of it sent to the IRS, that amount would not earn additional interest because the government would be using it interest free. Another appeal used by the ABA was equity; it asked, "Should honest taxpayers be required to give up some of their rightful income from savings and investing because the government is unwilling to use administrative procedures to find the few who cheat?" The advertisement ended with the call to action: "The government wants a piece of your savings. Instead, give

Congress a piece of your mind." The nationwide ABA magazine campaign was so broad that it could hardly fail to reach stakeholders; the resulting volume of mail demonstrated that key members of the public agreed with the association.

Appeals coupled stakeholder interest with that of the thrift institutions; the self-interest of stakeholders was pitted against the federal tax system, thereby providing a powerful campaign. Persons with the time and inclination to protest, the graying population—responsible middle-aged and elderly savers—proved politically potent (Elmendorf, 1988).

Examples such as these suggest the value of companies' seeking to optimize the interests of their stakeholders (Ewing, 1987). One primary outcome of coalition building is increased credibility (Tucker & McNerney, 1992). Corporate credibility continues to be low, primarily when people worry that businesses are selfish, narrow, and willing to engage in one-way communication. Coalitions demonstrate efforts to foster two-way communication and seek outcomes that are mutually beneficial and prone to increase harmony.

Conclusion

Proactive, constructive problem solving is preferable to combat. Communication cannot win all battles. Sometimes, the only way to solve a problem felt by activists is for industry or government agencies to implement strategic change. A win-win attitude fosters constructive communication and joint problem solving, which leads to mutual interests and harmony. A long-term commitment to inform and cooperate with key stakeholding publics about the challenges facing businesses is a prerequisite for a stable society. All sides in public policy controversy must feel they have prospered from open exchange of ideas and constructive problem-solving negotiation and collaborative decision making.

Issues Communication

Argument Structures and Zones of Meaning

Issue managers recognize the need for using communication as tough defense and smart offense (Adams, 1995). That observation can be made regardless of whether the issues managers work on behalf of private-sector organizations, activist groups, nonprofits, or governmental agencies. The past 35 years have demonstrated that corporations and government agencies do not have a stranglehold on opinion. Society is a complex of many voices, opinions, and interests. Politicians often do not agree with one another. They take stances that carve out or identify with prevailing opinions. Regional differences can be substantial. Interindustry and intraindustry differences work against consensus. Activists challenge companies, industries, governmental agencies—and one another. Media reports and commentaries affirm some points and oppose others—often in dramatic and hyperbolic style.

Issues communication entails reaching audiences and publics with vital data, key premises, and conclusions relevant to public policy matters. The goal for all parties in this dialogue is to forge policies that meet the needs and satisfy the values of all stakeholders. In this dialogue, each party presents what it believes to be compelling argument to support its conclusions. Opinion leader groups contest vital propositions of fact, value, and policy. By listening (issues monitoring and analysis as well as collaborative decision making) to these publics, organizations can decide when they need to agree with or challenge the views of those publics. A public contest of issue positions can increase the chances of all parties becoming more satisfied with the way each issue is resolved.

One guiding assumption behind issues communication is that if companies, activists, and governmental agencies get involved in public discussion before issue positions become fixed in the minds of key publics, communication efforts may have greater impact (Chase, 1984; Crable & Vibbert, 1985; Dionisopoulos, 1986). Early intervention increases the chance of having competing points of view thoroughly discussed while they are malleable (Lesly, 1984; Schmertz, 1986). In a republic, can we be responsible if we conclude anything other than "Let the dialogue continue"?

An array of communication options exist. Communication options range from placed advertisements to news stories, feature articles, books, and published studies, to name only a partial list. They range from massive issue advertising campaigns to negotiation between leaders of critical groups. They include the private communication of the organization. It may entail testimony at legislative and regulatory hearings. It can involve advisory councils. What is important for the discussion in this chapter is not so much the venue of the communication as its structure and content. We want to know about the substance and formation of opinions because ideas count. Issues discussion uses all vehicles to ensure that public policy is best for the relevant parties and establishes a community of shared interest for society at large.

Strategic communication should complement strategic business and public policy plans to balance corporate, governmental, and key publics' interests. In the absence of these plans, the communication plan has no firm rationale and is likely to be reactive rather than proactive. Communication planning maximizes the advantage of addressing issues important to opinion leaders and key publics to foster informed opinions and constructive evaluations (Adams, 1995).

Issues communication is inherently two-way. An issue position favored by one group or organization is likely to suffer some opposition from another group or key public. Corporations must be listeners as well as advocates if they are to provide useful "what's-in-it-for-me" information about their operating conditions to key stakeholders. They must respond with information each public wants. Businesses and other organizations cannot survive or thrive by only telling what they want audiences to know—and not telling what audiences want to know.

Ideas are contested and debated. As Burke (1969b) aptly observed, our society is a marketplace of ideas, facts, values, and policies: "the Scramble, the Wrangle of the Marketplace, the flurries and flare-ups of the Human

Barnyard, Give and Take, the wavering line of pressure and counter pressure, the Logomachy, the onus of ownership, the War of Nerves, the War" (p. 23). In this wrangle, private-sector organizations, Sproule (1989) warned, "try to privatize public space by privatizing public opinions; that is, skillfully (one-sidedly) turning opinion in directions favorable to the corporation" (p. 264). Analyzing this hegemonic effort, Dionisopoulos and Crable (1988) concluded that organizations "attempt to secure a desired outcome by aiming their messages toward leading and dominating the terminological parameters of emergent issues" (p. 143). Discourse is important "because of the creative and evocative power of language, the very 'essence' and 'boundaries' of the organization are things to be managed symbolically" (Cheney & Vibbert, 1987, p. 176).

Organizational rhetoric can have what Cheney (1992) called "an individualistic bias" (p. 166). As organizations become larger, they become less personal. Identities of people involved with each business—as well as its products or services—are caught up in this symbolism. For these reasons, Cheney reasoned that corporate rhetoric is moving beyond individual rhetors to develop an analytic model "that accounts for the corporate, collective nature of much of contemporary rhetoric, while avoiding the danger of reifying the organization (i.e., separating it analytically from its individual contributors)" (p. 178).

Without actual people to know and trust as representatives of an organization, persons external to it are asked to trust it as a symbolic identity. Large organizations' personae are manufactured; each becomes real to persons involved with it by what it does and what it says about itself. Zones of meaning are the shared information and opinion that members of organizations and publics understand and hold dear. Zones are expressions of the meaning, the interpretation and judgment, groups and publics believe to be true representations of reality. Through their zones, groups and publics view reality.

Activists, for instance, share a zone of meaning that champions environmental protection. That zone defines key issues in ways that are unique to their organizations. Sharing those zones constitutes a vital part of individual identities and identifications. A manufacturing concern shares zones of meaning with other manufacturing concerns. Outsiders may not know and may not need to know much about those zones. The key focal point, however, is when a manufacturing zone is in conflict with an environmental zone, for instance. One must give way to the other—in whole or part—unless the differences can be reconciled. Issues managers would seem to become more effective to the extent that they can see and appreciate others' zones of meanings, spot where they are in conflict or agreement, and reconcile or eliminate those differences through various kinds of communication or by changing policies and procedures.

This privatizing effort is legitimate and wise because organizations argue over the principles that provide the rationale for, and thereby bring order to, their activities and policies. The strategy can be misguided. However, selfish attempts to privatize opinion are limited by the counterattempts by activists, governmental agencies, and other voices of interest. In the past three decades, activist groups have employed rhetoric to redefine the personae of government and private-sector organizations and alter the premises of society. Such groups reframe the power bases of society; they strive to "publictize" the private sector in the public interest. This dialectic of public and private interests is the heart and soul of issues communication (Burke, 1969a; Heath, 1980, 1993; Pearson, 1989).

A critic of corporate communication practices, Sethi (1977) encouraged issue advocates to narrow the legitimacy gap between business performance and societal expectations. He was outraged by firms that tried to narrow the gap by denigrating societal expectations or by asserting that business performance meets them when such is *not* the case. He noted that companies that cry the loudest about their inability to gain access to the media are often the most irresponsible. Sethi (1981) concluded that "a great number of advocacy campaigns contribute little or anything to the public's information base. Issues are presented with catchy headlines and simple messages that are conclusatory and deterministic. The primary emphasis is on reinforcing the sponsor's position" (p. 12). Despite misgivings, experience has demonstrated that companies cannot manage issues by dominating communication channels even though they ostensibly have the deep pockets needed to drown out voices of opposition. Opinions continue to be at odds with one another.

Issues communication is most effective when it is informative, fair, nonthreatening, and direct (Kelley, 1982). As Grey Advertising Inc. noted, the best issue campaigns "do not seek to be all things to all people. Rather, they focus on a single important idea that can be developed over time and presented in a variety of creative executions" (Bell, 1983, p. 16). Issues communication provides opportunities for creating, altering, and using zones of meaning that can bring entities together in harmony rather than leave them pitted against one another. Issues communication helps activist groups gain members, attract reporters' attention, frame issues, and lay the basis for a multiplier effect, whereby reporters comment on positions expressed in ads and thereby increase the number of people who become aware of the group's position.

Publics can be defined by how people communicate and what they communicate about. As Vasquez (1994) reasoned,

> A public represents individuals that, through the process of configuring, reconfiguring, and evolving an explanation of a problematic event, have created, raised, and sustained a group consciousness around the problematic

event or issue. The public's view of the event represents the public's symbolic reality and provides a deep structure explanation of the event. (p. 271)

Issues communicators should consider publics (and audiences) as segmented by the opinions they hold, as well as their communication patterns, instead of as demographic groups (Berkowitz & Turnmire, 1994; Vasquez, 1994).

Publics become cognitively involved because they see a self-interest in an issue, believe that problems exist, and estimate the extent to which they are constrained from acting on their opinions (Grunig & Hunt, 1984). Stakeholders are audiences or publics that have identifiable stakes of value to the issues communicator. Organizational spokespersons should frame messages in ways that address audiences as potential spokespersons for the position advocated (Black, 1970). Such message design addresses the audiences' needs to participate constructively on behalf of their own interests.

Framed on those principles, this chapter considers the strategic role of issues communication in the issues management process. Although this chapter features private-sector activities by the illustrations offered, that focus is not intended to slight the abundant number of examples that demonstrate how activists and governmental leaders use issues communication to advance vital causes. The illustrations used in this chapter feature the components of issues communication regardless of the kind of organization employing them. This discussion draws examples from issues advertising, not necessarily to advocate the use of that vehicle but to examine the kinds of arguments organizations set forth. In its examination of issues communication, this chapter explains (a) issues communication as argument, (b) organizational persona, (c) issue content, and (d) campaign options, including (e) understanding and targeting stakeholding publics, (f) designing messages, and (g) assessing campaign success.

 The Issue of Issues Communication

Instead of communicating in public view, some organizations remain mute or resort to behind-the-scenes lobbying. Total lobbying expenditures in the United States run into the billions each year. In contrast to this virtually silent communication, annual grassroots spending (including issues campaigns) exceeded $1 billion as early as the mid-1970s (U.S. Congress, 1978a) and had increased to nearly $2 billion by 1986 (Sethi, 1986). Industry associations annually spend $150 million to $350 million on related campaigns (Pincus, 1980). Activist groups commit large budgets to publications and public issue communication campaigns and often enjoy free access to audiences through reporters and commentators.

Corporations evolved three lines of reasoning to justify spending their funds to address contested issues. First, each business is an aggregate of the persons who own it; because they have a stake in what happens to the company, they should be willing to spend money to defend it and its industry. Second, employees deserve a collective voice in the outcome of issues. Third, corporate money spent to communicate during controversies can lead to constructive discussion of regulatory options, resulting in a more informed electorate, lower costs, and better customer service (Stridsberg, 1977).

The public seems to accept issues advertising. Opinion Research Corporation data indicated that 60% of the respondents in one of their studies favored the idea of companies using paid advertising to present controversial points of view on policy issues. In addition, 90% reported having read or heard corporate advocacy advertisements within the previous 2 years. Of that 90%, two thirds thought the ads were at least fairly believable, and nearly the same number believed issues ads helped them better understand key issues. Respondents believed that advertisements had changed their minds on crucial issues. Because of what they had learned from the ads, 84% had discussed the issue with others. Forty percent would attempt to change others' opinions on the issues. Not only did the respondents see company issues more favorably because of this advertising, but they also reacted to the interest groups engaged in issue debate with corporations. Fifty-one percent believed that interest groups had taken unfair advantage of corporations because of the amount of unfavorable news the interest groups were able to generate. Although they favored corporations publicly debating issues, respondents voiced concern that businesses had an unfair advantage because they could spend large amounts of money on issues advertising (Ewing, 1982; Opinion Research Corporation, 1981b; see also, Coe 1983).

How do issues advertisements compare with other mediated messages in terms of impact? One study discovered that when compared to news stories, advocacy ads were "more interesting and more informative, and hence, to be more persuasive than a message presented in a news format" (Salmon, Reid, Pokrywczynski, & Willett, 1985, p. 562). Impact increases if the audience realizes that it is less well informed on the key issues than it believed (Mendelsohn, 1973). Burgoon, Pfau, and Birk (1995) found that ads reinforce by inoculating supporters of a position against its critics. However compelling that finding is, evidence suggests that attitudes do change because of ads.

Even though it traditionally accounts for less than 10% of corporate advertising spending, issues advertising's penchant for the controversial commands attention. Making advocacy pay off has proved to be a problem for some users; thus, it receives mixed acceptance (Dougherty, 1983). Researchers do not know much about the long-term impact of this effort except anecdotally. In the midst of an earlier robust period of issues communica-

tion, Sethi (1977) concluded that "advocacy advertising, as it is being cur-
rently practiced by major corporations and industry groups, with some notable exceptions, is of largely questionable value and doubtful effectiveness"
(p. 237). This failure to achieve immediate and dominant communication
impact offsets the concern many critics have regarding its deep pockets effect.
Organizations find that sustained, tailored issue communication is likely to be
needed rather than a burst of issue advertising.

The bottom-line rationale for issues communication is the need to advocate points of view, set forth important facts, and advance policy positions.
Organizations operate in an opinion environment that is the product of
statements by activists, members of an industry, members of other industries,
governmental officials, and media reporters and commentators. At the
macrosocial level, this opinion contains archetypes and assumptions that
define the character of society. These opinions are held by vast numbers of
people as well as opinion leaders. At a more specific level reside opinions of
smaller groups and communities, which are confirmed or disconfirmed by the
dominant points of view. People in a stakeholding public may not agree with
the prevailing, widely held view on some issues. Between stakeholders and
stakeseekers, a communication tug of war often occurs.

Companies and other complex organizations speak out on opinions basic
to vital zones of meaning. Dominant opinions—prevailing points of view—
constitute a hegemony that privileges the policies and operations of some
organizations or industries and marginalizes others.

> Such hegemony does not refer to simple or outright domination but rather to
> control over the (value) premises that shape basic and applied policy deci-
> sions. In essence, corporate discourse seeks to establish public frames of
> reference for interpreting information concerning issues deemed important
> by Corporate America. (Cheney & Dionisopoulos, 1989, p. 144)

Such response needs to be strategic and selective, a daunting task. As
Goodman (1983) observed, issues management is frustrated when "corporations spend more time trying to label issues than they devote to manage
issues. . . . [B]usiness is bombarded with too many issues—and must come
up with ways to handle them" (p. 20). The problem is exacerbated if issues
management is fractured into three separate options: (a) strategic business
planning and management, (b) corporate responsibility, and (c) issues communication.

Issues management is not merely communication, opinion surveying, or
corporate planning. If these activities are integrated at the executive level, an
organization can participate as a citizen in a rapidly changing political and
social environment. What is required is getting messages to appropriate
audiences and working to satisfy the needs of key publics to understand and

appreciate the organization's point of view. The process is best when it is two-way—speaking and listening. Communication cannot fix problems that require improved operations. Organizations must listen to and adopt well-reasoned points of view advocated by other opinion leaders and key publics. The wisest response by an organization is to change its policies and operations because it cannot defend them.

 Images and Issues: Complements and Counterparts

One proactive issue response is to clean up the organization. Once the job of cleaning house is finished, the organization can benefit by putting its image forward for the judgment of its stakeholders. In that sense, issues management could be conceptualized as image management—what some call *reputation management.* An organization that is viewed favorably—meets key publics' expectations—is likely to suffer less criticism and public policy constraint than is its less favored counterparts. Thus, issues and image complement one another.

One way to think of organizational image is as the attitude key publics hold regarding the company or other organization. An attitude is an expression of the belief that an attitude object—that about which an attitude is formed—is associated with key traits and an expression of the evaluation of those traits—favorable or unfavorable (Fishbein & Ajzen, 1975).

By definition, an *issue* is a point of controversy, a dispute. Factors that key stakeholders use to assess a company's image may not be controversial. If controversy exists regarding an organization's image, it may be less of a matter of which criteria should be used to judge it than concerns about whether the organization meets those criteria. Considering ingredients relevant to the attitudes that constitute corporate image, Garbett (1981) defined corporate image advertising by stressing its unique outcomes:

1. To educate, inform, or impress the public with regard to the company's policies, functions, facilities, objectives, ideals, and standards.

2. To build favorable opinion about the company by stressing the competence of the company's management, its scientific know-how, manufacturing skills, technological progress, product improvements, and contribution to social advancement and public welfare; and, on the other hand, to offset unfavorable publicity and negative attitudes.

3. To build up the investment qualities of the company's securities or to improve its financial structure.

4. To sell the company as a good place in which to work, often in a way designed to appeal to college graduates or to people with certain skills. (p. 13)

The IAA believed that

> corporate image advertising treats the company as if it were a product,
> positioning it with care within its industry or industries, giving it a clear
> differentiation from others resembling it, and basically 'selling' it to the
> audiences selected. The selling objectives are usually financial, legal, and to
> a lesser extent governmental support, to facilitate the company's pursuit of
> its business objectives. (Stridsberg, 1977, p. 32)

On one hand, attributes that key publics use to form the image (think
attitude) regarding a company, product, service, or industry seem relatively
uncontroversial and innocuous. However, critics of corporate behavior may
not see these attributes as supporters do. Trying to distinguish between
commercial and political communication, Meadow (1981) advised critics to
differentiate between product and nonproduct advertising. The first falls into
what some call commercial communication, and the latter is political, the
result of contests between critics whose values differ. Nonproduct ads include
a range of statements from those that support company images to those
encouraging public support of political candidates and issues. Meadow reasoned that political communication results when controversy exists over the
criteria by which organizations, products, or services are evaluated. Writers,
such as Parenti (1986) and Gandy (1982), reasoned that premises that guide
organizational choices and behaviors are in fact political. They challenge
companies, their supporters and critics, to examine political and hegemonic
implications basic to the rationale for corporate activities.

This rationale may not be easily or widely accepted, especially when
product and service advertising dollars are spent to reaffirm aspects of our
lives, such as driving automobiles, as merely commercial; however, unlimited
use of automobiles is a political issue—with implications for mass transit, a
more environmentally friendly mode of transportation. In the past three
decades, increased scrutiny of all aspects of corporate behavior has honed in
on the political implications of business activities. Decades ago, for instance,
cigarette smoking in public (and even in private) was thought to be a private
or perhaps a social issue. Now, it is a political issue.

How have others dealt with the problem of definitions, dichotomies, and
criticisms? The sociopolitical significance of issues advertising has been
captured by many researchers, especially Crable and Vibbert (1983), Ewing
(1982, 1987 especially Chapter 11), Garbett (1981), Heath (1988b, 1991a),
Heath and Nelson (1986 Chapter 3), Marchand (1987), Meadow (1981),
Raucher (1968), Sethi (1977, 1987a, 1987b; see also Fram, Sethi, & Namiki,
1991), Simons (1983), Stridsberg (1977), Toth and Heath (1992), Walty
(1981), and Waltzer (1988).

Sethi (1977) asserted that issues advertising is a type of corporate image advertising. It is, he reasoned, "part of that genre of advertising known as corporate image or institutional advertising. It is concerned with the propagation of ideas and the elucidation of controversial social issues deemed important by its sponsor in terms of public policy" (Sethi, 1987a, p. 281). If one view of corporate activity or policy is preferred, it is a matter of image. Developing that analysis, Sethi (1987b) placed advocacy advertising in two contexts. The behavioral and social context of advocacy advertising entails

> changing public perception of a corporation's actions and performance from skepticism and hostility to trust and acceptance. The political context of advocacy advertising is that of the constitutional safeguards for freedom of speech where a corporation is asserting its right to speak out on issues of public importance without any regulation or censorship on the part of other private groups or government agencies. (p. 7)

Issues are contestable opinions, unsettled matters, disputed points. To the extent that criteria used to evaluate a company or its products or services are contested, issues exist. For this reason, Sethi (1977) concluded, a precise taxonomy differentiating image and issues advertising is difficult to produce because "most such campaigns not only may use one or more types of advocacy appeals, but may also have elements of pure corporate goodwill or image advertising, and also include some product advertising" (p. 10).

To minimize negative connotations about issues communication, the IAA in 1977 proposed using the term *controversy advertising* for "any kind of paid public communication or message, from an identified source and in a conventional medium of public advertising, which presents information or a point of view bearing on a publicly recognized controversial issue" (Stridsberg, 1977, p. 12). The IAA preferred the use of controversy advertising to strident alternatives such as public-interest advertising, public-affairs advertising, cause-and-issue advertising, viewpoint advertising, strategic advertising, opinion advertising, advocacy advertising, public-issues advertising, and adversary advertising. In public debate,

> The purpose of controversy is not to create a passively favorable climate for actions the company wants to take, but to inject the company's interests, points of view, and objectives into the outside controversy where other people are taking actions. (Stridsberg, 1977, p. 33)

Issues advertising typically results from the desire to defend or promote a socioeconomic point of view and establish a platform of fact on which to judge and resolve issue. This vehicle "bears a strong resemblance to corporate image advertising. The advertisements are factual, do not present demands for action or justification of past events, and represent a selection of information intended to put the corporation in a good light" (Stridsberg, 1977, p. 36). As Sethi (1979) concluded,

> Corporate image advertising is not concerned with a social problem unless it has a preferred solution. It asks no action on the part of the audience beyond a favorable attitude and passive approval conducive to successful operation in the marketplace. (p. 70)

Direct image advertisements differentiate the sponsor, its products or services from its competitors and in doing so, apply criteria that are widely accepted and without much, if any, controversy. Such ads are designed to cast the sponsor in a favorable light for taking the stand that it does because the issue is thought to be of general concern. The organization is thought to be good because it takes a popular stand on an issue that concerns interests well beyond its own.

Other image ads are *indirect;* these discuss topics to help key publics and audiences appreciate the organization's operations. Indirect image ads address social, financial, or economic issues basic to corporate responsibility and feature goodwill efforts such as environmental responsibility of products or services. These ads take informational or issues stands but do not emphasize traditional marketing concerns. Such is the case for goodwill ads, which, although featuring charitable efforts, are not directly associated with services, products, or operating reputation. By presenting controversial stands, they can indirectly or directly influence the image of the sponsoring organization.

Although not free from conceptual complication, distinctions between types of ads should be based on *content* (the points being made), *imputed purpose* (the presumed reason the ad was placed—given what it says and where it is placed), *context* (where in the evolution of an issue this ad intervenes), *audience* (persons targeted with the ad content and purpose), and *channels* (where the ad is placed). Interaction between these variables helps define the attributes by which an ad can be defined.

The following list features this continuum of advertisements. It begins with **direct ads** that can be taken at face value; they demonstrate admirable attributes of commercial value.

- ※ Directly affects image through a favorable description of the company's products or services that are not the subject of public debate
- ※ Directly affects image by providing facts about the organization's operations or activities
- ※ Directly affects image through a description of how an organization's activities and policies agree with values that meet key publics' expectations of appropriate corporate behavior

※ Directly affects image through a description of the organization's support of charitable community service activities, expected and appropriate community relations

Indirect image advertising asks publics and audiences to assign positive attributions to the sponsor, based on the position it takes on issues; the image of the organization results from associations with values and attributes held in positive regard.

※ Indirectly affects image by providing noncontroversial information of value to the public, such as pharmaceutical companies explaining how their products work or what the symptoms or treatments of certain ailments are

※ Indirectly affects image through the organization's association with traditional values, such as when it demonstrates its commitment to freedom of expression or sanctity of life

※ Indirectly affects image through stands on social, economic, or financial issues by favoring a noncontroversial or popular point of view, such as the wisdom of saving for one's retirement or supporting public education as a foundation for the future of a community

※ Indirectly affects image through a favorable discussion of the need for corporations (implying the value of the sponsoring company in specific) as vital to the American and global economies

The sponsoring organization may directly address facts or conclusions about itself—as image—or ask the audience to make indirect attributions based on the stance the organization takes.

Such ads may be direct or indirect; the outcome is to affect the organization's image as well as adopt what the sponsor believes to be the correct stance on the underpinning issue.

※ Indirectly or directly affects image by challenging facts reported about a company, industry, activist group, nonprofit organization, or governmental agency, thereby answering criticism

※ Indirectly or directly affects image by taking controversial stands on facts, values, or policy

※ Indirectly or directly affects image by calling for participation in the legislative or regulatory process

Issues ads have an image component to them, but the desired outcome is not to create image as much as to have publics and audiences adopt a stand on issues.

* Issue ads call to publics to be involved in efforts to create, mitigate, pass, or defeat legislation.
* Issue ads seek to foster or blunt regulatory or legislative activities.
* Issue ads rebut facts about products, services, or operations to allay calls for policies that would force appropriate change.
* Issue ads discuss sharply contested norms and values of organizations' behavior.

Issues communication may mobilize or reinforce supporters rather than convert opponents. A substantial portion of issue advertising targets readers of specialty publications and of editorial sections of major newspapers and news magazines.

Thoughtful consideration of types of ads, and other issues communication options, is not designed to help issues communicators solve idle riddles but to challenge them to think through their objectives and the attendant communication requirements. The real concern is the use that communication has for the organizational mission and strategic business plan. Thinking about communication options is brought into sharp focus by considering how the money spent on such campaigns creates, restores, or maintains stakeholder relationships in ways that foster harmony and a fair exchange of stakes.

Issues communication is best conceived of as a two-way process, whereby organizations listen to and reasonably consider positions that agree with as well as differ from theirs. It is best when it is tailored to specific audiences, is stylized, is sustained, and imaginatively approaches the audience and the issue. Issue campaigns not only provide information and influence opinions, but they also make statements about themselves. Wise and honest issues advertising demonstrates that the sponsoring organization is so confident in its position that it makes its position public. It is willing to spend money to help inform others and put out opinions for consideration and challenge by a variety of stakeholding publics.

As this section demonstrated, the content and role of the communication in ongoing discourse help define its character. Knowing the kind of communication and seeing it positioned into an array of options can help issues communicators to decide what needs to be said and how the message should be tailored to specific needs.

 The Good Organization Communicating Well

In ancient Rome (1st century A.D.), Quintilian set as the standard of rhetorical excellence, the good person speaking well. That standard, which is explained and examined in this section, asked people to be morally sound and to learn to communicate in ways that enhanced the likelihood that their influence would prevail against persons of inferior moral character and inadequate rhetorical ability. Today, in this age of the large organization—the corporate rhetor—we may adopt Quintilian's challenge to be this: The good organization speaking well. As Coombs (1992) reasoned, "Members of publics will not support the position of an organization unless they believe that the issue is a legitimate one and that the issue management and the organization's policy proposal also are legitimate" (p. 101). This corporate rhetor could be speaking and writing for a business, an industry, a governmental agency, or an activist group.

Character is the persona created by what organizations say and do—and how they present their issue position and go about their activities. A persona can affect how key publics react to the organization's public policy stance, and its public policy stance helps establish its persona. As well as being vital to its public policy plan, the persona becomes a factor in how well the organization is received in the marketplace. Advocacy communication, for instance, can advance or harm the organization's interests—in the public policy and marketplace arenas.

Advocates of issue positions exhibit personae that are vital to the campaign they are waging. Differentiation, association, identity, and goodwill are outcomes of issues communication. *Differentiation* results when products, services, issue discussions, procedures, and policy positions advocated by the sponsoring organization make it unique. *Associations* result from attributions that come to mind as a result of the actions, values, and traits that typify the company or industry—such as being proenvironmental. *Identity* is the metaphoric residue of the archetype characteristic of the organization—bold advocate, technical expert-adviser, 800-pound gorilla, or defender of national security. *Goodwill* results when policies and actions of the organization benefit others and advance community interests: those of stakeseekers and stakeholders.

These functions should not be thought of as separate and independent but interdependent. The attributes that become associated with an organization may differentiate it from others; that point could be contestable, as in the case of one activist group being more conservative or outraged on environmental issues. These associations and differentiations merge to establish identity in the minds of key publics (and lead them to identify with it). This identity may exhibit goodwill for the interests and identity of the targeted audiences—the persona of the organization being one that takes stands and acts in ways that are in the interests of its stakeholders. Combined, these factors constitute the persona of each organization.

Issues ads are likely to increase the awareness, readership, and impact if they increase or capture targeted audiences' cognitive involvement by demonstrating how the issue affects the self-interests or altruistic concerns of these audiences. One way to do that is through graphics—as the U.S. Council for

Energy Awareness (USCEA) did when it pictured Middle East characters, such as Saddam Hussein, as villains who could control the supply of oil to the United States. These ads depicted a cobra-headed snake with a body made up of barrels of foreign oil that is poised to strike U.S. citizens. Emphasizing the point that 40% of all oil used in the United States comes from abroad, the ad alleged that "excessive dependence on foreign oil could poison America's economy and our national security if our supply were ever disrupted" (1990). In another ad, USCEA used graphics to depict foreign oil as bait in a bear trap ready to spring shut on the United States (1989).

Based on this overview of the elements of issues communication, the remainder of this section will explicate them. This discussion begins with an examination of organizational personae: differentiation, association, identity, and goodwill.

Differentiation

Chevron Oil Company seeks to demonstrate its corporate responsibility to the environment to differentiate itself from other members of its industry, one long associated with environmental damage. Using television and print ads in a long-running campaign, Chevron asks whether people care about the environment and answers, "People Do." At first, these ads directly attributed environmentally friendly acts to Chevron company or its personnel. Recently, the ads have applauded acts of environmental responsibility. The ads also address environmental issues, such as one circulated in 1989 titled, "Will there be room for all in Eden?" which addressed the problems of coexistence between animals and humans in the vast plain of the Serengeti in Tanzania. Chevron voiced its commitment to seek balance between people, industrial growth and operations, and wildlife: "The people of Chevron are learning about that kind of balance—and are working to meet the needs of nature as well as humans." Chevron indicated that it interrupts drilling activities at any time or in any fashion when they might disrupt the natural activities of wildlife. Using this message, Chevron differentiated itself from the image that oil companies are uncaring about the environment. Such ads have strong image components, and they address policy issues emphasizing the success of voluntary compliance with environmental standards, to blunt the argument that such standards need to be imposed through legislation and regulation (Porter, 1992).

As do their private-sector counterparts, activist leaders seek to take stands and present personae that differentiate them—from business and government—and from one another. Groups seek to define and differentiate themselves. For instance, Greenpeace continues to be strident in contrast to its more staid and centrist counterpart, the Aubudon Society.

Association

Fear and mystique have surrounded the use of nuclear energy. Safety is an attribute associated with the use of this fuel to generate electricity. There is concern that a catastrophic event could kill or seriously harm millions of people who live near nuclear generating facilities. After nearly 15 years of issues communication, the nuclear-generating industry has come to believe that its technology is widely accepted and that antinuclear activism has been countered. For that reason, the campaign has been discontinued.

The campaign began when survey results by Opinion Research Corporation (1981a) revealed that nearly all of the sample (99%) believed control of radioactive wastes was important. Almost as many respondents (94%) wanted close federal supervision of nuclear reactors. Eighty-five percent thought the government should "require companies to give public notice of toxic substances they are making or handling." Ecology won out over energy; people wanted solutions to technical problems and shortages while not abandoning environmental protection.

Part of the problem with nuclear fuel resulted from projects such as Three Mile Island, Diablo Canyon, and Washington Public Power Supply System (also known as WHOOPS). The Diablo Canyon generating facility in California was the target of special-interest protest over claims that it was not designed to withstand an earthquake. In 1983, the Washington system defaulted on several billion dollars of bonds—costing thousands of people to lose their life savings. Many ratepayers in Mississippi worried that Grand Gulf I unit (eventually called "Grand Goof") would increase the cost of electrical service in Claiborne County by 30% once it went on line. Three Mile Island has been the icon of near nuclear disaster in this country.

The nuclear accident at the Soviet Chernobyl site drew international outcry and prompted legitimate concerns in the United States. The USCEA responded with an ad to explain factually the differences in design between the plant in Chernobyl and that at Three Mile Island. The question posed, "Why what happened at Chernobyl didn't happen at Three Mile Island" (1986). The answer associated U.S. plant design with safe design criteria. Using graphics as well as text to explain, the ad indicated that radiation was unlikely to escape in the event of an accident because it would be contained by a steel-reinforced concrete containment structure with walls four feet thick. Additional concrete and steel walls existed. The concrete floor was 11 feet thick. The ad stressed the following point: "One important part of 'defense in depth' is that America's commercial nuclear power plants (and most nuclear plants throughout the world) have multiple protective barriers to contain the effects of an accident." The ad associated the concept of nuclear generation with the attribute of safe operation, even in the event of an accident.

The tobacco industry suffered severe scrutiny in the 1980s and 1990s. This assault included a grueling hearing by a subcommittee of the House of Representatives during which tobacco company executives were charged with encouraging research and production that increased the addictive effects of tobacco and with ignoring or underestimating research findings that linked their product to health problems. Freedom is an attribute the tobacco industry has associated with itself and the use of its products; it argued that adults must be free to choose whether to smoke. Addressing this issue, R. J. Reynolds Company used an ad (1994) that contrasted freedom in Berlin, Russia, and South Africa with congressional proposals to raise the tax on cigarettes to a prohibitive level and with OSHA's efforts to limit the use of tobacco products in public and private places. The theme, along with freedom, was accommodation—adults being left to solve problems with wise choices and politeness. In a series of ads, Philip Morris featured the attributes of accommodation, choice, and courtesy. The industry stressed its responsibility to lessen the likelihood that minors were attracted to cigarettes. In one of its ads, Philip Morris indicated that it "has taken legal action more than 1,800 time in cases where our tobacco brand logos were used illegally, often on products intended for use by minors" (1994). The attribute is the desire for equity—smokers being treated equal to nonsmokers.

Activists seek associations typically drawn from their cause. Opponents of traditional shrimping methods that lead to drowned turtles associate themselves with those turtles. The World Wildlife Federation uses the logos of the giant panda, one of the most familiar of the endangered species.

Identity

Liar, Liar, Pants on Fire—Lying to the public is fatal. One incident involved a coal producers association advertisement in the *Wall Street Journal* featuring a "coal miner" as the "man of the year." Rather than being a real miner, the spokesman was later revealed to be a vice president in the association's advertising agency. When this fact became known, the coal producers' image dropped dramatically (Stridsberg, 1977).

Organizations take aggressive stances (*bold advocate* or *technically expert adviser* archetypes). During the issue campaign waged by American Electric Power Company, Inc. (AEP) in the mid-1970s, a series of advertisements discussed technical, energy, and environmental issues. Several ads blasted methods proposed by government to prevent high coal pollution byproduct levels. Addressing this issue in a discussion of antipollutant scrubbers, AEP argued that the technology was available "to eliminate most of the sulfur-oxide emissions" but such devices created "horrendous problems." The reason: "Scrubber systems do remove sulfur oxides. But in the process all of them are plagued with one or more problems that make them unreliable and impractical for a major electric utility." The company alleged that 10 square miles of the United States would be destroyed by the limestone sludge created as a part of the pollution-reduction system. The issue posed by AEP was air quality versus land quality. The company argued that the best solution was

> to release the enormous reserves of U.S. Government-owned low-sulfur coal in the West. And at the same time continue the investment of time, energy and money in the development of the technology to clean high-sulfur coal before it is burned.

Several appeals were used by AEP, such as asking readers to imagine what would happen if OPEC decided to stop the supply of oil again. Many critics felt that this theme amounted to little more than a xenophobic attack on Middle Eastern oil producers that could damage international relations. Both the *Washington Post* and *New York Times* editorialized against the campaign. More than 200 letters were sent to the EPA protesting the content and tone of the ads. AEP did not do evaluative pretesting and posttesting, but according to a 1980 Gallup & Robinson poll, theirs is one of the most successful advocacy campaigns in recent years (Hush, 1983). Nevertheless, scrubber technology was implemented. Archetype? Bold, technical adviser or xenophobic, self-interest pleader?

Technical Adviser

One of several industry public information organizations, USCEA undertook an issue campaign to help the public understand and accept the technology and economic benefits of nuclear generation. Magazine and television ads used pastel colors and lively graphics to attract audience attention and highlight the issue position being set forth. Aware of public concerns about the dangers of nuclear power, one ad announced that a poll conducted by Cambridge Reports, Inc. indicated that 54% of adults favor nuclear energy. Of this number, 22% "strongly favor" and 32% "somewhat favor" nuclear generation (1984). This campaign tried to create an expert-adviser persona by citing technically qualified individuals; one ad reported that 53% of all scientists, 70% of energy experts, and 92% of nuclear experts believe that nuclear construction should proceed rapidly because risks are acceptable (1983). One ad cited Dr. Lynn E. Weaver, Dean, School of Engineering, Auburn University, who concluded, "Nuclear-generated electricity has become one of the basic props supporting the entire national economy" (1985).

In pursuing the advantages of nuclear generation, the USCEA, while avoiding anti-Arab stereotypes, coupled balance-of-payments deficits with apprehension of energy dependence on the Middle East. A telling comparison is that over 3 years, one 1,000-megawatt plant would require one uranium fuel core versus 30,000,000 barrels of oil. Cost advantages are such that nuclear power, in the decade since 1974, "saved electric rate payers an estimated $40 billion, and continues to save rate payers $4-$6 billion each year" (1984). A 1984 ad explained how a "blizzard of changing, costly, complex government rules and regulations" have slowed the growth rate of nuclear generation. Constructing nuclear generating facilities is very expensive, so the first years' costs are much higher than those in plants using other kinds of fuels. Over time, costs become more favorable to nuclear power because of dramatic differences in fuel costs. A January 1985 ad, showing a nuclear plant under construction, opened with this headline: "Good morning. Today and every day this year, nuclear electricity will reduce America's trade deficit by over $11 million." Over the next decade, the campaign was so successful that in 1995, USCEA terminated this issues advertising campaign.

Activist leaders strive to position themselves as experts, advising key publics and audiences on the perils of not seeing problems and seeking solutions featured by the activists. Their expertise depends on their ability to define problems and craft socially viable and useful solutions.

Goodwill

Issues advocates adopt the persona of speaking to the goodwill of society. In the midst of auto safety controversy in the 1980s, General Motors sought to demonstrate its public service commitment by discussing drunk driving and the use of seat belts to help the public cope with the perils of driving. Likewise, environmental activists position themselves as goodwill advocates for the focal point of their cause. They fight for endangered species, virgin redwood forests slated for harvesting, or humane treatment of laboratory and farm animals. Goodwill is the lifeblood of activism.

For a quarter century, Mobil Oil Company has worked to establish a persona as the most visible—and feistiest—corporate practitioner of advocacy communication (Connor, 1975). For several years, Mobil presented a persona of Gulliver in the land of the Lilliputians, its view that American business is artificially tied down by swarms of ill-informed bureaucrats and journalists. In covering an array of topics, three messages emerged: (a) bias exists in the media, (b) the integrity of free enterprise must be protected, and (c) government is guilty of many unintentional sins ranging from ill-conceived regulation to ineffective management. The bottom-line argument is that businesses create jobs, foster prosperity, and provide valuable products and services.

According to former Mobil Vice President for Public Affairs Herbert Schmertz—creator of the campaign, the company's objective is "to present our views and our ideas along with established facts to assist the public in making decisions." Mobil wanted an alliance, an identification, with targeted audiences who also suffer from irresponsible reporting and incompetent government. Schmertz told *Madison Avenue* magazine that Mobil targets print and broadcast journalists plus "all the other opinion molders and thought leaders who shape public discourse in this country" (cited in Hush, 1983, p. 9; see also, Schmertz, 1986).

This persona provokes extreme reactions, positive and negative. Reflecting on the first decade of the program, Verne Gay (1982) observed, "No other major advertising campaign has generated as much controversy or major media news coverage as Mobil's" (p. 87). Among respondents to a Grey Advertising Inc. survey of chief executive officers at 50 prominent U.S. companies reported in *Grey Matter,* some professed admiration for Mobil's aggressive stance and praised it for "recognizing opposing views and presenting corporate positions in a positive way;" others accused it of being "too strident" and "preaching to the converted." Examining these views, the Grey agency concluded that "strangely enough," divided opinions and heated debate are probably the reactions Mobil wanted (Hush, 1983, p. 9). As Gay (1982) noted, "Mobil's voice is distinctive and highly idiosyncratic— reflecting the personality of the company's top brass" (p. 87).

As petroleum costs skyrocketed in the mid-1970s, consumers, reporters, and Congress sought someone to blame. In defense of itself and its industry, Mobil centered on the critical question, Are oil companies withholding gasoline to falsely escalate prices? Although many were quick to blame the industry, the Media Institute demonstrated the need for an open contest of ideas in its report on news coverage during the oil crisis. The major problem was imbalance (Fletcher, 1982; Theberge & Hazlett, 1982). In a 1982 op-ed, "A Post Audit," Mobil agreed with Media Institute findings that print and broadcast journalists failed "to properly describe the economic size of the crisis" through "overreliance on the government for information."

Over the years, the Mobil campaign has assumed many forms. In the 1970s and 1980s, the backbone of the campaign was three kinds of print advertisements. The mainstay was a quarter-page op-ed placed periodically in business publications, national magazines, and the opinion section of major daily newspapers. A second kind of ad ran in Sunday supplements of major newspapers and some national magazines. Titled "Observations," this series featured interesting information, typically about the energy industry or capitalism in general. A light writing style and cartoon graphics enhanced readability on what could be considered uninteresting themes. "Observations" often highlighted a fable designed to attract a broad audience, whereas op-eds were targeted at an elite readership. The third kind of ad promoted public service activities by the company, for example, its underwriting public television's "Masterpiece Theater."

The company created a Mobil Corporation civic action program newsletter, titled *Mobil re:cap*. This newsletter series, "published periodically for active employees, annuitants, and others on request," provided timely information to these stakeholders regarding the gasoline shortage and other key issues of material interest to them. Headlines in *re:cap*'s June 1980 issue suggested the array of topics and stances Mobil took in its campaign: "TV: Still pulls the plug on voices not its own," "Who was responsible for gasoline lines? Us? No, U.S.!," "How states are hampering energy goals," and "Governments take more than Mobil makes in a year." Compare this with the June 1984 issue that discussed information relevant to these topics: "Truth vs. freedom of the press," "Gas recontrol bill would cut supplies, hurt consumers," and "Oil company mergers: The healthy result of a changing market," and "Study shows 'big oil' pays higher tax rates."

To create its persona, Mobil placed ads to discuss media reporting practices, oil industry operations, and government policies. In a widely debated five-part series, Mobil sought to answer the question, "Are the media giving us the facts?" The first ad, "The myth of the villainous businessman," cited communications professor George Gerbner of the Annenberg School of Communications at the University of Pennsylvania. He claimed that television helps create a view of the world. The more television people watch, the more they adopt television's view of reality; for instance, people who watch a lot of television believe more violence exists than is factually true. Thus, if television gives a distorted view of violence, it does the same for business. Here, Mobil relied on Media Institute findings of antibusiness television bias (Theberge, 1981).

Because of the controversial topics and rhetorical stance Mobil adopted, it was prone to foster dialogue. Countering public distrust, Mobil agreed in a 1983 *Wall Street Journal* ad,

> To be sure, businessmen make their share of mistakes. However, business is the direct source of livelihood for millions of Americans and the indirect benefactor of many millions more. It is the producer of virtually all of the goods we as a nation consume. And if free private business is destroyed or threatened, all the institutions in society, including a free press and free mass communications network, would be threatened.

Jan R. Van Meter (1983) published a rebuttal in the *Journal* 10 days later, titled "TV didn't invent evil businessmen." Van Meter, a senior vice president of a New York City-based public relations firm, argued that long before television, novels and films have used the villainous businessman as a central character. For Van Meter, the bottom line is not malicious bias but the need for television revenues. Programs featuring fictional bad-guy business executives such as J. R. Ewing in the long-running television program "Dallas" are perceived by the broadcasting industry to be more interesting than their often stodgy real-life counterparts to the viewing public. After making this point, he responded to the theme of Mobil's op-ed:

> What is clear is that Mobil and Accuracy in Media and The Media Institute had better find another scapegoat to blame and another hobbyhorse to ride. It's fun to attack television entertainment programming, and it may even scare some television executives. But it won't change how the culture looks at business.

In the second op-ed of the media series, Mobil continued its good guys-bad guys discussion by comparing political stereotypes prevalent in the media. The "liberal politician" is a "defender of consumer interests and environmental protection." In contrast, the "conservative politician" is "in the pocket of big business." The "social activist" is a public interest representative who "has unruly hair and wears folksy clothes." The "business executive" is "motivated by greed for more profits, unwilling to put the country's good ahead of his company's." Mobil offered these personae of political leanings to demonstrate its commitment to fairness as a balance to the unfairness of the media.

In the third op-ed, Mobil challenged "the myth of the crusading reporter" by suggesting that many media corporations are virtual monopolies. "The journalist has the power to shape the agenda, edit the story and place it prominently before the public eye." To demonstrate how the problem perpetuates itself, Mobil pointed out that 40% of Columbia School of Journalism students in that era "advocate public ownership of corporations." So much for print media balance.

In the fourth advertisement, Mobil turned its attention to "the myth of the open airwaves." Here, the villain was the Federal Communications Commission's Fairness Doctrine, its mandate to pursue vigorous debate undercut by programming executives seeking to prevent controversy from being aired. As Mobil pointed out from its own experiences and those of other corporate communicators, broadcasters are reluctant to sell time to those wishing to respond to public-affairs stories. The ad's conclusion is drawn from the 1978 Supreme Court Bellotti decision: "The press does not have a monopoly on either the First Amendment or the ability to enlighten."

The fifth ad condemned the proclivity media have for hiding behind the First Amendment. In assuming that the Constitution protects them against irresponsibility, Mobil warned that the media may be in for a rude awakening because there is no absolute shield preventing libel and bias actions. Mobil cautioned that "By crying 'wolf' too often, the media may well bring the wolf to their door."

In a reflective follow-up ad, Mobil concluded in a play on words that "The customers always write." In this op-ed, Mobil shared excerpts from several letters by people who agreed with Mobil's criticism of the media. The company acknowledged it received some brickbats, such as one from a reader who thought Mobil dollars could be spent more productively than on ads criticizing the media. This reader challenged Mobil to be a more responsible steward of investor and consumer dollars.

As well as defending itself, Mobil diligently presented the U.S. oil industry in the most favorable light. Aside from detailed examinations of the profit picture, Mobil sought to broaden and deepen the public's view of oil company corporate responsibility. In a 1980 op-ed, Mobil gave us pause to "Count our blessings." The broad message was the effectiveness of business as "provider" and "creator." The oil industry creates jobs, provides oil for other industries, "helps the little guy," and is an investor. In a related op-ed titled, "When golden eagles nest near a coal mine," Mobil described its effort to relocate nesting golden eagles so that they would be outside its Caballo Rojo coal-mining property. The ad extolled Mobil's virtues as having generated baseline data on the wildlife in the area. This discussion proclaimed, "The environment can be preserved while needed energy is produced" (1982). A cynical reader could imagine that without federal and state regulations, corporations would be less "socially responsible."

To describe its efforts to increase oil field production, Mobil used the headline, "Plop, plop! Fizz, fizz!" The catchy title played on Alka-Seltzer's popular commercial jingle to attract readers to a technical discussion of how carbon dioxide is injected into old wells so that it will mix with crude oil, thereby thinning it for increased recovery. The companion "Observations" of July 17, 1983, gave a folksy version of the technical material. After describing technological advances in discovering new oil fields, the column said,

> We're also using science to squeeze more out of what we've already found. We inject carbon dioxide—the fizzy stuff that adds zip to soda pop—into "mature" wells to increase oil recovery . . . and set fires down below to make thick, gooey oil flow to the production wells.

This technical theme continued into the 1990s. In a 1996 op-ed (which included Mobil's website address), the company addressed new technologies used to discover oil and natural gas. New methods are used to rejuvenate older oil and gas fields. Drilling techniques have advanced to allow exploration in deeper water and to tap old fields. Technologies have also lessened the environmental damage associated with obtaining oil and gas reserves to fuel consumers' demands.

During the energy crisis, the public believed oil companies were using crude oil for more profitable lines of plastics rather than gasoline for automobiles. "Observations" devoted a column to this issue. After a brief, chatty discussion of the history of plastics, Mobil noted that plastics save energy and improve the quality of life. But, said Mobil, "in 1982 less than 1.5 percent of the oil and gas supply" in the United States was used in making plastics (1983).

Nor has the government received high marks in Mobil's grade book. In January 1985, Mobil's op-ed asked, "Is this any way to run a business?" The center of attention was federal waste of tax dollars through use of obsolescent computers. The conclusion was "Clearly, no private business could operate the way the government does and hope to remain in business." Regulatory agencies have also been singled out for criticism, but in "An invitation too good to refuse," (1984) Mobil praised former EPA head William Ruckelshaus for his call to scientists to assist in establishing sound guidelines. Mobil applauded his action: "Too often, U.S. environmental policy has been based on political considerations or has been influenced by one-sided TV reportage." Mobil continued, "Without the guiding hand of science in environmental policy-making, the results have been predictable, confusing, contradictory, duplicative and punitive rules and regulations." In the conclusion, Mobil centered on the belief "that government officials, working together with scientists, Congress and industry, can forge better environmental laws that protect both the health and economic welfare of all the people."

An op-ed published after the November 1984 elections typifies Mobil's commitment to debate. Titled "Since you asked, Mr. Haskell," the ad was addressed to Floyd Haskell, a former Democratic senator from Colorado who headed the Taxpayers Committee. At issue was his contention that the 1981 tax law should be repealed because it gave too many breaks to industry. Mobil built its refutation on several contentions. The first was "that all taxation distorts the marketplace" by robbing companies of investment capital. Second, Mobil favored the Accelerated Cost Recovery System provision that allows companies "to take deductions for plant and equipment at a faster rate than before." Moreover, Mobil challenged Haskell to advocate repeal of the windfall profit tax on oil that took $61.4 billion from oil companies between 1980 and 1983. In a letter to the editor of *The Denver Post,* Haskell (1984) responded to Mobil regarding the effects of the 1981 tax measure. He contended that instead of fostering capital investment, the opposite occurred; fewer dollars were devoted to capital investment in 1982 and 1983. He challenged Mobil by countering that "there is no discernible correlation between corporate taxation and economic health." To close his portion of this dialogue, Haskell parried, "As a Mobil stockholder, I wonder why they [op-ed dollars] are spent at all."

Good question. Mobil continues its campaign, as it said in a 1984 op-ed, because it does not

> want to be like the mother-in-law who comes to visit only when she has problems and matters to complain about. We think a continuous presence in this space makes sense for us. And we hope, on your part, you find us informative occasionally, or entertaining, or at least infuriating. But never boring. After all, you did read this far, didn't you?

Whereas those themes dominated ads of the 1970s and 1980s, a new variety has become prominent in the 1990s. It consists of serial discussions of single issues, especially proposals to improve air quality. The ads have featured a single theme, "clearing the air," which carried a double meaning—conveying the point of view preferred by Mobil—clearing the air—on the issue of environmentally friendly fuels. The policy issue was which fuels were environmentally most friendly. The value premise was accepted—that which is environmentally friendly, satisfying to consumer expectations of availability and use, and fairly priced is preferred to that which is not. At issue were the facts used to reason through that premise to the conclusion regarding which fuels are best for society. Facts: Liquefied petroleum gas (LPG), compressed natural gas (CNG), methanol, ethanol and electricity "are impractical and uneconomic today for widespread use" (1995). What is available is reformulated gasoline, RFG, "a new generation of motor fuel engineered to reduce auto emissions and improve air quality." The ad discussion included details on how this gasoline works to satisfy the expectations of regulators, activists, and manufacturers. A single ad (1995) further demonstrated the characteristics of alternative fuels. LPG can only be used in limited quantities because "there are no facilities to import large volumes and no pipeline system to distribute them." Large investments would be needed to supply LPG and CNG, the latter fuel having limitations for personal use because vehicles using this fuel "can go only one quarter the distance of cars powered by gasoline," an issue of convenience. Methanol is expensive to manufacture, even when it is derived from garbage; it has limited distribution facilities and like CNG, allows drivers limited driving distances. Ethanol is made from corn, which requires substantial amounts of fuel to cultivate and harvest. Electric fuel cells: "It's expected to take decades before the large cost and engineering problems can be solved." The solution presented is RFG. The persona of Mobil is the benevolent engineer and manager who is planning, conducting research, and operating in the public interest—exhibiting goodwill—and letting the public in on its thinking. The policy solution (1994) was this: Use RFG, and

> If we observe all the laws now on the books, promote mandatory emissions testing in states that don't now have it, and enforce those standards strictly, we'll all breathe easier. What's more, we won't threaten our economy with unreasonable burdens that hamper growth and jobs.

With arguments such as these, Mobil wanted to free the corporate Gulliver from the petty Lilliputians who would keep it from realizing its potential; it asked readers to realize the excellence in engineering and business planning in which Mobil engaged. It invited key publics to recognize the attributes that differentiate Mobil from its competitors because of its aggressive political, economic, and social stances. It adopted the identity of the gentle, benevolent giant that acts with goodwill. Not all critics saw Mobil's persona in a favorable light. For instance, Simons (1983) criticized it for reiterating versions of the standard theme, Things are better for everyone when the free enterprise system can work to its fullest extent. This disarming theme, Simons reasoned, led Mobil to present a persona of the bower bird, which creates an attractive nest to lure and deceive a mate. In contrast, Crable and Vibbert (1983) employed the famed Prometheus story to examine the rhetorical impact of "Observations." As the "bringer of fire," Mobil, by its own estimation, is sorely misunderstood and punished for the exact reason it should be applauded.

Through its issue advertising, Mobil has worked to present a goodwill persona, champion of the public interest. More than other compliance-gaining strategies, Mobil has employed moral appeal and drawn on its expertise to predict positive consequences for compliance and negative ones for noncompliance (Smith & Heath, 1990).

In its issues communication, Mobil adopted a persona to differentiate itself from other companies that will not boldly take stances on vital issues. Mobil champions free expertise in behalf of the public interest, environmentalism, free speech, fairness in pubic debate, and efficiency in governmental actions and policies. Schmertz (1986) reported that the aggressive issue campaign stance of Mobil Oil Company attracted consumers who admire that corporate persona. This issues communication program was part of the company's cause-related and affinity-of-purpose marketing plan. The result was measurable, in so far as 31% of a public survey preferred Mobil products compared to 16% for Exxon, 15% for Chevron, and 10% for Texaco.

This section has discussed the value of organizational image, reputation management. Key elements seem central to any organization's persona: differentiation, association, identity, and goodwill. These factors become featured in what each organization does and says. They are essential rhetorical components in the efforts of businesses, industries, activists, and governmental agencies. They guide the organization's efforts to manage its reputation.

 Issues Communication as Argument

Some discussants of organizations' communication believe that argument is not two-way or symmetrical and wish that argument did not occur. Close examination reveals that an argument is inherently two-way. It takes two parties to disagree. Parties disagree because facts often are subjected to different evaluations and interpretations. Predictions frequently are based on subjective probabilities, estimates of what will occur. Concerns that argument is not symmetrical can derive from disparity in the ability of one organization (a large corporation) to spend more on its effort than another (a small environmental group). Other factors than money enter this equation. Reportage can balance the equation, at least to a degree. Goliaths do not always win but are often defeated. The best advocates are those who listen to the views of others and know when to agree, disagree, and supply information and opinion to continue a mutually beneficial discussion. We should not be alarmed by the terms *advocate, argue, debate, assert,* or *capitulate.* Those terms are used to dissect and analyze issues communication. They characterize the rhetorical issues of all public policy segments, including—perhaps especially— activists (Wallack et al., 1993).

Issues managers do not want to go forward with a strategic business plan, a public policy plan, or a communication plan without having a firm sense of the facts of the case, knowing the premises and values that are used to reason about the facts, and understanding the policy positions that are being advocated. A wise organization uses sound argument to support its own decisions and those of its stakeholders.

Opinions relevant to strategic business planning and operations of organizations exist at macrosocial, community, and personal levels. Macrosocial opinions are unlikely to yield to efforts by a single company, an industry, activist group, media commentator, or governmental agency. Formation of macrosocial opinions requires years, even decades. The glacial movement of such opinions is the result of concerted and sustained efforts by activists, industries, and political parties. At lower levels—community—closer to the firm and the issues, communication efforts can be more successful as the persons involved use macrosocial opinions to make localized decisions.

Under consideration are relevant facts, values, and policies. Propositions of fact are objectively verifiable. Value judgments center on principles regarding right and wrong, better or worse. Propositions of policy are "ought" statements basic to choices, the most rewarding or beneficial of which are preferred. These argument components are valuable for analyzing what advocates should and do say when considering the public policy stance they choose to take. Advantage can be gained by contesting or adapting principles to performance options and image components of companies and industries. The contest will decide what principles are applicable, in what ways, and to what conclusions—thereby creating a zone of meaning shared by stakeholders and stakeseekers.

In this argument, issues communication *uses widely accepted premises, defends contested premises, advocates new premises,* and *challenges or champions policies.* Issue stances enlist audiences to take actions in support of policies; they stress the reward-cost basis for supporting or opposing those policies and the actions that result from them. The following review suggests the diverse platforms of fact that companies, activists, and governmental officials consider as part of public policy decision making:

> Profit margins, such as that on a gallon of gasoline, an issue contested during the oil embargo years of the 1970s
>
> Amount of secondary tobacco smoke nonsmokers inhale during a month
>
> Costs and problems involved in generating and transmitting electricity
>
> Costs of overregulation, such as a report by the tobacco industry that some businesses that banned smoking suffered financial harm
>
> Amounts of pollutants produced by companies, municipalities, and individual families
>
> Improvements in operating procedures and results of those changes
>
> Policy by tobacco companies, including contested claims that they do not target minors with their product advertising and do not spike cigarettes with nicotine
>
> Safety record of operations, especially for industries that ostensibly create risks, such as chemical companies or electric generating utilities, including those that use nuclear fuel
>
> Quality of products and services
>
> Health effects of eating foods that have been sprayed with pesticides or that result from biotechnology

Such facts, often widely and sharply contested, provide insight relevant to operations of companies and industries as well as to the rhetorical stances of activists and governmental agencies.

In addition to facts, issues communicators discuss values to establish the standards of acceptable corporate responsibility, the foundations of corporate policy and operation. The following statements illustrate typical value positions discussed:

Virtues of free enterprise as the basis for enhanced lifestyles and increased quality and variety of goods and services

Virtues of regulation or deregulation

Virtues of environmental quality

Virtues of companies' being allowed to discuss controversial issues in public

Virtues of achievement through innovation, hard work, and profit incentive

Virtues of working together to solve problems

Virtues of having companies large enough to solve problems, especially those requiring sufficient capital to search for and produce oil

Virtues of commitment to safety and health of persons who use specific products and services

Virtues of using technology to solve problems, such as the use of nuclear energy to reduce greenhouse gases

Rather than meeting absolute standards of verifiability as is possible with facts, value issues require personal or collective judgment that draws conclusions based on principles central to the good of society. One major rhetorical advantage of value appeals is their ability to be used to achieve common ground with key publics through the identification of mutual interests.

Based on the interaction of fact and value, issues communicators contest the wisdom, advisability, and expedience of policy. Policy recommendations are characterized by "oughts" or "shoulds." The logic is this: If specific facts are true and if certain values prevail, a policy should be created (defeated) because it is reasonable (unreasonable). The overlap between fact and value gets us squarely at the importance of propositions of policy, as evidenced in the following examples:

Should require state or federal legislation to foster innovation and corporate reorganization for citizens and companies to take full advantage of communication technologies required to create the information superhighway

Should cut government spending to lower taxes and enhance personal and corporate finances

Should implement or modify air and water quality legislation

Should restrict products that produce health or safety problems

Should change domestic mineral exploration policies, such as allowing oil exploration in environmentally sensitive areas

Should support the natural gas industry as an environmentally friendly fuel

Should regulate tobacco as a drug

Such policy positions are debated by opponents who supply key audiences with information about advantages or disadvantages of specific legislation or regulation.

Policy statements appear to be most persuasive when they foster the self-interest of targeted publics as well as the sponsors. In issues communication, propositions of fact are important as people engaged in a debate attempt to understand an issue. Evidence has to be obtained and weighed to determine which policy choice it and the appropriate values support. A case study demonstrates that point. It centers on dioxin, which, according to researchers, is a potent carcinogen that is pervasive in the environment. Abatement has already cost, and will cost, millions of private and public dollars. For this reason, the parties involved with dioxin have had reason to reconsider its effect on health.

New evidence produced in 1992 led the Center for Disease Control (CDC) in Atlanta and the EPA to reconsider their stance on the harmfulness of the chemical. This reconsideration was welcomed by the paper manufacturing industry, which was suffering extensive costs to abate the emission of dioxin. The stance by the CDC and EPA resulted from research touted by the American Paper Institute (API) and the Chlorine Institute. Both circulated data from research that challenged previous reports that linked dioxin to cancer. According to Bailey (1992), these reports were questionable because they lacked scientific objectivity. The API revisited a 14-year-old study and the Chlorine Institute commissioned findings that it reported selectively. Ellen Silbergeld, a toxicologist at the University of Maryland, called the studies lies. Indeed, other studies suggested that dioxin may be more harmful than was previously concluded. Some researchers fear that dioxin may work in combination with other known carcinogens to increase the potency of the attack on cell structure.

The ongoing debate between the EPA and paper and chlorine makers focuses on the level of exposure a test animal or human must have with dioxin before damage results, a recurrent theme in risk assessment and risk communication. Many substances can be harmful, but the issue is dose response, the amount of a chemical a person must be exposed to for any period of time before harmful effects occur. This equation is the crux of this debate. Environmental and community action groups argue for conservative measures regarding how much dioxin exposure is safe, whereas the paper and chlorine industries argue that higher levels are safe. Such debates lead government, activists, and companies to commission research. People pore over old findings looking for flaws that have resulted in false conclusions. Facts are debated in this case, not values. If the chemical is harmful, the values warrant policies to govern its control.

Platforms of Fact: Information as the Basis of Issue Arguments

Campaigns should provide information that publics want to understand key aspects of business operations and policies. People pay attention to and carefully consider information when it helps them make decisions that are confronting them (Atkin, 1973; Heath, Liao, et al., 1995; Petty & Cacioppo, 1986). Company spokespersons complain that they cannot get audiences to listen to what they have to say. Perhaps what they have to say is deemed irrelevant by the audiences.

Mendelsohn (1973) found that information campaigns are effective when they (a) provide information in a neutral fashion, (b) show people that they know less than they thought they knew, (c) and give information that the audience perceives to be valuable. In a 1983 series of op-eds, Mobil used this strategy to address the question, "Just how profitable is oil?" At the top of each ad in the series, Mobil posed a true-false quiz. In one, Mobil stated, "Oil companies make a large volume of dollars," followed with the answer, "That's true." It posed another statement, "Oil companies are therefore very profitable." The answer: "That's false." The message was designed to prove these propositions. In a second advertisement, Mobil asked, "In 1981, the 25 leading U.S. oil companies spent $44 billion, up from $33 billion the year before, to try to find and produce oil and natural gas around the world." This answer was, "That's true." The second question was "Two thirds of those investments were made right here in the United States," followed by, "Also true." The rest of the quiz went this way:

> But the payout in oil and gas is so great that such huge sums can be risked safely, producing almost surefire big profits. That's false, even though a lot of people seem to believe it. The oil industry, despite all its complaining about high taxes, could afford to pay more. Also false, and there a real danger of killing the goose in the quest for more golden eggs.

Most people enjoy quizzes. Once readers think they know what answer is correct, they may be more receptive to information that confirms or disconfirms that belief.

In 1984, USCEA ads asked, "Do other countries know something about nuclear energy that we don't know?" These ads, called "Energy Updates," presented snippets of information in a reportorial style. Appearing in newspapers of the caliber of *The Wall Street Journal,* the series briefed the reader on the progress of the nuclear generating industry. Advertisement headlines in 1984 suggest the themes discussed: "Without nuclear power, U.S. trade deficit would be worse;" "U.S. electric use hits new peak; coal, nuclear meet the added demand;" and "Record-setting plant shows clear benefits of nuclear energy to U.S." Ad content such as this could help establish a platform of fact useful in making informed—if controversial—regulatory decisions.

Allstate Insurance, for example, participated in the automobile air bag safety controversy to help increase public awareness and bring pressure for acceptance of the device. In 1972, only 17% of the public viewed air bags as viable safety devices; 5 years later, this number had risen to 55%, even though the bags still were unavailable on U.S. passenger vehicles (Ewing, 1980).

The chemical industry and its counterparts are confronted with massive challenges to spend billions to reduce emissions that can result in improved environmental quality and safer health conditions for people and animals that reside near chemical plants. Using national news magazines and television news channels and in proximity to news and commentary segments, the Chemical Manufacturers Association used three ads in 1994 and 1995 to describe improvements in engineering technologies and plant operations. One ad began with the image of a chemical plant emitting particles into the environment. It depicted an animated character climbing the smokestack and bending it back into the plant to indicate that the industry was containing and using what it had previously emitted into the environment. A second ad addressed the question, "What if someone found a way to convert some of our chemical waste into energy?" The answer: "In just one year, the member companies of the Chemical Manufacturers Association captured over 1 billion pounds of toxic chemical waste for conversion to energy." The third ad asked: "What's the most important thing to do after keeping 93% of our toxic chemical waste out of the environment?" The answer: "The EPA and the Chemical Manufacturers Association have targeted 311 compounds as top priorities for action. We kept 93% of these compounds out of the environment through treatment, recycling, and energy conversion." Each of these ads indicates that the Chemical Manufacturers Association companies are not resting on these accomplishments but seeking to achieve even greater successes.

Values as the Basis of Issue Arguments

According to Wallace (1963), rhetorical statements raise ethical considerations and address the choices that confront people—and organizations: "When we justify, we praise or blame; we use terms like right and wrong, good and bad; in general we *appraise*" (p. 243). Through public debate, people contest the "goodness" of reasons. As Weaver (1970) reasoned, "Rhetoric is advisory; it has the office of advising men [and women] with reference to an independent order of goods and with reference to their particular situation as it relates to these" (p. 211). Such stances rest on assertion and counterassertion as the expression of self-interests. In light of tensions between evaluation and counterevaluation, we are forced to answer the question Burke (1946) raised: "How can a world with rhetoric stay decent, how can a world without it exist at all?"

In the mid-1980s, United Technologies conducted a campaign to laud free enterprise and individual initiative. To counter what the firm believed to be a broad attack on free enterprise, it championed freedom and individual achievement. It reasoned that if free enterprise is vital to the nation, then an attack on it weakens the foundations of the nation. One ad championed commonsense (1984). Another praised courage and conviction, as exemplified by Susan B. Anthony (1984), and ability to rise in business as did Conrad Hilton and John Paul Getty (1984). The company rejoiced in the virtues of personal thrift and blasted governmental deficit spending (1984). A rawboned faith in competition permeated its ad that reflected on the changes in corporate giants. It noted that every year since 1955, *Fortune* had listed the top 500 corporations. Each year, some names drop off and new ones are added. From these data, the ad generalized, "Resting on past results doesn't keep you in the 500. Remember: Every day another product goes the way of the buggy whip. So don't abdicate. Innovate" (1984). United Technologies reminded readers that no matter how humble someone is, he or she may think up a new product or service that changes history. "Remember, someone had to invent the paper clip, contact lenses, and the clothespin. So start thinking. Your clothespin may be waiting around the corner" (1984). The ads were simple and to the point. They stressed the value perspectives that define the U.S. character. In this way, they constituted statements on issues of value.

Platform of Policy

Policy statements are contestable recommendations that if specific steps are taken, desired outcomes will be achieved or undesirable consequences will be avoided. Making a policy argument, the Asphalt Institute appealed to readers to let "your lawmakers know where you stand on preserving our streets and highways. The deterioration of the nation's road system must be stopped, before it stops us" (Garbett, 1981, p. 21). The objective of policy arguments is to assert the wisdom of preferred choices—the creation of a zone of meaning with key stakeholders.

W. R. Grace & Company's 1979 campaign against a proposed increase in the capital gains tax is another example of a firm's attempt to create a zone of meaning in support of a policy position. Fighting the tax increase, Grace compiled statistics to support its belief that more taxes would harm the economy. Those statistics became the basis for a series of ads bearing headlines such as "Taxes Up, Productivity Down, Could We Be Doing Something Wrong?" That particular execution was so convincing that it also ran as an editorial in the *Wall Street Journal* and as an article (bylined J. Peter Grace, chief executive officer of W. R. Grace) in both the *New York Daily News* and *Los Angeles Times*. In addition to advertising, Grace incorporated its statistics into a 49-page memorandum delivered to every member of Congress. The results were gratifying to Grace, to say the least: Instead of increasing the tax from 49% to 52%, Congress reduced it to 28%. Grace officials believed their advocacy campaign played an important role in fostering a zone of meaning that influenced the outcome. The campaign has paid dividends ever since. As Stephen B. Elliot, director of Corporate Advertising at W. R. Grace, told *Madison Avenue* magazine, "This campaign opened relations with Congress we never had before. . . . Grace suddenly became an authority in Washington." Subsequently, J. Peter Grace emerged as a celebrity by heading the Private Sector Cost Control Presidential Commission that spotlighted practical ways to reduce government waste (Hush, 1983, pp. 8-9). In 1986, Grace sponsored an televised issue ad titled, "The Deficit Trial," which depicted a courtroom where youths in the year 2017 brought criminal charges against their elders who had not stanched the growth of the national debt. The children were in a dimly lit courtroom, in tattered clothes, as an elder apologized for the fiscal indiscretion of his generation.

The electric, natural gas, and telephone service industries operate in a stormy political climate in which issues involving rate are raised. For decades, various interests took stances on the issue of utility rates, looking to regulatory bodies to keep them within reasonable bounds. In the 1990s, a new direction occurred in this policy contest. Advocates for lower rates as well as corporate entities seeking to develop or expand a niche market looked to legislation to allow competition in industries that traditionally had been regulated monopolies. Throughout the United States, state legislatures have been debating the best ways to introduce competition into the sale of electricity, natural gas, and telephone service.

Another key policy debate of the 1990s has been the balance of interests that clash over myriad topics under the umbrella policy issue of environmentalism. Wanting individuals to share their portion of responsibility for pollution, industries have pressed for careful investigation and the development of policies that place blame where it deserves to be lodged. If industry pollutes, then it must change its policies. The same can be said for individuals who damage air quality by driving their automobiles and using backyard barbecues. The nation—indeed the globe—became increasingly aware that policies in one part of the world were not independent of other venues. For instance, shrimpers were constrained from using traditional harvesting methods in an effort to protect sea turtles. Once the cost of gathering shrimp rose, farming efforts could produce shrimp at a competitive rate. That method, however, led to substantial environmental damage along the coasts in developing nations seeking increased revenue.

Policy deliberations feature discussions of fact, interpretations of evaluative premises, and considerations of policies. These three focal points constitute the similarities and dissimilarities in the zones of meaning used by issues communicators. They are the key aspects of advocacy, opinion formation and change, and negotiation.

▶ Campaign Planning

An issue campaign may progress in cycles: set goals, select audiences, state messages, use channels, assess impact, reevaluate goals, reassess strategies, redesign campaign, select channels, execute new strategies, ascertain impact, and reevaluate commitment to the campaign. This section and those that follow consider the strategic stages and options of communication planning, implementation, and evaluation. Issues communicators use a wide array of options ranging from protests to issues ads, congressional hearings, and collaborative decision making.

How issues communicators conceptualize the communication process is likely to influence their success or failure. Contemporary approaches to issues communication avoid the assumption that "if you knew what I knew, you'd make the same decision" (Gaudino, Fritch, & Haynes, 1989, p. 299). Issues managers succeed in understanding the information and opinion needs of all discussants and work to satisfy those needs. When opinions cannot be sustained, the wise issues communicator quickly realizes the limits to which some policy and action can be justified and sets about changing it. The wise issue manager recognizes the virtue of negotiation and uses constructive strategies to maximize mutually beneficial outcomes needed by stakeholder and stakeseeker relationships. Throughout the stages of issues management, organizations are wise to provide preventive maintenance of their reputations.

Communication efforts may attempt to marginalize opponents by denying them proper identity, challenging the rationale of their position, and ignoring them as players in the public policy marketplace. In contrast, communication may empower key stakeholding publics with vital information and invitations to participate in the formation of policy positions.

Issues managers can think in terms of combinations of independent and dependent variables as they plan, execute, and assess their communication efforts. Changes in independent variables are intended to affect dependent variables, such as in the way message content can be thought of as an independent variable. What is said by the organization can affect the understanding or opinion of a public. That change in opinion, for instance, in turn becomes an independent variable that can affect a dependent variable, such as a decision to oppose or support the policies of the sponsoring organization.

One important point to keep in mind is that as independent variables, messages should be tailored to the self-interests and opinion development needs of each audience, public, or stakeholder. Totally different messages need not be created for each audience on the assumption that it has unique self-interests and opinion needs; rather, campaign planners should decide on the specific theme to get across and express that theme in messages tailored to the interests of each group (MacEwen & Wuellner, 1987).

International Paper Company, for instance, in a 1995 ad, featured the theme of using forest technology to develop better, faster growing trees and to plant more than are harvested. The message of environmental responsibility was designed to meet activist expectations, to demonstrate current and long-term profit potential to investors, to applaud innovative and responsible employees, and to provide a forest legacy to future generations while meeting demand for paper products. The challenge is to maintain a single theme tailored to the interests of each audience.

Issues managers should realize that audiences tend to accept what they want to learn about issues and reject what they do not want to know or believe. Breaking through the barriers of doubt and refutation can be difficult. Advocates of social judgment theory (Sherif, Sherif, & Nebergall, 1965) postulated that people consider ideas in messages through latitudes of acceptance, rejection, or noncommitment. These latitudes lead individuals to strategically assimilate, filter, reject, and ignore information, based on whether or not it confirms their attitudes. For this reason, people who champion corporations and the role they play in our capitalistic society will be likely to accept and even seek confirming information. If an issue is presented to highly involved publics, even those that initially oppose the issue, with sufficient supporting evidence and reasoning, attitudes can be changed (Petty & Cacioppo, 1986). Key attitudes and values change over time and bring about new standards of what the public will accept or reject (Heath, 1976).

Campaign planning may seek to confirm the attitudes of some stakeholders and to change those of others. Reaching uncommitted segments of the population is difficult because they may have no incentive to learn about the issues or images involved in a particular campaign. The uncommitted may become aware of an issue and realize the need to have an informed opinion only after activists and reporters have made the issue salient. Issues communication is best when it addresses issues people want discussed.

The persuasion theory of information integration (Fishbein & Ajzen, 1975) and the theory of reasoned action (Ajzen & Fishbein, 1980) supply rationales for analyzing attitudes and fostering changes in behavior regarding an organization. Of related importance is the compatibility between those theories and the rhetorical assumption that facts, value premises, and conclusions shed argumentative insights into the ways people make decisions. Information integration features attributes that people use as they think about an organization, industry, activist group, governmental agency, idea, situation, condition, policy, and so forth. These attributes may be positive and negative, a way of understanding that people may have positive and negative reasons for favoring or not favoring something. They balance and integrate these positive and negative attributes as they derive their opinions and attitudes on the topic. The theory of reasoned action suggests that people use norms and expectations they think others have of them, as well as their own attitudes, as they decide to act in one way as opposed to another.

This analysis gives campaign planners rationales for several options. One can be to make negative attributes more salient, or important, in the audience's decision process, thereby increasing the negative valence or decreasing the positive valence in the attitude. More positive (or negative) attributes can be supplied to shift the opinion. Attributes that are thought to be negative may be changed to be positive. The degree to which the attribute is associated with the target of the opinion (such as a company, industry, policy, or process) may be increased or decreased through information relevant to the topic. On matters of actions, the key is the ability of the campaign to address the targeted audience's desire to support and to act favorably toward that which they think brings rewards to them personally or is an expression of their altruism.

Issues communicators should think about targeted populations as the more extreme, less moderate positions on a bell curve. The people nearer the outer or extreme positions on that model are more likely to be in a support or opposition mode and experience higher degrees of issue self-interest (Heath & Douglas, 1991). People who have negative attitudes toward corporations are ripe for information on issues that can lead to regulatory constraints.

Communicating before an event to pave the way for its occurrence may prevent concern from becoming outrage. For example, in 1994, at the dictate of the EPA, the chemical industry began to prepare to create and make public worst-case scenarios. Each company and the industry as a whole was required to define the possibility *and* likelihood of massive, cataclysmic explosions and releases of toxic materials into the atmosphere, including residential neighborhoods. It was expected to reanalyze its emergency response measures as well as take preventive measures to lessen the chance of catastrophe. Concern was expressed by the industry, particularly the technical personnel who were preparing these cases and the corresponding emergency response plans. What would be the news story, that the chemical industry was preparing for total holocaust, or merely complying with an EPA-mandated study that gave the industry added incentive to think through and prepare to avert massive explosions and releases of toxic materials? The key seemed to be establishing liaisons and involving the media, community leaders, and concerned citizens in the process before the announcement so that it can be presented for what it is—a mammoth planning effort to increase the likelihood that no catastrophe will ever occur.

Setting Campaign Goals

Issues communication campaigns can intervene early in the evolution of an issue to prevent—or increase—the likelihood of it becoming ingrained into key publics' mentality. The objective is to keep each stakeholder group attentive to the issue while demonstrating commitment to foster community and countering incorrect information and false changes. Five bits of advice offered by James O'Toole (1975b) warrant consideration. First, organizations should make their identity part of their issue stance. Second, dialogue should begin when key publics become concerned about an issue. Third, each issue campaign "should be based on a healthy respect for the reader's intelligence." Fourth, the campaign position must relate to the self-interests of readers and listeners. Fifth, measurements should test the effectiveness of the campaign (p. 16).

Offering advice on how to position issue communication, Stridsberg (1977) featured several desirable functions: (a) to correct misinformation and misunderstanding, (b) to warn targeted publics of dire outcomes that will result if they do not support a specific issue position, (c) to mobilize constituent support, (d) to counterattack, (e) to compare and contrast both sides of an issue, and (f) to request supporters to do something in behalf of the cause.

Careful issue analysis is needed because of the nature of issue decisions and people's ability and willingness to simplify issues to their basic components. Planning and design should assume that carefully selected key points are much more likely to succeed than enormous amounts of information and opinion. Research and issue analysis should help reveal the bits of information and decision criteria that truly make a difference.

Campaigns must adapt to the needs and interests of targeted audiences and are more credible when they make statements that the audiences can verify. The IAA reported the difficulty public relations and advertising agencies have had in helping corporate managers realize that in many instances, they are communicating a message they want heard rather than the message an audience wants to hear. Because of the tendency to blame misunderstanding on ill-informed statements by activist groups and media reporters, corporate communicators may have difficulty acknowledging that their company must first level with the public (Stridsberg, 1977).

Issues management is more than fire fighting. It maintains dialogue and collaborative decision making with key publics. Long-term commitment can establish a platform of information and create zones of meaning. It can forestall the criticism that companies only go to publics when they are being picked on by the media, activists, or governmental agents. In conducting an audit, the International Association of Business Communicators suggested that companies determine what information key publics require to make sound decisions and commit to get that information to them (Reuss & Silvis, 1981).

Issue messages should be tested before they are placed into channels. Matrix organization of issues management teams brings together many disciplines (and outside topic specialists) that can be used to develop arguments and design messages. The issue needs to be addressed in a way that is relevant to the targeted audience. One of the worst mistakes an issues campaign can make is to tell an audience what it already believes or acknowledges, while not addressing key issues on the audience's mind. Such campaigns may work against the sponsor's credibility because poor campaign design can reinforce the opinion that the organization does not care to provide sufficient and worthwhile information.

 Listening to Key Publics and Targeting Audiences

Careful stakeholder and key public analysis needs to be central to issues monitoring and analysis as well as all phases of the planning, design, implementation, and assessment of issues communication. Issues managers should determine which publics demonstrate the greatest concern and which stakeholders' support is vital to the issue at hand. Crucial audiences, in the form of key publics, come to the organization rather than the organization having to seek them. Stressing the value of this analysis, Garbett (1981) advised, "It is essential to understand the current climate and environment within which the corporation operates" (p. 156).

Corporate issue messages need to be vetted through responsible activist groups to avoid unfortunate rebuttals and eventual admissions of error or bias. At least one timber company has worked in coalition with environmental groups to discuss the responsible growth and harvesting of woods products and the responsible use of natural resources by people—students and their families—as well as companies. The USCEA allowed activist groups concerned about nuclear power plant safety to review and edit its pronuclear issue ads.

A valuable audience is the membership of the organization sponsoring the issues campaign. Employees of the corporation, the industry, and related industries have a vested interest in the outcome of policy formation and regulation. Labor groups represent a community of interest that could be detrimentally affected by dramatic changes in the operating requirements of their industries. Political education for employees is a valuable part of the corporate communication program. Companies should establish legislative and political support systems to help employees learn when and how to write letters to legislators, conduct meetings with officials, and speak in behalf of the company. Keeping everyone accurately informed and carefully coordinated becomes a difficult but vital issues management task.

Employee's willingness to engage in political activity on behalf of their company, such as writing letters and contacting legislators, is the result of several variables working together: organizational commitment (based on the employee's position in the corporate organizational hierarchy, the amount of company stock owned, and tenure with the company), prior record of non-company political activism, amount of information seeking to become informed on public policy matters, and degree of cognitive involvement. The profile of the employee who would be most likely to engage in governmental relations activities is one with more organizational commitment and more noncorporate political activity. Coupled to that is a high amount of information seeking and higher cognitive involvement (Heath, Douglas, et al., 1995). One could argue that this is the profile of the external activist as well as the procorporate activist.

Despite obvious advantages to be gained by building employees into the issues management team, some companies take the stance that employees must be mute regarding corporate mistakes. Otten (1984) concluded, "Slowly but steadily, states are beginning to protect employees who blow the whistle on dangerous or improper business behavior" (p. 11). Even Mobil, a strident advocate for open communication, settled out of court with an employee who had been fired as being incompetent. She had reported two toxic chemical accidents that occurred at Mobil's Environmental Health and Sciences Laboratory. Such incidents demonstrate the inconsistency between corporate policy and behavior and counteract efforts to involve employees in efforts to achieve corporate responsibility. Provisions in the Mine Safety and Health Act, the Toxic Substances Control Act, the Occupational Safety and Health Act, and the Water Pollution Control Act protect workers who report violations. Some companies have established programs to protect employees who report corporate mistakes.

Media reporters and broadcast managers are targeted audiences whose gatekeeping determines what information gets to the public and how it will be phrased. As Wallack et al. (1993) demonstrated, activists focus their issue advocacy to gain attention of reporters and program directors. In this way, their concerns and solutions make their way into the public dialogue. Reporters and program directors have substantial impact on the issues agenda because they decide the content of the news and how much of the news hole each item receives. They tell people that certain topics are worth thinking about because they are important enough to appear on the front page or at the top of the news hour.

Most issues managers recognize that media representatives pride themselves on their objectivity. They have their own perspectives on issues that govern what is said and how the information is presented. Not only do these persons inject their opinions in the presentation of the news, but they also are influenced by the news policy of the organization for which they work. Investigative reporters seek stories about corporate and industry failure to comply with standards of public acceptance. To deal proactively with this power, issues communicators often address the press in an attempt to build a platform of understanding. An important responsibility of issues communicators is to be sure the press receives accurate and reliable information so that it can cut through the enormous flood of information available. Issues communicators can provide information that helps reporters understand the organization's point of view and operations.

Attempts to inform media leaders and reinforce their commitment to fair and informed reportage have been made by corporate leaders. In this fashion, Robert W. Lundeen (1983), then Chairman of the Board of Dow Chemical Company, was the keynote speaker at the annual Business Journalism Awards banquet of the Interstate National Gas Association at the University of Missouri—Columbia. He took as his theme the words of Thomas Jefferson who had come to believe, "Nothing can now be believed which is seen in a newspaper." The relevance of this observation was the gap between the "media elite" and the "business elite." He observed, "A very wide cultural gap lies between working journalists in newspapers, television and radio and most, if not all, industrial executives and professionals." The problem is that "neither side quite understands what the other is up to. Neither side quite trusts the other's. And so there is hostility." The gap translated into divergent perceptions. Dow executives saw themselves as savvy, competent, and responsible. When they read about themselves, they got the picture of "arrogant polluters, insensitive to the health of their own workers, of consumers of their products, and of plant neighbors." One problem is the expectation by journalists that business problems have simple solutions. He begged the press to double-check facts and to seek them from a variety of sources. He asked writers to try to understand that the company is not inherently evil and therefore should not immediately be approached with suspicion. He championed a dialogue, but encouraged writers "to get it right and then tell it right so that 235 million Americans can judge it right."

Another corporate representative, T. M. Ford (1984), CEO of Emhart, spoke as he received the 1984 Leadership Award for excellence in communication from the International Association of Business Communicators. His theme centered on the challenge and cooperation that can exist between corporations and professional communicators to increase the quality of communication. Such messages may build a more supportive climate for corporations.

As they grow in size and stature, organizations—business, media, governmental, and activist—shoulder a stewardship responsibility to engage with others who are concerned about important issues and pressing problems. Through careful listening to one another and by fostering public dialogue, these organizations can advance society and create mutually beneficial relationships. To do so, they must be willing to listen, speak openly and candidly, and work for the betterment of the community—the collection of publics and audiences whose interests are interpenetrating.

 Communication Vehicles

Sophisticated campaigns strategically use every communication channel available to reach key publics and build or adapt to zones of meaning that are mutually beneficial. In this effort, many modes of communication are worth consideration:

Issues advertising

Sponsored books, editorials

Negotiation

Executive comments

Public affairs programming

Press releases, media relations

Personal contact with opinion leaders by key staff and management personnel

Video and satellite presentations to internal and external audiences

Congressional testimony, public hearings

Mailings to constituencies

Bill stuffers

Conference paper presentations

Trials

Open houses, issue workshops

Educational information relevant to activist, government or industry issues that can be distributed through schools

Joint research efforts

Placed and commissioned articles

Employee communication

Internal and external newsletters

Speakers bureaus

Annual financial or special topic reports

Videos mailed to key audiences and on request

Op-eds placed on editorial pages

Talk show appearances

Electronic mail and bulletin boards

Billboards

Special issue documents

Scholarly papers (commissioned)

Citizens advisory committees

Lobbying

Web sites

Legislative position papers

Collaborative decision making

Consumer 1-800 numbers can be useful for assisting customers in the proper use of a service or product; in addition, those numbers provide access for individuals who want to complain about products or services—potentially useful information for issue scanning and analysis. Those numbers can be provided for key publics to use to obtain key bits of information during a crisis or on some issue. Organizations use e-mail to interact with key publics on their inquiries and comments, especially via Internet, Netscape, or World Wide Web. Communication technologies allow for interactive means for delivering and receiving public policy information.

Enterprising company, trade association, and activist groups make available interactive computer-CD systems that allow students or concerned members of a community to manage a forest profitably and in ways that are environmentally responsible. Or they might solve problems related to community air or water quality standards and regulation of the source of those pollutants. Coalitions with stakeholder groups can be used—through their communication channels—to reach persons who are interested in their opinions.

New communication technologies are offering options that increase the response rate to concerned persons and narrow casting, with the personal touch of quick response to questions by concerned citizens. Companies, governmental offices, trade associations, and environmental groups can establish electronic bulletin boards and discussion groups that allow concerned influence leaders to ask questions and receive speedy responses and engage in issue discussion.

Annual reports can explain challenges and efforts undertaken to meet social responsibility expectations. As well as discussing these efforts in the financial annual reports, firms publish special "corporate responsibility" reports, as did Phillips Petroleum Company in 1994. This publication contained a mixture of attractive copies of nature paintings, graphics, and photographs of plant operations and personnel. A typical theme presented in this report was captured in the following conclusion:

> After adjusting for the sale of three facilities, Phillips reduced releases of SARA III chemicals by 3 percent in 1993 and increased on-site treatment and off-site recycling of the chemicals by 40 percent and 34 percent, respectively. We also closely monitor what happens to materials that are released to the environment. (Phillips Petroleum Company, 1994, p. 14)

Reports can be sent to key legislative, regulatory, company, and activist personnel, demonstrating not only the organization's progress and commitment to solve important problems but also its openness to public scrutiny regarding its efforts.

Issues communicators find advantages to using several media to increase the reach of their messages; they optimize the advantages each medium offers for issue presentation. Print media and video are useful for giving detailed presentations and have a permanence that television and radio lack. Print media are easily photocopied by persons who want to share issue positions with friends and acquaintances. Television and video offer dramatic presentations; color, sound, and movement can add impact. This electronic medium allows for the personalities of key personnel to be brought to life.

Mass dissemination of issues messages has limitations, such as not reaching people who need and want the information. Thus, issue communicators develop narrower, more tailored forms of communication. Companies often buy ad space in magazines of critics to reach that group of readers from whom they have tended to be alienated in the past. For instance, company or industry ads are placed in environmental group publications, thereby reaching a highly involved audience rather than spending millions on a campaign that only reaches disinterested readers and viewers. Companies and other organizations are learning the value of using public hearings and workshops to reach concerned citizens, such as those who worry about the route to be taken by a new electric transmission power line or a natural gas or other product pipeline. It is not uncommon to hear about utility companies, solid waste management companies, or petrochemical companies creating advisory panels of concerned citizens to solve problems of citing facilities (Heath, 1995).

Open houses and public hearings allow face-to-face contact, an opportunity for concerned citizens to ask questions and get to know key personnel involved with issues and controversial processes. These opportunities give the organization and its publics the opportunity to create or share zones of meaning that foster mutual interests of all parties, fostering compromise and joint decision making. Such strategies can empower concerned persons in a community who monitor their experience as tangible evidence of their ability to get the company, activist group, or governmental agency to respond to and address their concerns.

From an era where most of the issues communication was mass mediated, the trend is toward more open and dialogic interaction in more intimate opportunities. People on all sides of issues recognize the advantages of getting to know persons with whom they have disputes. Developing personal rapport is a major step toward collaborative decision making.

 Campaign Assessment

Tracking issues communication is a counterpart to issues monitoring. The goal is to track what is being said by whom and with what effect on the life cycle of each issue. From a corporate perspective, campaign tracking has the same advantages as does tracking operating costs, production, profits, and employee turnover and satisfaction. Measuring the impact of issues management efforts is difficult, because many variables and players interact to affect how an issue develops. Rarely is any factor decisive in the outcome of an issue. No organization can totally "manage" an issue. Issue assessment can go awry when executives expect or demand change that is daunting given the nature of issues, publics, and attitude formation or change.

Standard methodologies for campaign assessment feature precampaign and postcampaign image and issue position comparison. Organizations can be unnecessarily frustrated by ostensible failure or self-satisfied by success that simply is not true. The foundation of assessment is knowing what can and is to be gained, having reasonable measures, gathering data by proper methodologies, and analyzing it candidly and honestly.

To accurately and honestly assess the success of their issues communication campaign, the first step is to know what objectives are desired. Issues communication plans should be designed and executed with specific objectives in mind. These objectives should be framed as dependent variables that are planned to be affected by changes in a complex chain of independent and dependent variables.

In conjunction with data generated from instruments such as surveys and focus groups, assessment can be integrated with the issues monitoring process—looking for indicators, such as activist-group or company position changes regarding an issue. Issue campaign design and execution are more impressive in boardroom discussions when they are attached to tangible measures and translated into stakes granted (or withheld) by stakeholders. Measures are difficult to generate and employ in accurate and candid ways unless the issue communication is based on how people receive and think about information, become knowledgeable on an issue, make judgments, form attitudes and beliefs, decide on appropriate actions, and act or fail to act in the predicted way based on their attitudes.

Behavioral measures can include formation or changes in alliances, shifts in reporters' positions and reporting styles from unfavorable to favorable, and issue support or opposition. Tracking strategies can be used to determine shifts in opinion and may ascertain what influences are having the greatest impact on opinions held by key publics.

Tracking and monitoring measures need to be carefully integrated with the issues management objectives. One measure might be information level. If a key public knows more on the issue after the campaign or at milestones, the issues manager can conclude that that aspect of the campaign is working. By taking the facts, values, and policies approach, an issues communicator can estimate shifts in levels of knowledge, understanding, and appreciation of what values are relevant to the issue and understand the policy and its implications for the company, industry, and public. Persons who assess issues communication can increase their sensitivity to stakeholder concerns and differences of opinions by establishing rapport with stakeholders.

Each survey should not try to encompass all of the opinions embedded in a large public policy debate but should consider those most relevant to the organization's interest in the issue and the opinions of key publics. Evidence of this point was found in a survey conducted by Yankelovich, Skelly, and White regarding the effectiveness of the Mobil Oil Company and the American Forest Institute issues communication campaigns in the late 1970s. Data indicated that opinion leaders were aware of Mobil ads; 90% of congressional and other government leaders had read them. But 66% of those readers believed the ads to be of little value for understanding energy deregulation. Mobil advertisements had done little to influence key public opinions on the energy crisis; only 6% of the respondents considered them to be credible, whereas 53% believed they lacked credibility (Adkins, 1978).

Looking at an issue from the macrosocial level, the Yankelovich study concluded that the American Forest Institute was effective in winning public favor when it provided information helpful for readers' understanding of its industry; effectiveness fell when the communication became adversarial (Adkins, 1978). The Institute's "trees are the renewable resource" campaign demonstrated impact on opinions. In 1974, 34% of the sample thought that the forests were being managed well; by 1980, this percentage had increased to 55 (Pincus, 1980, p. 63).

If issues management is going to help the sponsoring organization achieve its strategic business plan, then assessment needs to be built into the communication plan. If assessment is an afterthought, issues managers are prone to use research to justify what they have been doing. A well-designed issues management program builds assessment measures and milestones into the campaign design and ties it to the corporate mission and strategic business planning efforts. The ultimate outcome of issues communication is to create harmony and foster mutually beneficial relationships with all key audiences and publics.

 **Conclusion**

Recognizing that no organization can dominate the course an issue takes, this chapter addressed issues communication as dialogue—argument reflecting and forming competing and compatible zones of meaning. The substance of that debate leads to policy formation. Although no organization can dominate the debate, each one—as a steward of the democratic process—is obligated to assert its point of view, offering support and reason for its conclusions. In public, each position is debated and policy moves forward.

Legislative, Judicial, and Regulatory Constraints on Issues Communication

Courts and legislatures recognize that corporate entities are "artificial" or "unnatural" persons. As a "person" in the eyes of the law, these entities have rights, privileges, and responsibilities. Among those is the right to speak responsibly in public—to make statements—on issues of public interest for public policy formation. To "speak" takes many forms, whether paid or unpaid; for instance, advertising—whether using television, a billboard, a newspaper, or radio—is a form of paid speech. Speech can include making financial contributions; to spend money for or against public policy issue positions or political candidates is a form of corporate speech.

Critics of business practices have sought constraints on corporate communication primarily because they worry that the ability to spend substantial sums of money to buy time and space as well as use professional communicators distorts the public dialogue. Deep pockets, some worry, increase the ability to make financial contributions for and against ballot positions, thereby increasing the chances that the corporate interest can prevail over what the public interest otherwise would have been. If businesses have disproportionate impacts on issues and if the stance they take is incorrect, ordinary persons or poorly funded activist groups have limited ability to properly balance the public policy dialogue. The result can be an incorrect and unwise public policy stance, one that is not based on all of the relevant facts or does not give fair hearing to all of the information and opinion that should be brought to bear. Critics of business speech seek to (a) prohibit or limit the amount of money spent on issue campaigns, (b) require all advertising and public relations claims be factual, and (c) bar issue advertisers access to the electronic media—radio and television.

Despite problems, government officials acknowledge the right, indeed the responsibility, of corporate entities to speak on issues that affect their well-being—especially when that interest is tied to the public interest. This principle recognizes that public policy decisions can be wise and informed only if the interested parties put their ideas and information out for public scrutiny. As collectivities of persons acting for a shared interest, organizations are designed to express interests that people cannot make individually. People are allowed to create and join corporate entities on the assumption that such membership is a useful form of financial or public policy power.

Observers acknowledge that interested publics must have the opportunity to obtain accurate, balanced views as to the faults and strengths of corporate behavior, operating requirements, and corporate responsibility (Lukasik, 1981). The question is how to balance that dialogue and limit those players who have the potential of undue influence. On this point, Sethi (1987a) reasoned,

> In order for society to operate in a reasonable, socially equitable and politically acceptable manner, some restrictions are inevitable to curb the excesses of one group while facilitating greater expression for other groups that would otherwise be squeezed out of the market-place of ideas. (p. 281)

Rather than accept this dire view, a more positive one is that by allowing maximum communication by those who have vested interests in each issue's outcome, the dialogue is enriched rather than corrupted. If corporations or activist groups, for instance, place paid advertising asserting their preferred view on an issue, reporters and news commentators become aware of issues they might otherwise not notice or ignore. Alerted to the issue, their reporting of competing points of view can enrich the public policy dialogue, increasing the likelihood that key publics will obtain relevant information and create wise policy conclusions.

Government control of corporate speech is problematic to implement under the best circumstances. Establishing public policy guidelines is complicated by the complex nature of communication and our country's commitment to keep speech as free as possible. American Civil Liberties Union Executive Director Ira Glasser (1983) argued that supporters of restrictions "see the free flow of information as a threat, and seek increasingly to insulate governmental decisions from public debate" (p. 2). However privileged they are, corporations are limited in what they can say, when they can say it, and how they can say it. Issues managers who do not know and appreciate these privileges and restraints are likely to make mistakes regarding the advice they give senior management regarding the design and execution of communication campaigns.

The purpose of this chapter is to examine regulatory, legislative, and judicial constraints regarding issues communication. To this end, this chapter discusses (a) the status of corporate speech, (b) the Federal Communications Commission (FCC), (c) the Internal Revenue Service (IRS), and (d) the FTC. The FCC can influence advertiser access to broadcast channels by overseeing media managers' performance so as to ensure balanced presentation on issues of public interest. The IRS influences what advertising campaign costs may be deducted as ordinary and necessary business expenses. The FTC has made strides toward regulating the content of advertising when it is deemed to be political; the rationale is that information used in public policy debate serves the public interest best when it is accurate.

 ### The Rationale for Organizations Speaking as Citizens

As persons in the eyes of the law, what privileges and responsibilities do organizations enjoy? That question frames this chapter's analysis, which addresses the right or privilege companies and other organizations have to communicate in public. From that basis, the chapter discusses the dialogue regarding the limits on messages that issues communicators wish to present in public. Central to this analysis is the awareness that the courts feel strongly committed to protect individual citizens' rights to know—to receive information and ideas.

Supreme Court decisions grant corporations limited protected rights to speak on issues of public interest (*First National Bank of Boston v. Bellotti,* 1978; *Consolidated Edison Company of New York v. Public Service Commission,* 1980). The basic premise in these decisions is the public value of having companies supply information and argument on public policy issues. The key in such decisions is public interest, the right to know.

The Bellotti case asked whether companies could make financial contributions in support of or in opposition to state referendum questions that did not materially affect their property or business activities. The state of Massachusetts had prohibited such expenditures. First National Bank of Boston and four other corporations wanted to spend money to defeat a referendum item that would have created a graduated personal income tax. The majority view of members of the Supreme Court on this case was that the discussion of public policy issues is central to the First Amendment, the right of persons—whether natural or artificial—to address public issues to inform public policy. If the public's interest is served, the speech is protected. The issue of whether the speaker is materially affected is not relevant to the right of the individual to speak. The larger issue is the value of enlightened public opinion. The public interest is the vital criterion in deciding whether to protect speech. To prohibit companies and other organizations from speaking on referendum issues even when they do not have a direct interest in that issue, the state needs to demonstrate a compelling state interest.

The Supreme Court considered the potential contamination of deep pockets on the political process and concluded that unlike unlimited spending to support political candidates, corruption was unlikely to occur merely because one side could spend more on an issue position than its opponents. Politicians can be "bought" with indebtedness gained through campaign contributions. But issue positions cannot be similarly bought. Ideas are put forth for public consideration without inherent bias that they will play a disproportionately large role, despite the amount of advertising purchased. If a state wishes to limit spending on ballot issues, it must demonstrate a compelling public interest for that restraint.

Even if the advertising purchased by large organizations can influence election outcomes, that does not mean that the influence is inherently contrary to the public interest. Concern about balanced public discussion was addressed by the Court, with the majority view pointing out that *Buckley v. Valeo* (1976) rejected the concept of "equalization" of speech. Buckley, however, affirmed the conclusion that to spend is to speak: If a company contributes or uses money in behalf of or against some issue, the expenditure is speech. The importance of the *Bellotti* case is its affirmation that public discussion of issues is valuable and any restriction on such speech must be founded on a compelling argument that such restriction enhanced the political dialogue.

In *Consolidated Edison of New York v. Public Service Commission of New York* (1980) the justices ruled that Con Edison had a First Amendment right to send out bill stuffers advocating nuclear generation without giving equal time to opponents of the use of nuclear fuel. Nuclear generation, although controversial as an energy source and, therefore, ostensibly political, has substantial commercial importance. Likewise, increased use of electricity has "political" implications. Opponents of the use of nuclear fuel to generate electricity sought to force Con Edison to include their position on the bill stuffers—a kind of balanced discussion of the issue of nuclear generation. Citing *Bellotti,* the Court justified its verdict by reaffirming the public's right to acquire information and downplayed the fear that a captive audience—the persons who received the bills—are likely to be easily and decisively swayed by Con Edison's communication campaign. One issue in this case was the economic incentive the company had for conducting its advocacy campaign. The *Consolidated Edison* ruling found that the bill stuffers were political speech—due to the controversy surrounding the use of nuclear fuel—and not commercial.

In *California Medical Association v. FEC* (1981), the Supreme Court began to be more cognizant of issues that had been raised by minority justices in the previous cases. They questioned whether deep-pockets spending skewed the ballot campaign process. Evidence was entered into the case that indicated that large contributions weakened the individual's influence in the ballot process and skewed the results. Justices writing for the minority applauded the efforts of the election commission to define limits on corporate participation in the ballot campaign process. To spend was to spoil: That was the minority position.

The *Austin v. Michigan Chamber of Commerce* (1990) decision reexamined principles basic to the *Bellotti* decision and laid a foundation for subsequent prohibition or at least restrictions on the rights of organizations to speak on issues of public policy. The chamber sought to fulfill its organizational mission by spending money from its treasury to buy newspaper advertising space to promote a specific candidate running for office in the Michigan House of Representatives. The chamber's message was that this candidate would work to foster jobs and strengthen the economy. A Michigan election statute prohibited such expenditures. The Supreme Court upheld the election statute, based on the public's need and right to know the issues in public policy debates, including those central to political campaigns.

The theme that survived in this case was one that had been raised before. Does the power to spend more money lead to greater political influence? The Court's answer was yes. The Court wanted to distinguish between the value of placing ads and engaging in other forms of communication as compared with spending money on behalf of a specific candidate. Stressing the desire to maintain or achieve a level playing field so that all ideas have an equal play in the public policy debate, the Court was willing to allow limitations on corporate speech, thereby suggesting that "state-created" (artificial) individuals could be limited in their political communication and that this limitation could include restrictions on spending. In this regard, the Court weakened the *Buckley* prohibition on equalization. (For an extensive review of this case, see Casarez, 1991.)

The cases reviewed in this section deal with the constitutionality of limiting corporate political speech. Of related interest are court decisions that have clarified or blurred the distinctions between political (noncommercial) and commercial communication. In *New York Times Co. v. Sullivan* (1964), the Supreme Court ruled that advertising that is valuable to public opinion may be protected even if it is commercial. First Amendment protections were extended to commercial speech in *Bigelow v. Virginia* (1975). Commercial speech, said the Supreme Court, is protected when it discusses issues of value to society, in this case, the availability of abortions.

The prevailing interest scrutinized by the Court is not so much the right of the organization to speak but the right of the public to hear what is said. Similarly, the Court protected individuals' right to receive information in *Virginia State Board of Pharmacy v. Virginia Citizens Consumer Council* (1976). In *William F. Bolger et al. v. Young Drug Products Corp.* (1981), the issue was whether a company could advertise a birthcontrol product (commercial speech) and discuss venereal disease and family planning (political speech). The Court ruled that discussion of family planning and venereal disease made the mailing of sufficient public value to extend First Amendment protection to commercial speech.

Because the right of commercial speech under the First Amendment is not absolute, the Supreme Court has followed the premise that truth and the value of information to the public are the essential criteria for regulating communication. A four-part analysis set forth in *Central Hudson Gas & Electric Corp. v. Public Service Commission of New York* (1980) held that (a) advertising that concerns lawful activity and is not misleading is eligible for First Amendment protection, (b) the state government must demonstrate a compelling interest to restrict advertising content, (c) regulation must directly advance the government's stated interest, and (d) regulations may not exceed the boundaries necessary to serve that interest. In striking down a blanket ban forbidding utilities from advertising to stimulate the use of electricity, the Court concluded that even though the state was correct in wanting to conserve energy and, therefore, sought to prohibit speech that advocated the use of energy, the state could not justify its legislative action by merely wanting to suppress information about electric devices or services even when that advertising would cause no net increase in total energy use. This case defined commercial speech as that which is in the economic interests of the speaker and its audience and which proposes a commercial transaction.

Commercial speech proposes and promotes a commercial transaction (*Edge Broadcasting*, 1991; *Board of Trustees v. Fox*, 1989). It is relevant to the exchange of goods and services for pay: price, quality, location, and availability. Commercial speech relates to the economic interest of the sponsor (*Bolger*, 1981) and is used by consumers to make better buys. Not so easily included in this definition are discussions of attributes of the company, its image, or reputation. Some image components do not directly suggest commercial outcomes but are related to public policy issues, such as safety of plant operation. As will be seen in the following section to on the FTC, statements that have public policy implications but are made to protect the public policy integrity of a product, such as cigarettes, can be considered to be commercial speech. The key to this analysis is that commercial speech is less protected by the First Amendment.

These cases suggest that corporate entities have a protected right to speak on issues of public interest as long as their influence does not corrupt the public policy process. The rationale for that opinion is not merely the entity's right to speak but the public's right to receive information and opinion in its effort to form thoughtful opinions. Commercial speech is not protected unless it is accompanied with messages that are vital to the community's need for information and opinion and presented in ways that are candid, honest, and verifiable. With these principles in mind, the remainder of the chapter considers the influence of the FCC, the IRS, and the FTC over corporate communication. The guiding principle is the concept that issues communication should foster the good of the community (Kruckeberg & Starck, 1988).

History of the Federal Communications Commission—and Its Future?

A decade ago, the FCC played a dominant role in determining what issues communication made its way through the electronic airways. Today, the FCC plays virtually no role. However, an understanding of the past can be instructive regarding the kinds of practices that would prevent the return on this regulatory control. Reflections on past policies of the FCC may shed light onto what could become its new stance on public policy discussions, a topic that reemerged during discussion of the 1996 Telecommunications Act.

Section 326 of the Communications Act of 1934, as amended, forbade the FCC from censoring broadcast programming; however, Section 307 directed the Commission to grant and renew licenses "based on its assessment of the licensee's ability to serve the public convenience, interest, or necessity." Contained in Section 315(a) of the Act, as amended, the fairness doctrine charged station licensees "to devote a reasonable amount of broadcast time to the discussion of controversial issues" and "to do so fairly, in order to afford reasonable opportunity for opposing viewpoints" ("Fairness Doctrine and the Public Interest Standards, 1974; and Report on the Handling of Public Issues Under the Fairness Doctrine and the Public Interest Standards of the Communications Act, 1974).

The fairness doctrine expected broadcasters to seek balanced and contrasting views on controversial issues. In practice, as Henry Geller, former FCC General Counsel (1964-1970), observed, "In its post-1962 reach for perfect fairness, the Commission has lost sight of the real goal—robust, wide open debate. However well-intentioned, its actions now thwart or tend to discourage such debate" (Friendly, 1977, p. 223).

In the late 1980s, through a series of decisions by the FCC, federal Congress, and President Reagan, the fairness doctrine was abandoned and has been replaced with the principle that the marketplace of ideas will take care of the public's need and right to become informed. Once this FCC requirement was abandoned, persons seeking to place advertisements on the electronic media or wanting to respond to conclusions made by issue opponents or media reports could follow this principle: Electronic media outlets are not required to accept issue advertising, under any principle, including the need to balance the record being made available to the public.

Part of the rationale for the current status of the fairness doctrine grew out of the Supreme Court ruling that the First Amendment rights of advocacy advertisers are not abridged if they are denied access to electronic or print media. This means that no program director is required by law to air any particular organization's issue advertisement. For electronic media, this principle was established in a complex of cases: *Columbia Broadcasting System, Inc. v. Democratic National Committee*; *Federal Communications Commission v. Business Executives' Move for Vietnam Peace*; *Post-Newsweek Stations, Capital Area, Inc., v. Business Executives' Move for Vietnam Peace*; and *American Broadcasting Companies v. Democratic National Committee* (1973). Basing its decision on broadcast media's special status, the Court majority expressed its desire to avoid making electronic media common carriers.

Because the electronic media constitute a special public resource, said the Supreme Court, their regulation is best left to government and the journalistic discretion of those who prepare the programs. The justices supported the need for the public to be informed fully and fairly, arguing that if those forces with more money to spend on advocacy advertising were also allowed to demand time, the broadcast media could become their tools. The majority opinion concluded that financial differences could be diminished if stations provided free time for one group to respond to the editorial advertisement paid for by another group. As laudable as that strategy is, it offends the concept that journalists should have the say over the broadcast coverage of public issues. Any change in policy would shift that responsibility from the journalists who are accountable to the public for their editorial policy to private citizens who are not similarly accountable.

Siding with corporate and special interest commitment to inform the public, Justices Brennan and Marshall dissented. They acknowledged the usefulness of the fairness doctrine to regulate the broadcast industry by forcing balanced airing of controversial issues. Citing *Grosjean v. American Press Co.* (1936), these justices emphasized the need for policy that at least partially corrected the imbalance of issue presentation. Groups should not dominate public policy discussions because of their superior ability to spend. With these arguments, the decision pitted the fairness of journalistic discretion of licensees as regulated by the FCC against the imbalance that could result from deep-pocket spending by advocacy advertisers. The decision blocked private access to the broadcast media.

Little over a year later, in *The Miami Herald Publishing Company v. Pat L. Tornillo* (1974), the Supreme Court granted newspapers the privilege of rejecting advocacy advertising. At issue was a Florida statute that required newspapers to print replies. The Court decided that the statute was contrary to the principles of the First Amendment because it interfered with the primary function of editors: to determine what news and opinion deserves to be presented to readers. A newspaper is not a passive vessel through which advertisers can supply information and opinion to audiences. Journalists have a right and a responsibility to participate in the editorial decisions regarding what should be made available to readers.

The changes in FCC doctrine resulted in part because managers of electronic media argued that the public is best served by choices broadcasters make in regard to regular news and public affairs programming and not by companies seeking to spread "partisan viewpoints on the basis of who is first in line . . . because of their ability to pay" (Kaiser Aluminum & Chemical Corporation, 1980, p. 19). Under fairness doctrine guidelines, judgment to accept issue ads was a personal call made by network or station "standards and practices" executives along with their legal counsel. This group evaluated each advertising message submitted on an ad hoc basis and did so without clear, published guidelines regarding what was acceptable to be aired on that station or network. Such committees had virtually absolute control regarding whether an ad would be aired. For the most part, gaining access to television audiences for issue advertising was usually easier at the local than at the network level. Networks worried that if they allowed the airing of an ad, its affiliate stations could be placed into a local controversy regarding the balanced discussion of that issue in that community.

Some advertising practitioners believed that television should not carry advocacy advertising. President Edward Ney of Young & Rubicam International concluded that broadcast media are so inherently persuasive that they should be barred from use in public controversy. Ney feared the use of the 30-second spot commercial is insufficient for a comprehensive discussion but could lead viewers to believe that they have received valuable information (Stridsberg, 1977). In contrast to this concern, 85% of the respondents in a 1981 study believed that television companies should not exclude advocacy advertising (Ewing, 1982; Opinion Research Corporation, 1981b).

The fairness doctrine gave substantial discretion to broadcasters, as is evident in the cases that arose from the refusal of radio station WTOP in

Washington, D.C., to sell time to Business Executives' Move for a Vietnam Peace (BEM) to air 1-minute spots during the Vietnam conflict. WTOP argued that its news and public affairs coverage adequately presented full and fair coverage on the important public issues involving Vietnam. BEM had also produced television issue advertisements that it was having difficulty airing because broadcasters felt the ads might lead to fairness doctrine problems. BEM was joined in its suit by the Democratic National Committee (DNC), which sought a declaratory ruling by using the First Amendment and the Communications Act to reason that a broadcaster does not have the power to deny air time to responsible parties. Arguing that it was a responsible party, the DNC claimed that it should not be denied air time, which it wanted to purchase to solicit funds and comment on issues of public importance.

The FCC upheld the broadcaster's paramount editorial rights but was reversed in a two-to-one decision by the Court of Appeals for the District of Columbia, which held that a blanket ban against public interest advertising violated the First Amendment by leaving responsible groups without broadcast voices. The Supreme Court overturned the Appeals Court's decision in *Business Executives Move for Vietnam Peace v. FCC* (1973), and *Democratic National Committee v. FCC* (1973). The Court agreed with the FCC that balanced news coverage alone was sufficient to act responsibly in the face of this controversy. Stations did not infringe on complainants' First Amendment rights by refusing to sell them air time.

The FCC is charged with the positive obligations implied in the right of the public to be informed. In *Red Lion Broadcasting Co. v. FCC* (1969), the Supreme Court narrowed the rights of broadcasters when it affirmed the right of the public to receive suitable access to social, political, environmental, moral, and other ideas and experiences. Over the years, the FCC adhered to this principle:

> The sole function of the fairness doctrine is to maintain broadcasting as a medium of free speech not just for a relatively few licensees, but for all of the American people. As such it is not only consistent with the First Amendment, it promotes the underlying concept of the Amendment. (*American Broadcasting Co.*, 1969)

In one of its most seminal statements of its regulatory philosophy, the FCC interpreted the Supreme Court as requiring the fairness doctrine "to promote robust discussion of controversial issues." As a consequence, the FCC accepted a broad mandate for its activities:

> There is no conceivable legal reason why views should not be expressed, notwithstanding that they be distasteful, incorrect or even absurd. The burden of the licensee is to give opposing views a chance for utterance and to protect

persons who might have been attacked by giving them a chance to reply. (*Brandywine-Main Line Radio, Inc.*, 1968)

Special-interest advocates periodically contended that they should be allowed air time to respond to product advertising because it was associated with larger political topics. The FCC found most of these complaints unpersuasive because the particular product was not the issue (rather, its use). Efforts such as these evidenced the impossibility of drawing neat lines between commercial and political advertising. Uncertainty led station managers to refuse issue advertising

The FCC said the fairness doctrine normally applied "to ballot propositions, such as referenda, initiative or recall propositions, bond proposals and constitutional amendments" (Fairness Doctrine, 1974). But whereas political campaigns were considered "to be controversial issues of public importance within the meaning of the fairness doctrine" (*Radio Station KKHI*, 1980), there was a loophole. The FCC ruled that although changing the Virginia constitution was prima facie evidence of a controversy, a broadcaster could talk about the revision's constitutionality without inviting a response because the discussion did not touch on the controversy of the issue itself (*George R. Walker*, 1970).

Once stations allowed corporations or PACs to purchase advertorial advertising on ballot issues, the fairness doctrine prescribed that free air time must be made available to responsible representatives of the opposing view. Clarifying the FCC's stance was a case involving the 1982 Proposition 11 statewide bottle-recycling campaign favored by Californians Against Waste (CAW). Because of the heavy bottler-canner advertising blitz to defeat the measure, CAW was able to invoke the doctrine to gain access. Its own ads featured actor Eddie Albert as a spokesman explaining how the proposition, if adopted, would lessen litter. These were run throughout California at no expense to CAW (Waz, 1983).

In estimating the degree of controversy, a broadcaster needed to look both to the specific issue and the larger topic of which the issue was a part. The FCC ruled that a licensee had unreasonably denied a response to spot announcements opposing a ballot proposition relating to nuclear waste disposal. The broadcaster could not defend itself against the charge of unfairness by demonstrating the broad coverage that had been given to the issue of nuclear energy but not to the specific ballot issue (*Radioactive Waste Policy*, 1982). Advocates for controversial issues had imprecise guidelines—whether established by the commission or the courts—to use when they sought to determine the likelihood that they could have their advertisements or other message forms aired. Those who would engage in advocacy advertising risked having to lay out production costs to prepare advertisements that might be denied air time. Issue position advocates often decided to say nothing rather than waste money on advertising messages that would never be aired. The media had monetary incentives for not granting time for controversial discussion. They had to defend themselves, often at substantial cost, against those who believed they had been adversely affected by the controversy.

Exercising its mandate on electronic broadcasting, the FCC ruled that an issue did not require response or balanced coverage unless it centered on a controversy. In an attempt to assist broadcasters and other interested parties, the FCC broadly distinguished between controversial and newsworthy topics. The FCC stated that even if an issue was newsworthy, it might not be "a controversial issue of public importance" (*National Football League Players Association,* 1973). Likewise, the FCC consistently ruled that a licensee's freedom of speech would be infringed if the commission prescribed what persons were invited to provide the views that balanced the coverage (*WCMP Broadcasting Co.,* 1973). The fairness doctrine did not quantify the amount of coverage and did not involve equal time requirements. No attempt was made to support those who would seek equal time because the coverage was biased.

Two broad approaches were available for corporations and activists seeking air time. The *low profile* strategy worked to create cordial relationships with the network or station. In such cases, the entity seeking air time access for its ad might create a coalition with its likely respondents and allow them to comment on the accuracy and tone of the ad, along with any conclusions or recommendations, as part of the inquiry process to determine whether network or station lawyers were concerned that running that ad would bring forward groups that demand their share of air time in which to present their messages. *High profile* tactics included applying pressure on a reluctant station or network, including threats of litigation and FCC intervention. Such challenges could include the allegation that the station or network was not addressing vital issues in a balanced fashion.

Low profile methods for gaining access to national networks or local stations depended on four conditions:

1. The extent to which the content presented in each message was factual and accurate. Part of this determination rested with the likelihood that some concerned player would come forward with a list of complaints about the objectivity of the ad message. Vetting the message through critics prior to seeking access to the air waves could lessen the likelihood that this concern would constitute a problem.

2. The rapport between the sponsor's advertising management team, including its legal counsel, and the members of the station, with its legal counsel.

3. The credibility of the opponents who oppose the position taken in the ad and who might request the opportunity to air their reply.

4. The way the ad was worded vis-à-vis the controversy: The more objective
and harmony building the tone of the ad, the more likely the advertising
management team would not be denied.

These criteria offered constructive means for presenting a case for the airing
of an advocacy message; they also conformed to the underlying principle that
the public should not be denied access to information that is useful to its need
to be informed on controversial issues.

The sponsor needed to support its case that the advertisement's content
was factual and constituted an accurate interpretation of the facts: The better
the documentation, the stronger the case. Network review committees often
sent ad copy to the sponsor's opponents, such as activist groups, and authorities on the topic to ascertain whether the message was factual and the issue
was fairly presented. The more sensitive the controversy surrounding the ad,
the greater the likelihood that it would be sent out for review. The committee
also studied the graphics and pictorial representations to determine whether
they were biased or misleading.

Good personal rapport between the review committee and the sponsor
seemed to increase the likelihood that the review process and negotiations
went smoothly and were successful. Savvy ad sponsors got to know the
persons involved and worked with them in the review process rather than
approaching them as adversaries. Astute sponsors opened dialogue with the
review committee and sought their advice to develop and defend the ad. To
save money and effort, story boarding was used rather than creating and
presenting a completed commercial on a take-it-or-leave-it basis. Several
versions might have to be presented before it became reasonable to show the
final version to the review committee.

The third criterion did not always allow for a constructive response by
the sponsor of an ad. If the opponents to the position taken in the issue ad were
irrational zealots, the network or station would likely pay less attention to their
objections to the advertisement. But if the opponents were rational, scholarly,
and authoritative, they posed a formidable opposition that might be too great
to overcome.

To satisfy the fourth criterion, the advertisement needed to be framed so
that it was more informative than polemic. Ads could be designed to convey
the necessary information without baiting a hostile rejoinder from adversaries,
scholars, or activists. Network programmers seemed particularly sensitive to
ads that criticized the government. Fear of government reaction—even retri-
bution—perhaps more than the potential clash of contestants led to the
frustration W. R. Grace Company experienced when it attempted to air its ad,
"The Deficit Trials, 2017 A.D." (See Chapter 6 for a description of this ad.)
This advertisement criticized government spending and the seeming unwillingness of federal legislators to curtail the growth of the national budget

deficit, a public policy stance that Grace feared would leave a legacy of financial ruin for subsequent generations. For this reason, national television networks were reluctant to air the ad.

FCC rulings slowly established guidelines that issues communicators used when filing a complaint against a licensee:

> The burden of carrying the complaint required precise definition of the issue that was alleged to be controversial.

> The complainant must demonstrate that a significant amount of debate was transpiring in the relevant legislative bodies and media. An issue was controversial when it was being debated by relevant legislative bodies or when it concerned action taken by them.

> The case must be based on a test of the depth and breadth of public sentiment reflected in the controversy. The public discussion of an issue must be extensive. A substantial part of the so-called news hole must be devoted to the issue. Poll data probing the depth of public sentiment, particularly by comparing the issue's sensitivity to other issues, could provide a measure of the depth and breadth of public concern. The presence of several activist groups could suffice as an indicator.

> An issue must receive careful attention when it has substantial implications for public mores and public policies. The complainant could not win its case if it did not show that the licensee's coverage failed to address the controversy or was unbalanced.

> Even when the complainant was sustained, the licensee had substantial editorial discretion when deciding how the issue was to be treated and by whom.

> Any ballot issue or one central to a political campaign was controversial.

> Entertainment programming was controversial only when it constituted a "discussion" rather than a dramatic or comedic "depiction."

These guidelines continued to become more precise as complainants pressed their cases. One of the most precise implementations of guidelines resulted from *Syracuse Peace Council v. WTVH-TV* (1987). The case arose over WTVH's decision to allow the Energy Association of New York to advertise that "The Nine Mile II nuclear power plant is a sound investment for New York's future." The council sought air time to reply and carefully documented the fact that the issue was controversial and unbalanced, a conclusion with which the FCC agreed (*Syracuse Peace Council,* 1987). The case was based on comparisons of (a) the total time afforded each side, (b) the frequency with which each side was presented, and (c) the size of the respective audiences. The record demonstrated that WTVH had allocated 187 minutes to the proponent point of view and 22 minutes to the contrasting view, a total time ratio disparity of approximately 9:1. In terms of frequency, the proponent view was aired 261 times compared with 20 times for the contrast view, a ratio of 13:1. The proponent view aired throughout the broadcast day; a substantial number of ads ran during prime time. Such quantification was necessary to balance presentation on controversial issues.

The *Syracuse* case was vital to the decision on the part of the FCC to abandon its support for the fairness doctrine (McCoy, 1989), adopting instead a commitment to the ability of the idea marketplace to provide the information people want and deserve in their public policy decision making (Hazlett, 1989). Hazlett (1989) reasoned that the FCC abandoned its support of the doctrine because it inherently contradicted the principles of the First Amendment and was largely used as a means by which powerful members of government could bludgeon broadcasters into restraining their editorial policy. McCoy (1989) reasoned that "the development of the technologically more sophisticated marketplace rendered the very constitutionality of the fairness doctrine questionable, then obsolete" (p. 70).

Today, such guidelines are best used proactively while issues communicators breathe a sigh of relief and apply these rulings as they propose advertising that could prompt reimplementation of the fairness doctrine (Hazlett, 1989; McCoy, 1989). The good news: As issues communicators seek to place issues advertising with television and radio stations, they no longer need to worry that network affiliates will reject the advertising to avoid the intrusion of the FCC into news reporting and commentary programming prerogatives. The bad news: This breath of freedom is offset with the ruling in the *Columbia Broadcasting System* case that program directors are not required to sell time to any entity that wants to communicate about issues.

Although for the moment a benign policy, the issue of fairness could reemerge. Discussion that occurred during the 1996 debate over new telecommunications policy raised the question that led to the fairness doctrine. What must broadcasters—those who are granted control of broadcast frequencies—do to demonstrate their public responsibility in balanced broadcasting? How do they demonstrate their efforts to ascertain the problems and issues prevalent in the community of license? That underpinning concern sustains interest in a doctrine of fairness (Holsinger & Dilts, 1997; Schneider, 1996). Deploring the move by the federal courts to end the fairness doctrine, Lentz (1996) claimed that action violates a crucial principle: "Truth should prevail in a market-like struggle where superior ideas vanquish their inferiors and achieve audience acceptance" (p. 1).

▶ Internal Revenue Service

As was reasoned in the *Bellotti* and *Austin* cases, to spend is to speak. Business critics and some governmental officials assert that if an entity can spend more, it speaks more—with greater impact. A 1978 House of Representatives hearing brought forth persons who advocated using a broad interpretation of what kinds of advertisements should not be deductible under IRS Regulation 162-20 as necessary and ordinary operating expenses (U.S. Congress, 1978a). Business critics sought to use IRS guidelines to force companies to decide not to use paid advocacy communication because the impact on their budgets would be too great.

How Tax Code provisions regarding business deductions are interpreted affects companies' participation in public discussion of issues, because corporate communicators are reluctant to allocate nondeductible advertising dollars. For instance, Shell Oil Company decided not to engage in the windfall profits tax debate because advertisement costs on the pending piece of legislation were nondeductible. Participating in this campaign would have meant that "half of Shell's advertising budget would go for taxes" (Iverson, 1982, p. 18). Willing to spend such funds, Mobil has taken a conservative stance regarding the tax deductibility of its campaign expenses. Mobil Tax Legislative Counsel Thomas J. DuBos (1982) observed, "If in doubt we would decline to deduct the expenses. This position was conscientiously taken to reduce the public criticism that large companies, particularly Mobil, receive from time to time from the media and even elected officials."

A substantial advantage of proactive issues management accrues from the ability to monitor issues and communicate about them before they progress to the stage where they become pending legislation. If a company incurs costs in its efforts to enhance its ability to meet corporate responsibility expectations, it can deduct those expenses. If an advertising campaign is undertaken to prove the company is acting responsibly and should not be punished as is being threatened by legislation or regulation, the costs are likely not to be deductible. If corporations are unwisely constrained, the public may lose a valuable—and often unique—source of information, thereby defeating a well-established principle of court review of communication policy—the right of the public to receive valuable information on policy issues.

Business critics attempt to politicize corporate communication. Reflecting the ideology of this position, Meadow (1981) argued that nonproduct advertisements are

> of questionable deductibility. Although they may not relate to a specific bill or pending legislation, it is difficult to conceive of them as other than political. Messages that purport to show the benefits of a capitalist system clearly are messages of system political support, and to the noncapitalist are debatable messages, more appropriate for legislative, electoral, or other reform. (p. 73)

Efforts have been made to determine whether corporations have undue public policy influence. They may spend a great deal of money but whether they reap disproportionately large rewards is unproved. In the 1978 Hearings

(U.S. Congress, 1978a, pp. 77-78), Harvey J. Shulman, executive director, Media Access Project, pointed out how much more money had been spent by pronuclear forces than by antinuclear generation advocates. In retrospect, the case may be made that corporate spending does not invariably translate into undue influence.

Case in point, despite large advertising expenditures, nuclear generation did not proliferate; the intensity of its regulation increased. And the public became more comfortable with the ability of U.S. generators to operate safely. Gun control offers another example where undue influence may not be true. Bordua (1983; see also Schuman & Presser, 1977-1978) contended that gun control measures have been unsuccessful because public sentiment opposes them. To support his case, he examined the survey data that he concluded are often distorted by antigun advocates.

The principle here is relevant to an interpretation of corporate speech that Supreme Court Associate Justice Powell made in *First National Bank of Boston v. Bellotti* (1978). On behalf of the majority position of the Court in this case, he argued that those supporting the right to regulate corporate communication must prove that undue influence occurs; such influence, he argued, could not be assumed merely because one side outspent another. Those who champion changing the Tax Code to allow deduction of advocacy advertising costs argue that the money is spent in pursuit of profit because it is designed to prevent unnecessary and costly regulation (Ehrbar, 1978).

The rationale behind legislative constraint of corporate speech is the belief that their deep pockets and grassroots lobbying can unduly influence public campaigns on referendums or pending legislation. In contrast, legislators believe that no such influence can prevail in direct lobbying because they have experience in dealing with such efforts (Krauskopf, 1979). Passage of the current Tax Code provisions changed the decision in *Commarano v. United States* (1957), which established the principle of tax equity by prohibiting all deductions in an attempt to make an individual seeking to influence public opinion equal to corporations. Subsequent legislative revisions, although attempting to maintain the principle of equity, have removed that restriction except for grassroots lobbying.

For years, companies enjoyed the advantage of being able to deduct the costs of lobbying, whereas citizens could not. In 1993, Tax Code limits were placed on costs of direct and indirect lobbying activities. Prior to that time, companies were allowed to deduct lobbying costs when those activities related directly to the business activities of the organization. Section 162(e)(1) disallows deductions for money spent to (a) influence legislation; (b) participate or intervene in political campaigns on behalf of specific candidates; (c) influence one or more publics' opinions on election, legislative matters, and referenda items; and (d) communicate directly with executive branch officials in an effort to affect regulation. Section 162(e)(2) eliminated deductions for expenditures for lobbying efforts other than (a) on matters addressed by local legislation of material interest to the taxpayer, (b) on behalf of another party, and (c) some minimal in-house expenditures specified in Section 162(e)(5) (Taylor, 1995).

Dues are often paid by companies to trade associations and other tax-exempt organizations that engage in lobbying efforts. 1993 Tax Code provisions removed that allowance for expenses the tax-exempt organization spends on lobbying. The Code requires the tax-exempt organization to report to the funding company the portion of dues that was allocated to lobbying (Taylor, 1995).

Analyzing issues of this kind, Sethi (1979a, 1979b; see also, U.S. Congress, 1978a, pp. 384-387) recommended that regulators carefully distinguish between political and commercial speech. He interpreted IRS Regulations, Section 162-20 (a) and (b) as distinguishing between deductible image ads (which he equates with "commercial speech") and nondeductible issue ads (or "political speech"). However, as noted earlier, such a distinction is becoming more blurred than delimited. This recommendation, rather than simply interpreting the IRS Code, would change tax policy. This artificial distinction between commercial and political speech fails to eliminate the gray area in the Tax Code and is neither supported by Code language nor tax rulings.

To eliminate this gray area, Sethi's second recommendation during the 1978 Hearings was to abolish the provision that allows companies to deduct expenses incurred for the general discussion of social, economic, or financial issues even if they do not address legislation. He argued that such discussion is made by a corporation only when it thinks it has a good solution to the problem. Such issues, he continued, are "within the domain of legislative matters", which would put them into the category of grassroots lobbying. The only advertisements that should be deductible, therefore, are those that distinguish the sponsoring company from others in the industry and for goodwill advertisements, those typically called "Red Cross" (Sethi, 1979a, p. 386).

Despite efforts such as these, overlap between image and issues ads is inevitable. Such advertisements often provide information about a company's operating procedures and requirements, facts that can lead to more informed decisions about the company or industry. Attempts to differentiate clearly between the types is often difficult. Issue ads, unlike more commercially oriented messages, do not carefully position and clearly differentiate the sponsoring company from others. They are not ordinary and necessary business expenses, and consequently should not be deductible.

This rationale is contrary to Section (a), which allows the discussion of nonlegislative issues. Somewhat confusingly, the test of whether these expenditures are directly related to profit or even the survival of the company is not at issue because the courts have consistently ruled that this defense does not protect the deductibility of expenses (as in *Commarano*). Such is the case even where the legislation being opposed by grassroots lobbying would adversely affect the company (Krauskopf, 1979, pp. 322-326; see also Reg. Sec. 1.162-20(b)(1)). Public-service advertising supporting groups and causes such as the Red Cross are specifically deductible according to the Code. One could argue that taking a policy stand demonstrates a similar kind of citizenship as "Red Cross" advertising does by looking at free enterprise and other issues basic to the national economy. Because "Red Cross" advertisements do not differentiate among corporations, they certainly evoke responses other than purely commercial ones—yet remain deductible.

In light of this interpretation, a more valuable conceptualization of such advertisements would include the following categories that intertwine image and issue positions. As defined in Chapter 6, direct-image advertisements are those that carefully and clearly differentiate a company, its products, or services from its competitors', and indirect-image advertisements deal with social, financial, or economic matters. This latter type of advertisement can demonstrate corporate responsibility or goodwill in a fashion similar to "Red Cross" advertisements, but it does not provide details about the sponsor's products, services, or reputation. The advertisement may associate the sponsor with popular causes or values but does so without identifying characteristics of the company. The ad is indirect because the company's services, products, or reputation cannot be identified from the content of the advertisement (Heath & Nelson 1983a, 1983b, 1985). This taxonomy would treat as nondeductible only those advertisements that address issues in the presence of pending legislation, encourage direct contact with legislators, or discuss taxation. This position fosters the good that can be done when companies offer opinion on issues of economic, social, and financial importance.

As these issues develop, issues communicators are advised to follow a simple guideline: Do not assume that the costs for engaging in issues communication will be tax deductible. Call on expertise in the strategic design of a campaign to determine the actual likely costs if expenses are not deductible.

 Federal Trade Commission

The FTC is empowered to regulate the substance of commercial communication and retains broad power to define and regulate unfair or deceptive advertising claims (Carson, Wokutch, & Cox, 1985; Cohen, 1982; Section 5 of the FTC Act as amended, 15 USCS Section 45). Former FTC attorney H. Robert Ronick (1983) observed that even a "cursory reading of the FTC's implementing statute will show that the agency has enormous latitude and can literally use its imagination in deciding what is and what is not unfair, deceptive, or unlawful" (p. 38). The FTC's substantiation program requires factual support for advertised claims regarding a product's safety, performance, efficacy, quality, or comparative price.

The nature of issues advertising is such that traditional FTC guidelines on factual verifiability are extremely difficult to apply. Issues ads involve arguable interpretations of fact, value, and policy. As Sethi (1977) has written, "It is well nigh impossible to develop reasonably objective measures of proof of accuracy for most advocacy advertising without making them so onerous as to be unimplementable, or ad hoc and therefore capricious" (p. 258). In fact, it is easier to determine whether claims are unsubstantiated than to determine whether they are true and establishing criteria to operationalize verifiability often lags behind the need to apply them ("Perspectives on current developments," 1983).

Not until December 1974 did the FTC staff take steps to regulate image advertisements and differentiate between them and issues advertising. The staff defined image advertising as that "which describes the corporation itself, its activities, or its policies, but does not explicitly describe any products or services sold by the corporation." Such ads would cover a range of topics, including "such diverse areas as research and development" and corporate "activities and programs reflecting a sense of social responsibility towards, for example, the community or the environment" (U.S. Congress, 1978b, pp. 1450-1451). The staff urged the commission to proceed against unfair or deceptive image advertising in situations where the dominant appeal and likely effect of the advertisement is commercial under powers given it by Section 5 of the Federal Trade Commission Act.

Because "claims in certain corporate issue advertisements may arguably be capable of eliciting both commercial responses and political ones" relating "to the formation of public opinion about or action on a public issue," the memorandum suggested that the following six factors determine if an advertisement fell within regulated commercial limits. These included whether (a) ad claims relate to the sponsoring corporation's activities rather than assert facts, opinions, or views about general subjects or conditions; (b) corporate logos, tag lines, and so forth are present; (c) a brand name is identifiable in the ad; (d) the dominant purpose for disseminating the ad is economic; (e) persons viewing the ad are likely to perceive it as an expression of facts or opinions about a public issue; and (f) an advertisement refers to or depicts a product or service in which the sponsor has a financial interest (U.S. Congress, 1978b, pp. 1469-1471).

Over the years, FTC personnel suggested extending regulatory control to ads in which the public could be fooled into believing the advertising message was "political" when it actually was "commercial." That recommendation took effect in June 1986 when the commission ruled that an ad, titled "Of Cigarettes and Science," placed by R. J. Reynolds Company in March 1985, was deceptive. This charge was substantiated by the claim that the ad misrepresented the purposes and results of a scientific study regarding the health effects of smoking and could lead readers to doubt the seriousness of health consequences of cigarette smoking despite the fact that the federal government, particularly the Surgeon General and Congress, had on several occasions ruled to the contrary (22,522, R.J. Reynolds Tobacco Co., Inc.—FTC Opinion, Dkt. 9206, announced April 11, 1988, *FTC Complaints and Orders*).

The study, known by the acronym MR Fit (Multiple Risk Factor Intervention Trial), was alleged by R. J. Reynolds to provide credible scientific evidence that smoking is not as harmful as the public has been led to believe by other scientists and antismoking advocates. In its ad, Reynolds reminded the reader:

> This is the way science is supposed to work. A scientist observes a certain set of facts. To explain these facts, the scientist comes up with a theory. Then, to check the validity of the theory, the scientist performs an experiment. If the experiment yields positive results, and is duplicated by other scientists, then the theory is supported. If the experiment produces negative results, the theory is reexamined, modified or discarded. But, to a scientist, both positive and negative results should be important. Because both produce valuable learning.

The ad applied this principle to studies that examined whether a link existed between smoking and certain diseases. The conclusion of this research was that

> much of this evidence consists of studies that show a statistical association between smoking and the disease. But statistics themselves cannot explain *why* smoking and heart disease are associated. Thus, scientists have developed a theory: that heart disease is *caused* by smoking. Then they performed various experiments to check this theory.

Having placed this set of assumptions on the table, Reynolds drew the reader's attention to an important study: MR FIT, which cost $115,000,000 and took 10 years to conduct. Over 12,000 men served as subjects in the study. They were selected because they fit a high-risk profile for heart disease because they smoked and had high blood pressure and high cholesterol levels. The researchers divided the sample into two groups. One received no special medical intervention and the other received treatment that reduced all three risk factors. The hypothesis was that the subjects in the group with reduced risk factors "would, over time, suffer significantly fewer deaths from heart disease than the higher risk factor group." The key point, according to Reynolds, was this: "But that is not the way it turned out. After 10 years, there was no statistically significant difference between the two groups in the number of heart disease deaths."

Given these findings, Reynolds admitted that the study did not prove that smoking does not cause heart disease; however, "Despite the results of MR FIT and other experiments like it, many scientists have not abandoned or modified their original theory, or reexamined its assumptions. They continue to believe these factors cause heart disease." The caution asserted by Reynolds was this: "But it is important to label their belief accurately. It is an opinion. A judgment. But *not* scientific fact." The ad indicated that Reynolds' commitment to the pursuit of truth on this issue led it to commission research as well. It made a plea for fairness:

> But we do not believe there should be one set of scientific principles for the whole world, and a different set for experiments involving cigarettes. Science is science. Proof is proof. That is why the controversy over smoking and health remains an open one.

The FTC complaint against R. J. Reynolds charged that the ad was deceptive because it failed to disclose vital information about the study's findings. To make its ruling in the Reynolds case, the FTC relied on *National Commission on Egg Nutrition v. FTC* (1978), which allowed the FTC to rule against an ad placed by sponsors who claimed that no scientific evidence supported the conclusion that eating eggs increased the risk of heart disease.

One crucial factor in the MR Fit case was whether the FTC has jurisdiction to rule on issues (political, noncommercial) advertising as well as commercial advertising. Political communication, such as claims about political candidates or positions on referendum issues, is thought to be outside of the purview of the FTC because the facts presented or claims made are more a matter of subjective opinion rather than facts that can be verified by independent scientific scrutiny. First Amendment protection of political communication is based on the assumption that factual interpretations and conclusions are best debated in public. The government need not intervene to protect uncritical audiences from misleading claims as it does for product and service advertising. Part of the rationale for this position is the chance that the aura of regulation can have a chilling effect on political communication.

The latitude of review changed when the FTC ruled (4-1) on April 11, 1988, that a print ad by R. J. Reynolds Tobacco Co. was false or misleading because it made false claims that the study provided credible scientific evidence that smoking is not as hazardous as the public or the reader has been led to believe. In June 1986, the FTC had issued a complaint charging that R. J. Reynolds's ad misrepresented the purpose and results of the MR Fit study.

In response to this charge, R. J. Reynolds filed a motion to dismiss the ruling claiming the ad was an editorial (thus, noncommercial speech) fully protected by the First Amendment and therefore beyond the regulatory reach of the FTC. Taking a view that was overturned by the FTC, the administrative law judge on the Reynolds case and FTC Chairman Daniel Oliver agreed with Reynolds that the ad was not commercial speech and, therefore, was outside the jurisdiction of the FTC. Oliver argued,

> From the face of the document itself we can determine that the communication is a direct comment on a matter of public debate. The piece is not a solicitation for a commercial transaction with a gratuitous reference to a public debate thrown in the evade laws relevant to commercial advertising. (*FTC Complaints and Orders*, p. 22,188.)

This criterion was explicit in the *Bolger* case. Despite this argument, the majority of the FTC panel did not agree with this interpretation and ruled that Reynolds's ad misrepresented key facts and conclusions.

Oliver reasoned that the ad should not be regulated because the Supreme Court has allowed corporations full protection for making "direct comments on public issues." In this view, the statement by R. J. Reynolds was a direct comment in which the company "questioned the objectivity of the scientists who examine the issue of smoking and health." He stated,

> If the editorial is deceptive, or not believable, or runs counter to other information on the health question that the public is aware of, consumer are free to reject the message in the editorial. But it is critical for First Amendment purposes that the public, and not the government, decide the answer to this question.

He continued by noting that "the Supreme Court has never looked to the subjective intent of the speaker" in deciding whether speech was fully protected or commercial" (*FTC Complaints and Orders*, p. 22,188). Oliver reasoned that content alone cannot be the deciding factor in this kind of ad, and drawing on the *Bolger* case, he concluded that protection exists unless the sponsor is using political comments merely to protect the commercial speech.

Oliver directed attention to the commitment of the Supreme Court to protect speech that is political, philosophical, religious, artistic, or literary. Limited protection is granted to discourse that advertises products, services, or corporate images. By being able to rule on the content of these latter kinds of communication, the FTC serves the public interest by fostering informed commercial decision making. The core element in commercial speech is a commercial transaction, particularly one where there are economic interests for the speaker and the audience.

Oliver based part of his reasoning on cases regarding commercial statements that could not have been made public if they had not been accompanied with political statements that gave umbrella protection to the commercial speech. The Supreme Court has extended protection to commercial speech that links a product to important public issues on matters subject to current public debate. The point is this: If commercial speech, which otherwise would not be allowed to be made public, is presented in conjunction with relevant political statements, the political statements serve to protect the commercial speech. Political (noncommercial) statements must be relevant to the product or service being advertised. In contrast to commercial speech, political speech does not involve direct benefit to the sponsor. The *Bolger* case defined commercial speech as that which poses or implies a commercial transaction. The *Central Hudson* case took a broader view that commercial speech is that which addresses an issue of commercial interest to the sponsor. The concern is whether the commercial speech would have occurred on an occasion if the political speech had not also been present and could not be present without the protection of the political speech.

In June 1986, the majority of the FTC panel overturned the administrative law judge and disagreed with Chairman Oliver. The panel made specific distinctions in its reasoning that R. J. Reynolds's ad was intended solely to be commercial speech, although presented as political speech. In drawing that conclusion, the panel featured the following premises: (a) Speech containing a message promoting the demand for a product or service is commercial. (b) Commercial speech typically refers to a specific product or service. (c) Commercial speech addresses attributes of a product or service offered for sale. This criterion could extend to the health effects associated with the use of the product. (d) Commercial speech usually is paid for. (e) Placement of the advertisement is a relevant criterion; if it is placed on an op-ed page, for instance, where it is obviously editorial comment, it is less likely to be commercial speech than if it is presented in places where other ads appear and is associated with a company's logos. (f) The ad is more likely political if it addresses, directly or indirectly, legislators and calls for grassroots support; it is treated as commercial if the appeal is to individual buyers on matters such as product safety. The essence of these criteria is a determination of whether the sponsor of the advertisement could or seeks to benefit commercially from audiences' accepting and acting on the speech. In terms of the mission of the FTC, the incentive is to prevent ad sponsors from being able to publish false or deceptive statements about a product by associating it with a political, public policy issue.

The FTC decided the Reynolds ad was commercial speech because it included words and messages that are characteristic of commercial speech. (a) The ad referred to a specific product—cigarettes. (b) It discussed an important product attribute—the connection between smoking and heart disease. A message that addresses health concerns that may be faced by purchasers or potential purchasers of the sponsor's product may constitute commercial speech because it bears on the wisdom of purchasing and using the product. (c) The means used to disseminate the Reynolds ad—paid-for advertising— were typical of commercial speech. (d) Reynolds is in the business of selling cigarettes and, therefore, has a direct, sales-related motive for disseminating the ad. Even though no product brand name was identified in the ad, R. J. Reynolds is well-identified, a company firmly associated with tobacco products. (e) Economic, rather than political, motives indicate the presence of commercial speech.

Time will tell whether other cases will be similarly interpreted. Tobacco use may be a unique instance, whereby, for example, the government believes that its sponsored science will be definitive. Nevertheless, precedent exists for FTC interpretation that ostensible issue advertising is commercial speech when it is used to defend a product or service against allegations and scientific conclusions widely accepted to be true. At issue in such decisions is the extent to which the information put out for public consideration is of value to the public or only expressed in the interest of the advocate.

Such interpretation has been provided by Cutler and Muehling (1989) who stressed the potential benefits of the advertisement: to the sponsor, the industry, the business community, or to society as a whole. The farther the ad moves from the narrow interest of the sponsor to the concerns and well-being of others, the more likely it is not to require FTC intervention. In this sense, the telling distinction between commercial and political speech is the degree to which the resolution of the issue has a competitive impact favoring the sponsoring organization. If the advocated position benefits the industry and the society, it is political rather than commercial.

Taking issue with this stance, Middleton (1991) responded that competitive advantage is only one of several criteria that are useful for distinguishing commercial and political speech. Other criteria include the ad's contents, the context of the ad, competitive-environmental factors, and the identification of the sponsor. The content of commercial speech makes a commercial offer, is paid for, refers to a specific product or service, and is economically motivated, a conclusion based on *Bolger.* Believing that Cutler and Muehling took a position that would make the First National Bank's position (adjudicated in *Bellotti*) commercial instead of political, Middleton advocated a position that conformed to the court's ruling that the business activity of the organization is not a primary factor in whether its speech is political. The need is for more precision in delineating the standard that distinguishes political from commercial interest. Rejoining the criticism of Middleton, Cutler and Muehling (1991) stressed the purpose as interpreted by court review as one of the major defining criteria.

The key to distinguishing commercial and political communication, no matter how subjective, is the imputed purpose behind the placement of the ad. That analysis returns us to consider who is making the statement, the context of the statement, the imputed purpose, and the conversants that are implied or made explicit in the case. Subsequent applications of these criteria by the FTC may clarify the distinctions at hand, as will court cases. At least from the point of view of the FTC, the defining criterion to be used in distinguishing commercial and political speech is the purpose the ad sponsor has for making the case and the motivation its sponsor has for distorting its presentation and making misleading comments. To the extent that the purpose is largely related to commercial advantage for the sponsor, the ad is more likely to be interpreted as commercial than political. If others can benefit from the issue position, especially concerns other than members of the same industry (such as tobacco manufacturers in the case of R. J. Reynolds), the speech is more likely to be treated as political, thereby enjoying First Amendment protection.

The FTC guidelines regarding what is regulatable speech seem to be narrowing the latitudes available to organizational spokespersons. The apparent attempt is to assist the public in its efforts to obtain honestly developed and fairly presented fact and information. This section demonstrated that organizations that wish to avoid FTC intrusions are advised not to use product or service contexts to discuss public policy issues.

Conclusion

Sponsors of issues communication are likely to be more successful if they frame the content of their messages and the purposes of their campaigns in terms of the demonstrable need and desire of key stakeholding publics to obtain information relevant to public policy discussions and decisions. Beyond this rubric, guidelines are specific to the particular regulatory agency: FCC, IRS, FTC. Although key organizations can be faulted for speaking in ways that are self-serving of their own interests and preferences, by putting ideas into the public arena for scrutiny by others they meet their stewardship responsibility.

Media Technologies—New and Old— as Communication Infrastructures

We live in an era of massive change in communication media, routinely called the *information age* and often expressed in hyperbolic terms as the information superhighway. Network television's dominance is grudgingly giving way to alternative information and entertainment channels that allow people to be more selective and demanding of what they view. Increasing numbers of channels become available each year, both on cable and through satellite transmission. Entertainment, news, and commentary formats are tending to be more varied, seeking niche markets. Talk radio, exposé programming, and television talk shows focus on issues that have sociopolitical ramifications— and use the bizarre and unusual as lures for audiences. Computer-assisted communication through networks such as Internet offer electronic billboard space—available to wealthy corporations and financially challenged activist groups.

Agencies such as Medialink sell satellite transmission services that allow issues managers to transmit a still photo or graphics to TV newsrooms; those images arrive in digital form easily positioned into the news organization computer for transmission into layout and printing rooms. Using satellite links, companies and other users can monitor issues as they develop into news stories. New communication technologies allow for dialogues between people and organizations through listservs and discussion rooms.

Mass media clutter can be daunting to individuals who supply public policy information to audiences and for those audiences who seek to be informed on public policy issues. The World Wide Web became so popular in 1996 that it added to this clutter, even though various search engines helped users locate topics and web pages. Computer-assisted technologies allow people to search for and obtain information and opinion in ways that are quicker, more targeted, and more vast than before. But to use such technologies requires access to equipment and some expensive services and databases. Print publications have developed in pursuit of niche markets based on narrow themes and public policy issues. Academics as well as professional communication specialists who use print and electronic media realize that society is becoming demassified.

A plethora of nonmainstream publications, including slick magazines and informative newsletters, are created by an amazing array of organizations, including those devoted to activist causes. Nonmainstream publications and electronic devices, such as video and audio cassettes, allow "sovereign" viewers, listeners, and readers to pass up a great deal of information and avoid persuasive influence that various organizations work hard and spend substantial sums to provide.

Internet and other computer-assisted communication options give people the ability to obtain and share information and opinion positions, often through over-the-backyard-fence interpersonal influences. Through the Internet, persons can receive and forward a vast array of documents, ranging from formal publications and position papers to comments by friends and acquaintances. Although broadly diverse in geographical location, people cluster into tightly knit groups of cognitively involved stakeholding or stakeseeking publics who share views as to which problems require solutions. In this mixture of communication networks and infrastructures, zones of meaning become refined, at times elusive, and ever more global.

Thousands of voices compete for attention—that of the media, potential followers, and targets of their concerns, information, and policy recommendations. Each voice influences a few or perhaps many others, sometimes intentionally, whereas at other times, quite accidentally. Organizations try to get their information into these channels, sometimes working to prevent other groups from communicating through these channels. For instance, lawsuits have been used by corporate giants, such as those in the tobacco and automobile industries, to suppress stories and force accurate news reporting or feature commentary.

Persons who manage organizations often engage in issues monitoring and strategic communication planning on the assumption that mass media have dominant effects. According to this reasoning, if something unfavorable is said about their organization, cause, or issue position, the general public will immediately and uncritically accept that report as true. Perhaps the report is true and widely believed; perhaps not. Some media reports about companies or other organizations are accepted uncritically by readers or viewers in the absence of competing facts or opinions. Even then, many people do not see, hear, pay attention to, understand, perceive in the same way, recall, form opinions, and act on the information in the same manner. Media reports and commentary tend to reinforce as much as or more than they change opinions (Klapper, 1960).

In addition to the role media play in the formation of opinions on the part of widely diverse publics, interpersonal communication, influence of friends and acquaintances—over-the-backyard-fence conversation—has a powerful role in the way people receive and are affected by information and opinion (Basil & Brown, 1994; Heath, Liao, et al., 1995; Rice & Atkin, 1990). Interpersonal conversations can enhance agenda-setting effects of the media as well as mitigate that influence; a key factor in predicting persons' perception of the salience of an issue is the frequency with which they discuss the issue (Wanta & Wu, 1992). A key factor in the impact of information and the role a medium plays in a person's information acquisition and opinion formation is the degree to which that person thinks the information is useful (Atkin, 1973).

Issues managers are ill-advised to assume that they—or any other entity—can satisfactorily communicate with publics and audiences by assuming that "if you knew what I knew, you'd make the same decision" (Gaudino et al., 1989, p. 299). Organizations may be overly sensitive to and concerned by what is said and written about them and the issues they hold dear. Although media news, commentary, and entertainment programs can seem to plant opinions in the minds of key audiences, it is likely that the influence is more informative and reinforcing than resulting in cataclysmic change. However, one powerful influence of the media is the ability to repeat themes and opinions that may create, but at least confirm and popularize, widely held opinions.

Exploring these assumptions, this chapter examines how old and new media portray business activities, considers the role of media in the creation of issue agendas, and speculates about alternative communication technologies that are the frontier of issues management. This analysis assumes that media reporting and entertainment programming practices affect in varying degrees the growth of image and issue problems for organizations engaged in issues management. The chapter explains how media extend the reach of messages and augment or reinforce zones of meaning to which people and organizations contribute, in which they participate, and from which they draw premises and assumptions. Chapter 3 suggested ways that computerized databases could be used in monitoring issues, a topic that will be expanded in this chapter as we explore the burgeoning new technologies. Chapter 6 discussed communication channel options, a topic expanded in this chapter featuring the possibilities for obtaining and providing information through new technologies that allow for dialogue.

Media-Fostered Cynicism about Business, Government, and Activism

The media not only constitute means by which organizations (business, government, and activism) can reach targeted audiences and interact with key publics but they also play a formative role in the public policy issues agenda. Whether media reports and entertainment create, foster, or merely reflect ideas that fuel the growing cynicism in this country is difficult to assess. What is less difficult to recognize is the cynicism regarding the sociopolitical system of this country, which was uncovered by " 'The Dream' in Danger" (1995) study commissioned by the Public Relations Society of America. People increasingly have lost faith in many organizations and institutions that ostensibly arose to promote their material interests and protect their health, safety, and welfare. Some of the impetus for this cynicism results from media news reports, entertainment programming, and politicians' continued negative campaigns and cynical—perhaps politically expedient—indictment of government. Even though they do not dominate the public's thinking, programs, news reports, and political campaigns emphasize the negative and unusual, thereby fostering or reinforcing distrust rather than enhancing appreciation of the institutions of society.

A concern of issues managers is the role the media play as they interpret events and portray problems and their solutions. In such efforts, the media may follow while seeming to lead. In their reportage, as Reese and Danielian (1994) concluded, "The media follow each other's lead as they 'converge' on the same topics and interpretations, often limiting the range of views on important policy debates" (p. 84). Such is the case because editorial power elites exist as a composite of major journalists, newsmakers, government officials, and expert commentators. Elite players interact in a self-confirming infrastructure whose participants comment on each other's policy stances in forums, whether mediated or in other venues. These networks become a closed system that outsiders cannot easily penetrate to interject comments and new information.

Business executives, like most people subjected to scrutiny, are uncomfortable with the portrayals they see of themselves in newsprint or on the screen. More so than any other medium, the unblinking eye of television serves as an electronic pop-culture window into company practices, presenting a picture of U.S. business seen by nearly everyone in the country. For at least three decades, TV has opted for stereotypes of executive ruthlessness, foolishness, or incompetence, which some audiences may uncritically accept as true. Not surprisingly, given the antiestablishment opinions of the antiwar years, corporations reached new image lows in news and entertainment programming during the 1970s and early 1980s (Aronoff, 1979; Chickering, 1982; Divelbiss & Cullen, 1981; Lichter, Lichter, & Rothman, 1982, 1983; Nelson-Horchler, 1982). These developments reflect broad societal trends in which assumptions as to the role of government, the press, business, and other institutions have undergone reevaluation (McKenzie, 1983; Nimmo & Combs, 1981, 1982; "Private enterprise and public values," 1979).

News by its nature is selective and often a cyclical repetition of events. It tends to focus on problems, mistakes, controversies, and crises. Good policies or activities, whether by business, labor, government agencies, or activists, unfortunately, are rarely perceived as newsworthy. If a chemical company spends $5 million to $10 million to reduce the emission of some chemical, that announcement is unlikely to be treated as news. If the same company has a truck turn over due to the driving negligence of another motorist, the perpetrator of the accident is unlikely to be the focus of the news story, whereas the company is—a bigger news target. Even if the company is not irresponsible, media portrayal can create or leave that impression, especially for headline readers.

Addressing reasons for increased cynicism about business, Dominick (1981) contended that bad news about business heavily outweighed neutral and positive news. The Institute for Applied Economics, a nonprofit organization sponsored by 39 major American corporations, confirmed this conclusion in a report analyzing all evening TV newscasts of ABC, CBS, and NBC for the last 6 months of 1983. The study concluded that although the amount of economic news had increased over previous years, "television's coverage of the economy continued to highlight bad news, not healthy economic trends. . . . Good economic news was simply not reported—or, more often, not reported in depth" ("Study sees too much emphasis," 1984, p. 74). Investigative reportage usually concentrates on conflict between public and corporate interests and features the worst side of business life. Nefarious acts, such as toxic waste dumping, cost overruns, misleading advertising, and irresponsible real estate development, receive disproportionately large amounts of media attention. Ethical malfeasance in corporate America is far rarer than the day-to-day production of high quality products and services.

One reason for this reporting trend is that people want to assume the narrative of good companies doing good, making positive change, and providing proper services and products at fair prices. That assumed narrative of the free enterprise system occurs through myriad routine business activities. The news story occurs when a crisis or violation of the accepted narrative happens. The news value is the information that alerts people in a community to the potentiality of a problem that may relate to their interests and about which they may want to take action as a consumer or a concerned member of the community. (For further discussion of the concept of narrative in organizational communication, see Heath, 1994.)

No company or industry can expect media to serve as unthinking conduits that businesses, activists, or governmental agencies can use to force-feed key publics. Likewise, businesses should not have to contend with reporters who make predetermined conclusions and know what their report will be before arriving for interviews, seeking useful "sound bite" or "actuality" video and audio quotes rather than new information to complete the story package. Commenting on the credibility gap between reporters and companies, Finn (1981) observed,

> Reporters suspect that businessmen often lie and more often fail to tell the whole truth. Businessmen are convinced that the press is out to get them whatever the facts may be, and they are wary of saying anything lest they be quoted out of context. (p. 6)

Unless it pays for the space or time to place advertisements, businesses, activists, or government agencies have little control over what appears or is printed. Some notable cases demonstrate organizations' willingness to wage a frontal attack of openly refusing to cooperate with a publication or broadcaster they may disagree editorially with, as Mobil did with the *Wall Street Journal*. Lawsuits are also a favorite tactic of organizations that believe their point of view is not fairly represented or, worse, the media portrayal is contrived or falsified. Lagerfeld (1981) suggested 15 years ago that free enterprise does not necessarily receive fair or balanced treatment even in the popular business press. Although his analysis of *Business Week* is skewed toward a conservative view of corporate practices and economics, he charged that the magazine performed "a tremendous disservice" to readers by editorial policies "undermining and attacking the very ideas and values that give their work meaning and moral status" (p. 75). These issue battles slowly redefine the premises by which the facts are interpreted and conclusions drawn regarding business policies.

Even in science reporting, bias and distortion unintended by journalists affect conceptions of social reality. Reporters react to disasters and other events for which they could have more adequately prepared themselves and their readers-viewers-listeners. For example, based on precoverage of the nuclear industry and later developments from the Three Mile Island nuclear generating plant incident, S. Friedman (1981) concluded that the media and power utility communicators were both in error for failing to adequately warn the public of possible dangers.

Often, when issues involve technical details, journalists lack competence to judge and accurately present them. Space and time limitations restrict what can be said. One cost of communicating on terms dictated by broadcast journalists is the need to compress information—however complicated—into 20-second segments, because TV and radio people think in that timeframe. A story requiring a couple of pages of print or an hour of television rarely receives full treatment.

Mazur (1981a, 1981b) demonstrated how "reaction against a scientific technology appears to coincide with a rise in quantity of media coverage" (p. 106). Taking a hard look at nuclear issues, B. Cohen (1983) reported that pack journalism leads some reporters to become blinded to alternative interpretations of facts. He charged that public perceptions of nuclear reactor safety had been shaped by those who did not understand nuclear energy but who recognized the popularity of a negative stance. The press used the safety issue to rail against nuclear generation when many other more immediate safety concerns received lesser treatment. To support his argument, Cohen reviewed the number of entries in the *New York Times* to compare the frequency of reporting on certain safety topics. Some 40,000 people die in car crashes yearly; Cohen found 120 stories on automobile safety. Industrial accidents, resulting in 13,000 fatalities each year, received only 50 entries. Reports on asphyxiation dangers got just 20 mentions even though they account for 4,500 deaths. Other issues were largely ignored. In contrast, although not a single person has died directly from radiation exposure due to nuclear generation, over 200 entries discussed its safety, technology, progress, and regulation.

Motion pictures and television series often present negative views of business activities; the routine is not as dramatic as the unlikely. Nuclear disaster, whether viewed from military or peacetime use, is a recurring theme in films such as *On the Beach, Dr. Strangelove, The China Syndrome, Silkwood, Special Bulletin,* and *The Day After.* Irresponsible operations and lackadaisical and poorly trained employees has been a recurring topic in the television show, *The Simpsons.* In the 1950s, nuclear material was portrayed as the cause of mutant animals of many species, each of which was the featured villain in horror movies. Nuclear weaponry has been a recurring theme of adventure films, including several in the James Bond series. This was a central narrative theme in the Cold War.

Compare those portrayals to movies or television programming that have featured the benefits of radiation in medicine, thousands of industrial uses, or as a harnessed energy source, including generation of electricity. When these safe and productive uses of radioactive materials have been feared, perhaps unwisely, sponsors of their use have had to counter an apprehension that was fostered not by scientific studies but by portrayals in popular culture. In such portrayals, the persons involved seem to have no responsibility to present fair and accurate information and opinion but have used and fanned fears and anxieties for profit. Such portrayals create and augment cynicism.

Another point of comparison is made by considering the amount of property damage and loss of human life in this country in the past few years due to bombs constructed from readily available materials such as ammonium nitrate, a form of chemical fertilizer frequently used by farmers. This substance was a primary ingredient used in the bomb that destroyed the Murrah Federal Building in Oklahoma City, Oklahoma, in April 1995, an explosion that caused at least 168 lives to be lost, including children in the day care center. A similar combination of readily available chemical ingredients was used in the bomb attack on the World Trade Building. Based on those examples, the lives of U.S. citizens and visitors were more at danger as a result of ordinary substances rather than from nuclear energy, a comparison lost in the analysis of the news and comparative risk assessment.

The relationship between corporations and television programming is paradoxical. Despite reliance on corporate advertising, television tends to show the darkest side of corporate life in entertainment programming as well as investigative journalism. A glance at entertainment broadcasting reveals that the J. R. Ewing-type of scoundrel holds much more prime time interest than the generally unspecified businessman roles exemplified by earlier TV shows, such as *Father Knows Best* or *Leave it to Beaver.* Examining popular culture portrayals through content analysis, the Media Institute discovered that

* Two out of three businessmen on television are portrayed as foolish, greedy or criminal.
* Almost half of all work activities performed by businessmen involve illegal acts.
* The majority of characters who run big businesses are portrayed as criminals.
* Television almost never portrays business as a socially useful or economically productive activity. (Theberge, 1981, p. ix)

The Institute concluded that the typical crook, conman, and clown portrayals of business leaders forms and reinforces opinion hostile to business people and private-sector organizations.

Reinvestigating this crooks, conmen, and clowns syndrome, Thomas and LeShay (1992) argued that the bias is more a matter of economic class than antibusiness. Content analysis of 200 episodes in the 1979-1980 season conducted by the Media Institute revealed that two thirds of the 118 business characters were crooks, conmen, or clowns. Immoral behavior overshadowed sound, socially responsible business ethics. Only 25% of business characters were portrayed positively, and 8% were presented in a neutral fashion. Such findings, Thomas and LeShay reasoned, are counterintuitive given the fact that free enterprise business is a sociopolitical icon:

> Considering that business is a cornerstone of U.S. society and that the viewing public's commercial dealings are essential to the U.S. economy, one would not expect business, of all things, to be so harshly characterized on network television. This is particularly true given that television writers and producers typically create their productions in conjunction with sponsors to deliver implicitly commercial messages. (p. 97)

Thomas and LeShay concluded that the portrayal of business was more accurately one that condemned wealth rather than business. Middle-class characters are portrayed as caring, supportive, and sympathetic toward one another. Wealthy characters take on the opposite persona; positive traits are assigned to them only when they live a middle-class lifestyle despite their wealth. This study agreed with the Media Institute finding that more than half of the television business characters exhibited negative traits and behaviors, but even here, the bias seems to be one toward wealth more than occupation. Whereas characters may have been presented negatively, especially due to extreme wealth, "commerce, consumerism, and capitalism generally are given positive endorsement on television" (p. 104).

The danger of regulation by false stereotype leading to cynicism is real. Users of television classified in the heaviest network-viewing quintiles have their access to information artificially restricted when the major networks take outraged stands on corporate behavior. Often, knowledgeable publics come away believing they have been misled (L.H. Young, 1981). Expose, news commentary, and talk show formats abound on network and cable television channels. Each week, private-sector and public-sector managers, as well as activists, tune in to a variety of programs, such as *60 Minutes, 20/20, 48 Hours, Nightline, MacNeil-Lehrer,* and *This week With David Brinkley.* Magazines also have learned the marketing advantage of exposes, especially on large business activities and government agencies. Program directors know the business value of outraged audiences who tune in to see what offenses have been committed by business, government, and even their neighbors.

The cynicism that abounds in this society leads to, results from, and allows the easy characterization of activists as hopelessly unrealistic, overly moralistic, and simplistic "do-gooder tree huggers." Government officials are easily stereotyped as pompous and spineless vote seekers who are out of touch with the communities they serve and gridlocked in an effort to seem to solve all problems although solving none.

Images of leaders—business, religious, government, education, and activist—are scrutinized to discover what is wrong about them rather than what is redeeming. Constant negative attention may create images that justifiably lead people to be cynical. This cynicism challenges issues managers who try to foster harmony and cooperation with key publics. Without trust based on accurate and positive images, harmony and cooperation are difficult to establish. All parties that respond to and attempt to gain favorable attention in mediated news stories should realize the lack of neutrality in the general media. For this reason, and many others, large organizations—private and public—seek to use channels of communication over which they have greater control. Companies use newsletters and paid issues advertising. Activists use issues advertising and rely on their newsletters and specialty publications and videos.

 Media Effects in a Multitiered Society

Despite reporting, editorial, and entertainment programming biases, we cannot assume the whole story is told in regard to the formation of opinions on the part of cynical publics. "Today," as Noelle-Neumann (1983) noted, "most researchers assume that the mass media have a decisive effect on people's conceptions of reality" (p. 157). However, media often reflect sentiments that form in the minds of publics, some of which are closely identified with issue activism. Television programming and other media presentations probably reflect rather than create opinion that has become formed. If a sizable segment of the public were not convinced that corporations are corrupt and acting against public interests, negative broadcast portrayals of business on entertainment and information programming could not maintain their ratings with such programming. Although in times of issue crisis, people turn to government agencies and activist groups, that does not mean that they do not doubt the objectivity, sincerity, and efficacy of such organizations.

Media appear to have dominant impact because the points they express seem to correspond to opinions of their audiences. In actuality, people may have formed or are in the process of creating opinions that they avoid discussing in public until those issues are presented in the media; once the topics are discussed in the media, people feel they can legitimately express opinions they had formed quite independently of media reporting and commentary (Noelle-Neumann, 1984).

Because media follow publics' opinions as well as reinforce them, the extrapolation of this analysis is that if groups of people receive different information from different media and interpersonal contact, they develop different conceptions of reality, a multitiered society of different and conflicting zones of meaning. Instead of the media playing a singular role in the formation of opinions on key issues, media *and* social interaction—conversation among people—influence key publics' issue priorities (Zhu, Watt, Snyder,

Yan, & Jiang, 1993, p. 8). People seem not to acquire much of their factual information from media news reports and commentary (Neuman, 1986). People discuss news more with one another when they believe that it is personally relevant (Basil & Brown, 1994).

Opinion leaders are prone to read upscale magazines and newspapers carrying issues ads explaining public-sector and private-sector points of view. Hawkins and Pingree (1981) argued that televiewing and demographics interact so that social realities are created, amplified, and reinforced. These viewing and reading patterns are strongly influenced by socioeconomic status. Higher income persons are more knowledgeable of sociopolitical issues and consume more media news and commentary (McLeod & Perse, 1994).

Another perspective of this problem was provided by Kenneth Burke (1969b) who contended that one of the most powerful social forces involves living a shared view of reality, what he calls *identification.* If reporters take their leads from the same sources—other media reports—the trend would seem to be to reinforce the mediated reports on business topics instead of to look for nonconfirming or disconfirming evidence. Reinforcing the danger of media-based reality; researchers discovered that network claims of momentum shifts in candidate popularity during the 1976 presidential election were often based not on poll data but on subjective opinions—feelings—of the reporters. Such shifts, as reported, could lead viewers to believe a contrived social "truth" (Meyers, Newhouse, & Garrett, 1978).

On political communication, which employs some of the most skilled audience-targeting techniques, Graber (1982) viewed "media as active creators of political reality, rather than mere mirrors of the passing scene and transmitters of the views of others" (p. 557). As a consequence, perhaps because of the attempted balance of television, heavy viewers call themselves political moderates and avoid liberal or conservative labels (Gerbner, Goss, Morgan, & Signorielli, 1984).

This analysis of media impact brings us squarely to the topic of how issue and policy agendas become set in this country—how they become visible and adopted, whether because media personnel decide an issue is important and raise it to invite responses from politicians, corporate spokespersons, or activists or because pressures exerted by these key players motivate reporters to cover stories and take editorial positions (McCombs, 1977; McCombs & Shaw, 1972). Reflecting on this theme, McCombs (1992) acknowledged that even if people do not acquire much of their information or opinion from the media, they do use media to decide what to think about and how to think about the information they acquire. Perhaps the agenda-setting function of the media is more the symbolic presentation of what is important—whether that portrayal raises or confirms what people think is important.

The status of this view of media impact is captured in the encompassing, if indecisive, conclusion: "The media agenda is constructed through an interactive process between the news media and their sources, in the context of competing news organizations, news-handling conventions and routines, and issue interest groups" (Rogers, Dearing, & Bregman, 1993, p. 73). Considerations of media impact feature the salience of topics and issues, what people think about. Thus, salience discrimination "is operationalized as the importance that media and audiences accord to an event, and the causal relationship that exists between media and audience judgments about that importance" (Edelstein, 1993, p. 85).

"Problematic situation" is a criterion variable that predicts whether media reporters or other players believe some change is or has occurred in the agenda. People—media professionals, government officials, activist groups, private sector organizations, or the general public—begin to think an issue must be a problem because it is widely and thoroughly reported and discussed (Edelstein, 1993). Newsworthiness is the result of some occurrence being discrepant from what people want or expect (war is newsworthy because people want peace). People want corporations to manufacture safe rather than unsafe products. In this vein, agendas result when the media report that some set of events has occurred, noting the connection between (or allowing the audience to make the association) the event and what is desired or expected.

Persons appear to monitor the media to determine the extent to which a problem may exist. This monitoring focuses on the amount and duration of coverage. Health and safety concerns, those that typically are addressed under the heading of "risk communication," can be made salient by widespread news coverage (Mazur, 1981b; Sharlin, 1987). In the formation of opinions, such as those related to risk estimations, media and interpersonal influences prevail (Coleman, 1993) in complex ways that may be idiosyncratic to the specific risk.

As much as media reporters, editors, and program directors might like to believe that their gatekeeping role translates into issue leadership, they must acknowledge that they may also stifle the rise of an issue's visibility. One primary instance of that phenomenon is the controversy over the health and socioeconomic effects of cigarette smoking. Most of the impetus for this issue came from the medical profession and antismoking advocates who challenged politicians and media personnel to take an aggressive reporting and editorial position on the issue.

Counterbalancing those efforts are the tobacco industry's advertising dollars. According to Warner, Goldenhar, and McLaughlin (1992), magazines and other media that rely heavily on tobacco ad revenue are less likely to report health hazards than are their counterparts that are less dependent on those revenues. Fear of losing revenue because of editorial stances that might offend tobacco companies with huge advertising budgets mitigates what might otherwise be a more aggressive editorial position (Weis & Burke, 1986).

According to Gandy (1982) and Parenti (1986), advertising dollars play a primary role in the gatekeeping and editorial policy of the media.

During the late 1960s, corporations began to realize that their communication practices could prove quite damaging (Steckmest, 1982). Awareness that society would no longer accept business practices as usual startled some leading communicators and corporate leaders into the development of new strategies. Focusing criticism where it was due, Ronald Rhody (1983), former Vice President of Public Relations for the Bank of America, observed,

> Most of the misimpressions, or errors, or unfairness that so many are concerned about is business's own fault. We, in our institutions, (just like the media and government) have been guilty of ignorance, arrogance, bad judgment and negligence. Silence, evasiveness, the lack of candor, the unwillingness to respond, have been like lead weights pulling business down lower and lower in public esteem. The fact that the public may be misinformed on key economic or business issues, may be misled about our respective operations and intentions, is largely our own doing. We have permitted this because, out of fear of either criticism or controversy, we have failed to take the initiative. (p. 46)

Rhody challenged business leaders to "stop grousing about the media and really learn how to work with it" (p. 47).

Sage prescription was voiced by Kevin Phillips (1981) speaking as President of the American Political Research Corporation:

> The battleground of business-media relations is changing. Television network news is still simplistic, inflammatory and more than occasionally biased, yet it is a problem corporations have begun to take seriously. The larger context of press coverage of business-economic issues is one of improvement, however, and in the growing area of corporate-related First Amendment interpretation, press groups are now frequently emerging as allies of the business community. (p. 60)

Frustrated by lack of access to the mainstream media, private sector organizations, government, activists, and labor groups created alternative sources of communication that they could control and shape to their purpose. These sources of communication have supplied substantial amounts of information and opinions. Although the media may lead on some issues, they likely follow and confirm the growth of key publics' concern that problems exist that need remediation. The media may be a mainstream beacon of the point at which an issue, discussed by several publics, has achieved visibility.

If that model of the role of the media obtains, then it offers additional support for the concept of a multitiered society, which consists of many overlapping and conflicting zones of meaning. Key publics with various opinions, rather than a single public opinion, is the accurate model. In addition, these publics are likely to have a different sense of the importance and content of an issue and the priority of values by which it should be judged and solved. Viewing opinions in public and media influence in this way suggests that issues managers engage in balancing acts between many key stakeholders and stakeseekers, each of which may not agree with and interpret issues in the same way as the others. They may have their own media preferences and are likely to view the same media stories in idiosyncratic ways.

Many lessons were learned in recent decades as organizations matured in their understanding of and response to media reporting and commentary. Part of the lesson is a realization that media do not dominate opinion and do not report or portray accurately. Issues communicators realize that narrowly targeted audiences and appropriate channels to reach key publics are more likely to be useful than is high cost advertising designed to reach mass audiences. Society is multitiered. Zones of meaning conflict with and overlap one another. What seems to be public opinion is a variety of opinions often at odd with each other. Some zones are laden with information and thoughtful analysis; others contain hyperbole and outrage with little substance.

Issues communicators seek to reach each audience or public at its own level of knowledge, awareness, and concern. The daunting task facing issues communicators is to put out (listen to and appreciate) as much information and opinion as they can so that people who want it can obtain it. Even if the clutter seems turbulent and daunting, it privileges audiences and fosters public debate, discussion, and dialogue.

 ## New Communication Technologies: Accessing and Supplying Information and Opinion

A multitiered society sharply contrasts with Marshall McLuhan's (1969) prediction that advancing communication technology will congeal "the entire human family into a single global tribe" (p. 17). Television is the crucial channel, McLuhan argued, because it can allow millions of people to have common viewing experiences—to view the same event or news item at the same time or in slightly different times—and thereby to form similar opinions. The assumption of McLuhan's prediction is that what we see will be interpreted in exactly the same way. If that prediction by McLuhan ever was likely to become reality, it is probably less true today.

New communication media offer many opportunities for organizations to reach audiences and respond to critics and counterparts. For all of the effort to put out more information and to receive others' information and opinion, issues monitors along with others in society suffer information overload. Nevertheless, the abundant availability of information privileges audiences to learn and evaluate. New communication technologies privilege wealthier organizations in some instances, but in others, the cost of reaching vast global audiences can be quite low, thereby balancing the economic dynamics of the opinion playing field.

Unlike any previous time in history, viewers and readers have a plethora of mediated sources of information and opinions. With e-mail and computer-assisted bulletin boards and discussion groups, interpersonal influence is electronic, nearly instantaneous, and global. Society is becoming demassified and more interactive. The dialogue is electronic but not necessarily on network television or radio. Multitudes of discussions and arguments occur each day on new communication technologies, especially those that are computer assisted.

In seeking to supply information and exert opinion influence, organizations look to widen their reach, employing the available media to gain audiences and respond to critics (Friendly, 1977; Maher, 1982; F. Rowan, 1984). To meet their programming needs and news responsibilities, TV stations or systems regularly request promotional public service films and other visual or audible materials (DeWitt, 1983; Klein, 1983). Despite this openness to material supplied by other organizations, network broadcasters have argued that news and public affairs programs created by their own staffs are the best way society has to explore issues and keep informed (Pool, 1983).

Cable programming offers alternative avenues for issue discussions because each new channel option can disperse substantial amounts of information each day. Cable TV is one of the greatest potential avenues into people's homes. As of 1992, 90% of U.S. households had cable television available to them and 60% actually subscribed to it. Despite this proliferation and the potentiality for cable as a carrier of an unlimited array of points of view, this micro multimedia has disappointed some observers. According to Aufder-heide (1992),

Cable today is hardly a thriving marketplace of ideas. There are harsh limitations on the current cable industry's ability to provide diversity of sources and viewpoints on issues of public concern, much less to be a service that fortifies civic activism. Those limitations lie in the conditions of commercial television programming, whatever the delivery vehicle, as well as the current structure of the cable industry. (p. 54)

Industry biases against creative programming options and public space, coupled with horizontal and vertical integration of the corporate structure of the industry, have led to markedly less variety in programming that can address controversial topics as opposed to formats and content controlled by program directors. Four cable companies control 47% of the market (Aufderheide, 1992).

Nevertheless, substantial segmentation arises from cable television, such as C-SPAN programming that includes hearings, forums, and in-depth book reviews of policy discussants. Nonmainstream channels allow the discussion of topics unpopular to major networks, such as programming by the Audubon Society that periodically runs on TBS and environmentally slanted programs on the Discovery channel. Hours of public policy, business, and financial programming go out each week through Cable News Network (CNN), Public Broadcasting Service, and syndication.

The future is not limited to network and standard print outlets. Major growth areas of new communication technologies involve internal communication (corporate, agency, activist, labor television and video; CD-ROM; videoconferencing; and teleconferencing) and external communication (cable programming, direct mail, database retrieval, CD-ROM, videoconferencing, and teleconferencing).

Ahead-of-the-curve writers such as Patrick R. Williams (1982) encouraged corporate communicators to become proficient in using new technologies. Bleecker and Lento (1982) challenged public relations practitioners: "As people who manage and disseminate information, we should be in the vanguard of the information revolution. To play out our role in the transformation of our jobs, we must keep up with the technology" (p. 11). Taking this advice to heart, practitioners in the 1990s engaged in a substantial dialogue exploring the possibilities and challenging each other to push the envelope on the use of new technological means to reach ever more narrowcast audiences. Through new technologies, the era of mass narrowcasting is firmly established. In this way, issues discussants can communicate with one another without network intrusion.

Internal communication can be supplied to employees and activist group members by closed-circuit television and by videos that play continuously in kiosks or migrate among departments throughout an organization. Internal corporate-institutional (or business) video is a multibillion dollar industry. Issues discussants—business and activist—routinely use other video formats as well: video news releases, video brochures, video annual reports, informationals, advertorials, and newsitorials. In one video, produced by the Chemical Manufacturers Association (CMA), former CBS commentator Rod MacLeish affected a stand-up microphone reporter pose to describe how the chemical industry is solving pressing waste and environmental safety problems. Another video sponsored by the Association featured Meryl Comer as correspondent to show the precautions taken by the chemical industry during the transportation of its products. The story made two important points: (a) Federal figures indicate a continued drop in the frequency of chemical transportation accidents, and (b) Chemtrec, a CMA-funded agency, is on the job assisting fire protection and police agencies when they encounter a chemical accident.

Videos have become so cost effective as a narrowcasting device that environmental groups, for instance, use them. "Making a World of Difference" and "Saving Life on Earth" were sent by the World Wildlife Fund to thank contributors to its environmental projects. These videos reminded viewers of the beauty of nature, the ravaging effects humans have on nature, the success that has been accomplished by the environmental group, and the problems that remain to be solved. These videos reinforce environmentalism and encourage contributions to be spent in that cause.

The U.S. Chamber of Commerce fostered the creation of the American Business Network (BizNet), a business-oriented, closed-circuit private television subscription service transmitted via satellite from the chamber's studios in Washington, D.C., to its members (local chambers, companies, associations, and law firms) and nonmembers (colleges, hotels, and cable companies). BizNet supplied a teleconferencing interactive on-line network with receiver sites throughout the country for private use. It has been used to bring PAC managers together by video to coordinate lobbying efforts.

Members of the U.S. Chamber could receive 2 to 4 hours of weekday programming. Programs included in-depth reports on legislative, political, and regulatory events in Washington as well as the 50 state capitals. BizNet featured business and political experts, forecasts and trend analyses, educational workshops, and seminars. Through BizNet's state-of-the-art two-way audio capability, subscribers could interact with program participants in Washington for an annual subscription fee. Nonmembers of the U.S. Chamber were also targeted to receive *BizNet News Today,* a daily 1-hour talk show patterned after *Good Morning America,* with hosts Meryl Comer and Carl Grant. *BizNet News Today* offered policy analysis reports on issues affecting business and financial sectors. The U.S. Chamber produced *Ask Washington,* an hour-long call-in talk program aired daily with leading Capitol Hill figures, and *It's Your Business.* In this half-hour syndicated program available on over 155 stations and cable systems, chamber President and different guests used a moderated discussion-debate format to discuss topical issues.

Members of Congress, for example, have ready access to the professionally equipped congressional television studios, complete with a backdrop of the Capitol, for video news releases directed at TV-cable constituents in their home districts. Many political, public interest, religious, labor, and educational groups seeking greater exposure for their views are also exploring similar opportunities opened up by 30-channel cable, low power TV, direct broadcast satellites, and electronic bulletin boards. C-SPAN has been a vital part of this link to constituents.

The AFL-CIO established a media affiliate in the 1980s, the Labor Institute of Public Affairs, with a $3 million annual budget to create informational television programming. The union has also helped form an ambitious "CableLINE" service test-marketed in Pittsburgh, Atlanta, and Seattle during late 1983. Included were prolabor feature films, such as *Harlan County, U.S.A.* and a half-hour *Labor Visions* weekly news magazine that presented worker views on issues such as the Greyhound Bus Company strike. The AFL-CIO spent an additional $600,000 producing the 12-part issue-oriented *American Works* to screen in nearly 40 selected local television markets. The initial episode described the economics of plant closings and the resulting impact on workers. The United Auto Workers spent $2 million to air commercials aimed at bolstering support for domestic content legislation and offsetting improper Reagan administration interference in GM-Ford labor contracts. The Communications Workers of America aggressively communicated their union's positions on issues such as high technology, airing the television and radio public affairs series, *Rewiring Your World.*

New communication technologies allow for the use of interactive means for delivering public policy-related information in interesting ways that can be rapidly changed as issue development demands. Technical innovation has added many communication tools to be used by issues managers whether on behalf of businesses, government agencies, activist groups, or media programmers. This list contains electronic mail, electronic bulletin boards and discussion groups, computerized mailings targeted at key constituencies, and electronic billboards. Consumer 1-800 numbers can be useful for assisting customers in the proper use of a service or product and in fielding as well as monitoring complaints and diffusing issues. Those numbers provide access for individuals who want to complain about products or services—potentially useful information for issue scanning and analysis. Such insights could foster other research strategies, such as surveys and focus groups.

Companies are setting up on-line Web sites and Internet equivalents, as well as 1-800 numbers, to field and respond to consumer inquiries and comments. For instance, in 1996, McNeil Consumer Products took out a series of print ads in publications such as the *Wall Street Journal* to engage in dialogue with its concerned customers, supporters, and potential regulators. The issue was the effect of alcohol on pain relievers. The ads began with the cognitively involving advice that if the reader consumed three or more alcohol-containing drinks per day, he or she was advised to discuss this matter with a physician before taking over-the-counter pain relievers. Of special interest were those medications that contain acetaminophen, aspirin, ibuprofen, ketoprofen, and naproxen sodium. *Run to the medicine cabinet and read the ingredients!*

Because of potential harms, the Food and Drug Administration Advisory Committees recommended that all over-the-counter pain relievers carry warnings. The sponsors of this ad—exhibiting the persona of proactive corporate responsibility—proudly announced that this company was the first to carry such warning and is considered by physicians to be one of the most trusted over-the-counter sellers of pain killers. Demonstrating its commitment to customer safety—self-imposed control of its product—and fostering positive relationships with its consumers, it offered a 1-800-4-Tylenol number that consumers could call to receive answers to questions and to voice concerns about this issue. Instances such as this demonstrate how technologies increase the openness and responsiveness of proactive issue managers. The assumption is that such efforts employ technologies to reduce barriers and increase access and a sense of personal control by consumers over the companies with which they have business relations. That sort of positive relationship is predictably a better solution than regulation.

Some businesses, such as members of the tobacco industry, offer incentives for people to call 1-800 numbers to voice concerns, for instance regarding their rights as smokers. Once they have made this contact, the company has the person's name, address, and telephone number, in exchange for some issue promotional material. This list offers access to active and cognitively involved publics that support the industry cause. Similar technological options exist for persons who contact companies, activist groups, and governmental agencies by e-mail and bulletin boards. Once they have made themselves known to the sponsoring organization, they can be targeted as a key audience whether they support or oppose the points addressed by the organization. In this case, tobacco companies combine product-service marketing and issues management efforts.

Enterprising companies, government agencies, activists, and industry trade associations create and make available interactive computer systems that would allow access to information and opinion. One innovative instance is educational, interactive programs using CD-ROMs that can be operated on personal computers by students or concerned members of a community to obtain information and solve problems. One program challenges users to manage a forest in ways that are profitable and environmentally responsible. Similar programs might encourage students and concerned citizens to solve problems related to community air or water quality standards and regulation of the source of relevant pollutants. CD-ROM capabilities are readily adaptable to special exhibits, such as open-house presentations by utility companies seeking to allay public concerns about electromagnetic fields created by electric transmissions and distribution power lines.

The EPA oversees the creation and availability of databases that report lists of chemicals that are toxic or harmful to health. Such databases and computer access were mandated in subsection 313 of the Emergency Planning and Community Right-To-Know Act of 1986, section three of the Superfund Amendments and Reauthorization Act of 1986 (SARA Title III). Often in conjunction with local emergency planning committees, the chemical industry has become more proactive, in its Responsible Care program, to using meetings and databases to provide lay publics with technical information regarding the presence of harmful chemicals in each community. These databases report the amounts of these chemicals, symptoms from exposure to them, and remedial actions.

Instead of relying on mainstream outlets, alternative channels play powerful roles in the generation and exchange of ideas that constitute a public dialogue. Substantial concern was voiced about these alternative sources of information following the bomb attack on the federal building in Oklahoma City in 1995 when it was made public that militia groups could share information regarding how to manufacture bombs via computer networks. Issues management is launching into cyberspace. Mainstream organizations routinely employ communication technologies, including computerized databases that are available to subscribers to use, in scanning issues and creating legislative alerts. One of the earliest and most successful systems was NAMnet created by the National Association of Manufacturers. With it, subscribers could obtain legislative and regulatory alerts and issue updates. It included business, financial, and economic news.

Trade associations have offered on-line databases to subscribers for several years. The EEI-on-line service of the Edison Electric Institute, a major trade association for the electricity-generating industry, supplied news, background on issues, and issue alerts of interest to companies that generate electricity, manufacture equipment for that industry, or perform contract work related to the industry.

With the enactment of the High Performance Computer and Communications and National Research and Education Network fostered by the Clinton administration, the United States is moving closer to the realization of an information superhighway. As Ithiel de Sola Pool (1983) observed, such technologies without boundaries weaken central controls when no place (and no source of information) on the globe need be more than a few seconds away electronically. Traditional media often represent the social power interests they supposedly monitor, reinforcing the disenfranchisement of interests and organizations outside the mainstream.

New applications of technologies such as fax, e-mail, Internet, and cable channels are proving effective alternative vehicles for relatively unfiltered and uncensored direct communication to target audiences. Internal e-mail net-

works (intranets), for instance, offer managements and activist group leaders
the opportunity to communicate "directly" and instantaneously with employees and members. Such communication can remain in computer memories, be
read on screen and deleted, or printed for filing or further distribution. On-line
communication translates easily into other forms once it is entered on computer. It can, for instance, make an easy migration from the computer to an
organizational newsletter.

On-line services make E-mail addresses of reporters and media organizations (newspapers, radio stations, and television stations) available to issues
communicators who want to supply these targeted audiences with news
releases and issue backgrounders. That access also allows for quick response
to reporters and program directors when a comment is needed on a news story.
The story angle and coverage could be complemented because of the fairness
and accuracy demonstrated with the reporter. Or suggestions and corrections
could be offered that might be used in subsequent stories. E-mail has an
advantage of providing text that the reporter can use without having to type it
into his or her computer. Rather than responding by telephone—and risking
having to leave a voice mail message—E-mail can wait for the time when
the reporter can be attentive to it. Conventional mail is slow, and fax requires
that the reporter type (or scan) parts of the commentary into his or her
computer.

Burgeoning consulting and placement services are adding dimensions to
issues communicators' access to technologies. One such service is Interactive
PR provided through Lawrence Ragan Communications of Chicago, Illinois.
Other services include CyberSpace PR Report, MediaNet, Inside the Internet,
Internet Week, Multimedia Wire, on-line Tactics, and Technology for Communicators (Bobbitt, 1995). Electronic clipping services, such as Burrelle's
and PR Newswire's eWatch, scan for issue discussions in Internet Usenet
groups.

NAPS-NET (North American Precis Syndicate) is an on-line press release
and clipping-broadcast time service. It takes press releases and other tailored
messages that can be placed on Internet where they can be located by media
editors. This electronic bulletin board gives editors the opportunity to download computer-ready copy that can be easily edited and entered into news and
commentary copy. This electronic message dissemination service gives issues
communicators access to 1,600 large and small daily newspapers as well as
8,500 weeklies and thousands of television and radio stations. This service
can track what outlets accessed the messages and report that data along with
a geographical and demographic profile of the areas reached. Another on-line
outlet having a similar reach is News USA, Inc. CompuServe is a commercial
service provider that sets up address sites that reporters can use to contact
experts on relevant aspects of issues.

Niche agencies and services have grown in response to the burgeoning new communication technologies. News Broadcast Network specializes in helping organizations place radio or video news releases. Services such as SNET assist organizations that want to use teleconferences to reach key audiences, especially through an interactive medium. SNET also offers a fax service that allows clients to place their stories and news items with thousands of outlets in minutes. Video news releases are accessible through World Wide Web and Internet.

Interactive setups enable specialized users immediate, "face-to-face" access to communication experts and corporate executives. One major success story in this use of videoconferencing was Johnson & Johnson's (J&J) response to the September 1982 Tylenol crisis. When several people died in Chicago after taking cyanide-laced Tylenol capsules, crisis response was employed to protect the company's product image and establish new levels of social responsibility by preferring caplets to capsules and improving tamper-proof containers. This crisis gave J&J an excellent opportunity to demonstrate its commitment to achieve the highest corporate social standards. One primary commitment was to show that the company cared by stressing its concern for people and emphasizing the statement on corporate responsibility J&J adopted 40 years before. As the backbone of the crisis management effort, the executives opened J&J operations to public scrutiny.

The company allowed Mike Wallace and a *60 Minutes* crew to video a strategy session. Chairman James E. Burke volunteered to appear on major national television programs. A highlight of the crisis management effort was a 30-city teleconference used to introduce new triple-sealed Tylenol capsule safety packaging. The satellite teleconference attracted representatives from over 6,000 news organizations and gave the company impressive visibility in major markets while solidifying reporter perceptions that J&J executives were telling the truth.

Striking Air Line Pilots Association (ALPA) in 1983 used a national videoconference to charge that Continental Airlines planes were being flown by inexperienced and psychologically stressed crews shortly after the carrier voided labor contracts, eliminated routes, and declared Chapter 11 bankruptcy. ALPA president Henry Duffy's claim that Continental committed 152 safety violations was featured on *60 Minutes*. ALPA executed a video press conference beamed by Telstar 301 to media representatives (including 200 commercial television stations) in the 32 cities served by Continental. ALPA used telex to notify stations that the broadcast would be available for airing. The short-term result: Approximately 11 million homes with 28 million viewers saw the releases (Hattal & Hattal, 1984).

On-line commercial databases are a window onto the world. Persons interested in keeping abreast of the available commercial databases can periodically consult *Gale Director of Databases,* which is likely to be available through most large public libraries and those in colleges. Catalog listings or marketing brochures supplied by the vendors reveal almost endless research options—the future of which is limited only by the lack of imagination.

New on-line services appear each day. One that is valuable for issues monitoring went into service in 1996. It is CQ Washington Alert, an on-line service from the organization the published the *Congressional Quarterly* that provides access to primary and secondary information about U.S. federal legislation and the legislative process. This allows an interested party to see where a bill is in the legislative process, research legislators and their voting records, as well as to search and read *CQ Weekly Report, CQ Researcher,* and *Governing.*

Some large corporations subscribe to satellite-fed news services, the primary sources of information for print and electronic newsrooms. These services put out a stream of information that can be captured through the end users' computers and brought into print or placed into newsroom copy via computer networks. The advantages to companies that can afford such subscriptions, which are quite expressive, is the ability to have individuals and computers maintain constant vigilance for the name of the company and its products and services as well as those of its industry and competitors. If news reports appear on the service during a day and the company (or industry) becomes aware of them, immediate response can be made. Such responses could include correcting facts or putting into the service the comments of the company to interpret and correct judgments and interpretations that are likely to make their way into final electronic or print news stories. Factual errors can be difficult or impossible to correct once they are made public. If the news organization wants comment from a company spokesperson, the subscriber can make such persons available during the time the story is developing.

CompuServe not only allows electronic mail but also offers the following reference databases: Academic American Encyclopedia, Books in Print, Computer Database Plus, Computer Directory, and Newspaper Library. Data-Star offers more than 300 databases that provide worldwide coverage of news reports. Available through this commercial service are business news, financial information, trademarks, market research, trade statistics, industry analysis, health care and pharmaceuticals, chemicals, petrochemicals, chemical industries, biomedicine, biotechnology, and various other technologies.

One of the largest commercial services is Dialog Information Services, Inc., which gives subscribers access to approximately 400 major databases. It supplies the American Library Director, Book Review Index, Books in Print, British Books in Print, Business Software Database, Buyer's Guide to Micro Software, Computer ASAP, Computer Database, Computer News Fulltext, Computer-Readable Database, Conference Papers Index, ERIC, Everyman's Encyclopedia, Findex, Gale Director of Publications, Information Science

Abstracts, LC Marc-Books, Library and Information Science Abstracts, Microcomputer Software Guide, Microcomputer Index, on-line/CD-ROM Database News, and REMARC. Those databases, among other options, give access to an array of newspapers and scholarly publications in all disciplines.

Among other resources, DataTimes supplies subscribers with over 5,000 leading sources ranging from U.S. newspapers to U.K.'s huge FT Profile and the information contained on five Reuters business wires as well as the top TV news programs. Full-text national publications, such as *Fortune, Forbes, Money, Inc.*, and *Business Week* are available, as are abstracts from the *Wall Street Journal* and the *New York Times.*

Mead Data Central provides Lexis (60 legal databases) and Nexis (16 databases on a variety of topics) as well as Lexis Public Records on-line Service (4 databases) and Medis Service, which includes MEDLINE. Dow Jones News/Retrieval sells access to full-text versions of major business publications as well as financial materials on 750,000 companies listed by Standard and Poors. WLN offers 8.2 million MARC bibliographic records as well as access to Internet.

Orbit Search Service offers access to more than 100 databases on a range of subjects. It serves National Union Catalog Codes, Microsearch, Power, and Scientific & Technical Books & Serials in Print. CDP on-line offers access to 160 databases with a focus on biomedical data. NewsNet features industry newsletters that cover topics relevant to business and the professions.

As a supplement to traditional media efforts, on-line options offer participating companies and industries the potential to bypass reporters to speak directly via articles, fact sheets, position papers, and other useful data to a willing audience. This ideal issues communication vehicle serves the public interest by expanding access to issue discussions. Rather than relying on editorial discretion, readers can go into large data systems and find authoritative, unedited information (which would otherwise be unavailable) about corporate operations and industrial practices. Multiple addressing via electronic mail services, such as Western Union EasyLink, offer additional message-tailoring options.

Some groups, especially activists, provide their own news stories. One of several stories supplied by Investor Responsibility Research Center focused on details about environmental damage to South American rain forests. Of related interest would be a protest circular used by the Rainforest Action Network to call for a boycott of products by Texaco Oil Company. The circular offered data about Texaco's environmental irresponsibility over 25 years. A focal point in this analysis was the damage these business practices had on the Amazon natives.

World Wide Web pages are being used to supply information as well as to elicit commentary and problem solution advice from stakeholders and stakeseekers. Such pages are established by all of the traditional organizations engaging in issues management. These pages can supply information and opinion that is updated as revision becomes necessary. These pages are locatable by users through netsearch capabilities. Such capabilities facilitate key issue or topic searches and allow for easy location of sponsoring organizations' Web addresses. Once a user locates one of these addresses, it can be entered as a bookmark for later easy access.

Web sites offer text and visual images. That kind of presentation is ideal for organizations that wish to present issue-position-relevant information and opinion. One additional feature is the ability of various Web sites to be cross-referenced with other sites. For instance, a site sponsored by an organization discussing an issue can provide details about that issue—and can refer the reader to other Web addresses where additional issue-relevant information and opinion can be found. Both on Web and Internet, for example, organizations engaged in issue-relevant discussions routinely ask for and supply addresses—electronic and regular postal—as well as telephone numbers that give issue discussants access to one another.

Listservs and Web discussion pages exist. Some are provided by environmental groups such as Greenpeace and the Aubudon Society. Others are created by other interested parties. Web pages often provide search engines to locate relevant databases and discussion groups. Companies as well provide issue pages and discussion sites. For instance, in 1996, Shell Oil Company prepared a page that explained its stance on the Nigerian controversy. Shell made available a discussion room for those who wanted to participate in the dialogue. Mobil places its issue ads at its Web site and invites commentary.

Earth Island provides a Web site with its Journal and ReThink Paper. It supplies the Bluewater network that gives interested users access to related groups and topics. The Audubon Society Web page describes the organization, its membership, education program, and publications, as well as provides a public policy and advocacy page. A search could bring the interested surfer to the Environmental Organization WebDirector. Greenpeace has a series of interlocking sites that featured reports: Greenpeace Toxics Reports, Greenpeace USA Energy and Toxics Reports, Greenpeace USA Nuclear Reports, Greenpeace USA Ocean Ecology and Biodiversity Reports, Greenpeace USA Toxic Trade Reports. Greenpeace offers interested parties discussion pages and supplies its own search engine for those looking for additional information.

Dow Chemical Company used its Web pages to summarize court decisions regarding the breast implant controversy that plagued the company during the 1990s. A search of documents using the term "Dow Chemical Company breast implant" generated 7,602 documents available on October 1, 1996. As Dow used the Web to reach publics and audiences, a site was established by critics of Dow to assist women and other interested users who wanted to know how to file a suit against Dow. Of related interest, on October 1, 1996, the Consumer Law Page reported having had 270,149 visitors since its creation.

This brief review of communication technologies glimpses the burgeoning and quickly changing array of options that issues communicators have to supply and receive information and issue commentary. Some of these, especially the Web, allow for interactive dialogue, collaborative decision making, and negotiation. Perhaps the most synthesizing conclusion from this review is to observe that we have not yet seen the future of innovation that will give individuals and organizations more immediate and personal access to one another for debate, discussion, and negotiation. Narrowcasting and dialogue rather than mass dissemination of information and opinion is the paradigm of the future.

 Conclusion: What Is the Future of Issues Communication?

Rather than McLuhan's (1969) vision of one global village, society may be inexorably drifting toward polarized "global villages" where consubstantiation and identification on many serious issues is impossible. Assuming the need for a common platform of fact and a shared evaluation of the activities by business and other large organizations, some constructive alternative is necessary so that society can forge supportive rather than contradictory and inharmonious zones of meaning. Arenas of open public debate and collaborative decision making are vital.

The future? Issues communicators may create interactive computer-assisted communication options that allow them to challenge communicants to download informational games. Activists may make available games that allows persons to test their ability to manage solid waste or regulate air and water quality. Chemical companies might challenge communicants to operate a chemical plant in ways that make money, protect employees and area residents' health and safety, and generate jobs and tax revenue for the community. Timber companies can offer their own versions—adapted by age—of how to operate timber resources as a renewable and sustainable resource. Who knows where the human imagination will lead?

Issues Management
and Crisis Communication

Preparing for the Worst

Consumer safety—Cyanide in Johnson & Johnson's Tylenol capsules. Environmental quality—Exxon Valdez oil spill in Prince William Sound, Alaska, March 24, 1989. Fairness—60,000 Chrysler Corporation executive cars with odometers disconnected to not record miles so the cars could be sold as new. Public safety—Bhopal, India's Union Carbide chemical plant release of methyl isocyanate (MIC), a deadly poison. National security—Assassination of President John Kennedy. Student safety—Students killed at Kent State University and at Jackson State University. Worker safety—Selikoff studies link asbestos to lung cancer and asbestosis. Customer safety—Pan American flight 103 blown up by terrorists over Lockerbie, Scotland, December 21, 1988. Customer safety—Dow Chemical silicone breast implants. Public health and safety—Times Beach and dioxin, the Alar scare regarding chemicals on apples, Three Mile Island and nuclear power plant radiation, Love Canal and oozing chemicals in a residential neighborhood. These crises have become iconic, a part of the popular culture of our society. They define the types of events that we think of as crises and the responses expected in their aftermath.

Crises come in all kinds and exhibit degrees of severity. Some become issues. Many involve loss of life or property damage—or both. Others result from events such as bankruptcy, loss of a senior officer, or scandal that portend harm to concerned parties. Some occur because of actions by the organization, such as a major change in policy, sudden closure or relocation of facilities, or a violation of law or regulation. Some are the products of what others do, as in the case of a terrorist attack on an airliner.

Most crises have little if any likelihood of maturing to the public policy stage as issues. Most are likely to have consequences only for the marketing (revenue generation) or funding-raising activities of the organization. Failure of banks and savings & loans as well as the unwise use of charitable dollars by the head of United Way are examples of crises that affected revenue generation. False advertising is a recurring practice that can reach crisis level. This activity is against the law. Unless the law needs clarification or more stringent interpretation, however, the interests of the customer are adequately protected. In similar fashion, product recalls—even product tampering—are more likely to be a marketing and operational concern rather than something that matures into a public policy issue.

Crisis management and issues management are linked. Some crises have the potential for becoming issues if they create or add to a key public's sense that a problem exists that needs public policy remedy. Some issues may become crises as key publics press organizations and industries to achieve higher standards of performance. In rare cases, the issue can threaten the existence of the company or industry, as is the case of the antitobacco critics' efforts to destroy the tobacco industry. A crisis can be an event that creates an issue or keeps it alive or gives it strength.

Discussion of crisis response and issues management might open by posing a hypothesis: If a company acts responsibly and engages in the fundamentals of issues management, it will not be surprised; it will not suffer the unsettling experience of a crisis. That statement is fraught with wishful thinking. A more accurate prediction of the connection between crisis and issues management is this: If a company is engaged in issues management before, during, and after a crisis, it can mitigate—perhaps prevent—the crisis from becoming an issue by working quickly and responsibly to establish or reestablish the level of control desired by relevant stakeholders.

A variation of control is trust, the extent to which party A can rely on actions and statements by party B when party A is vulnerable to those actions or statements. Crisis management is designed to exert control on behalf of the organization and its stakeholders, and Marconi (1992) featured trust as "the cornerstone of business relationships" (p. 3).

The theme of this chapter is that crisis management is an issues management function that entails issues monitoring, strategic planning, and getting the house in order, to try to avoid events that trigger outrage and uncertainty and have the potential of maturing into public policy issues. If all of these management pieces are in place, then crisis communication—especially media relations—is easier to manage. In discussing this theme, this chapter considers the circumstances that can lead to a crisis event that has negative effects—or at least their potential. It stresses the need for crisis prevention—to maximize the sense of control the organization exerts over its affairs and the mutually beneficial relationships it should create and maintain with its stakeholders. Featuring an issues management approach, an argument will be made that crisis conditions and events can be lessened by effective strategic business planning and an appropriate sense of corporate responsibility that is implemented by effective operational and personnel procedures. Only a fool or the most optimistic writer and planner would assume that if planning and management are effective, a crisis will never occur, but that is an interesting point of departure. Based on an issues management approach to crisis management, discussion centers on the precrisis efforts as well as the communication options that are available during and in the wake of a crisis—or at least what seems to be a crisis.

 Crisis Management: The Search for Control

What is a crisis? Not all newsworthy events are crises. Nor must the definition of crisis be limited to those that threaten the existence of an organization. For example, the Exxon Valdez oil spill did not threaten Exxon's existence, but it has been widely considered to be an archetypal crisis. Whereas the magnitude of the Exxon spill might have destroyed many companies, Exxon had sufficient financial and technical reserves to weather that storm. Framed in this manner, this section defines crises and suggests that they occur in degrees of severity, threats to the integrity of the organization. It views crisis management and response as a search for control, either by the offending organization or by society. Issues management is a search for order—for control.

A crisis is an untimely event that can be anticipated, that may prevent management from accomplishing its efforts to create the understanding and satisfaction between their organization and interested parties needed to negotiate the mutually beneficial exchange of stakes. If unattended or poorly managed, the crisis can prevent the organization from making satisfactory progress toward achieving its mission.

> A crisis is an unstable time or state of affairs in which a decisive change is impending—either one with the distinct possibility of a highly undesir-

able outcome or one with the distinct possibility of a highly *desirable* and extremely *positive* outcome. (Fink, 1986, p. 15).

As Weick (1988) concluded, "Crises are characterized by low probability of high consequence events that threaten the most fundamental goal of an organization" (p. 305). A crisis threatens the physical system of the organization as well as "its basic assumptions, its subjective sense of self, its existential core" (Pauchant & Mitroff, 1992, p. 12).

A definition of crises must include an awareness that they come in degrees. For instance, a crisis event can be characterized in terms of its potential impact on the health of an organization:

- ※ Bed rest: an event that receives front-page, top-of-the-hour coverage. It attracts public attention but is unlikely to threaten the existence of the organization even if it fails to make a strategic response.

- ※ Medication: an event that requires the organization to respond to media inquiry and may demand changes in operations to prevent or lessen the likelihood of recurrence; explanation and sympathetic response as well as modest change are likely to suffice as crisis responses.

- ※ Chronic: an event that demands that the organization communicate with the media and formulate changes that are implemented to prevent recurrence of this event. Without such response, confidence is likely to be lost in regard to the organization's operations and key personnel. People will see reason to allocate their resources to other organizations.

- ※ Fatal: an event that ends the existence of the organization because it lacked the technical, financial, human, and communicative resources to restore faith with its stakeholders. The organization is so badly damaged that it cannot generate the resources it needs to sustain itself.

The first two conditions are likely to be corrected by routine actions of the organization working to put its house in order. The second two are more serious, implying the likelihood of public policy action, even if the organization does not survive the crisis. The tendency is to create regulation or legislation to prevent incidents from recurring.

Although this list addresses crises in terms of a hierarchy of health concern metaphors, it might feature concepts related to the integrity of materials: tension, strain, stress, and failure. Similar lists could be proposed to suggest a progression from the point where an organization is under extra pressure through a series of stages where its integrity fails.

Coombs (1995) created a four-part taxonomy that featured the locus of responsibility for the crisis and the degree to which it was the result of intentional acts: faux pas, accidents, terrorism, and transgressions. The locus of responsibility could be internal (poor operational procedures) or external (act of God or terrorism). Set against these options are considerations of whether the crisis resulted from intentional (transgressions of corporate responsibility) or unintentional (act of God) motives. As external and unintentional factors come together, we have a faux pas. When unintentional and internal factors occur, they produce an accident. Terrorism is one product of intentional motives and external acts. Transgressions result from intentional motives and internal acts.

The objective of crisis management is to exert control over activities in ways that assure stakeholders and stakeseekers that their interests are cared for and fostered by the organization. That is a best-case scenario. Even the best, most vigilant organization can suffer events that, even when foreseen and planned for, cannot be prevented. Effective planning and the exertion of corporate responsibility—as well as informed and responsive communication—are the tools an organization, even an industry, can use to avoid the imposition of external control.

Crisis response is likely to be better if it follows planning that includes all relevant specialists. Issues managers and public relations practitioners seem to benefit from the size of their organization and whether it has experienced a serious crisis; however, many organizations do not have a crisis plan. Of the respondents in a national survey of communication practitioners, only 36.3% reported that they worked in an organization that both had a plan and practiced it. Once a crisis is encountered by an employer, communication practitioners find themselves more included in the creation and practice of crisis response plans (Guth, 1995).

As a discipline, issues management can serve firms by engaging in reciprocal activities that increase the control stakeholders and stakeseekers have over the conditions of their lives, "the *optimization* of the satisfactions of its stakeholders" (Ewing, 1987, p. 32). Mintzberg (1984) asked, "Who should control the corporation" (p. 90)? As rationale for more sensitive and responsive management, Mintzberg concluded, "Our challenge is to find ways to distribute the power in and around our large organizations so that they will remain responsive, vital, and effective" (p. 113). They must control their activities—in the interest of their stakeholders, or control will be imposed on them.

Although control can have a negative connotation, in reality no stakeholder or stakeseeker wants to engage in stake exchanges with organizations that fail or are unable to establish and maintain proper amounts of control over their activities. In contrast to the difficulty Exxon had in responding to the events during the Valdez event, that company seemed, to Duhe and Zoch (1994-1995), to be much more successful in the aftermath of an August 2, 1993, plant explosion in Baton Rouge, Louisiana. This time, Exxon demonstrated an ability to understand and achieve corporate responsibility, showed compassion for those affected by the explosion, and brought its expertise to bear in ways that evidenced its control of the technical aspects of the event. Exxon helped its publics react to emergency measures and cope psychologically with damage to lives and property that resulted from the event. The theme: Exxon demonstrated its willingness and ability to work with the community to regain control—technically, emotionally, and in terms of health and safety.

Reflecting on the confluence of crisis management and issues management, Hearit (1994) concluded, "Given the terminological nature of crises, crisis management is a form of issue management, in which crisis managers attempt to control the terms used to describe corporate actions" (p. 122). Whereas this view partially corresponds to the definition of issues management set forward in this book, some major differences are worth examination.

Issues management entails strategic business planning and management with a sensitivity to the public policy arena of the organization: issues monitoring, efforts to define and implement standards of corporate responsibility needed to meet key publics' expectations, and issues communication. Hearit's definition tends to deal narrowly with the latter aspect, suggesting that crisis and issues management is exclusively associated with terminological functions. Any company or other organization may suffer a crisis because what it did does not satisfy stakeholder expectations; it may be dead wrong, doing the wrong things, and stupid given the circumstances of the organization vis-à-vis its key publics' expectations. Actions that prompt the crisis may be illegal. That is hardly terminological. Thus, crisis management must consider the total array of activities engaged in by the organization, set in the context of expectations held by its publics, and observed from their point of view.

Circumstances of a crisis may be, but do not necessarily constitute, an issue. An issue is a contestable matter of fact, value, or policy that results in conflict between concerned parties and entails the distribution of resources, either as threat or opportunities for the organization. The events of a crisis may be contestable, requiring—even expecting—informed persuasion to set the record straight. Beyond that circumstance, a crisis is likely to be best defined in terms of the organization's strategic business and public policy planning. Either the organization brings the crisis to an end by exerting proper control to resolve it, or a public policy issue has the potential of maturing into a regulatory or legislative change or an adverse court decision.

If strategic business planning uses issues management to calculate and navigate threats and opportunities, the crisis may require expenditure of moneys, which if wisely allocated can restore or build a mutually beneficial relationship between the organization and its stakeholders. Failing that effort, which may entail implementation of higher standards of corporate responsibility, key stakeholding publics may try—in the marketplace or the public policy arena—to force higher standards of performance on any organization that suffers a crisis and does not make responses needed to control its activities in the interest of concerned publics. These responses may require communication. They may require improved strategic planning or higher standards of corporate responsibility. They may mature into public policy battles. They are not merely terminological.

Crisis is about control. People want control of that which affects their self-interest and altruistic interests. Control springs from their desire to lessen the uncertainty that actions of some entity may adversely affect their health, safety, aesthetics, and well-being as well as that of animals or other aspects of the environment. Uncertainty is uncomfortable. As a personal trait, it is the perception of one's degree of certainty in a social situation (Berger & Calabrese, 1975). The concept can be viewed as "a lack of sure knowledge about the course of past, present, future or hypothetical events" (Driskill & Goldstein, 1986, p. 41). As Albrect (1988) concluded, uncertainty is "the lack of attributional confidence about cause-effect patterns" (p. 387). According to this approach to crisis and risk (a topic expanded in Chapter 10), people believe either that circumstances are so random and unpredictable, due to the crisis, that no favorable outcome can be predicted. Or they compensate for that discomfort by predicting that dire rather than favorable outcomes will occur. People tend to assume dire consequences will outweigh positive ones; therefore, they engage in self-protective thinking and behavior.

If actions of an organization actually or even seemingly interfere with an individual's effort for control, he or she is likely to seek to achieve or reassert control. One means for achieving control is to support activist criticism of an organization or industry, seeking to browbeat it into submission. Another means for exerting control is to call on government to intervene on behalf of the public and against the organization. Courts provide avenues for exerting control.

Crisis occurs when an organization actually or seemingly loses control of its operations and the consequences of that action appears or actually does have dire consequences. Viewed that way, crisis response is an issues management strategy that has as its outcome the maintenance or restoration of control over organizational procedures or operations in ways that do not demand interference by activists or government officials as a remedy. According to Renfro (1993),

> If issues are not anticipated and identified early in their development life, the response is crisis management on an issue-by-issue basis. While a stand-by crisis management capability is always necessary, it is planned to be just that: a stand-by capability and not one that is used. (p. 63)

Responsible organizations work hard to enact the persona that they are in control of their futures—and the futures of all that can be affected by them. Crisis strains the appearance and actuality of control. Crisis response is the enactment of control in the face of high uncertainty in an effort to win or restore audiences' and publics' confidence.

Given the need to assist organizations' efforts to achieve proper control, issues managers should have two major game plans, one for long-range objectives and one for crises. Many crises seem not to involve an issue—such as the Johnson & Johnson's Tylenol capsule-tampering case. If Johnson & Johnson had not proactively undertaken measures (partly to avoid liability and partly as a marketing strategy) to provide tamperproof packaging and adopt the use of caplets in place of capsules, legislation was likely. Capsules could be opened and toxic substances, such as cyanide, could be placed inside in place of the proper ingredients. Because of the responsible behavior evidenced by the company and the industry in this situation, the issue was not defined as a problem that would not be corrected voluntarily.

Some crises prove that an issue needs attention. For instance, the Three Mile Island nuclear generating plant incident increased national concern over the safety of such facilities. Public pressure focused on the Nuclear Regulatory Commission. This incident produced a domino effect of increased regulation of existing plants as well as those under construction. Some safety features were retrofitted to bring existing plants to new levels of safe operation.

Crisis response has become that aspect of issues management that entails imagining events that could become crises leading to issues and planning for the eventuality that an event will occur that has immediate negative consequences for the organization and its constituents—its products are unsafe, its procedures are unsafe, its values are corrupt, or its management is callous, uncaring, or incompetent. Given the paradigm that issues management is a discipline that is central to society's search for order, a crisis can become an issue when the offending organization seems unable or unwilling to exert sufficient control to create and maintain the mutually beneficial relationships its stakeholders expect.

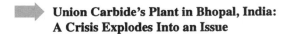 **Union Carbide's Plant in Bhopal, India:
A Crisis Explodes Into an Issue**

This section focuses on one of the most dramatic crises of the 1980s. It is a paradigm case of a crisis becoming an issue as society sought control over the chemical industry that seemed to violate public expectations. The focal organization in this case, Union Carbide, generated such concern and outrage that legislators and EPA regulators imposed new, stringent requirements on the chemical industry.

Issues emerge, become visible, and progress toward legislative or regulatory resolution for many reasons, one of which is a cataclysmic or sustained series of crises that violate expectations held by one or more key publics. Through negative news coverage and rhetorical efforts of activist groups, toxic chemicals have been associated with environmental destruction as well as public health and safety over the past three decades. To revamp their images, individual chemical companies and their trade associations, such as the Chemical Manufacturers Association, have responded by opting for a variety of public affairs approaches, including image and issue advertising. Typical ads featured either a safety specialist or member of the environmental protection team who announced that chemical facilities and procedures are safe and clean. Ads such as these were designed to assure the public that it need not worry about the safety of chemical plant operations: Facilities are safe; rest assured.

Such expert-informed conclusions could have assuaged public fears even when activist outrage and sensationalist reporting tended to overwhelm scientific data used in risk assessments (*Chemical Risks,* 1985; Copulos, 1985). However calming such ads were, the catalyst for public awareness of and concern about the health and safety hazards of living near chemicals was a series of catastrophic events, especially the Love Canal disclosures and the 1984 MIC leak in Bhopal, India, that killed more than 3,000 people and resulted in more than 200,000 injuries. Both incidents stunned the chemical industry, underscoring how smoldering issues become inflamed once graphically publicized.

Immediately after the Bhopal tragedy, Rosenblatt (1984) observed, "If the world felt especially close to Bhopal last week, it may be because the world is Bhopal, a place where the occupational hazard is modern life" (p. 20). Worry generated activist concern, which prompted passage of the Emergency Planning and Community Right-To-Know Act, section three of the Superfund Amendments and Reauthorization Act of 1986 (SARA Title III). It mandated each governor to appoint members to a State Emergency Response Commission, which in turn created local emergency planning committees. This was one step toward the Clean Air Act of 1990, which was projected to cost approximately $166 billion over two decades for chemical plant improvement (Sullivan, 1993).

Normally, a story about India would receive minor play in the U.S. press. Helping fuel interest in Bhopal was not only the magnitude and severity of the tragedy but also the fact that it involved a U.S. firm that was manufacturing the same lethal chemical in this country. After Bhopal, the media recalled prior instances of disaster, including Texas City, Texas, in 1947; Saveso, Italy, in

1976; Béziers, France, in 1977; and the BASF factory failures in 1921 and 1979. Discussions of classic cases of a crisis make an issue so salient that the likelihood of government intervention substantially increases.

A prescient *Wall Street Journal* reporter, Terence Roth (1984) speculated that because of Bhopal, "the chemical industry may be facing a fresh wave of legislation to tighten controls on uses of such lethal substances" (p. 4). Editorials debated the value of chemicals to protect lives and promote food production (Boffey, 1984) versus their safety and that of facilities where they are manufactured (Beck, Greenberg, Hager, Harrison, & Underwood, 1984; Grier, 1984).

Activists demanded stricter regulation as they pointed out that the manu-facture of dangerous substances in populated areas is common. At the time of the Bhopal incident, approximately 6,000 facilities were making toxic and hazardous chemicals, with 180,000 shipments occurring by rail and truck each day in the United States. A *Newsweek* article acknowledged,

> The U.S. chemical industry can boast of a strong safety record. But with more than 60,000 chemicals produced and stored in America, government regula-tors and watchdog groups can't even tell where potential time bombs are—let alone guarantee that they won't go off. (Whitaker, Mazumdar, Gibney, & Behr, 1984, p. 28)

Wall Street Journal writers similarly observed, "On the inside, the chemical and refining industries maintain the most exemplary safety record in U.S. manufacturing. But outside the plants, community ignorance of chemical risk remains widespread, and preparedness for the unlikely calamity remains spotty" (Petzinger & Burrough, 1984, p. 1).

A complicating factor—authorities did not know much about the dangers posed by the chemicals in use and under manufacture. The Toxic Substances Control Act, passed in 1976, required that new chemicals be studied before they go on the market, but that requirement had been applied to only about 20% of all products by the mid-1980s. Chemical companies developed inter-nal safety rules, created their own extraordinarily competent fire departments, and established precautions to protect workers, forestall regulation, as well as maintain proprietary control over various chemical products (Loddeke, 1984). Many positive steps taken by the industry were overlooked by reporters and concerned publics once fear entered the information and policy decision equation.

Henry A. Waxman (D. California), House subcommittee chairman, held hearings on this issue. He was asked on ABC-TV's *This Week with David Brinkley* whether "we let the industry continue to police itself or does the government step in?" In addition to measures designed to increase safety from toxic leaks, Waxman was concerned with the long-term effects of chemical exposure, particularly cancer. Underscoring his worry, the California Democrat recalled a 1981 study by Union Carbide that depicted periodic leakage of MIC and other chemicals during manufacturing and handling processes. In the midst of this controversy, Union Carbide was fined $55,000 for nine environmental violations it had reported having occurred since 1982 at its South Charleston Technical Center ("Carbide's U.S. plant," 1984).

One of the most damaging pieces of information surrounding the disaster was Carbide's claim that it knew a runaway disaster was possible at least 3 months prior to the Bhopal accident. A warning memo had been prepared by a Carbide safety inspection team and was received by the manager of the Institute, West Virginia, plant on September 19, 1984. This memo was made public by Rep. Waxman who indicated that he did not know whether corrective actions had been taken at any plants ("Carbide was warned," 1985).

Later, Carbide reported that it had revised its operating procedures several weeks before the Bhopal incident. Jackson B. Browning, Director of Health, Safety, and Environmental Affairs for Carbide, stated that the changes implemented in the operations at Institute were irrelevant to Bhopal because the two plants were designed differently. Browning noted that the company had undertaken increased safety measures at the Institute plant to detect the presence of water and other contaminants in the process for manufacturing and storing MIC. Training procedures were revised (Winslow, 1985a). The industry tried to play down the 28 leaks, whereas activists and governmental regulators charged that any leaks were unsettling. Carbide also operated an MIC facility in France, where residents asserted they were caught between working in possibly hazardous conditions and suffering unemployment (Kamm, 1984).

After the Bhopal catastrophe, Carbide ceased MIC production at Institute. By mid-February 1985, it was ready to resume producing the chemical there because corrective actions had been taken. One change was the addition of a computerized system to monitor weather and wind conditions and predict how they would disperse chemicals in the event of a leak. In opposition to this announcement by Carbide, Waxman claimed that starting up production was "premature." Rep. Robert E. Wise (D. West Virginia), whose district included Institute, welcomed the plant restarting (Winslow, 1985b).

Such publicity added fervor to those seeking to impose stringent national—even international—standards. Activist groups, including the Environmental Action Foundation, Washington Fair Share, and Public Citizen Health Research Group, used this opportunity to voice their opinions (Solomon & Russell, 1984). Several cities and states passed or at least considered legislation to require companies to inform workers of any hazardous chemicals they were handling. An EPA study reported that current law may be inadequate to protect people who live near such facilities (Meier, 1985).

Just how effective was Carbide in dealing with the press, government, and the public at large? That's hard to answer, given the considerable national and international attention to the incident and mixed news coverage Carbide received. It appears that the corporate players in this crisis believed that a low key effort was best because they were slow to mount a crisis response campaign. Union Carbide made itself available to the press and showed signs that it was interested in safety. It issued media releases on legal developments, scientific findings, new safety measures, and operating changes. The company provided funds for medical care and established a research program at a university hospital in Bhopal.

A 1985 opinion survey conducted by the Media Institute of 20 major daily newspaper and weekly news magazine editors and 20 major chemical corporation public relations executives found Union Carbide scored above average in its responsiveness to media requests. Editors and executives virtually agreed that the overall tone of media coverage toward the company had been neutral (*Chemical Risks,* 1985).

In their contacts with the media, company representatives were not always well-prepared. In the face of initial questioning by reporters, for example, Carbide admitted there were no emergency evacuation plans for Bhopal nor did the company understand the circumstances of the accident well enough to be able to explain how it happened and, thus, how it could have been prevented (Marbach, Gibney, Gander, Tsuruoka, & Greenburg, 1984). Even a month later, Union Carbide still was unable to account for the operating procedures that led to the release of MIC. Such information gaps raised uncertainty and assisted activists by sustaining audience interest in their policy agenda.

Despite Union Carbide's statement that it would pursue a total communication program as part of its 1985 marketing strategy, company spokespersons agreed that the program was slow to emerge because of continuing uncertainty over how to approach a post-Bhopal information and opinion climate (Editors, 1985). To its credit, Carbide volunteered to assist governmental efforts, United States and abroad, to put into play regulatory mechanisms that could prevent a similar disaster. Carbide worked with congressional agencies, scientific organizations, and reporters to generate information that could be used to assess the problems of producing, transporting, and storing hazardous and toxic materials. Much more could have been said publicly if not for liability claims so large they threatened the financial future of the company. At some point in every crisis, executives must listen to legal counsel; perhaps they listen too much and too soon to counselors trained to think only of court proceedings and not the court of public scrutiny.

The Bhopal incident harmed the image of chemical manufacturers and their operating environment. Aftershocks were not confined to Carbide. The industry had limited impact in playing down the seriousness of leaks, whereas

activists and governmental regulators proved effective in charging that any
leak is unsettling—because of immediate safety concerns or long-term health
reasons. Demonstrating a strong sense of corporate responsibility and a
prudent sensitivity to community outrage, many companies decided to enhance their operating standards.

Shortly after Bhopal, Du Pont Corporation plant managers in La Porte,
Texas, for example, publicized operating plant changes to limit on-site MIC
storage. Management decided to produce MIC in a "closed-loop" system, an
improvement that cost $10 million to $11 million. Thus, the chemical could
be used immediately after it was produced, to minimize the risk of large
amounts escaping from storage facilities. Insecticide manufacturers began to
relocate facilities closer to product sources. Surrounding communities became safer with production limited to several pounds rather than the estimated
45 tons that escaped in India. Such measures could improved attitudes by key
publics unsettled about chemical industry safety.

Concern and rage continued. The *Wall Street Journal* noted that "the idea
of applying criminal laws to corporate executives is getting increased attention
worldwide" because of the mass poisoning in India. The "tragedy," the
Journal reported, "is generating demands for tougher corporate-responsibility
laws." Quoted was 19th-century English judge Edward Baron Thurlow's
lament: " 'Did you ever expect a corporation to have a conscience when it has
no soul to be damned and no body to be kicked?' Then . . . 'By God, it ought
to have both' " (Trost, 1985, p. 14). This story captured the iceberg tip of the
controversy

In response to calls for criminal actions against chemical company
executives, the National Association of Manufacturers claimed that civil court
is the proper place for remedies. Quoted in opposition was Timothy Smith,
director of the Interfaith Center on Corporate Responsibility, a coalition of
church investors, who said "Let's send people to jail" (Trost, 1985, p. 14). In
this opinion atmosphere, the chemical industry decided to change operating
procedures and communicate quietly—if at all.

A crisis can become an issue if it demonstrates to a concerned public that
its worries are justified—an offending organization or industry is failing to
properly control its operations. To avoid further crises, society sets out to
correct the behavior that created the concern. This search for order is the
feeding ground of issues management.

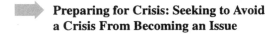 **Preparing for Crisis: Seeking to Avoid
a Crisis From Becoming an Issue**

One prerequisite for effective crisis management is an insightful concern that
specific events could constitute a crisis. As emphasized throughout this book,

issues management is a strategic planning and response option that organizations can use to create and maintain mutually beneficial relationships with key stakeholders and stakeseekers. If monitoring of issues and activities is sufficiently rigorous and if the house is in order, then the organization is more likely to avoid the trajectory of a crisis becoming an issue of public policy concern. This section addresses strategies that organizations may use to prevent crises and lessen their long-term effects.

Wise crisis management begins before a crisis occurs. It entails the fundamental functions of issues management: strategic business planning, issues monitoring, working to ascertain and implement high standards of corporate responsibility, and having key personnel coordinated and trained to communicate honestly, clearly, factually, and candidly—with minimal interference from legal counsel who understand court procedures better than they comprehend media relations and the consequences of being tried in the court of public opinion.

This observation brings us to one of the disciplinary battles that needs to be resolved prior to a crisis event: that between legal counsel and public relations. Typical counsel from lawyers is to say nothing that can be used in a court of law—which is quite different from the court of public opinion. The court of public scrutiny plays by different ethical and evidentiary standards than does a court of law. The public no longer believes there is such a thing as an industrial *accident*. Faith in engineering and operating expertise abounds. Accidents are blamed on carelessness and cutbacks, smacking of corporate irresponsibility along with its dire implications for corporate and industry reputations and images. Unwillingness to make statements is admission of guilt.

The training of lawyers is to put the burden of proof on the adversary and to operate on the principle that an organization (or individual) is innocent until proven guilty. Experience has taught savvy communication counselors that the world outside the courtroom works on the opposite heuristic. During a crisis, an organization is guilty until it proves itself innocent, and what it does *not* say can and will be held against it. A collaborative effort, in advance of and during the event, is likely to win a more favorable public and media response toward the organization in the event that it does end up in court (Fitzpatrick & Rubin, 1995).

Strategic business planning entails wise expenditures to assure a level of performance high enough to control the activities that can affect the financial well-being of the organization and the health, safety, and environmental quality of entities it affects. Strategic planning consists of allocating resources to achieve the mission of the organization. Crises can frustrate that effort. Executives can cut financial corners to such a degree that they increase the chances that a crisis could damage the organization. On the other hand, careful balance is required between making expenditures that are sufficient to minimize crises by meeting expected operating standards while not devoting so many financial and human resources to crisis prevention that—at least in competition with others—the organization becomes unable to generate income needed to profit and meet its obligations. To prevent such outcomes requires contingency planning, which is designed to manage risk, minimize loss, and ensure business continuity (Myers, 1993).

Contingency planning requires defining problem areas where crisis could occur. The organization needs to audit how well it would respond to a crisis. Strategic planning requires preventive measures to minimize the likelihood of a crisis, to develop an organized response if one should occur, and to formulate an operating plan for maintaining business continuity in that event (Myers, 1993). Strategic planning entails budgeting that can, for instance, include allocations for training personnel to increase the likelihood that they can work at a level that reduces the chance of a crisis event. Strategic business planning can require expenditures to establish manufacturing processes that reduce the probability that a piece of equipment could fail unexpectedly. Expenditure on research and development can increase the likelihood that the safety processes in manufacturing and high product standards can lessen the probability that the product will be found wanting in the court of public opinion.

Strategic planning can include choosing to create or abandon products or services, depending on the degree of risk associated with them—for instance, their manufacture or use. Strategic budgeting may be needed to assure that manufacturing processes are monitored with such precision that all parties who handle a product, such as Tylenol, can be screened, trained, and overseen so that the company can quickly ascertain where tampering might have occurred and by whom. Allocations may be needed to create a company fire department and emergency response team in the event of a crisis such as could occur at a chemical manufacturing plant. Strategic planning options should be guided by issues management to look for opportunities and avoid threats associated with predicted events that could outrage the media or key publics.

Mitroff and Pearson (1993; Pauchant & Mitroff, 1992) identified five stages of crisis preparedness, each of which demands higher levels of performance. Stage 1 entails minimal planning, doing nothing more than preparing contingencies for emergency response by security and fire personnel; this stage routinely does not even include training employees and a response team on the procedures to use in the event of an emergency. Stage 2 planning is limited to natural disasters or human error and consists only of measures for damage containment and business-recovery tactics. In-depth planning is a characteristic of Stage 3, whereby procedures are created for notifying key personnel who are trained to implement detailed response tactics. Efforts at this stage tend to grow out of quality assurance planning. The difference between Stage 3 and Stage 4 centers on the amount of coordination and planning needed to involve personnel from many divisions and keep them in the loop for purposes of emergency response, communication, and investigation. Stage 4 includes careful consideration of external stakeholders and preparation of responses to them vis-à-vis their needs and interests. Organizations that have progressed to Stage 5 implement

> early-warning signal detection, engage in preparation and probing actions and procedures, design and implement damage-containment mechanisms far in advance of actual crisis, invest in and implement business-recovery mechanisms, and incorporate learning without unduly assigning blame (unless specific stakeholders have been found directly culpable). (Mitroff & Pearson, p. 99)

Issues monitoring in support of crisis management is two-pronged. One prong results from the need to ascertain the status of sentiments that will surface if an action of the organization occurs that becomes a crisis. Research can ascertain, even second guess, performance expectations held by key publics regarding the impact of the organization on people, animals, and environment. The second prong requires internal surveillance to monitor the quality of personnel, service, and manufacturing processes. This process may require, for example, knowing how headache remedy capsules are manufactured, stored, and provided to retail outlets. It may entail using focus groups of employees to obtain their opinions regarding the high risk processes and weak links in the manufacturing system. Quality assurance and internal security can be vital when determining why events occurred that resulted in a sense of uncertainty and intense media scrutiny—a crisis.

As a monitoring tool, a crisis audit looks for the points in the organization's operations where if a problem were to occur it would generate public outrage and uncertainty. If a chemical vessel malfunctions, the media, concerned citizens, and government officials want to know what chemical(s) was in the vessel, how it was designed and operated, what its construction and maintenance specifications were, how well trained the personnel were that operated it, and how much of the material escaped. Inquiries can be endless. The company or other organization has to know its business intimately, have excellent records of its activities, know what persons are responsible for assessing the nature of the crisis and for predicting how quickly activities will return to normal or be improved to a level whereby a similar crisis will not occur.

Monitoring is vital at various stages in the crisis process. The first stage, *prodromal,* exists when warnings first appear, as warning clouds form on the horizon. This crisis phase is similar to an emerging issue. The second stage is *acute,* when some event has occurred and damage has been done. The *chronic* stage is only reached when responsible parties lose control of the crisis, as Fink (1986) said, and "the carcass gets picked clean" (p. 23). As crisis events play out, monitoring should ascertain whether the crisis is moving toward the chronic or fatal stages or whether events are settling down to a precrisis norm.

At a media relations level, the crisis can be monitored by the frequency of reporter inquiry, the amount of time-space devoted to the crisis, and the degree of outrage expressed by reporters and persons affected by the crisis. In this regard, once reporters have begun to report about reporters reporting on the event, it has taken a trajectory toward calming down. A second line of monitoring is specific to the policy issues that may arise from the crisis. Here the question is whether voluntary efforts of the organization or industry are sufficient to calm fears, reduce outrage, or lessen uncertainty on the part of affected parties or whether those parties are keeping the issue alive by commenting on it to their family and acquaintances, followers, reporters, and members of regulatory or legislative bodies.

One or more key publics, as well as media reporters and governmental officials, have a legitimate right to hold expectations regarding the performance of each private-sector firm. A similar expectation can be assumed to exist in regard to the performance of governmental agencies that are accountable to concerned citizens and corporate entities that can be affected by agency performance. A crisis occurs when an event or action introduces uncertainty into how well the organization manages its affairs so that they do not adversely affect persons who come into contact with them. The public does not, for example, expect a company to manufacture breast implants that can have adverse health consequences. Investors do not expect a company to irresponsibly invest and manage their investment dollars. A company does not expect a governmental agency to make gross errors in its judgment of financial or foreign affairs.

The list of examples is endless and contains sensor points that an issues manager wants to understand and monitor to be ready for crisis response. If the company did not meet public expectations, the crisis communication team will need to explain why flawed judgment or performance occurred. Perhaps the company could not foresee what is routinely called an act of God, one excuse for a crisis. If human error due to faulty training and the attribution of corporate greed are available to explain the cause of the crisis, the crisis response team has little moral ground on which to stand. If the crisis occurred despite reasonable and responsible efforts on the part of the organization, which voluntarily agrees to set and meet even higher standards in the future, the crisis response is likely to have more favorable outcomes. When an organization's activities can spark concerned public outburst, the monitoring and management efforts to know and meet standards of corporate responsibility must be high.

Examples: In its efforts to avoid a crisis, the asbestos industry commissioned studies on the harms of asbestos and, therefore, had reason to know of the dangers long before the Selikoff studies revealed them (Brodeur, 1985; Heath, 1991a). A. H. Robbins engaged in a cover-up of data about the harmfulness of the Dalkon Shield—the ability of part of the apparatus to conduct harmful bacteria into women's bodies. According to critics, many of whom have even taken to on-line (Internet) criticisms, Nestle continues to create crises by refusing to change marketing strategies to conform to public standards for the safe marketing of its infant formula in international markets.

By knowing how the organization creates and executes its strategic business plan, the crisis communication response plan can be formulated in a candid, honest, and informed manner. If the organization has wisely and thoroughly monitored to ascertain the expectations key publics hold in regard to its efforts, the response team is more likely to be prepared. If the organization has worked to set and maintain sufficient performance standards so that the affected groups are not shocked and therefore charge the organization with moral malfeasance, the response can be positive, and uncertainty can be quickly lessened. In this way, crisis communication is a planning, preventative, and emergency response activity that follows in the footsteps of careful strategic business planning, issues monitoring, and moral foresight.

To achieve the desired quality of response, crisis teams need to be vigilant and engage in training, especially the enactment of decision-making processes and the formulation of messages. As Williams and Olaniran (1994) observed,

> When confronted with a corporate crisis, crisis management personnel will also have their decision-making abilities challenged by the need to react quickly, the scrutiny of the press and public interest groups, and the threat of negative consequences resulting from poor decision making. (p. 8)

The quality of the decisions made under strain depends on the crisis team's ability to analyze the problem, establish or rely on preestablished goals and objectives, and evaluate the positive and negative qualities and consequences of available choices in message responses.

Early in a crisis, spokespersons who meet the press and regulatory agents may not know the facts. In terms of finding vital facts, regulatory agents, such as those from the Department of Transportation, may become the crucial fact-finding body. Their judgment of the fact may be final. The company—for better or worse—can rely on them and use their investigative time frame in responding to media inquiries. If the legitimate interest of the media is getting the story, they must wait until that story can be known. Months and even years may be devoted to learning the facts. In some crises, facts are never fully forthcoming because of the nature of the event. In those instances, the methodology used to find the truth may be the story that captures media attention.

At least for crisis marketing—the effort to recover markets lost or potentially lost due to a crisis—the first stage is to publicly acknowledge what went wrong. More than making an apology, the response requires reporting investigative findings. A final step is crucial: "Present and maintain the positioning of the company in a larger context than the problem" (Marconi, 1992, p. 30).

In the investigative process, organizations under pressure are wise to be cautious, precise, open, honest, and scientific in finding the truth. They should be collaborative in that effort. They do not serve themselves well if they work to be the only source of information. The quality of information—as a scientific product and in terms of public acceptance—increases as it is subjected to independent review. Organizational spokespersons who in their reports venture beyond what is known or knowable are fools.

This section has attempted to establish the point that a good crisis manager and communicator has the inclinations and mental discipline of the scientist while maintaining a genuine ethical commitment to resolve the issue in the interest of the relevant stakeholders. The goal of prevention and response is to understand operations, take the best available preventative measures, and be scrupulous in the pursuit of understanding why a crisis could or did occur.

 Crisis Communication Options

Practitioner and scholarly publications are replete with advice on how to communicate during a crisis. A typical list might advise some or all of the following. Be prepared by developing a strategic crisis communication plan. Practice the plan. Know who the key spokespersons will be in the event of a crisis. Train them for media response. Make senior management and other key spokespersons available to reporters during a crisis. If the crisis is one that could endanger lives, such as an explosion in a chemical plant, have places available for the press to meet with key organization members in safety—away from the flow of hazardous or toxic materials. Tell what you know and what you don't know. Be candid, honest, and truthful. Name the communication team and establish the communication network it will use in the event of a crisis. Plan how to communicate with reporters to give them details such as the names and phone numbers of crisis team members, command center location, 1-800 numbers, emergency responses, procedures to avert additional crises, and policies to display open and honest concern for persons affected by the crisis. For instance, a company may plan to provide counselors for victims' families, methods to redress damages, and other enactments of public apology.

Perhaps these prescriptions are sufficient—perhaps not. This section examines typical advice prescribed by crisis management and communication response experts. It reasons that regardless of such prescriptions, crisis communication needs to be driven by a central theme: Address the interests of persons affected by the crisis and downplay its effects on the offending—at least ostensibly offending—organization. Birch (1994) captured this theme: "Crisis management teaching stresses the need to show that the company cares and feels concern when something has gone wrong" (p. 32).

Preparation not only includes careful planning, drills, and a cautious approach to high risk operations but also includes the formation of a reputation that can help sustain an organization in time of crisis. An organization with a reputation for truth, openness, candor, safety, fairness, environmental concern, and honesty brings that persona with it to the first press conferences after the crisis event has occurred. An organization with the opposite reputation begins with media reporters and other participants doubting its accounts. Such doubt gives publics the incentive to look for sources of information that disconfirm rather than confirm the organization's version of the crisis event.

A crisis response philosophy is augmented by Chase's (1984) insights into communication styles that help people prepare for and engage in issues response. Communicators can adopt a *reactive* style—stonewalling; it involves denial, avoidance, and postponement. An *adaptive* style voices "openness to change, a recognition of its inevitability" (p. 58). Adaptive style assumes that the errors of judgment and performance that led to the crisis will be corrected largely as prescribed by outside forces, such as activists or governmental officials. The third style, *dynamic,* can respond aggressively to critics who do not understand the circumstances that led to the crisis. It can include refutation of claims and charges made about the performance of the organization. It can state what changes are pending or being implemented to decrease the likelihood that the event will be repeated. This stance includes comments about the proactive and collaborative decision-making measures the organization has taken or is initiating to improve its operations.

The key to these three styles is the locus of control. The reactive style ignores the desire for control on the part of parties affected by the crisis; this can be a saddening, even startling mistake to the management of the offending organization. The adaptive style evidences so much willingness to accommodate to others' expectations that it yields all of the control to them. The dynamic style assumes a shared sense of control, the outcome of which contains the best performance and management options to be exerted by the organization on behalf of all parties concerned with the crisis. The dynamic style assumes the organization is responsible for constructing appropriate corrections and making decisions—if necessary, in conjunction with other relevant parties. It seeks win-win outcomes and willingly takes crisis situations as opportunities to demonstrate the quality of operations and planning that is characteristic of the organization. It uses the crisis as an opportunity for collaborative improvement.

Failure to have designated persons to meet the media during a crisis will allow reporters to select the spokespersons based on those who make the most quotable statements or are easiest to contact—or both. Even when a communication plan calls for executives and skilled public relations practitioners to act as spokespersons, reporters do not limit themselves to those sources. As Ressler (1982) concluded, "Local media often know and trust local management; and comments from that person are more believable and create confidence that local leaders are in charge" (p. 8).

Operations personnel may understand technical processes and be able to explain them and answer technical questions more credibly than can executives or professional communicators. Even after a crisis, operations people are likely to be contacted by reporters because they were eye witnesses and may be able to give newsworthy details about events and operations. They often give a story of events that seems to be authentic rather than manufactured by slick communication personnel, executives, and lawyers.

Critics of Exxon's handling of the Valdez crisis pointed out that the number one person, Lawrence Rawl, was tardy in getting to the scene of the cleanup where he was needed to enact the persona of a concerned company. Some skeptics doubt the usefulness of chief executive officers showing up and seeming to be involved; others say that gesture is crucial. Herbert Schmertz, former vice president of public affairs of Mobil Oil Company, said that under Exxon Valdez circumstances, he would have sent his CEO immediately and would have included a group of prominent environmentalists charged with the task of advising the cleanup. Regardless of whether the CEO goes to the scene of the crisis, he or she is responsible for enacting the company's response (Small, 1991).

Employees need information, particularly if safety is a factor. Customers require information if product safety or reliability is at issue. Crises often resist neat and tidy explanations where the information is decisive and readily available. Responsible parties may have difficulty obtaining the facts, knowing the truth. A good example is Dow Chemical Company, through its Dow Corning division. The issue is breast implants. The question is one of fact: Are implants manufactured by Dow harmful to women's health?

Part of the difficulty in answering this question results from the reactive, moving-target crisis response of Dow. In all of its efforts, it has not demonstrated that it is committed to self-analysis or self-criticism, at least in the judgment of Rumptz, Leland, McFaul, Solinski, and Pratt (1992). Not being timely and forthcoming with information was only one criticism these experts had of Dow's response. They believed it also failed to nurture credibility, to make company representatives available to the press, and to demonstrate sympathy to the implant recipients. The company seems to have taken a reactive stance and suffered the criticism of having withheld data for 20 years that suggest a link between its product and health problems.

Was Dow covering up? The Federal Drug Administration issued a moratorium on silicone implants on January 6, 1992, because the data regarding health effects were conflicting and indecisive. In June 1995, the Harvard Medical School published a study in the *New England Journal of Medicine* that indicated results that failed to connect the transplants with immune-system illnesses, specifically rheumatoid arthritis, systemic lupus, and scleroderma. Does that end the debate? *Wall Street Journal* reporter Thomas M. Burton (1995) did not think so:

> The research, the latest of a number of such studies that don't connect implants with certain diseases, is likely to buttress legal arguments made by manufacturers of the devices. But for a number of reasons, including its relatively small size and statistical significance, the study won't resolve the debate over the safety of the silicone devices. (p. B11)

In its defense, in 1995, Dow took out full-page issue ads with the headline, "Here's what some people don't want you to know about breast implants." The ad summarized five conclusions relevant to its defense and offered to send copies of the studies to anyone who called a 1-800 number. One report contained a summary of 17 U.S. and international studies that did not find a link between breast implants and disease. Another report contained evidence used by the British government to conclude that it had not found evidence of connective tissue disease. A third document discussed routine medical applications of silicone, including its use in chemotherapy, kidney dialysis, and IV tubing. The last two reports blamed lawyers for the crisis. The fourth described plaintiff's attorneys, who stand to make huge incomes from lawsuits, as buying ads and conducting workshops to help women file lawsuits. The fifth report offered details on California, Texas, and Alabama where plaintiffs' attorneys gave $17 million to state and local candidates, including judges, during a 4-year period ending in 1994. The facts behind the crisis? The blame? Will time tell?

Crisis response teams have learned that they must demonstrate they are responsible and responsive to the needs and expectations of stakeholder and stakeseeker publics. This point is fundamental to the corporate responsibility function of issues management—to get the house in order. One example: Kraft created a contest designed to increase product visibility and buying preferences of Kraft cheese slices. On Sunday, June 12, 1989, a promotional contest was launched in the Chicago and Houston markets. The contest told persons who bought Kraft cheese slices that they automatically competed to see who would win one of the following prizes: A 1990 Dodge Caravan van valued at $17,000, 100 Roadmaster bicycles, 500 Leapfrog skateboards, and 8,000 packages of Kraft cheese. This routine promotion became a crisis when hundreds of people jammed Kraft's phone circuits to claim prizes. A printing error in the contest materials resulted in hundreds more customers' having winning game pieces than had been planned. More than 10,000 people claimed the van. Kraft canceled the ad and moved to change the contest rules. Instead of giving the prizes to winners as it had promised, it offered nominal amounts of cash but eventually settled for $10 million (Deveny, 1991). That decision led to a class-action lawsuit. Who was responsible? Could a Kraft person count and double-check all of those pieces to assure no printing error had occurred? Could Kraft suffer the image problems of placing all of the blame on the printer, who could never have sustained that kind of financial loss? Could Kraft truly be held responsible—totally—for all of its actions that were made responsibly and in good faith? Admission of responsibility can be extremely naive and dangerous, perhaps even unethical.

By the same token, blame placing—a risky crisis response strategy—can imply that an organization is unwilling or unable to accept the responsibility its stakeholders expect of it to achieve and maintain appropriate control of its activities. It is a surefire tactic for demonstrating that management is prone not to solve problems and prevent subsequent crises. An example: In 1995, Philip Morris had to recall millions of cigarettes because of a problem with the filters that caused some persons to experience dizziness and respiratory discomfort. At first, blame was placed on the company that supplied the fibers for the filters, Hoechst Celanese Corporation, which allegedly had allowed contamination from a harmful chemical used in pesticides, MITC. The problem with blame placing is shown in a headline that reads, "Philip Morris reassigns blame for its recall," and a story:

> The company said it now believes its cigarettes contained only tiny amounts of MITC, not enough to pose a safety problem. And adding to an already bewildering public relations effort, Philip Morris offered a new theory for the origin of the mysterious MITC. It said MITC is a "natural breakdown product" of thione, a preservative used in packaging of cigarettes and many other products. (Hwang, 1995, p. B1)

The search goes on. Who is responsible for the tainted filters? Philip Morris?

At times, a crisis response calls for the assigning of blame. *Dateline NBC* alleged that General Motors pickups were unsafely designed because their gasoline tanks could ignite on side impact. They demonstrated the problem. However, their demonstration was contrived. They had rigged the test vehicles with incendiary devices to make a more vivid dramatization. To correct the record, GM counterattacked in search for the truth and demonstrated that the story was fabrication and hyperbole (Hearit, 1996). That rejoinder did not prove the trucks were safe but that NBC was not committed to the truth.

Audiences are more attentive (less inattentive?) during a crisis. This situation can offer opportunities to communicate and demonstrate a corporation's commitment to responsible behavior and the measures it has and is taking to be responsible. Stephenson (1982) demonstrated how Dow Chemical turned a crisis to its advantage. Two train derailments (Mississauga, Ontario, in November 1979 and MacGregor, Manitoba, in March 1980) brought attention to Dow products that were being transported by rail. Dow took the opportunity to explain some of the properties of these products along with the safety procedures that were designed to ensure that no one was harmed. Such events, especially in industries with high outrage potential, offer the chance to explain how emergency response teams are trained and how they act to minimize harm to people and damage to the environment.

Organizations that suffer a crisis are often criticized for being unresponsive to media inquiry. This prescription assumes that not only do crisis managers and communicators need to understand the standard media, but they also must think beyond them to new communication technologies. Birch (1994) advised crisis communicators to be prepared to respond to a daunting list of challenges posed by new communication technologies. One challenge is the number of news channels looking for stories—CNN, for example. Another challenge is the enormous amount of detail that is available to reporters through on-line databases. In a bit more than the blink of an eye, reporters who have learned of a crisis event can go on-line and from vast databases call up stories and retrieve data about a company or other organization. In a few moments, this wealth of information can be compressed into stories that frame whatever detail becomes available to the reporters regarding the crisis. Such databases can contain and make continuously available false or deceptive information that reporters may rely on—perhaps without ever contacting the company for verification. For this reason, someone in the organization suffering a crisis (or an agency assisting the organization) needs to monitor the databases to look for incorrect information that can be recirculated in an infinite variety of inaccurate news stories. A good example of this problem was the continuing discussion on Internet that a TWA flight leaving New York City had been shot down by missiles—a story the U.S. government said lacked any substance.

Communication technologies are useful tools as well as daunting challenges. Precrisis planning may include considerations (and contractual arrangements) for the use of satellite communication, which allows two-way video links with internal and external audiences. Video news releases can be prepared to demonstrate how an organization manages delicate manufacturing processes or trains emergency response teams; drawn from storage, these can be used as feed for news gatherers who are trying to understand and report visually the efficacy of the organization in crisis. Faxing allows for widespread dissemination of printed material. Responding to inquiries can be extremely time consuming. Faxing can lessen that burden. Voice mail and electronic workstation messaging is a means for answering phone calls electronically. For instance, instead of personally answering each reporter's questions about the schedule of the next news release or news conference, that information could be placed on voice mail and periodically updated. If the release is sent by fax or e-mail, the reporter is ready for its arrival. Specialized databases can be established so that they can be used in the event of important information; a crisis would be such an event (Kotcher, 1992).

Differences exist in cause and severity. Each crisis deserves its unique response—the rhetorical situation that it poses. Based on this reasoning, Coombs (1995) laid out matrices of response options for each kind of crisis he identified: faux pas, accident, terrorism, and transgression. For each kind, responses need to be adjusted to consider the evidence regarding the interpretation of the responsibility for the crisis, the amount and kind of damage, and the organization's performance history. Based on these options, responses could feature ingratiation, mortification, distance, claims that a crisis actually had not occurred, or clarification. The upshot of these strategic selections is to help key audiences and stakeholding publics realize the proper cause of the crisis and the measures by which things would be set right.

Lerbinger (1986) classified crises as technological (a failure of technology), confrontation (expressions of outrage by a concerned public), malevolence (on the part of a person or group that does something harmful to the organization), and management failure (inadequate planning or execution by executives). Technological crisis response demands a demonstration on the part of the organization that it can and will use a technology properly or abandon it. Confrontation requires the organization to understand, explain, and resolve the motivation for the protest. Management failure requires that senior officials demonstrate that they can plan and execute on behalf of their stakeholders' interests. Malevolent crises require the organization, in conjunction with appropriate law officials, to move quickly and decisively to restore control and foster the interests of concerned publics.

A precrisis plan can specify what people need to be trained, what relationships are not to be created (especially those related to crisis-sensitive activities of the organization), and how reputation is to be built or restored. During the crisis, the team needs to identify the problem—to the best of its ability. It must implement a data-gathering and dissemination process to put its information into the flow. During the crisis, the organization needs to respond quickly, honestly, and people-to-people; to communicate continually the facts that are confirmed; and to report on the process of finding additional facts. After the crisis, efforts should be made to maintain and bolster relationships and to proactively put out relevant information regarding solutions to the problem discovered during the crisis (Birch, 1994).

This section has examined prescriptions that routinely guide crisis planning, management, and communication. These response options add to an organization's ability to enact a coherent voice and trustworthy persona. A culture of being wisely cautious and proactive lays a foundation for looking for problems that could result in crises and prepares employees and executives to enact a persona of candor and caring if a crisis occurs.

Apologia

Can words put a crisis right? Crisis communication may include strategies for saying, "We are sorry," making an apology to harmed or concerned publics. This section examines apologia as a communication response to a crisis. It acknowledges that performance outweighs communication in the long run. That means that an apology is typically insufficient to set things right, but it can help if it is a demonstration that the organization has recognized its failure to respond responsibly to the needs and expectations of its stakeholder and stakeseeking publics.

Crisis communication may employ the rhetoric of apologia, the use of terms to define and redefine events to give what the company or other organization postulates to be the accurate interpretation of events that led to and resulted from the crisis. As Hearit (1994) concluded,

> An "apologia" is not an apology (although it *may* contain one), but a defense that seeks to present a compelling, counter description of organizational actions. It functions to situate alleged organizational wrongdoing in a more favorable context than the initial charges suggest. This is done in an effort to neutralize the argumentative force of the initial charges of wrongdoing. The tone of most apologiae is that once key publics understand a corporation's explanation, then they will be unable to condemn the corporation. (p. 115)

What communication options are available as part of the rhetoric of apologia?

> An organization charged with wrongdoing seeks to accomplish three objectives. First, it attempts to present a convincing and plausible description of the situation in which the wrongdoing allegedly occurred that offers a

competing narrative to the one commonly reported. Second, to diffuse the anger and hostility directed at the company, the organization issues a statement of regret that expresses concern but acknowledges minimal responsibility. Third, the organization engages in dissociation to remove the linkage of the organization with the wrongdoing. (Hearit, 1994, p. 115)

A key strategy of apologia is to provide a different descriptive and interpretative (evaluative) name for the event than the one offered by the media or the critics. One common response is that an action (which seems to violate the expectations of key stakeholders) is not illegal.

Beyond noting how spokespersons select terms of positive, neutral, or negative attribution, Hearit (1994) identified three apologia strategies: expression of regret, persuasive accounts entailing definition and redefinition, and dissociation. Apologia through definition and redefinition can use terms to foster a more favorable or less unfavorable view of the event. It can assign blame, including acceptance of blame by the subject organization. This strategy can center on the matter of intent, raising the question of whether the outcome desired and means used by the organization were intended to produce good and avoid harms for the concerned public, whether the purpose was different than what the critics alleged, whether intent is ordinary and routine to an industry, and whether intent was misunderstood by how the organization acted.

An apologia is likely to carry an *expression of regret*. The veracity of this claim is less likely to depend on the assertion by the subject organization than it is to be based on the presentation of evidence to demonstrate its regret. Of related importance is the quality of the prior relationship. If the organization has had an honest, candid, and mutually beneficial relationship with the concerned publics, then reputation is likely to lend credence to its current expression of regret.

> One potential communicative benefit of a statement of regret is this: it implies that the problem that precipitated the wrongdoing has been isolated and resolved. This may explain why a strong denial does not necessarily resolve doubts about organizational wrongdoing; the organization may still have a problem that it simply has not located. (Hearit, 1994, p. 118)

Cultural differences offer marked contrast on how companies, airlines for instance, demonstrate their personae under crisis. The president of Japanese Airline was publicly active in his airline's ceremonies to apologize to victims and survivors after one of its planes crashed in 1985. A senior maintenance technician with the company committed suicide, an act not unlikely for personnel in a Japanese company. In contrast, airline executives did not personally appear at the scenes of crashes such as the Pan Am catastrophe in Lockerbie, Scotland, or United's crash near Sioux City, Iowa (Pinsdorf, 1991).

Events are subject to definition and redefintion. Knowing that terms used to define an event shape perceptions of it, spokespersons may propose the defining words for a crisis. In doing so, they divert responsibility from themselves or explain why key publics' concerns are justified. Ordinary words, such as "mistake," are offered as an explanation when, for instance, "moral malfeasance" is a more accurate term. A spokesperson may attempt to assuage concerned publics by indicating that the circumstances that led to the crisis are not illegal. Companies often confuse in their minds or attempt to assume that the public does not distinguish between that which is legal and that which is ethical.

The language of naming can tend to downplay wrongdoing. Often, neutral, even scientific or managerial, language is used. At the moment, perhaps no better example of the use of neutral language exists than these terms: *rightsizing, downsizing, or reingineering.* These terms mask harsher terms: *firings or layoffs* of working people with bills and obligations to meet, who have toiled loyally for a company whose management failed to wisely foresee downturns and who now enjoy huge bonuses for laying off lots of hardworking, middle-class taxpayers—all in the name of organizational efficiency and global competitiveness. If neutral managerial terms such as *reengineering* or *rightsizing* properly describe the process of reducing the size of workforces, why is a positive term, such as *growth,* used when the news is positive?

Dissociation is a strategy used to distance the organization from the cause of the event. Dissociation may involve one or more persons whose activities are disavowed as not being approved by the subject organization, whose characters are used as a scapegoat to establish the locus of blame because of the kind of persons they are, or whose intentions are not consonant with the subject organization's. Offending persons often must be sacrificed in some way—such as being terminated—to indicate this dissociation and begin the corrective process.

Without doubt, events that constitute a crisis are subject to interpretation. However, the standard by which crisis management is judged seems quite simple. Affected and concerned publics expect the organization that has created or experienced the crisis to exert control and to put matters right. For that reason, blame placing can be a tricky strategy, as likely to backfire as it is to succeed. Management does not serve the integrity of the organization and the persona of being in charge when blame is placed on subordinates. As was true when AT&T's system failed on September 17, 1991, stakeholders expect the organization to exhibit mortification and accept responsibility for losing control. If mortification, then correction and eventually bolstering. The organization can bolster its position as a reputation restorative or maintenance strategy by demonstrating its acumen, which at least momentarily failed. Placing blame and apologizing is usually an insufficient response (Benoit & Brinson, 1994). What is needed is evidence of the organization's concern and desire to restore appropriate control in the interest of its stakeholders.

Crisis communication seems best when it is framed in terms of what concerned publics want to know and how they make decisions. Facts evaluated in terms of established premises are valuable. Crises are likely to make established premises salient as decision heuristics; people want to interpret events according to established expectations. Crisis response is likely to be value laden. If an employee or customer dies because of a manufacturing process, that is an issue of value. As judgments of preference, values assist individuals in establishing priorities and making evaluations. Image and reputation seem strongest when organizations demonstrate as well as state that they share the values of the relevant community of interests and act in ways that affirm those values. Policy is a concern of control. If an organization, and related organizations, can demonstrate that it can manage its affairs in ways that meet or exceed community expectations, it is likely to suffer no additional burden from having policy imposed from the outside.

This section examines how a crisis is a test of an organization's ability to understand, accept, and respond to the appropriate standards of corporate responsibility. It assumes that failure to respond to these standards is one cause of a crisis. Mere apology is likely to be insufficient response, but it helps to demonstrate the organization's goodwill and willingness to understand and meet key publics' performance expectations.

 Crisis Response as Narrative

One framework for the evaluation of an organization's performance is the narrative of events represented by this organization, set in the frame of responsible and concerned operations and appropriate behavior. Events occur in context. That context exhibits the key aspects of a narrative, a story. How the story is resolved determines whether the crisis goes away or leads to an issue having public policy importance.

No crisis occurs in a vacuum. Reporters frame news events in terms of past events that are similar and relevant. People ask themselves whether an immediate event is a continuation of a story—a narrative—they have come to expect as they think about an organization or industry. Or they may ask whether this event is a dramatic shift in narrative—a new story. People think of events that occur in their world in narrative terms. Interpretation of the events treats them as acts by characters that have a past, present, and future.

Events are meaningful because they are part of a larger plot and have a plot of their own. Each plot can demonstrate some theme, some relevant point of view. The life of an organization is a narrative, a sequence of events played out by an arrangement of people (characters having various personae) over time (according to a plot that exhibits a coherent theme).

Companies and most other organizations work hard to enact the persona that they are in charge of their destinies and aware of the interests and concerns of the other characters—key publics—in the narrative. Crises strain the appearance of control. When a crisis occurs, a spokesperson is expected to explain publicly and quickly why it happened and what will be done to correct operations and protect people from further harm as well as repay and comfort those who have been harmed. Crisis communication is the enactment of the narrative of control (or at least its appearance) in the face of high uncertainty in an effort to win external audiences' confidence in ways that are ethical.

Viewed from a narrative perspective, a crisis is either a break—a dramatic interruption—or a shift in plot from one narrative—normal operations—to a crisis or emerging issue narrative. This analytic approach allows us to think of a crisis narrative as a subnarrative in the plot of the larger narrative of routine operations. The larger narrative forms a framework or point of view that concerned publics use to interpret and evaluate each unique event and decide whether it is a crisis. The dominant narrative gives continuity to the past, present, and future of the organization and other organizations of the same type. For instance, a plane crash is a subnarrative of years and millions of miles of safe operations. Or it may be viewed as a continuing narrative of unsafe operations by an uncaring industry indifferent to passenger safety.

Each narrative begins with "once upon a time." Crisis resolution is a narrative outcome of "happily ever after," "slowly recovering," or "death to the villain." The rationale for this analysis assumes that life is narrative: People are storytellers who live their lives as stories (Fisher, 1985, 1987, 1989). According to this reasoning, people structure their experiences and actions, as well as events around them, by thinking of them as narratives consisting of characters, plots, and resolution or outcome. Stories simplify what people think and know; they give coherence to experience. Facts, those of the events of individuals' lives, become meaningful when thought of and presented in terms of narrative form and content. The world is understood in terms of "once upon a time," "and then she said to him," "and after that, the company had to file for bankruptcy," and the final resolution of a story, "and all was well in the end."

The enactment of each event is compared with and becomes meaningful in the context of previous narratives. As Gergen and Gergen (1988) have reasoned,

> Narratives are, in effect, social constructions, undergoing continuous altera-
> tion as interaction progresses. The individual in this case does not consult an
> internal narrative for information. Rather, the self-narrative is a linguistic
> implement constructed by people in relationships and employed in relation-
> ships to sustain, enhance or impede various actions. It may be used to indicate
> future actions but it is not in itself the basis for such action. In this sense,
> self-narratives function much as histories within society do more generally.
> They are symbolic systems used for such social purposes as justification,
> criticism, and social solidification. (p. 20)

Narratives allow people to identify with and understand one another as participating in similar events and having had comparable experiences. Thus, people achieve a shared understanding of the world that helps them to predict the direction that events and actions will and should take.

Narrative frames people's understanding of the past, knowing what is occurring in the present, and projecting events into the future. A crisis is best framed in terms of what happened, what response is being made, and where that effort leads. "Time is critical because transactions have no mean-ing outside of their historical contexts: the expectations attendant upon an interaction moment are crucial for understanding the meaning of that inter-action" (Eisenberg, 1986, p. 89). Through their efforts to help create and enact narratives relevant to their activities and missions, businesses engage in sym-bolic processes by which they represent themselves and define their bounda-ries (Cheney, 1992; Cheney & Dionisopoulos, 1989; Cheney & Vibbert, 1987).

So do reporters. For instance, Nimmo and Combs (1982) identified three narratives used by reporters in comments on the nuclear-generating plant crisis at Three Mile Island: human interest, fact-finding—big picture, and educational. Treating war as crisis management, communication regards that military effort as narrative: The mighty and just good folks against their evil adversaries (Hiebert, 1991).

If life—personal and organizational—is a lived narrative, then its enact-ment exhibits the elements of narrative: narrators, auditors, plot or theme, characters, events, location of the act, acts, relationships, personae, scripts, communication plans and message design logics, and decision heuristics (Heath, 1994). Vasquez (1993) demonstrated how narratives can be used to identify publics. At issue is what people believe, the stories they know and hold dear as being meaningful to their lives. What they believe leads them to a point of view that determines whether they are a member of a public and, if so, which public. In this sense, each public shares a narrative that constitutes a definable zone of meaning. It is a prediction of how events progress: what will happen and how people will act.

Stories are not vacuous, figments of persons' imagination. They are understood, compared against other narratives, and subjected to scrutiny to determine whether they are accurate and coherent. Judgment of the rhetorical integrity of a narrative is based on "probability and fidelity," which are vital "considerations for judging the merits of stories, whether one's own or another's" (Fisher, 1985, p. 349). Narrative probability is a judgment of the extent to which a story holds together, rings true, and is free from internal contradiction. Narrative fidelity refers to the weight of values, good reasons, consideration of fact, consequence, consistency, and the degree to which a story has a bearing on relevant issues.

The company suffering a crisis must be able to tell a credible story, one that has factual fidelity that can withstand the scrutiny of reporters, governmental investigators, and concerned citizens. Stories provided by company spokespersons, for instance, shape details in ways that portray the company as favorably as possible. This response is strongest when it is sincere and probable, given the characters involved and the theme relevant to the crisis. Subsequent accounts of crisis events must be consonant with early accounts if crisis communication is to have the desired narrative impact (Hobbs, 1991). Inconsistencies in stories suggest the presence of deceit and falsehood and a lack of control by the organization under scrutiny.

Narratives, especially those enacted during a crisis, give audiences, internal and external to an organization, the chance to know (test hypotheses) what accounts are reliable and whether the organization, if at fault, will properly atone for its mistakes and take responsibility to understand what led to the crisis and to prevent its recurrence. As Mumby (1987) reasoned, "Political reading of narrative draws attention to the relationship between narrative structure and the process of interpretation" (p. 113). Narratives serve people as decision heuristics to frame facts they encounter. If a company or other organization has a history (narrative) for honest reports and responsible actions, the crisis as a part of that narrative or as a crisis narrative will be interpreted in light of the past narrative. If the past narrative is favorable and gives a favorable interpretation of the current event, it is likely to make management of the crisis easier.

A crisis shifts the narrative being enacted by an organization from one of routine events to one that may not be routine. If it is routine, the offending organization is likely to be caught in the development of a public policy issue to put an end to a narrative that appears to be contrary to the interest of key publics. Crisis occurs when interested parties have reason to wonder whether the organization is likely to regain or maintain control of its operation and its effect on others.

Control is a dominant cultural archetype. The performance of an organization through the enactment of its personnel or members is expected to meet publics' sense of an organization that is in control, one that can develop and implement policies and procedures that allow it to properly manage the balance of its interests with those of its key stakeholders and stakeseekers. Narrative interpretations of crisis ask audiences to consider whether the acts that were committed are consistent with the characters in the case and constitute a reasonable theme. This theme has to meet standards of fidelity and probability. Audiences use those standards to understand and judge whether the account as given is plausible and justified under the circumstances.

Stories have order. As enacted by organizations, they must lead to order, through the dialectic of what happened during the crisis, what is learned from what happened, and what will be done in the future based on what was learned. Narrative is a dialectic, Burke (1969a) observed, "a process of *transformation* whereby the position at the end transcends the position at the start, so that the position at the start can eventually be seen in terms of the new motivation encountered enroute" (p. 422). Part of the transformation of an organization during a crisis is to learn from it and make appropriate corrections. Concerned publics expect the organization to have learned how to exert control more appropriately, to become better at meeting public expectations (Gold, 1982).

Narratives that lead only to positive outcomes for the ostensibly offending organization may leave concerned publics dissatisfied. Policy statements appear to be most persuasive and satisfying when they consider the self-interest of the public as well as the organization. Activist groups build their cases by arguing that corporate behavior conflicts with the public interest.

How should companies respond to such crises? Rowland and Rademacher (1990) observed that a crisis can be approached passively by spokespersons who reaffirm the values that are relevant to the event and publicly recommit themselves to those values. Thus, a plant manager whose plant blew up may reaffirm that he or she remains committed to worker safety. One that allowed a toxic release is expected to proclaim commitment to environmental responsibility. In crises, blame may be placed on someone (perhaps a subordinate) or some thing (environmental factors—an act of God or a regulatory agency). In such situations, no actions are announced that are likely to result in actual changes. Rather, the appearance of change may be part of the symbolic response to the crisis. Passive response is possible if the atmosphere around the event is not adversarial and if reporters do not challenge the characterization of the event presented by the spokesperson. Given what is typical of many crises, some reporters are likely to assume an adversarial role. Different reports can result from various news services' agendas (Dyer, Miller, & Boone, 1991). In any event, the organization's account for the crisis is judged by the standards of narratives: a credible and ethical accounting for the event by the persons involved and the values that guided their actions.

Such responses require planning, procedures for internal and external communication in the event of a crisis. Planning allows participants to create a drama that consists of scripts that can be enacted under pressure. Part of the drama is the creation of interpretative premises that can be used to explain how and why events occurred and responses were taken. Issues management should create a single voice that increases trust and makes timely responses to media inquiries. Members of the organization should prepare to provide a trustworthy story of events using scripts that are familiar to them as well as ethically comfortable and persuasive to the audience. It must fit narratives relevant to the event, the organization, and most important, the community. Trust is unlikely to be achieved if the narrative is only framed in terms of what is said and done during a specific crisis event. If the press and affected publics only use the intrinsic credibility of the spokespersons and the extrinsic credibility of research efforts to assess the truthfulness of the statements of the spokespersons, credibility will not be as strong as it would be if it resulted from a long-term, positive relationship. Key publics assess how faithfully the organization has responded to the needs and interests of others instead of only responding to its own needs (Marconi, 1992). An effective crisis plan supports effective crisis response that is open, candid, and honest.

The crisis communication plan sets the tone, specifies in advance who will be the players in the event of a crisis, and establishes the role each person will play. Decisions need to determine the statements that can be made without breaching what legal counsel believes to be corporate liability. Accounts will be subjected by the audience to tests of factual fidelity and the probability that the events are as asserted by the organization given what people know of that organization and the persons who enact it. In that sense, the narrative—as is true of all narratives—is subject to interpretation and evaluation by key publics, other organizations, and media reporters who strive to enact the narrative of responsible investigative reporting. This is a daunting audience to satisfy during the drama of crisis response.

Whatever report of events is made by organizational spokespersons, they need to recognize that this report is interpreted in the context of the narrative of that organization, the narrative of its kind (industry, agency, or activist), and the narrative ideology of society. Spokespersons are limited or privileged in their report by the narrative that surrounds the event.

 **Conclusion**

Crisis management gives issues managers an opportunity to engage in planning and foresight that can lessen the likelihood of a crisis event. Such effort can lessen the loss of control and negative consequences in the event that a crisis occurs. For this reason, thoughtful preparation is a major part of preventing crises from maturing into issues.

Each crisis is a rhetorical exigency; it requires responsible parties to enact control in the face of uncertainty, with the objective of winning audiences' confidence and meeting their ethical standards. A crisis is an event that threatens lives or well-being of stakeholders and stakeseekers and the ability of the organization to enact the narrative of responsible change and continuity. Control assumes order, and people desire a sense of order and predictability that leads to positive rather than negative outcomes. Crisis narratives feature mistakes and dreaded outcomes. The goal of issues management before, during, and after a crisis is to restore and strengthen the relationship between the entity suffering a crisis and its stakeholders and stakeseekers.

Issues Management and Risk Communication

Balancing Public Well-Being With Technology

Few issues management challenges loom as ominously as those that arise from risks people fear they suffer in their places of work, neighborhoods, and daily activities. History is a drama of people assessing, communicating about, and creatively preventing or adapting to risks (Plough & Krimsky, 1987). Ancients predicted hazards and risk outcomes. They used myths, metaphors, and rituals to communicate knowledge needed to accommodate to or avoid hazards. Today, techniques for assessing and responding to risks may have matured little beyond those of the ancients (Douglas, 1992). The issue to be managed is how to understand and control risks as well as how to gain acceptance for these measures in ways that foster the wisest outcomes in any community of interests (Freudenberg, 1984). In their struggle to control risks, people seek and contest facts, evaluative premises, and conclusions to be derived from those facts and premises.

People have legitimate reasons to be concerned for their safety and health as well as that of others for whom they have an altruistic interest. For instance, they might worry about the safety or health of a spouse employed in a high risk occupation, for their children, for animals, and for the environment. A primary motivator of activism is people's desire to be safe and healthy, coupled with their vigilance for problems of that sort that need remedying. Such worry is fed by news stories as well as comments by friends and relatives about the safety or healthfulness of an array of daily activities—foods people eat, water they drink, and their exposure to toxic chemicals or radioactive materials.

Alarm and outrage result when people believe they are exposed to technologies that can hurt them, whether they live and work near the risk or encounter it while using or consuming a product. Friends and family discuss risks. Magazines, newspapers, radio news, and television programming feature health and safety, topics that have viewer, listener, and reader appeal. Companies, industries, government agencies, trade associations, unions, environmentalists, health specialists, journalists, and advocates of the public interest discuss risks such as chemicals in work and living environments, electromagnetic fields, AIDS, drunk driving, alcohol abuse, tobacco products, radioactivity, medical procedures, and crime in the streets or at home. The nation has become chemophobic while relying more on chemicals than ever before.

Safety, fairness, equality, and environmental quality are motivators people use when deciding whether a problem exists that affects them and deserves their attention, including the option of making personal responses or collaboratively seeking collective solutions by engaging in a public policy battle. All four motivators have been at the forefront of the public policy debates regarding risks over the past three decades. Translated into consideration of the benefits and harms of technologies, these motivators play a major role in the discipline called *risk communication* (Singer & Endreny, 1987).

As emphasized in Chapter 9, a crisis results when publics are confronted with events that lead them to feel uncertainty, concern, and even outrage regarding some condition that threatens their well-being and violates their expectations of responsible organizational performance. Paramount in the thinking of persons in this century are the hazards they encounter as they seek the benefits of technology. Science has dramatically improved the quality of life, but key publics are convinced that innovation is not without dire consequences. Such worry is not new. As Chapter 2 stressed, the concerns publics had regarding railroad and product safety led to major pieces of legislation around the turn of this century. A review of the plethora of legislative enactments in the past three decades reveals how heightened concern translates into legislative and regulatory reform—all aimed to increase publics' ability to control technology and lessen the risks they suffer.

What risks do people face daily? The list in endless. Automobile and traffic safety. Medical treatment. Financial investments. Pesticides on food and in living and work locations. Herbicides in agricultural and residential locations. Food additives that increase the color and shelf life of products.

Electromagnetic fields associated with the transmission and use of electricity—power lines, computer screens, backyard transformers, and household appliances. Automobile transportation. Releases of toxic and hazardous chemicals during manufacturing processes as well as the transportation of those materials by truck, railroad car, and pipeline. Crimes against people and property. Harmful chemicals in water supplies. Airline safety. Recreation. Exposure to chemicals and addictive components in cigarette smoke and other tobacco products. Fat in foods. A long of list of carcinogens that seems to be associated with all of what people eat and the things they come in contact with. Natural hazards, such as earthquakes, fires, hurricanes, floods, and tornadoes. Occupational safety, particularly in farming, mining, fire suppression, and police patrol. Safety in the home. Biotechnology that may open the door to superior foods but could, some people worry, create mutant strains because, for instance, we have no idea where gene splicing will lead. Radiation used in medicine, the generation of electricity, and warfare. This illustrative list features an array of choices people face each day and year while engaging in routine activities. Case studies are emerging to define the appropriate and inappropriate risk assessment and community response practices (See Heath, 1995, for instance).

Despite the exposure they suffer, people find that their life is better because of the risks they incur. Risks are offset by benefits, some of which people accept and even gladly seek, such as gambling or engaging in recreation, including mountain climbing and bungee jumping. People earn their living by working in occupations with high risk exposure: chemical workers, power line workers, miners, timber cutters, urban commuters, air commuters, and farmers.

Risk is a dialectic of benefit and harm. We engage in games of chance, such as buying a lottery ticket on the prospect of financial gain, while being cognizant that we will likely lose our dollar. We have a trained technician spray our homes to reduce the presence of undesirable insects. We fertilize our lawns and gardens to feel satisfaction and meet or exceed the expectations of our neighbors. We believe that seeing friends, relatives, business associates, and recreational sites offset the risk of traveling by air, car, bus, foot, water, or rail. Farmers engage in work involving dangerous equipment, hazardous chemicals, and powerful animals—all in the name of income and personal freedom. In such dialectical balances, what is a body to do?

Whether individually or as members of groups, people make decisions when risks—especially those controlled by someone else—conflict with their self-interests and the interests of others. For instance, do residents have to choose between tolerating a chemical plant operating in their community or lose it as a source of wages and taxes? A homemaker must balance the risk of serving foods that contain preservatives against the risk of serving dangerous spoiled food. Each person—whether a member of the public or an executive of a company—has to weigh competing beliefs and evaluations to estimate rewards and losses. In this sense, beliefs (degrees of certainty that one or more attribute is associated with an object or situation) interact with evaluations (positive or negative judgments). Each party in such decisions weighs different estimates of their actions and the associated risks defined in terms of positive or negative outcomes (Ajzen & Fishbein, 1980; Fishbein & Ajzen, 1975; Griffin, Neuwirth, & Dunwoody, 1995).

Risk communicators may falsely assume that understanding and agreement are the same. As variables, they may interact or be independent of one another. Two parties may understand one another but disagree. As Vaughan (1995) saw the challenge, "Communication and participatory strategies will be considered successful only if diverse communities can be engaged as partners in the policy process" (p. 169). One dimension of this challenge is to strive for environmental justice so that the risks of technologies do not unfairly fall to persons of color or those who have lower socioeconomic status.

Risk communication and issues management merge at the point where key publics feel deep concern that companies and governmental organizations create or allow risks to occur that will affect the health, safety, environmental quality, and economic well-being of community residents and users of products. Of related importance is the emerging concern that the placement of manufacturing companies, waste disposal facilities, and hazardous occupations do not equitably expose rich persons to risks as often or as severely as poor persons and those of color—the issue of environmental equity. The challenge of issues management has many aspects: ascertaining the degree to which a risk exists, learning to manage that risk within tolerable limits, ascertaining those limits, and communicating with key publics about those risks. This communication is a means to receive information and expressions of concern from key publics, to learn scientific opinions, and to express facts and opinions that enrich the community decision-making process.

A risk is an uncertainty of whether outcomes will occur and be positive or negative. Uncertainty results from doubts and predictions about what will happen (*state*), what the *effect* will be, and what response will occur, whether on the part of nature or human-created events (Gerloff et al., 1991). In a game of chance, for instance, the risk is that on a roll of the dice, a player might get a number that helps or harms his or her chances of winning or losing. During the board game Monopoly, a person might land on costly property and have to pay rent, land on unpurchased property and have a chance to buy it, or go by "GO" and collect $200. People love scary rides at an amusement park. They climb sheer rock faces. They invest in the stock market. This list illustrates that some of these uncertainties or their consequences are tolerable, even desirable. But such is not the case for all risks.

Enter issues management of risk; this chapter addresses the evolving effort on the part of communities to impose control on the sources of risk.

This topic sets the foundation for discussing the decision-making and legis-lative or regulatory efforts to impose control as a counterpart to the uncer-tainty that defines risk. The chapter addresses communication options, factors that characterize the communication infrastructure of communities where risks exist, and through that analysis, it expresses preference of a version of risk communication as the collaborative management of risk issues through dialogue.

 The Difficulties of Risk Assessment, Management, and Communication

Risk forces individuals, companies, activists, communities, and governmental agencies to balance many interests and to consider all of the dynamics that shape communities where risks exist. This section features those difficulties as a foundation for discussing response options in sections that follow.

Uncertainty is central to each risk because, by definition, people experi-ence doubt as they decide whether a risk exists and whether it is tolerable. Similar feelings come to mind as they consider who to trust and how much trust is warranted on matters of health and safety. Frank Press, as President of the National Academy of Sciences, said that "an uncertainty principle operates in science and the communication of *risk*" (as quoted in Davies, Covello, & Allen, 1987, p. 12). The standard definition of *risk* implies uncertainty, "a combined measure of the probability and magnitude of undesirable effects" (Hadden, 1988, p. 137; Rayner, 1992). As a technical concept, risk is conven-tionally defined as something that can be given a numerical value by multi-plying the probability of an outcome, typically one with negative conse-quences, with its severity. This expectancy value is used to estimate and compare risks (Hansson, 1989) that are perceived differently depending on the heuristics and biases each person uses to judge them (Tversky & Kahneman, 1986).

These decision models offer approaches to understand beliefs and values that underlie public judgments of risk acceptability and predict people's personal and public policy responses, as does Fishbein and Ajzen's expectancy value theory (1975; Ajzen & Fishbein, 1980). Risk judgments are affected by persons' attitudes toward the risk, attitudes toward the individual or collective measures to be taken to mitigate the risk, and the desire to conform to the social norms of a community (Griffin et al., 1995).

Sizable numbers of people distrust the operations and spokesperson reports regarding the safety and health implications of many business and government activities. Hyperbolic reports in newspapers, books, and maga-zines, as well as on television and radio, heighten apprehensions and foster distrust of business or governmental activities. These reports, framed as they are, often lead people to doubt the technical competence and fairness of reporters to obtain and provide valid and valuable information. Part of the lack of trust in risk communication comes from the uncertainty that is inherent in scientific processes that deal in probabilities and not certainties. Scientists tell people that one in 100,000 persons (or some other probability) will suffer the health or safety effects of exposure to something, but they cannot predict who that person will be. Scientists disagree. Politicians disagree. Scientists use technical terms and concepts that in the judgment of laypersons obscure truth rather than reveal it. Reporters sensationalize, dramatize, overgeneralize, and oversimplify rather than explain (Cohn, 1990; Covello, 1992; M. Moore, 1989).

People look to government and other sources of sociopolitical power to help discover risks, assess their severity, solve them by reducing their chances of occurring, or mitigating their negative consequences. Grave sociopolitical implications lead to public policy discussions, whereby harmed parties seek to regulate those entities that are liable for the risks. No single, universally accepted standard of risk estimate is available to help people know whether they should be concerned, for instance, about the presence of toxic materials in their neighborhoods and workplaces. Thus, government often becomes an unwilling and even inexpert arbiter.

Companies have a different choice to make than do other parties—to upgrade operations to lessen public criticism—which may increase operating costs and lower the ability to compete and attract investors unless all members of an industry adopt the same standards. In today's economy, governmental agencies are caught between competing stakeholder interests, which include the costs of regulation, safety of citizens, and the ability of domestic companies to compete in global markets where other countries do not impose the levels of constraint typical of the United States. Government agencies become the playing field for tugs of war between legislators, members of the executive cadre of government, business spokespersons, and citizens who are convinced that specific intolerable health, safety, or environmental quality risks exist.

Considerations of risk acknowledge that not all members of a community have the same tolerance for a particular risk, as they may have different information and opinions regarding it. What is a tolerable risk for some is intolerable for others. What some think is a risk that is intolerable deserving to be subjected to greater control, perhaps through legislation or regulation, to others may be a trivial, inconsequential risk not deserving the burden of governmental intervention. Even when members of a public perceive a risk to exist, they may conclude that its benefits are worth the risk. In this way, key publics—many of them—form and become active toward various outcomes, all of which have the potential of becoming major controversies.

Two major overlapping scenarios of risk exist. In one, organizations such as public health agencies attempt to alert and inform people about health or safety risks over which they have personal control, such as driving with fastened seatbelts, eating low cholesterol foods, immunizing children against diseases, or having safe sex. A second scenario involves responses by industries and government agencies to help people understand and agree to regulated levels of risk—such as those created by chemical or biotechnology companies. In this mix are reporters and activists, both of whom have self-interested reasons to treat simplistically and with hyperbole the conceivably harmful aspects of risks and the avarice of businesses coupled with the ignorance or cooptation of governmental regulators—the wolves sent to guard the henhouse.

A key issue regarding the role of corporations, and other large organizations, is the new sense of community stewardship. Discussions of issues management address the ways in which companies, such as those in the petrochemical industry, join together to impose higher levels of operating performance on themselves. Indeed, that process is underway in the form of reduced emissions as part of the Chemical Manufacturers Association's Responsible Care Program. Companies have adopted new strategies, other than merely assuming that their proficiency at manipulating the licensing or permitting process can allow them to continue business as usual. They are learning the value of proactively acknowledging the possibility of toxic releases into a community and teaching people how to take protective measures in that event (Heath & Abel, 1996a). Activists have learned to use public policy channels to their interests, even halting projects by some of the largest companies in the world. For example, the Texas Copper Company division of Misubitshi Corporation was stopped from going into construction and operation by determined citizens (Heath, 1995).

Companies find reason to implement programs whereby they increase publics' understanding of technical processes as a means for lessening the fear of the threatening unknown and of increasing trust. To do so requires that the companies evidence public interest in how they operate and communicate. They often have the best information to use to determine whether or how some commercial process should be conducted. If that information is hidden or otherwise withheld from the public, it cannot serve the wise formulation of public policy. Recognizing the new stewardship, companies pool information and share technologies to solve environmental problems—the fostering of community interests through strategic issues management.

When private-sector organizations fail to understand and exhibit appropriate levels of corporate responsibility, those standards will be advocated and perhaps imposed. For instance, government became deeply involved in chemical-related risk assessment and communication processes due to the Bhopal tragedy. The calamity in India motivated citizens to worry whether similar risks loomed near their homes or at their work locations. Questions of that sort led federal legislators to create the Emergency Planning and Community Right-to-Know Act of 1986, section three of the Superfund Amendments and Reauthorization Act of 1986 (SARA Title III). Legislators believed SARA would create a communication apparatus and strategic business planning process to empower people regarding risks they worry they might suffer.

Codifying environmental risk communication, SARA requires chemical companies to inform citizens regarding the kind and quantity of chemicals that are manufactured, stored, and emitted in each community. The EPA established risk communication as a subdiscipline committed to open, responsible, informed, and reasonable scientific discussion of risks associated with personal health and safety practices involved in living and working in proximity to harmful activities and toxic substances. The underpinning assumption was that as companies report the toxic and hazardous materials they produce, transport, and store, people can become informed of the level of risk in their neighborhood.

The EPA (1988b) characterized this initiative in noble terms:

> The Emergency Planning and Community Right-to-Know Act creates a new relationship among government at all levels, business and community leaders, environmental and other public-interest organizations, and individual citizens. For the first time, the law makes citizens full partners in preparing for emergencies and managing chemical risks. (p. 3)

Defined this way, issues management of risks, including communication about them, is successful to the extent that people who fear that they may be harmed become more understanding and confident that sufficient control is imposed by the sources of the risk and by government.

Reviewing the Right-to-Know provision for the Public Relations Society of America, Newman (1988) concluded, "The theory behind these toxic laws is that this information will not only help answer citizen questions about [chemical] releases, but will also assist them in pressuring government and industry to correct practices that threaten their health and environment" (p. 8). Understanding the nature and impact of a source of risk is not the only factor involved in risk assessment, management, and communication. Another factor is power—a rhetorical struggle by parties engaged in negotiating levels of risk and standards of regulative or legislative control.

This section has provided insights into these variables as a preamble to considering the community-based decision processes that aim to assess and control risks. Issues management enters this process to consider the strategic business planning options, issue monitoring, efforts to properly achieve corporate responsibility, and risk communication.

Issues Management of Risk: Decision Making Aimed at Control

An issues management approach to risk assessment and communication argues that these activities are more likely to be successful when they increase the control of key publics have over the technical information, risk assessment process, and regulation of any threatening product as well as its manufacture or transportation. That theme guides the analysis supplied in this section.

Groups that assess risks not only try to control risk decisions but also the availability and interpretation of relevant information. Experience led Ellen Silbergeld, speaking as Senior Scientist with the Environmental Defense Fund, to conclude, "Equal access to resources is needed to understand the issues, to go behind the presentation being made by the communicator—to reassess the risks, if you will, to reevaluate the grounds for decisions and discussions" (as quoted in Davies et al., 1987, p. 34).

Concerned publics realize that if they accept risk experts' assessments of risk, they are obliged to concur with the consequent recommendations, including the decision that a specific level of risk exposure is tolerable. When publics worry that they are at the mercy of risk assessors, their recourse is to refuse to accept those expert evaluations. Reflecting on this quandary, Covello, Sandman, and Slovic (1988) claimed,

> A risk that the parties at risk have some control over is more acceptable than a risk that is beyond their control. A risk that the parties at risk assess and *decide* to accept is more acceptable than a risk that is imposed on them. (p. 6)

In the face of unknown or unacceptably high risks, noncompliance by key publics forces risk assessors to strive toward zero risk or to bear the burden of justifying any level higher. In this feeding ground, activists attempt to force companies and government agencies to prove that no harm exists. That rhetorical stance contrasts with the assumption that concerned citizens must prove that a risk is intolerable.

In this battle, concern about risks matures into power politics, a realization of issues managers. Such insight is warranted, William Ruckelshaus (as quoted in Davies et al., 1987) reasoned, because our adversarial form of government features advocacy:

Ours is a government of the people in this country, and it derives, as we have been told since we were children, its just powers from the consent of the governed. If the governed withhold that consent or take a portion of it back, it simply means that the government has been forced to once again share the power to govern with those who had earlier given their consent. (p. 4)

The outcome of problem recognition without ready-made means for remedy, as described in Chapter 5, is the emergence, growth, and solidification of grassroots politics as people seek to reduce the risk they fear confronts them.

Any public that is unwilling to tolerate a risk is likely to work for its control. Activism results from detection of a problem, perception that minimal constraints are likely to be encountered during protest, and belief that the problem affects them (Grunig, 1989a). A constructive issues management response to concerned people is to encourage them to participate in decision making. Otherwise, they may assert that right. This recognition led the Chemical Manufacturers Association to advise chemical plant managers to "involve all parties that have an interest or a stake in the particular risk in question" (Covello et al., 1988, p. 2). Reflecting a high standard of corporate responsibility, such advice acknowledges that "people and communities have a right to participate in decisions that affect their lives, their property, and the things they value" (p. 2). Dialogue and decision-making participation by key publics in risk policy formation acknowledges that the decision regarding what level is acceptable "*is not a technical question but a value question*" (Covello et al., 1988, p. 6). Issues managers should recognize the political nature of risk assessment and control.

Scrutinizing the politics of risk assessment, EPA administrator Lee Thomas (as quoted in Davies et al., 1987) recognized that

We will never return to the days when we were content to let people in white coats make soothing noises. Citizens must share directly in decisions that affect them, and we must ensure that they do so with a fuller understanding of the inevitable trade-offs involved in the management of risk. (p. 25)

Evidence abounds that risk perceptions and estimates are affected by decision heuristics that reflect the cultures of key groups, based largely on their roles in society. For instance, policymakers' attitudes tend to be more favorable toward risk conditions than are the opinions of the lay public (Thomas, Swaton, Fishbein, & Otway, 1980). Krimsky (1992) believed risk assessments based on science must be couched in the social reality—zone of meaning—of the communities that are assessing the risks. Such is the case because "when faced with complex problems involving probability estimates or estimates of the frequency of events, people apply certain discernible rules of judgment called heuristics to simplify the problem. The use of heuristics often leads to judgment bias" (p. 17). Companies and governmental agencies can communicate to improve faulty heuristics, but they cannot dismiss or ignore them without dire consequences.

Risk managers need to acknowledge that risk communication is rhetorical and risk assessments are political and, therefore, must be treated through a communication process that is dialectical rather than linear: Expert-sender → concerned receiver (Heath & Nathan, 1991; Juanillo & Scherer, 1995; Rowan, 1995). Risk evaluation requires that values be imposed on risk estimations. Risk discussions fail when they ignore the fact that risk is a power issue that depends on agreement, evaluation, and compliance. Rather than blunting disagreement and downplaying differences regarding risk issues, the answer may be to make them public and explicit as a first step toward resolving them (Cannell & Otway, 1988). Based on this assumption, one means for responding to levels of risk people believe are intolerable is to spend the resources necessary to lower the risk to a level that meets key publics' expectations.

Expectations are subjective as well as scientific and are capable of being influenced through communication. The rhetorical struggle balances the degree of risk, benefits that offset it, ability to control it, and the collaborative participation of all stakeholders and stakeseekers. This section has featured those challenges as a prelude to considering what risk communication options are viable.

 Risk Communication Options

Risk communicators realize that each key public makes an idiosyncratic response to each risk based on its unique decision heuristic. Each concerned public has a proclivity to engage in or at least support activism to exert public policy solutions onto intolerable risks. That point was central to the discussion of the power resource dynamics in the previous section of this chapter. This section builds on that analysis to consider how communication can bring about the proper level of control and allay concerns on the parts of citizens regarding the degree to which they are at risk as they go about their daily activities.

Risk-relevant publics exist because people have different interpretive heuristics as well as conflicting understandings of whether something creates risk, whether that risk should be tolerated, and whether avoidance strategies or control measures are warranted. Publics arise because information and opinion regarding each risk do not uniformly exist throughout society. Pockets of concern become fertile ground for employing government to intervene between the public and the source of the risk. They constitute key zones of meaning—sometimes compatible and sometimes at odds.

Persons who design risk communication have at times reduced it to a list of simplistic prescriptions. One such list, the EPA's (1988) "seven cardinal rules of risk communication," advised risk communicators to tailor their messages to audiences and to use

> simple, non-technical language. Be sensitive to local norms, such as speech and dress. Use vivid, concrete images that communicate on a personal level. Use examples and anecdotes that make technical risk data come alive. Avoid distant, abstract, unfeeling language about deaths, injuries, and illnesses. (p. 4)

This advice assumes that "if people are sufficiently motivated, they are quite capable of understanding complex information, even if they may not agree with you" (p. 5). Such lists tend to miss the dynamics of technical ignorance, power, and controversy that frustrate the risk communication process. These lists can assume incorrectly that merely supplying information to people leads them to be educated, calmed, and risk tolerant.

This approach to risk communication predicts that if people receive credible and clear information regarding scientifically assessed risk levels, they will accept the conclusions and policy recommendations of risk assessors. This model overassumes the power of information and does not acknowledge the power resources that concerned publics employ to exert political pressure in their efforts to impose higher operating standards on the source of the ostensibly intolerable risk. The view assumes that "if people are given the facts, their subjective perceptions will begin to align with scientific judgments" (Liu & Smith, 1990, p. 332). That perspective reasons that if lay people understand the company's or government's side of the story, then confidence about risk would increase and complaints would go away (Gaudino et al., 1989).

Comparing those approaches, Hadden (1989) observed crucial differences between what she called "old" and "new" versions of risk communication. In the old approach, "experts tried to persuade laymen of the validity of their risk assessments or risk decisions." This option is "impeded by lay risk perception, difficulties in understanding probabilities, and the sheer technical difficulty of the subject matter" (p. 301). In contrast, the new approach is based on "dialogue among parties and participation in the choices among activities whose risks are being discussed" (p. 301). The new form of risk communication is impeded by the lack of institutions that are responsive to the needs, interests, and level of understanding of the publics affected by the potential or ostensible risk.

Hadden (1989) was concerned that institutional barriers stand in the way of meaningful dialogue in communities where people experience risks that they worry are intolerable. Such barriers result, at least in part, from statutes that do not specify what technical data are crucial and, therefore, should be collected. Even when data have been collected by industry or governmental agencies, institutional barriers prevent citizens from gaining access to them. People often encounter a maze of agencies, do not know where to acquire information, and suffer data dumps that provide huge amounts of information in ways that make it difficult to access. Encountering such barriers, people become frustrated or unsure that they have the data they need or want. Even when information is obtained, people run into barriers as they seek to exert changes they hope will mitigate the risks they believe they have discovered. A related barrier is the failure on the part of governmental agencies as well as industrial groups to agree on what data interpreted by what standards truly give meaningful insights. The institutions related to this process refuse—for various reasons, some of which are completely ethical and honest—to be precise in the reporting, use, and interpretation of data.

So what's to be done? Decide on what information is valuable, provide it, decide on what decision heuristics are appropriate, apply them. Organizations that are seeking to act in the mutual interests of themselves and their stakeholders work to make institutions yield to these changes. Organizations that are likely to be thought inadequate in their standards of corporate responsibility use bureaucracy to maintain barriers instead of to remove them.

Thus, risk is not only a communication problem but also an issues management challenge. Extending the EPA list of seven cardinal principles beyond communication prescriptions, the Chemical Manufacturers Association (1989) added four items that demonstrate a savvy understanding of the issues management approach to solving matters of risk. One prescription calls for refined strategic business planning, "Run a safe operation," whereas another demands a higher operating standard, "Reduce [toxic chemical] releases." Improved issues monitoring is required to "Find out the concerns of the community so you can decide what kinds of community outreach activities will be successful." One recommends better external communication: "Get involved in the community; establish a speakers bureau and join service organizations to make industry's presence known and to 'de-mystify' the chemical industry for local citizens." These four additions to the EPA list acknowledge the need to solve problems and meet community standards, an option that demonstrates the profound limitation of calming, soothing messages.

If zones of meaning—facts, value premises, and conclusions—in communities differ, then risk responses must be tailored to each public and convergence must be achieved. Addressing that theme, Rayner (1992) applied cultural theory to conclude "that risks are defined, perceived, and managed according to the principles that inhere in particular forms of social organization" (p. 84). This approach differs from "the dominant model of risk communication," which relies primarily on "information transmission with the goal of educating the recipient." In that option, which relies on a linear model of communication, the question

> is how to pass quantitative information about the probabilities and consequences of events from one information bearer (the transmitter) to another (the receiver) with the minimum of distortion. But information transmission is only one part of communication, which also involves developing shared meaning among individuals, institutions, and communities, and establishing relationships of trust. (p. 85)

The preferred risk communication model assumes that publics are active rather than passive information receivers and processors. Risk communication entails institutions trying to reach individuals in various states of collective behavior and engaging in collaborative decision making. Developing shared points of view may result from linear communication, but dialogue seems to be required because cultural relativism assumes "that the validity of public knowledge depends on its relation to the context of its creation through social activities such as science, technology, religion, and even magic" (Rayner, 1992, p. 93).

A linear risk communication approach can be faulted for assuming that the stakeholder relationship is limited to that between the organization or industry thought to pose risks and the public that feels concern. In contrast, von Winterfeldt (1992) reasoned that a multiple stakeholder analysis appreciates and balances the interests of all stakeholders. "The dilemma is thus clear: The experts should not control society's technological choices, but the public and their political representatives are not sufficiently informed to assume complete control themselves" (p. 324). An issues management approach (a) considers risks from the views of multiple stakeholders, (b) acknowledges and responds to their conflicting values, (c) analyzes data in light of best available expert interpretive approaches, and (d) integrates stakeholder values and scientific perspectives into outcomes seeking to maximize mutual interests through collaborative decision making.

Information becomes meaningful only if relevant parties are willing and able to use it in mutually acceptable ways in their assessments of risk. Persons differ in the ways they evaluate data and draw conclusions from them. To be avoided are risk response options based on "dissemination" rather than "communication" (Schultz, 1989, pp. 13-14), ones that do not embrace the politics of risk estimates and solutions. An information dissemination model is weak because the amount of factual knowledge individuals possess does not predict how much risk they will tolerate (Baird, 1986; Nathan, Heath, &

Douglas, 1992). Laypeople often are ignorant of the relevant facts pertaining to technical risks (Heath & Abel, 1996b).

The lay public does not understand technical aspects of risks. To complicate matters, risk messages often suffer from "deficiencies in scientific understanding, data, models, and methods, which result in large uncertainties in risk estimates" (Davies et al., 1987, p. 110). Evidence to support this conclusion was found in a survey conducted at 26 locations in the United States and Canada by Arthur D. Little, Inc. This survey revealed that plant personnel, community response personnel, and community officials had different interpretations of the risks associated with toxic fume releases and general environmental pollution. Plant personnel thought all of the risks in the survey were less significant than did either of the other groups (Young, 1990).

Because of inevitable controversies on how to assess risks, effective risk communication depends on trust among all parties (Hadden, 1988). If trust can be achieved by firms that ostensibly create risks and agencies that police them, citizens are less likely to want or use the information. People seek and use information and evaluation in their efforts to control sources of risk. When they believe that problems exist, they are prone to use public policy—regulation, legislation, and judicial review—toward those ends.

For these reasons, a community rather than an expert authority-based approach to risk assessment and communication is preferable. Thus, Palmlund (1992) argued against an authority-centered, linear communication approach: "I believe that a different vision of life is needed, one that emphasizes the role of social interaction, emotions, and power in public life." Continuing, he reasoned, "Societal evaluation of risk must be seen as a contest, where the participants offer competing views of reality. They compete to define what should be viewed as the benefits and the risks of prevailing production practices" (p. 199). Risk controversy results from a drama enacted by many personae, each of which attempts to create and live a different view of reality—zone of meaning. Conflict is the consequence of the interaction between personae playing narrative dramas in each community.

What view, therefore, is the best one in regard to what risk communication is? Our goal is to define risk communication according to the principles of issues management. Acknowledging the importance of taking a community approach lays the foundation for examining definitions of risk communication and investigating the dynamics of this process.

Definitions of risk communication feature information exchange while ignoring its outcome. What is that exchange supposed to accomplish? Featuring process, Covello (1992) defined risk communication "as the exchange of information among interested parties about the nature, magnitude, significance, or control of a risk" (p. 359). Featuring interaction between relevant parties, risk communication can be defined as "any purposeful exchange of

information about health or environmental risks between interested parties."
It involves "the act of conveying or transmitting information between interested parties about levels of health or environmental risks; the significance or
meanings of such risks; or decisions, actions, or policies aimed at managing
or controlling such risks" (Davies et al., 1987, p. 112). Why feature process,
not outcome?

Along with a stress on community dialogue, the National Research
Council (1989) featured potential outcomes. It treated risk communication as
*"an interactive process of exchange of information and opinion among indi-
viduals, groups, and institutions. It involves multiple messages about the
nature of risk and other messages, not strictly about risk, that express concerns, opinions, or reactions to risk messages or to legal and institutional
arrangements for risk management* [italics added]." This definition stresses
outcome. Risk communication is "successful only to the extent that it raises
the level of understanding of relevant issues or actions and satisfies those
involved that they are adequately informed within the limits of available
knowledge" (p. 21).

Is being informed the limit of risk communication? What about the
abatement of risks thought to be intolerable? What about the values unique to
assessing what risks are tolerable or deciding when each risk is tolerable?
Factors seem to be missing from this definition, particularly the desire on the
part of key publics to politically control intolerable risks—either their source,
their likelihood, or their consequences. We err if we feature only the process
of risk communication and fail to grasp the outcomes toward which it is used.
Beyond becoming informed, the product of the dialogue and interaction
typical of superior risk communication is an increased sense of control on the
part of the persons who feel themselves to be at risk. This desire for control
can be satisfied through dialogue or confrontation with activists, lawyers, and
regulators playing major roles. The sense of control is a counterpart of the
uncertainty that characterizes, indeed defines, risk.

The preferred outcome is a shared sense of control through which relevant
and concerned parties increase the harmony in the community and seek to
maximize mutual interests. This theme is further developed in the following
section, which focuses on variables that define the risk communication infrastructure in each community. Infrastructures are networks by which people
share and obtain information from one another, the media, and organizational
sources, such as businesses and governmental agencies. Activists and expert
groups, such as industrial hygienists, plant safety personnel, or university
faculty, are key players in this infrastructure.

One traditional weakness in the design of risk communication is the
assumption that people receive most of what they know about risks and learn
to respond if one occurs by watching television, reading a newspaper, or

listening to radio. This mass-mediated approach to the diffusion of risk information can fail to acknowledge the important role of conversation, interpersonal exchanges with friends and relatives (Heath, Liao, et al., 1995; Juanillo & Scherer, 1995; Salmon, 1992; Scherer & Juanillo, 1992).

As Fischhoff (1995) has modeled the risk communication process, it can be viewed as developmental: getting the numbers regarding risks correct, putting those numbers into a community at risk, explaining what is meant by them, showing that members of the community have accepted similar risks, showing the benefits of risks, treating the public with respect, and creating partnerships to understand and properly control risks. The strongest component of this progression is the creation of meaningful partnerships that respond to the concerns and needs of community members for information and to bring collective wisdom and judgment to bear on that problem. This stress on "we" gives a community grounding for two-way communication and partnership development (Chess, Salomone, Hance, & Saville, 1995).

We miss the point and, therefore, generate useless research and professional prescriptions when we approach risk communication as information exchange about risks while failing to acknowledge that people compete through persuasive exchanges to achieve greater control over the risks they believe to exist. Control is the motive behind efforts to define, estimate, and understand risks. For this reason, industry shares key publics' desire for control over risks—although their means may differ. Does industry sufficiently control its operations and employ proper research to understand risks it may create? Does the company or government agency share this information and foster dialogue and criticism so that people interact and form relationships with members of the industry in a collaborative fashion seeking to maximize the safety of all parties involved? Is industry ethical and responsive to the needs of its key publics and committed to building mutually beneficial relationships? Herein lies the essence of risk communication as conceptualized through the principles of issues management.

 Dynamics of the Management of Risk Issues

An issues management approach to health and safety risks requires a view that embraces several key variables. Ongoing research has yet to define these terms and their relationships satisfactorily; however, enough is known that we can lay out some conclusions and frame a philosophy of risk communication. Current research assumes that people's support or opposition for an organization that ostensibly creates or allows a risk to exist depends on whether they believe the organization subjects them (or relevant others) to a likely and harmful risk over which they have limited individual or collective control.

Rather than a linear communication relationship, whereby information and opinion influence flows from the firm to key publics, an issues management approach to risk views laypeople as a vital part of a complex communication, opinion formation, and decision-making infrastructure.

The primary outcome of the management of risk issues is not understanding or agreement, as some approaches argue. Rather, the outcome is control. Even to the extent that understanding and agreement are dependent variables, they in turn become independent variables affecting other dependent variables. This reasoning does not discount the importance of understanding or agreement. Rather, it acknowledges that they are often difficult or impossible to achieve due to the fact that corporate or governmental spokespersons often are not trusted sources of information, opinions, and advice. In addition, concerned publics typically lack the technical expertise needed to make independent judgments of complex risk issues, especially those requiring knowledge of scientific concepts and research methodologies.

Even if they do not have the scientific expertise to rely on their own knowledge and judgment but do not trust company spokespersons, they may conclude that a risk is tolerable if its benefits outweigh its harms. They may be assuaged in their apprehensions by knowing that mechanisms exist by which a dialogue can occur that considers their opinions and treats their concerns seriously. That last point stresses the importance of community dialogue—open, candid, honest, and responsive—as the basis for creating a harmonious, mutual-interest relationship between the key players where a risk may exist. For these reasons, *risk communication seeks to increase concerned publics' sense of control over the risks they believe can affect them.*

Drawing on his own research as well as that of others, Covello (1992) featured several variables to predict how people respond to risks. This list includes catastrophic potential, familiarity, understanding, uncertainty, controllability, voluntariness of exposure, effects on children, effects manifestation, effects on future generations, victim identity, dread, trust in institutions, media attention, accident history, equity, benefits, reversibility, personal stake, and origin.

Catastrophic potential is the product of estimations that many individuals or other entities will be harmed or killed at the same time as a consequence of the risk. *Familiarity* is a function of the extent to which people routinely encounter the risk. *Understanding* is the extent to which experts or laypersons comprehend the mechanisms that result in the risk or its consequences. *Uncertainty* is a defining construct of risk—the probability that an event will occur or that it will lead to positive or negative consequences of varying degrees of severity. *Controllability* refers to the ability of knowledgeable and responsible people to prevent the occurrence of the risk or its consequences.

Voluntariness of exposure addresses the concern that people have regarding how they become exposed to the risk: whether they opt to be exposed to it rather than if they are forced to suffer its occurrence or consequences against their will. When a risk has harmful *effects on children,* it is viewed as being less tolerable than if it affects older people. Another concern is how the effects are *manifested*—immediate or delayed. Impact of a risk can be immediate, but uncertainty increases as people attempt to predict its effects on *future generations.* Risks are uncertainties that experts attempt to reduce to probabilities that *some* persons out of a population will suffer. *Who will the victims be? Dread* refers to the seriousness or magnitude of the outcome: the number of people harmed or the agony of the effects of encountering that risk.

Increased media attention can magnify the degree to which people think a risk is in play. Risks are assessed according to *accident history,* their recurrence and consequences. *Equity* is an important dimension of risk because people of color and lower socioeconomic levels may experience disproportionately greater risks. Risks are not without *benefits;* a balancing act of risk assessment is to determine whether the positives associated with the risk overweigh the harms and whether the benefits are clearly recognized. A risk is thought to be less tolerable when its effects are *irreversible.* If people have a *personal stake* in a risk, they respond differently than if they do not. As people assess risks, they calculate the *origin*—whether natural or the product of human efforts—and respond accordingly.

Although research has yet to adequately eliminate some items from the list or completely define the interaction between them, it has helped experts to formulate hypotheses and frame useful conclusions. For instance, public concern is greater when the potential for many people dying at once is high, even when that same number of people might die at various times and in many places. For this reason, people fear flying—potential of many deaths at the same time—more than driving or riding in an automobile. Trends indicate that 40,000 to 45,000 people die in automobile accidents each year, but few deaths occur at one time or in one place. Few people die in all airplane accidents each year; however, during a plane crash, many people die at once. One additional reason for this difference in fear is that riding in an automobile is more *familiar* than is riding in a plane. People in a car think they are more in *control,* whereas they know they lack control while on a commercial flight. Of related interest is the bias that exists in media reporting that tends to respond in hyperbolic ways to catastrophic risks rather than routine ones. Media are more likely to express concern over a risk such as an airplane crash or exposure to radiation than they are to decry the number of people who die in automobile accidents—or cigarette smoking—each year. Public expectations—often expressed as potential outrage—become the bases for how a company or industry should identify, assess, and mitigate risks.

Given these factors, how do we progress to comprehend and create proactive responses to publics' concerns about the risks they believe they encounter? An issues management approach to risk assessment and problem solving begins by acknowledging the rhetorical nature of the dialogue and related power struggle that surround the assessment and control of risks (Heath & Nathan, 1991; Rowan, 1995). This view requires that issues communication allow for *rhetorical and political influence from community members.* It embraces the *uncertainty* people have regarding whether a risk exists and whether it can be controlled; *evaluation* regarding what is equitable, fair, safe, and environmentally sound; and *cognitive involvement,* which results from people's self-interest or altruistic concern for others. It should acknowledge the problematic role of *knowledge,* and focus on people's estimation of whether the risk *harms* or *benefits* them. In this analysis, *control* and *trust* are outcomes desired by the relevant parties, even though the definition and sociopolitical means for accomplishing them may differ. The outcome sought is public support for the risks—their sources, rewards, and controls.

This review of risk assessment and the communication of those assessments recognizes how important trust is, not only as an attribute of communication sources but also as part of each key public's awareness of and confidence in communication processes and business operations over time. This approach to risk communication assumes that narratives change and organizational activities both create risk narratives and must conform to narratives preferred by concerned citizens, especially activist publics. Because risk assessment is public policy resource-based, efforts to alter risk perception and behaviors entail the evaluation, weighing, and negotiation of stakes. To allay key publics' concerns, companies or government entities that create risks may have to spend money to improve operations to reduce those risks. As part of each company's or industry's public policy plan, efforts may be made to set standards that are required by law to lessen the effect of the so-called bad apples, the least responsible members of an industry. Community support is the fundamental outcome to be derived from the process of identifying risks as well as assessing their causes, magnitudes, and solutions and engaging in appropriate remediation.

Support is the outcome objective of managing the organization's response to the concern on the part of key publics. Either a risk exists or it does not. It is controllable in various ways and degrees—or it is not. It is controllable by collective, community, public policy actions, the self-regulation of the potential source of risk, or by persons who believe they suffer the risk and its consequences. The public policy contest (activist, company, and government agency) is to gain the support of key players. Companies desire to solve the problem through self-regulation without having regulation imposed through governmental actions as an expression of public will. Issues management of risks seeks to displace opposition with support by (a) making appropriate strategic business plans, (b) engaging in effective issues monitoring and analysis, (c) using public policy planning in the mutual interest of stakeholders, (d) seeking to meet key publics' expectations of corporate responsibility, and (e) communicating in ways that maximize the control people feel is reasonable to achieve harmony and foster multiple stakeholders' mutual interests.

People support that which benefits them and oppose that which harms them. That equation underpins issues management. One study of a town highly economically dependent on chemical manufacturing facilities discovered that perceived economic advantages correlated with support, whereas economic harms correlated with opposition. Advantages included personal income, business opportunities, community income, community tax base, real estate values, and job opportunities. In contrast, opposition correlated with personal medical insurance costs and environmental cleanup costs (Heath, Liao, et al., 1995).

Risk assessment and communication assumes that key players dispute propositions of fact, value, and policy. How people interpret risks may result from the facts they believe and the premises they use in their debate and decision making. Propositions of fact result from inquiries regarding what is known about a risk. Does a risk exist? If so, is it tolerable? This last question stresses the rhetorical and political nature of risks. Different cultures—zones of meanings—reflect premises that stress different, even conflicting, values. The argumentative outcome of risk assessment and communication is a product of facts interpreted through relevant premises and values. People seek to create public policies that exert the maximum control over the risk, given their understanding of it.

What rationale exists for this issues management approach to risk assessment and communication? For one, Nathan and Heath (1992) found that opposition correlated with the opinion that risks are intolerable. When considering whether they would tolerate the potential discharge of harmful substances—particularly lead—into coastal waters, nonsupporters were more likely to believe potential risks from a chemical manufacturing facility would be greater than did supporters.

In a similar fashion, persons who oppose or do not support the presence of a chemical plant in their community tend to think that harm from the plant outweighs its benefits—such as jobs, business income, and taxes (Heath, Liao, et al., 1995). Persons who oppose such a plant experience higher levels of cognitive involvement than supporters do; opponents believe that they need to be attentive to plant operations and information about them because of the likelihood that those operations adversely affect their self-interests. The longer people live near a chemical plant or similar facility, the more accommodating they become to it. Likewise, they become more willing to support its presence in their community (Nathan & Heath, 1992).

Uncertainty is a concept that is routinely used to define risk. Risk is the likelihood (probability) that an event will occur and that it is will be tolerable or severe. Focusing on this logic, Albrecht (1988) concluded that uncertainty is "the lack of attributional confidence about cause-effect patterns" (p. 387). Driskill and Goldstein (1986) reasoned that individuals suffering turbulent or unstable conditions become more attentive to information that will help them cope with their environment; they found that people are not always able to reduce their uncertainty with information alone. Uncertainty may not result merely from the lack of information but may occur when people lack appropriate premises to use to draw conclusions with it. Although people can tolerate a substantial amount of uncertainty regarding future events, their need for information increases when outcomes are thought to be harmful.

Exploring uncertainty as an incentive to communicate interpersonally, Berger and Calabrese (1975) stated, "When persons are unable to make sense out of their environment, they usually become anxious" (p. 107). Berger (1987) argued that when people place importance on outcome, they have more incentive to be attentive to and even seek information that can be used to predict or mitigate undesirable future events. Uncertainty, a function of the ability to predict and explain actions of other people as well as one's own, affects the way information is evaluated (Berger, 1987; Berger & Calabrese, 1975). If uncertainty exists, people are likely to devote more cognitive effort to thinking about the risk as well as seeking information about it (Kasperson, 1992).

Uncertainty is not only a variable that relates to how people perceive events and their effects or one that may lead them to engage in various kinds of communication behavior. It is also a compounding factor in the risk decision-making process. Weterings and van Eijndhoven (1989) observed that uncertainty inherent in technological risks and scientific complexity complicates risk communication. "Scientists' training, which teaches them to accurately represent certain types of uncertainties, comes into conflict with the pressure to give succinct, unambiguous answers that can inform the social and personal decisions non-experts must make about risks" (National Research Council, 1989, p. 44).

As people attempt to reduce uncertainty, they cannot always rely on their own judgments and may doubt the opinions and conclusions of experts. An essential part of the process, *trust* is a multidimensional construct that results from the amount of control an audience believes it can exert over sources of risk information and assessment. As Kasperson (as quoted in Davies et al., 1987) concluded, "There is not a single risk communication problem; there is not a single social trust problem. There are many problems, and they are different" (p. 45). Trust is affected by vulnerability, predictability, and reward dependability. Party A is vulnerable to party B if A's interests can be harmed or enhanced by what B does. If B can enhance rather than harm A, the trust relationship is different than if no prediction can be made or if B can be predicted to harm A. Emphasizing the multidimensionality of trust, Joanne Kauffman (as quoted in Davies et al., 1987) observed, "Government, in particular, suffers from a loss of credibility; it is often perceived to have a hidden agenda rather than to facilitate a process" (p. 74).

Self-interest or altruistic values predict whether publics and audiences will be cognitively involved with public policy issues leading them to recognize what arguments are relevant, to have more knowledge of a topic, and to communicate about it (Heath & Douglas, 1991; Heath, Liao, et al., 1995; Nathan et al., 1992). Persons who believe they are at risk become more thoughtful in their analysis of message content and work harder to obtain information and opinion through conversation, reading, listening to news, and televiewing.

Cognitively involved persons can be reached with information and argument even though they may resist them, whereas less involved persons are likely to ignore informational presentations and discussions of the risk. Involved persons are more critical of information and arguments than are their less cognitively involved counterparts (Petty & Cacioppo, 1986). Perception that risk exists and is unacceptable—or at least deserving of concern—correlates with cognitive involvement (Nathan & Heath, 1992). When people feel that the source of risk harms their financial well-being, they are likely to become more cognitively involved with the discussion of the risk and its abatement (Heath, Liao, et al., 1995). Persons who are frightened, angry, and powerless resist information that says that their risk is modest, whereas those who are optimistic and overconfident deny that their risk is substantial (Sandman, 1986).

Cognitive involvement and support or opposition exhibit a curvilinear relationship (Gay & Heath, 1995; Heath, Liao, et al., 1995; Nathan et al., 1992). That means that persons who strongly oppose or support an industry, company, product, service, or a regulatory agency are likely to exhibit higher cognitive involvement than will persons who neither strongly support nor oppose those players in the risk equation. This point is vital. In each community where a risk may exist, some persons are likely to be highly involved supporters, whereas others are likely to be cognitively involved opponents of the source of risk. For these reasons, risk communication should adopt a multiple-stakeholder approach to the management of risk.

Risk tolerance is an important concept. Just as everyone is not equally aware of the risks in a community or the emergency response measures they should take to increase their safety, all members of a community have a different sense of the degree to which a risk exists and whether it is harmful. They differ in their risk tolerance—a measure of how knowledgeable they are of a risk and accommodating to it. Women, for instance, tend to be less tolerant of technical risks than are men.

Control has particular relevance for the analysis of and strategic response to crises events and risks. Nathan and Heath (1992) found that persons who indicate that they do not support what they fear are high risk chemical facilities exhibit a greater need for control in comparison to supporters of such facilities. People tend to believe that they benefit more from sources of risk if they think the managements of such facilities, perhaps in conjunction with government regulators, properly control their operations. Chemical workers, persons employed by a source of risk, believe that the managements of such facilities exert more self-control over their operations than do persons who do not work in the industry. An increased sense of shared control over the risk and its potentially harmful outcomes is likely to lead to greater harmony between the organization and its stakeholders and stakeseekers. Addressing this issue by concentrating on industrial hygienists, Gay and Heath (1995) discovered that respondents who think that control over chemical facilities comes from government sought information from the general media whereas their counterparts who rely on business sources thought that chemical facilities would regulate themselves. The hygienists who worked in the industry were more supportive of it and less committed to the use of governmental regulation.

Knowledge is one of the most problematic variables in this analysis. One underpinning assumption in risk assessment is that experts can obtain scientific knowledge about the degree to which a risk exists, use that knowledge to properly abate the risk, and supply concerned publics with the details of the risk and means for its abatement. The assumption is that once key publics receive technical information, they make informed decisions and their concern will lessen. This model employed by the EPA leads it to require scientific analysis and reporting by thousands of companies and government agencies around the country. Despite its intuitive logic, that model does not seem to work—at least not very often or very well. For one reason, knowledge is unevenly spread throughout a community. Males tend to be more knowledgeable than are women—although both may lack a great deal of vital information (Heath & Abel, 1996b). People who work in an industry are more knowledgeable; those who live closer to risk are more knowledgeable (Baird, 1986).

Knowledge of the technical aspects of a risk does not account for much of the support or opposition that people express about it. Baird (1986) found that knowledge basic to risk estimates did not predict tolerance of emissions from a lead smelter. People tolerate risk for reasons that may have little to do with factual details, formal risk estimates, or details of risk abatement proposals. Even though smelter employees faced the greatest arsenic exposure, they were less likely to view the smelter as a personal health hazard and were more likely to voice confidence they would not become ill from its emissions. Although those who were less tolerant of the hazard had more information about it than those more tolerant, knowledge was not a useful predictor of risk tolerance.

In similar fashion, Nathan et al. (1992) discovered that knowledge about an alleged source of risk did not differ significantly for respondents who were less risk tolerant and those who were more tolerant. Part of the reason for this finding was explained by Chaffee and Roser (1986) who discovered that perceived health risk does not always create a desire for more knowledge but can produce erratic relationships among knowledge, attitude, and belief. People who know they are most at risk may actually make less effort to find and think about information that could increase their concern.

"Information to be communicated must fit into the frameworks of the receivers: because they will interpret the information according to these frameworks, we must be aware of what they are rather than bemoan their existence" (Davies et al., 1987, p. 81). Given this caution, we can discuss this issue using, for instance, the decision-making formula that seems to be at the heart of EPA regulation and SARA Title III. It assumes that if companies make information available, key publics will receive and use it. Examining that premise in the context of one of the most massive chemical manufacturing complexes in the world, Heath and Abel (1996b) discovered that knowledge in one community correlated with support, whereas it did not in another community. What is also important is the fact that members of the two communities differed significantly in the amount of knowledge they exhibited.

Respondents in this study were asked to name chemicals manufactured in their community, those that were on the EPA list of hazardous materials, and processes that were employed to abate the release of these materials—the standard EPA risk decision logic. Although support correlated with knowledge in the "high" knowledge community, both communities could be said to suffer from gross ignorance. Despite the fact that 75% of the people in both communities made their living directly from the chemical industry, 59% of the people in the high knowledge community could not name a single chemical or process; that number was 69% for the "low" knowledge community. When asked about benefits such as amount of taxes paid by industry or number of people employed, 31% of the low knowledge community respondents could not make a correct answer; the comparable figure was 25% for the high knowledge community. Even though people believed they were at risk due to their proximity to the industry, 72% (low) and 83% (high) could not name a company that had been found to violate a state or federal regulation. People in these communities were ignorant of outreach efforts by the companies to communicate with and involve laypeople in the conversation about plant safety and environmental responsibility. Nevertheless, in the high knowledge community, 85% of the people supported the chemical industry, whereas 58% of the low knowledge community supported it (Heath & Abel, 1996b). How can people who live and work in a chemical community be so uninvolved with its operations and risks?

The relationship between knowledge and support is perhaps more complex than straightforward. Knowledge of companies' outreach efforts correlated with knowledge of chemicals but not with support for the industry.

However, knowledge of chemicals correlated with support. For this reason, the relationship between support and knowledge of outreach may be indirect. Of related importance is the finding that knowledge of benefits correlates with support but not with knowledge of outreach. This relationship suggests that persons who know about chemicals and outreach become willing to support chemical plants for technical reasons, whereas other persons' support grows out of knowledge of economic benefits. This relationship also suggests that outreach features topics of safety and does not merely present economic reasons to support chemical companies' presence in a community (Heath & Abel, 1996b).

Harms and benefits are important aspects of the risk assessment equation. Krimsky and Golding (1992) observed, "Expected utility theory comprises a set of decision rules that define rational behavior. It is generally assumed that people would follow these rules if they had sufficient information and time to dwell on the consequences of alternative decision paths" (p. 356). People may infer that they receive benefits (or suffer harms) and then decide whether they suffer risks that are intolerable. Those who think they are harmed do not support the source of risk (Heath, Liao, et al., 1995). Females tend to rate the harms of technical processes greater than their benefits (Nathan & Heath, 1992).

These findings support the conclusion that the key factor in the issues management of risk is maximizing the sense of *control* people have regarding the risks they encounter. Risk results in uncertainty, although we may speculate that concerned individuals often are certain that dire consequences will occur. Perhaps they are only uncertain as to when those problems will arise. Control is a means for reducing uncertainty that something unpleasant, dreaded, or harmful can occur. One way to reduce uncertainty about hazardous operations by companies and government agencies is to give concerned citizens, especially activists, a constructive role in the dialogue.

For this reason, proactive companies use citizens advisory committees and other outreach mechanisms that disclose information that people want and allow them to voice their concerns. If people have control over the sources of information and the decision processes, they can exert more control and thereby reduce the risk to a tolerable level (Heath, 1995). When people have constructive means to control the source of risk or its consequences, they engage in that behavior, probably because it gives them a sense of self-efficacy. When they do not have knowledge of or confidence in a means to control the source of risk or its consequences, they are more likely to respond out of fear. This emotional response is likely to manifest itself in outrage or denial (Witte, 1995).

Along these same lines, proactive companies strive to inform community members about emergency response systems that are in place to warn them of an emergency and to assist their efforts to be safe. Firms such as these, often in conjunction with local government, formulate personal-response plans that people can use to shelter in place—to go or stay inside a residence or business, close the building to outside air, and to monitor the emergency by using special radio frequencies and emergency-response-activated telephone systems. Such measures, although potentially alarming to people, can increase their sense of control (coupled with a sense that the companies and local government help to exert control) over the effects of a risk should it occur (Heath & Abel, 1996a).

Is this good communication policy? It seems to be based on the discussion by Witte (1995) who reasoned that when spokespersons for ostensible sources of risks attempt to downplay a risk, either its probability or severity, without addressing ways to increase people's self-efficacy, public response is likely to be outrage or denial. Denial and outrage are unconstructive responses. Outrage can frustrate efforts of the participants to understand one another. Denial makes people hard to reach. For this reason, communities where risks exist do well to stress the expertise and preparedness of manufacturing plant personnel and community fire and police officials to respond during an emergency. Of related value is information such as instructions for how to shelter in place, which concerned citizens can use if an emergency occurs.

Rather than raising their fear, such information is a constructive, proactive response to that concern (Heath & Abel, 1996a). Without measures for responding safely in the event of an emergency—which reasonable people acknowledge could happen—community members are likely to engage in outbursts of rage, resort to the denial that an explosion or toxic release will not happen or will not affect them (or that they will die quickly), or resort to measures of self-efficacy such as deciding to attempt to evacuate in the event of an emergency. Experts believe that evacuation is unwise because it can expose persons to toxic materials and clog streets best left open to emergency vehicles and personnel. The exception to this policy is when the evacuation is ordered and guided by emergency response experts.

Control can be divided into two categories, personal and societal. People either prefer to take control of their circumstances, exert personal control, or they prefer that others—such as responsible industries, efficacious governmental agencies, or powerful activists—exert control over the source of potential harm. Is the risk too great, too high—particularly in proportion to the benefits that might be derived from it? This dimension of risk assessment is not only a matter of science and economics but of ethics. Of related interest are the scientific considerations of risk related to control. Some risks are more well understood than others. They have better developed controls or emergency responses to avoid becoming catastrophic.

Matters of control are sensitive to (a) personal control by individual members of the community where the risk exists, (b) authorized (authority) control, (c) activists' control, and (d) self-control by the source of the risk. The primary outcome of people's belief that sufficient or insufficient control exists is their support or opposition for the source of the risk and the governmental agencies that are expected to act on behalf of community members. If people believe that the agency of control can and will effect lowered risk or foster appropriate emergency response to it, they support that agency. If the agency, such as a business, has demonstrated that it understands the risk, knows the appropriate responses, and is willing to enact the proper control, it should enjoy support instead of suffer opposition. Lacking this control, people turn to other agencies of control and voice opposition to the source of risk.

  As control declines and a sense of risk increases, people's cognitive involvement raises if the risk is seen to affect their self-interests or the interests of persons and entities for which the person has concern. In this regard, uncertainty—doubt as to facts and conclusions—and cognitive involvement—belief that self-interests are at stake—lead to increased communication activity. Under such conditions, persons are more likely to teleview, listen to radio programs, and read books, magazines, and newspapers stories on the topic. They are more likely to attend meetings and to converse with others on this matter. Uncertainty and cognitive involvement motivate communication behavior—a desire to understand the risk, its potential harm and controls, and the likelihood those controls will be exerted. In this way, knowledge is sought as the means for control, but knowledge is idiosyncratic, inconsistent, culturally sensitive, and incomplete.

  In infrastructures, people obtain information from many sources (Gay & Heath, 1995; Heath, Liao, et al., 1995). These sources are the general media and narrowly specialized outlets. For instance, environmentalists prefer to receive information from environmental groups (Grunig, 1983). Trust predicts what they believe and the sources on which they rely. The infrastructure exhibits social amplification as various players receive, comment on, and pass along information and opinions. Making this point, Kasperson (1992) concluded,

  The concept of social amplification of risk is based on the thesis that events pertaining to hazards interact with psychological, social, institutional, and cultural processes in ways that can heighten or attenuate perceptions of risk and shape risk behavior. Behavioral responses, in turn, generate secondary social or economic consequences. These consequences extend far beyond direct harms to human health or the environment to include significant indirect impact such as liability, insurance costs, loss of confidence in institutions, stigmatization, or alienation from community affairs. (pp. 157-158)

As Kasperson (1992) observed, "Amplification stations can be individuals, groups, or institutions" (p. 159). In this communication infrastructure, interpersonal communication is instrumental in place of or in support of mass-mediated communication. Through media reports and interpersonal contact, people seek confirmation for their conclusions about risks. Information seeking is predisposed to confirm assumptions and goals of the persons involved. This infrastructure is a dialogue—many people discussing issues and sharing information—through media and interpersonal channels. People rely on experts as well as acquaintances. The flow of information and opinion is complex and multidirectional rather than linear—from an expert source to lay publics. They may trust the process of dialogue more than the content of the process.

Issues communicators need to understand the dynamics of this process, work to participate in it rather than dominate it, and seek to help people control their lives rather than to challenge that sense of control. One of the greatest challenges to that sense of control is to invite laypeople to implicitly trust the judgments and opinions of the source of the risk or even a government agency. Issues communicators dealing with risks should foster trust through dialogue. Dialogue is responsive to people's desire to exert control. For this reason, issues communicators should be prepared to tolerate and work with the idiosyncratic responses and interpretations people make in regard to whether risks exist and are likely to lead to serious harm.

This section has demonstrated how issues managers can enhance risk communication and increase support for their organizations when they help key publics become a part of the decision and information-sharing and interpreting processes, cater to the needs (information, advice, decision heuristics) people want and use, and deliver information and advice as well as help shape interpretative heuristics people think are useful.

 Risk Communication: Managing Issues Through Dialogue

At least three theoretical options guide the way in which risks are calculated, evaluated, and controlled: (a) scientific positivism, whereby data and methodologies of scientists dominate efforts to ascertain the degree of risk—once the decision has been reached, an elite manages and communicates about the risk on behalf of the community; (b) constructivism-relativism, which assumes that everyone's opinions have equal value so that no opinion is better or worse than anyone else's; and (c) dialogue—through collaborative decision-making processes, scientific opinion becomes integrated into opinions that are vetted by key publics' values (Renn, 1992a).

Scientists and some members of risk-producing industries scoff at any risk assessment and decision-making approach other than the first, but proactive issues managers acknowledge that community-based relativism should not be dismissed. Reflecting on the difficulties of incorporating risk assessments into policy, the National Research Council (1989) concluded, "To remain democratic, a society must find ways to put specialized knowledge into the service of public choice and keep it from becoming the basis of power for an elite" (p. 15). Resolution of risk controversies requires more than clear, candid, and honest information.

At the scientific-positivism end of the risk assessment and policy formation continuum, scientists, actuaries, and epidemiologists determine the extent to which people, as a community, are at risk. This risk assessment is driven by the scientific use of health and safety patterns and incidence of disease and harm, a macroassessment. Such analysis calculates the advantages of the risk in balance with community health patterns (Starr, 1969). At the other end of the theoretical spectrum (relativism), each key public expresses its opinions and insists on the integrity of its views, no matter how ill-informed they may be.

Comparing these choices, Renn (1992b) observed that a positivistic-objective approach fails to account for cultural differences, whereas the relativism of constructivism leaves the decision-making process "with no anchor for baseline comparison" (p. 179). Relying on the data at hand, which they believe and which confirms their predilection to support or oppose the source of risk, "social groups in a political arena try to maximize their opportunity to influence the outcome of the collective decision process by mobilizing social resources" (p. 180). If they opt for political activism, rather than a purely scientific approach to risk assessment and abatement, "individuals and organizations can influence the policy process only if they have sufficient resources available to pursue their goals" (p. 181). Community groups seek to have rules accepted and promulgated based on their values. In the absence of self-regulation by the ostensible source of risk, people turn to enforcement agencies to enforce the rules. "To be successful in a social arena, it is necessary to mobilize social resources" (p. 184). This is true both for responsible companies seeking community support and for activists working to wield their influence.

Social movements grow from people's concerns about health and safety as well as environmental quality. Concern is expressed rhetorically as the strain they feel between what is and should be the level of safety in their community. Believing that collective action can lead to increased safety, activists use rhetorical efforts to gather and mobilize power resources. With this power, they work to force confrontation over data and its interpretation relevant to the degree of risk: its potential, its likely severity, and the best means for abating or mitigating it. Through confrontation, the combatants seek means by which to negotiate and resolve their differences. If that occurs, the final stage in this protest scenario is the enforcement of appropriate standards and communication efforts to explain why that solution is appropriate.

Activists often go to great pains to define and explain the stakes various players have to use in social conflict. They battle over the degree to which risk exists and whether benefits outweigh harms. Typically, activists attribute negative motives to companies and other organizations that create or allow risks to occur: such as greed, laxness in operations, failure to care about people or the environment, stupidity, racial bias, or corruption. Public debate can get out of hand and truly decrease the potential for constructive outcomes especially if risk-related evidence is poorly defined and members of a community experience evidence gaps and, therefore, rely on scanty evidence from their own experience.

Even authorities cannot be free from such gaps. For instance, people are prone to exhibit risk intolerance and lack of trust for science and its use in risk predictions and abatement; evidence of such intolerance is captured in demands voiced as, "Can you assure the members of this community that they are not at risk?" Community members often rely on evidence and reasoning such as this: If a mother worries about the health of her children, who have moved with the family to a place where she or her spouse can work in an industry that potentially harms persons' health, is she going to rely on or dismiss the evidence she generates on her own of the incidence of health problems—such as colds or rashes? She is likely to use the data she experiences to confirm rather than disconfirm her fears.

For many reasons identified by Hadden (1988), risk management agencies suffer structural weakness. They deal with ambiguities and have ill-defined power and resources to exchange. The public policy arena is often fraught with confusion and distrust. As Renn (1992b) observed,

> The plurality of evidence, the weak role of rule enforcement agencies, the tendency of the risk debate to attract symbolic connotations and the public responses of moralization and polarization have all contributed to political paralysis: None of the actors is able to mobilize sufficient resources to force others to accept their viewpoint or to invest in a compromise. Evidence is contested, so that it cannot play a more integrative role in forging compromises; value commitment is polarized; social prestige is distributed among various adversarial camps; money experiences problems or legitimation in the risk arena; and power is insufficient. (p. 192)

As frustrating as these dynamics are, proactive risk communicators realize that reality. They adapt to those processes by involving concerned publics rather than denying them access to the political arena. Although it is not totally scientific, it is realistic and "avoids the relativism bind because it relies on intersubjectivity—shared perspectives; shared social reality" (Renn, 1992b, p. 195). The stabilizing force in risk decisions is the collective judgment of persons of the community crafted through dialogue. People feel that they enjoy more control when they have a say in the formulation of the factors that seem to lead to the control of risks.

Favoring an approach to risk that takes into consideration key publics' concern, Fischhoff, Slovic, and Lichtenstein (1978; Slovic, 1979, 1987; Slovic, Fischhoff, & Lichtenstein, 1987) initiated "expressed preference" research, which involves measuring a wider array of attitudes than merely weighing the benefits in the effort to ascertain tolerable risk levels. These researchers found that laypeople's risk ratings, unlike those of experts, are not just influenced by fatality estimates but also by their judgments of several "qualitative" factors. Of particular note, the public evaluates an activity or technology as more risky if it is involuntary, unfamiliar, unknown, uncontrollable, controlled by others, unfair, memorable, dreaded, acute, focused in time and space, fatal, delayed, artificial, and undetectable as well as if individual mitigation is impossible.

Drawing on this line of reasoning, Renn (1992a) favored an approach to risk assessment, based on the predictions and conclusions of science as well as the social reality of the members of the community that is assessing a risk.

> People are willing to suffer harm if they feel it is justified or if it serves other goals. At the same time, they may reject even the slightest chance of being hurt if they feel the risk is imposed on them or violates their other attitudes and values. (p. 77)

Dialogue, rhetorical community risk assessment assumes, as Slovic (1992) did in his psychometric paradigm, "that risk is subjectively defined by individuals who may be influenced by a wide array of psychological, social, institutional, and cultural factors" (p. 120). The underpinning theory, "the social amplification of risk, addresses the fact that the adverse effects of a risk event often extend far beyond the direct damages to victims, property, and environment and may result in massive indirect impacts" (p. 141).

Rather than a purely scientific and actuarial approach, a dialogic view stresses the likelihood that people's fears as well as their expressed desires for the benefits accrued from risks become part of a community of thought, the culture of a neighborhood or even a profession. For instance, persons who farm, serve as law enforcement officers, fight fires, cut timber, and mine ores are subjected to higher than average job-related risks. To cope with such risks, each culture weighs the benefits, costs, and strategic behavior needed to reduce or accept their likelihood.

Given such interpretations and personal choices, people either come to think positively or negatively about the risks they suffer. One factor that can influence that outcome is the likelihood that a stigma will result from the risks (Slovic, 1992). As they experience risks, people may become stigmatized. One aspect of a stigma is it concealability, whether it is hidden or open to public view. If people think they are likely to suffer a stigma that will become known to others, they are likely to oppose the risk. A stigma may involve aesthetics, whereby the person who suffers a risk becomes unattractive. Because of the possibility of stigma, people discuss and evaluate the effects of a risk. Discussion does not rely solely on empirical assessment but also on values. For this reason,

> Whereas experts define risk in a narrow, technical way, the public has a richer, more complex view that incorporates value-laden considerations such as equity, catastrophic potential, and controllability. The issue is not whether these are legitimate, rational considerations, but how the integrate them into risk analyses and policy decisions. (p. 150)

Unless scientists and managers of organizations that create risks take factors such as stigmas into account, they fail to properly monitor public expectations and track the evolution of issues. For these reasons, they become less able to formulate the appropriate sense of corporate responsibility and may miss the emergence of activism calling for the creation or change of public policy.

Because scientific data are hard to interpret and risk decisions are value laden, differences of opinion are not easily reconciled. Policy often is not the product of shared points of view but negotiated resolution of conflicting opinions. Such communication is likely to be disproportionately shaped by key players, industry, government, media, and activists. Although no group actually represents the public—because there are many publics—each of the dominant groups strives to speak and act as though it were the advocate and champion of the public interest. Such outcomes may leave all parties dissatisfied. Conflicting interests and epistemologies unique to the battlefield of risk often prevent communicators from finding "common ground between the social world of risk perceptions guided by human experience and the scientists' rational ideal of decision making based on probabilistic thinking" (Plough & Krimsky, 1987, p. 5; see also Fischoff, 1985).

Communities that are concerned about risks are not passive, waiting for scientists and corporate managers to define and assess risks. Rather, such communities, whether through media or activist leadership, tend to raise issues, even if flawed by lack of relevant and sound information or scientific methodology. For this reason, Otway (1992) emphasized a crucial point: "Policy decisions about hazardous technologies have the paradoxical quality that they are likely to be most urgent just where scientific knowledge is most uncertain" (p. 220). He too is aware that "what is commonly thought of as objective risk has a large subjective component, which may be based on one's experience of being at risk" (p. 220). These factors, coupled with the disparity in risk estimates by experts examining the same risks, lead communities to learn self-reliance and to formulate opinions and expectations, however crude, through dialogue. The outcome of this process is not orderly science but "political negotiations among stakeholders, informed by expert advice" (p. 222). Rather than immediately seeing that their interests match those of the source of risk, community leaders who recognize a problem—or at least its potential—ask and even demand "more democratic control of technology" (p. 226). "Risk communication is not an end in itself; it is an enabling agent to facilitate the continual evolution of relationships" (p. 227). The outcome of that process is a set of policies, whether self-imposed by the source of risk or through public policy planning, that results from a power resource and rhetorical struggle over standards, locus of responsibility, and the formulation of public expectations.

To enhance this decision-making process, Rowan (1995) reduced the sequence of steps to the acronym, CAUSE: credibility, awareness, understanding, satisfaction, and enactment. Step one calls on leaders to establish *credibility* with key publics. Credibility can increase or decrease, depending on how well the subsequent steps progress. The second step is to create or become *aware* of the likelihood or occurrence of the risk and its severity as well as measures for constructive response to it. This requires *understanding,* becoming scientifically insightful to the risk and its consequences. The linear risk communication (scientific-positivistic) model assumes that scientists become satisfied by the assessment and management of a risk and seek public concurrence. According to Rowan's scheme of things, *satisfaction* is community based. The last step, *enactment,* requires that appropriate measures—individual, by the risk entity, or by a government agency—to put into place the decision derived through the rhetorical processes of community dialogue.

An issues management approach to risks concludes "that the defining of risk is essentially a political act" (Kasperson, 1992, p. 155). Concern ripples move outward as from a rock thrown into a pond. Concerns expressed by some foster expressions of others' concerns. This leads to outcry for governmental intervention. Social amplification produces increased and extensive amounts of communication about the risk and its consequences. This dynamic process leads to opinion formation. In this community of discussion, people act as they do in part because of role-related considerations. Membership in social groups shapes the selection of information that each individual regards as significant.

Once amplification has begun, interpretations or comments that are inconsistent with previous beliefs or that contradict the person's values are often ignored or attenuated. They are intensified if the opposite is true. People evaluate risks through their own opinions—heuristics—and those recommended by significant groups. In this model, media reports contribute the basic step for the rippling effect to occur. Perhaps for this reason as well as the limited ability of many reporters to understand and report objectively on risks, media reports are not trusted by scientists and managers of the organizations that create risks. Often, media reporters do little more than to quote persons from opposing sides of a risk controversy without making any effort to decide and inform readers, listeners, or televiewers what point of view is correct. For this reason, the media at best are likely only to fan the fires of outrage. But even hyperbolic stories do not always lead to that end (Cohn, 1990; Moore, 1989).

As Kasperson (1992) accurately observed, "heavy and sustained media coverage of an event does not in itself ensure that substantial public concerns will emerge or that significant amplification of the risk through enlargement of secondary consequences will occur" (p. 173). Each key public uses its own heuristics to consider what is being shown, said, and written. For this reason, Kasperson concluded, "Preexisting levels of trust and credibility may allow risk managers to sustain an accident or event by 'drawing down' the reservoir of trust that has been built up over time" (p. 174).

Risk assessment that does not consider the dynamics—communication and opinion formation—of each community is likely to lead to frustrating outcomes—for the persons making the risk assessment and for the laypeople of the community. Information and the premises by which it is judged arise through a constant dialogue within a community. For this reason, persons who create risks—at least those that some people believe to exist—are savvy when they acknowledge rather than dismiss the existing communication infrastructure and opinion formation processes. Such responsible individuals are wise to work with that infrastructure and opinion formation process rather than to dominate it. If trust leads to control, people are prone to trust those entities that listen to them and acknowledge their concerns. People like to believe their concerns and cultures have been given credence. If risks are acknowledged and people are armed with the means for mitigating the consequences of those risks, they feel empowered (Juanillo & Scherer, 1995).

Based on the reasoning and research data presented in this chapter, several conclusions seem worth stating as guidelines for issues managers who deal with risk issues.

Accept the desire on the part of key publics to exert control over factors they worry affect them and other entities for which they have concern.

Collaborate with them to engage in information gathering, risk assessment, and risk control.

Empower community members by demonstrating to them through their participation in decision making that they are a constructive part of the risk assessment and control process.

Recognize the value-laden personalized decision process they apply, and frame the risk assessment accordingly.

Build trust over time through community outreach, collaborative decision making, and demonstrations that community expectations are met or exceeded by product design, manufacturing procedures, and emergency response.

Empower relevant publics by helping them to develop and use emergency responses that can mitigate the severe outcomes in the event of a risk event.

Acknowledge the uncertainty in risk assessments; do not trivialize this uncertainty, but use it as an incentive for constantly seeking better answers to the questions raised by the members of the community.

Accept criticism of data and decision processes in a collaborative manner; use objections to define the standards and goals to guide decision making to increase safety, health, environmental quality, and the likelihood that all people suffer risks equally, regardless of color or economic condition.

Feature legitimate benefits while acknowledging harms, but do not assume that all persons' decision heuristics or values lead them to the same weightings of risk harms and benefits.

Participate in the risk assessment and communication process; don't attempt to dominate it.

Frame all questions and concerns in terms of the experiences and values of community members.

Recognize that harmony can be increased by strategic planning, proactive measures taken to reduce concerned publics' sense that risks exist, that they are likely to result in harms greater than their benefits.

Innovate to reduce operating costs and increase customer satisfaction by proactive reduction of risk through strategic business planning.

Have as your goal the outcome of the members of the community believing that through the risk assessment and decision-making process, they have achieved better conclusions or have been unable to honestly and candidly find fault with the decisions of others.

An issues management approach to risk assessment, management, and communication aims to empower the persons in a community rather than to deny them access to information and processes that they do not have the technical knowledge and expertise to understand and evaluate. Dialogue and decision making may be more important than the ability of people to play constructive roles as participants. If they cannot understand the scientific assessments, they know when they feel that their concerns and interests have been responded to and regarded. Even if they do not know science, people know when they are taken seriously. For this reason, proactive responses to risk concerns see great value in the open, rhetorical, and honest discussion of issues to achieve outcomes that reflect mutual interests.

 Conclusion

Companies engaged in risk communication face obstacles as they work to form, change, or reinforce opinions and behavior regarding risks. Zones of meanings contain themes and principles that reflect competing self-interests of companies, regulatory agencies, and activist publics. Risk assessments and policy formation entail the enactment of control, opinion formation, evaluation, and collaborative decision making. As Rayner (1992) concluded, "Risk behavior is a function of how human beings, individually and in groups, perceive their place in the world and the things that threaten it" (p. 113). The rightness of decisions depends on which version of their self-interest key audiences believe needs to be advanced (seeking rewards and avoiding losses). Corporate managers and governmental officials make a grave mistake when they miss that point, arguing that some action is legal—as though that will satisfy the critic's sense of ethics and security.

Conclusion:
Issues Management—2000

As they approach a new century, writers become especially prone to speculate about the future. What will issues management be after the year 2000? What changes may result in the research and practice of issues management in the next century? Perhaps, none will be new. Central to such speculation is the constant belief that no company or other complex organization can totally manage public policy issues that affect it, but it can only participate in that process. It can respond constructively to meet or change the performance expectations that are espoused by its key stakeholders. Much remains to be done to achieve the promise of issues management, as it emerged in the 1970s and has been refined and redirected since.

Two broad kinds of response seem typical. One is to act in ways that are less offensive to other organizations and key publics. The second is to press ideas, information, opinion, evaluative premises, and conclusions into every venue of discussion. Sometimes, that discourse will be shrill and strident. At other times, it will be calm and collaborative. But it will occur and will be the product of the dynamics of each issue.

Issues management increases the ability of complex organizations to balance their interests with those of their stakeholders, to operate in the public interest. These challenges demand that organizations of all kinds—business, government, labor, and activists—vie for influence in a marketplace and public policy arena, which at the global level lacks a central public policy authority.

Issues management occurs in response to performance gaps—between expectations and performance. In a society with a relatively similar culture and value system, the reduction of key gaps is daunting but feasible. Such is less likely to be the case globally. Even the most passing glance notes enormous disparity in wages, income, and wealth distribution around the globe. Similar differences are evident in the values and cultural norms regarding the treatment of individuals. Varied and conflicting religions translate into cultural, business, and public policy differences. Business ethics and environmental responsibility are not uniform. In several countries, public policy change is the result of violence, not parliamentary debate. Regulatory standards differ substantially as is evidenced by conflicts regarding copyright and trademark infringement and the protection of intellectual property. The difficulties experienced in creating the economic union among European countries offer a perspective on the future of global issues management.

The second dominant challenge is the fact that no global governmental body is constituted for organizations and key publics to use in a coherent and structured effort to formulate the public policies by which commerce and other essential activities are made regular. Each country has its own public policy process. Some organizations bridge and span national boundaries, but the lack of a central global authority suggests the continuing need for a constructive, informed, articulate, and persuasive dialogue on the part of complex organizations in the United States as well as other countries. Public policy is going to be forged through dialogue, not promulgated—at least, not promulgated for long. It is forged through the expression of interests and reconciled into mutually beneficial guidelines, typically by some central authority. Each individual country and a few global organizations can help create system and force of law, but entanglements and frustration seem likely to be typical of the future.

A daunting challenge that will affect the practice and scholarship of issues management is the reshaping international marketplace and its accompanying public policy demands. Globalization of the marketplace challenges issues management to perform constructively in an arena that lacks a central public policy authority and involves countries that have not encountered or implemented standards of corporate responsibility that have been achieved through the learning curve experienced in this country, Canada, and Western Europe in response to the increasingly powerful and sophisticated citizens' grassroots groups.

Companies based in Western Europe, Canada, Japan, and the U.S. have established their global presence. So far, however, these companies are far from ending the search for order, which is a natural outcome of private-sector and public-sector activities and interests. One reason for this process being slow is differences in policies and processes by governments, each of which learned its own lessons through years of international exposure. Experience with colonialism, development of routine business and policy practices in their own countries, and the desire to have things their way—all of these factors will be stumbling blocks to achieving order in the global marketplace.

Lack of such authority poses the crucial question of how public policy will be created as the marketplace or products, services, labor, and ideas continues to globalize. Nations, as well as the companies and activist groups that exist within countries and cross boundaries, will compete in the effort to form policy that advantages their citizens or followers and their status in the world. As populations rise, and labor as well as product pricing is subjected to global forces, the resolution of this struggle is not easy to predict. Nevertheless, it will shape the next century.

Of importance in this globalization is the challenge to monitor and analyze issues, difficult at best when at home and vastly more complicated when multiplied across distances and frustrated by cultural differences and varied governmental and legal systems. Powerful sections of the world may experience chaos for decades, making business policy development uncertain due to potentially violent and wrenching efforts to change government and market systems. Ancient hatreds die slowly and manifest themselves in violence and uncooperative efforts that prevent the orderliness preferred by business and achieved through public policy. Problems such as those of the environment will be difficult to solve in countries starved for capital and committed less to environmental quality, fairness, security, and equality than to survival or short-sighted prosperity. Of related interest will be the volatility of new communication technologies that change daily—making yesterday's innovation obsolete today.

Issues management is not a barrier used to prevent an organization from having to change in response to demands by key stakeholders or other public policy pressures. It is a strategic means for managing an organization's response to public policy change—either by taking advantage of opportunities or mitigating unreasonable external demands. One obstacle in this regard is executives' unwillingness to act on issues, perhaps by striking agreements with their stakeholding critics, before an issue matures to the point where government intervenes or while an array of positive and socially responsible opportunities exist. Stressing this point, Renfro (1993) concluded his book with this line: "In the dynamic world of public issues, CEOs and their corporations must continue to reinvent themselves, anticipating and adapting to the rapidly changing rules of the public issue process—by which they prosper or perish" (p. 149).

As a narrowly construed rationale for issues management, systems theory treats information as the only dimension of communication or interaction and can assume that each bit has the same meaning for all participants. As such, we can miss the rhetorical dynamics of the dialogic process whereby engaged parties seek to establish interpretative frameworks by which information, their actions, efforts of others, and resources become understandable and are evaluated. At least one case has been made for a systems approach to ethical judgment, one that rests on "a thorough examination of the interests of all claimants, and a review of concomitant obligations" (Bivins, 1992, p. 376). This dialogic view, reflecting competing and conflict interests, assumes that evaluation and thoughtful, informed evaluation are central to the operation of complex human systems.

Rhetoric assumes evaluation and judgment, a contest and collaboration of interpretations or evaluations regarding fact, value, and policy. At point are considerations of which facts are important, true, and relevant to an issue; the weight of various facts given the case to be decided; and their integration into evaluations and conclusions. Evaluations place judgments into perspective and provide the basis for problem recognition and acceptable solutions. They often entail considerations regarding what ideas are preferred because of their association with larger ideals or end states and normative means by which to achieve them. Problem recognition and policy express preferences. As such, systems do not function merely in the framework of reading and adjusting to constraints and opportunities at play between themselves and their environments, in a neutral cybernetic fashion.

The dynamics of that adjustment are influenced by constraints and opportunities that are forged through rhetorical debate, symbolic processes, and power resource management. Each entity in this field of analysis seeks its self-advantage—in varying degrees of harmony with others—by asserting its cause and engaging in discussions of the merits of conclusions and policies related to those interests. In this sense, for instance, the definition of an industry—such as chemical manufacturers or tobacco manufacturers—is derived from the dialogue that exists in a community of expressed opinion and evaluation at a given moment. Such dialogue entails considerations of costs and rewards.

For this reason, the dynamics of communication and adjustive interaction central to issues management can be better understood by incorporating principles of dialogue—public debate—as the rationale for the study and practice of issues management. Dialogue frames this relationship in terms of what one entity does that is meaningful to another, which in turn has consequence for the original entity. For this reason, the act of saying nothing is meaningful;

all that an organization does can be used to form an attitude about the organization—positive or negative—hence its need for corporate responsibility. When a chemical plant flares some chemical as a means of disposing of it, that would not constitute communication (viewed from the perspective that communication only exists when a messages is prepared, conveyed, received, and interpreted). But it does communicate—and creates apprehension about exposure to chemical risks. If the plant ceases to use that method or communicates successfully that it is nothing that should be alarming, that is rhetorical and in some definitions, public relations. But is the prepared message the same as the decision to cease using flares? Both could lead to the same end— improved relationships with members of the community. Both choices seem to be vital to issues management—because they entail the strategic use of resources to take advantage of a public policy opportunity or to avoid a threat.

Contests over definitions are vital today and for the future of issues management. How an organization, an industry, or even a nation asserts itself into its environment defines the environment—and adapts that environment to itself (Cheney & Dionisopoulos, 1989; Sproule, 1989). As Prior-Miller (1989) reasoned, "Organizations will play roles in relation to each other. Organizations will act to create their own realities. Organizational structures will be a result of patterning roles" (pp. 70-71).

Some writers about public relations and issues management aver the concept of contest, or debate, or controversy. That, it would seem, is asymmetrical. Such discussion and critique, one might imagine, is a contest and debate. It is a rhetorical thrust and parry. Through such interaction, a dialogue exists that has at least three dimensions.

One product of dialogue is the creation of zones of meaning, shared realities that define the relationship between entities. The second is meaning that is forged, expressed, confirmed, and challenged through words and actions of entities engaged in the management of their self-interests. The third is values—evaluative frameworks—that are central to such debates, not pure information, which have substantial public policy implications as entities search for advantage. They do so by seeking harmonious relationships through appeals to common interests and through the creation or mitigation of public policy to advance their interests in compromise with the interests of others. Viewed this way, we can see the challenge of issues management as being the satisfactory reconciliation of conflicts that result from a clash of cultures— that of the organization being represented and those of key publics whose expectations arise from cultural perspectives that are or at least seem to be different from those of the organization.

This principle takes us beyond information as the foundation of relationships and emphasizes how self-interests and concomitantly mutual relationships between organizations and their shareholders are the foundation of those relationships. For instance, in terms of the relationship between chemical companies and their surrounding communities, supporters of those plants believe that benefits are greater than costs associated with living and working around chemicals or that the costs are not too great for the rewards. Opponents hold the opposite opinion.

Another example: In battles between timbering proponents and their opposition, both sides agree that harvesting trees alters the environment; the key concern is whether rewards from that process offset costs. Therein lies the foundation for the rhetorical and public policy battle. Two advantages offered by social exchange theory are that it is comfortable with a microeconomic analysis of the relationship between an organization and its stakeholders and that it features the quality of the relationship—and the factors that shape it. If systems theory is to be an underpinning rationale for the practice and research in this discipline, we must have a dynamic explanation for the adjustive mechanisms at foot, which are inherently evaluative and cost-reward driven. In a multiple stakeholder model, systems theory does not account for the mix of positive and negative feedback that is inherent in the kinds of relationships crucial to issues management. Second, it does not explain the reasons why some responses are favorable and others are negative but merely operationalizes those evaluations.

The agenda that arises from this array of perspectives may lead us to refine our views of how corporate organizations—as the expression of these factors at play on the individuals who enact them—and others groups of stakeholders enact their self-interests through efforts that are rhetorical, reflecting a dialogue to understand and define circumstances so that opportunities can be exploited and threats avoided. Although information is useful as a means for defining the circumstances of each choice—thereby lessening uncertainty and increasing a sense of control—the key to this process is the kinds of evaluative frameworks that operate as compatible or incompatible zones of meaning. These zones yield to influence through discourse—a dialogic process—and rationalize the kinds of actions that are seen to be responsible or irresponsible, depending on how well they satisfy the expectations of those whose interests are affected by the decisions and actions. If the outcome leads to a rewarding relationship, actions and choices are accepted and encouraged. If the outcome creates costs greater than the rewards, an effort may lead to the use of public policy to bring those to dimensions more into balance. The extent to which issues managers can help to maximize the opportunities and minimize the threats is an expression of the ability to add value to the organization and is a function of the short-term and long-term relationship between the organization and its stakeholders. All of this analysis has a rhetorical dimension, one that must be cast as dialogue—statement and counterstatement—which is comfortable with the principles of symbolic interaction. The essence of issues management is not in the messages brought into or conveyed from an organization but in the ways resources vital to relationships between organizations and their stakeholders are enacted.

This view suggests that opinions and judgments count. People influence and are influenced. Judgment and conclusion are forged on the anvil of debate, negotiation, and collaboration. Opinions change. Compromise is achieved.

Whether featuring individuals, members of sociopolitically involved groups, or members of corporate entities, several concepts are central to people's communication processes, opinions, and actions. They plan, assess the terrain around them to form useful opinions and reduce uncertainty, influence judgments and behavior through information and evaluation, exert and yield to control in a dialectic of competing and compatible interests, and manage their interests (Heath, 1991b). These principles, as the basis of research and the practice of issues management, offer us key elements of the unfinished agenda, one that forms the foundation for achieving a sense of community (Kruckeberg & Starck, 1988). Looking to the future, Renfro (1993) framed this theme:

> As both the legislative and executive branches have declined in their ability to serve as a forum for the resolution of public issues, the role of the private sector has grown. This shift of leadership from the public sector to the private is, for this quarter of the twentieth century, to equal the great changes of each previous quarter-century: the birth of mass production in the first quarter-century, the growth of centralized government in the second, and the explosion of human and civil rights in the third. (p. 1)

 The Agenda?

Ever insightful, Renfro (1993) gave us reason to pause and think about issues management trends for the coming quarter century. He conjectured

> that the private sector now plays a larger role in the public issues process than government. A new contract between business and the public is being written, one of a much greater social dimensions. Issues is the driving force of this fundamental shift in the roles of our largest institutions. (pp. 1-2)

If this is the case for this country, then it is even more likely to be true in the global market community.

As issues become more complex and forums are increasingly global, conflict between and among businesses as well as their critics may occur more in legislative chambers and other limited forums than in public media. Many issue battles occur between technical specialists, particularly natural or behavioral scientists or engineers. Some researchers are unwilling to take stands on issues, but others translate their science into issues politics or vice versa. For instance, on matters of toxic waste, nuclear generation, pollution, or chemical toxicology, special-interest groups have their scientists, as do companies. Government often has its cadre of specialists. Even when public opinion is for or against some issue position, the weight of scientific evidence and political efforts of politicians will be key factors in how the regulatory battle is played out. Politicians, whether representing any specific constituency on an issue or not, have their own agendas. Some favor the special-interest group side of the issue on a technical question, and other politicians take the corporate side.

The heart of issues management: It must balance the legitimate interests of a company with community interests and engage in the distribution of resources that are subject to public policy. Issues management must strive to develop a platform of understanding and agreement shared by key publics and corporate management. This outcome must be the composite of efforts by both sides. Use of facts to lessen conflict fails when sides defend themselves out of fear of change—not knowing what to agree to in the way of facts and evaluations because of their political implications. Agreement and understanding are not necessarily at odds with one another, but we may agree without understanding. And we can understand without achieving agreement.

Issues management grew out of a clash between corporate and public interests; that is its past and will be its future. Our sense of this discipline must be larger than an interest about the relationships between an individual company, for instance, and any key public. Organizations have many key publics. Opinions differ. Some opinions must change for progress to be made, agreement and compromise to be achieved, and mutually beneficial decisions reached.

The future of issues management resides in the distribution of power resources. Its future rests with the dynamic need of key publics to have harmonious and mutually beneficial relationships with companies and other major organizations. The goal of issues management is to assist organizations and key stakeholders to create a community of interest by which all are benefited.

References

Aaker, D. A. (1992). *Developing business strategies* (3rd ed.). New York: John Wiley.

Ackerman, R. W., & Bauer, R. A. (1976). *Corporate social responsiveness: The modern dilemma.* Reston, VA: Reston.

Adams, W. C. (1995). Marrying the functions: The importance of media relations in public affairs planning. *Public Relations Quarterly, 40*(3), 7-11.

Adkins, L. (1978, June). How good are advocacy ads? *Dun's Review, 111,* 76-77.

Ajzen, I., & Fishbein, M. (1980). *Understanding attitudes and predicting social behavior.* Englewood Cliffs, NJ: Prentice Hall.

Albrecht, T. L. (1988). Communication and personal control in empowering organizations. In J. A. Anderson (Ed.), *Communication yearbook 11* (pp. 380-390). Newbury Park, CA: Sage.

Alexander, H. E. (1988). Soliciting support through political action committees. In R. L. Heath (Ed.), *Strategic issues management: How organizations influence and respond to public interests and policies* (pp. 258-275). San Francisco: Jossey-Bass.

Alexander, H. E. (1989). *Comparative political finance in the 1980s.* New York: Cambridge University Press.

Alinsky, S. (1971). *Rules for radicals—A practical primer for realistic radicals.* New York: Random House.

Anderson, R. L. (1982). Foreword. In J. S. Nagelschmidt (Ed.), *The public affairs handbook* (pp. ix-xv). New York: AMACOM.

Andrews, J. R. (1983). *The practice of rhetorical criticism.* New York: Macmillan.

Anshen, M. (Ed.). (1974). *Managing the socially responsible corporation.* New York: Macmillan.

Ansoff, H. I. (1980). Strategic issue management. *Strategic Management Journal, 1*(2), 131-148.

Arcelus, F. J., & Schaefer, N. V. (1982). Social demands as strategic issues: Some conceptual problems. *Strategic Management Journal, 3,* 347-357.

Armour, J. O. (1906, March 10). The packers and the people. *Saturday Evening Post, 178,* 6.

Arms concerns called heavy donors to PAC. (1985, January 20). *New York Times,* p. A19.

Armstrong, R. A. (1981). The concept and practice of issues management in the United States. *Vital Speeches, 47*(24), 763-765.

Aronoff, C. E. (Ed). (1979). *Business and the media.* Santa Monica, CA: Goodyear.

Arrington, C. B., & Sawaya, R. N. (1984). Managing public affairs: Issues management in an uncertain environment. *California Management Review, 26*(4), 148-160.

Atkin, C. K. (1973). Instrumental utilities and information seeking. In P. Clarke (Ed.), *New models for communication research* (pp. 205-239). Beverly Hills, CA: Sage.

Aufderheide, P. (1992). Cable television and the public interest. *Journal of Communication, 42*(1), 52-65.

Baglan, T., Lalumia, J., & Bayless, O. L. (1986). Utilization of compliance-gaining strategies: A research note. *Communication Monographs, 53,* 289-293.

Bailey, J. (1992a, February 20). Dueling studies. *The Wall Street Journal,* pp. A1, A6.

Bailey, J. (1992b, February 20). How two industries created a fresh spin on the dioxin debate. *The Wall Street Journal,* p. A1.

Baird, B. (1986). Tolerance for environmental health risks: The influence of knowledge, benefits, voluntariness and environmental attitudes. *Risk Analysis, 6,* 425-435.

Bandrowski, J. F. (1990). *Corporate imagination—Plus.* New York: Free Press.

Barnes, B. (1988). *The nature of power.* Urbana: University of Illinois Press.

Barnet, S. M., Jr. (1975). A global look at advocacy. *Public Relations Journal, 31*(11), 17-21.

Barnouw, E. (1978). *The sponsor: Notes on a modern potentate.* New York: Oxford University Press.

Barrett, P. M. (1995, April 14). Supreme Court prepares to decide if regulators have gone too far to aid endangered species. *The Wall Street Journal,* p. A12.

Basil, M. D., & Brown, W. J. (1994). Interpersonal communication in news diffusion: A study of "Magic" Johnson's announcement. *Journalism Quarterly, 71,* 305-320.

Bateman, D. N. (1975). Corporate communications of advocacy: Practical perspectives and procedures. *Journal of Business Communication, 13*(1), 3-11.

Bates, D. (1982). Signal trends in not-for-profit public relations. *Public Relations Journal, 38*(11), 22-23.

Beck, B., Greenberg, N. F., Hager, M., Harrison, J., & Underwood, A. (1984, December 17). Could it happen in America? *Newsweek, 104,* 38-44.

Bell, C. (1983, December 18). Advertisers see link between sales, corporate ads. *Houston Chronicle,* p. D16.

Bennett, J. T., & DiLorenzo, T. J. (1985). *Destroying democracy: How government funds partisan politics.* Washington, DC: Cato Institute.

Benoit, W. L., & Brinson, S. L. (1994). AT&T: "Apologies are not enough." *Communication Quarterly, 42,* 75-88.

Berger, C. R. (1987). Communicating under uncertainty. In M. E. Roloff & G. R. Miller (Eds.), *Interpersonal processes: New directions in communication research* (pp. 39-62). Newbury Park, CA: Sage.

Berger, C. R., & Calabrese, R. J. (1975). Some explorations in initial interaction and beyond: Toward a developmental theory of interpersonal communication. *Human Communication Research, 1,* 99-112.

Bergner, D. (1982). The role of strategic planning in international public affairs. *Public Relations Journal, 38*(6), 32-33, 39.

Berkowitz, D., & Turnmire, K. (1994). Community relations and issues management: An issue orientation approach to segmenting publics. *Journal of Public Relations Research, 6,* 105-123.

Bernays, E. L. (1955). *The engineering of consent.* Norman: University of Oklahoma Press.

Bevk, K. L. (1979). Literature search and analysis: Key to vital information. *Public Relations Journal, 35*(2), 12-13.

Birch, J. (1994). New factors in crisis planning and response. *Public Relations Quarterly, 39*(1), 31-34.

Bird, L. (1993, April 9). Marketers miss out by alienating Blacks. *The Wall Street Journal*, p. B8.

Bivins, T. H. (1992). A systems model for ethical decision making in public relations. *Public Relations Review, 18,* 365-383.

Black, E. (1970). The second persona. *Quarterly Journal of Speech, 56,* 109-119.

Blalock, H. M., Jr. (1989). *Power and conflict: Toward a general theory.* Newbury Park, CA: Sage.

Bleecker, S. E., & Lento, T. V. (1982). Public relations in a wired society. *Public Relations Quarterly, 27* (1) 6-12.

Bobbitt, R. (1995). An Internet primer for public relations. *Public Relations Quarterly, 40*(3), 27-32.

Boe, A. R. (1972). The good hands of Allstate: A *Spectator* exclusive interview with Archie Boe, Allstate's Chairman of the Board. *Spectator*(10), pp. 1-3.

Boe, A. R. (1979). Fitting the corporation to the future. *Public Relations Quarterly, 24*(4), 4-5.

Boffey, P. M. (1984, December 23). Bhopal: The case for poison factories. *Denver Post,* pp. 1D, 12D.

Booth, M. (1978). Single-issue advocacy: A new trend in nonprofit PR. *Public Relations Journal, 34*(12), 13-14.

Bordua, D. J. (1983). Adversary polling and the construction of social meaning. *Law & Policy Quarterly, 5,* 345-366.

Botvin, G. J., Goldberger, C. J., Botvin, E. M., & Dusenbury, L. (1993). Smoking behavior of adolescents exposed to cigarette advertising. *Public Health Reports, 108,* 217-224.

Bowman, C. (1990). *The essence of strategic management.* New York: Prentice Hall.

Bradt, W. R. (1972). *Current trends in public affairs.* New York: Conference Board.

Bremner, R. H. (1956). *From the depths: The discovery of poverty in the United States.* New York: New York University Press.

Brodeur, P. (1985). *Outrageous misconduct: The asbestos industry on trial.* New York: Pantheon.

Brodwin, D. R., & Bourgeois, L. J., III. (1984). Five steps to strategic action. *California Management Review, 26,* 176-190.

Broom, G. M. (1977). Coorientational measurement of public issues. *Public Relations Review, 3*(4), 110-119.

Broom, G. M., Lauzen, M. M., & Tucker, K. (1991). Public relations and marketing: Dividing the conceptual domain and operational turf. *Public Relations Review, 17,* 219-225.

Brown, J. K. (1979). *The business of issues: Coping with the company's environments.* New York: Conference Board.

Buchholz, R. A. (1982a). *Business environment and public policy: Implications for management.* Englewood Cliffs, NJ: Prentice Hall.

Buchholz, R. A. (1982b). Education for public issues management: Key insights from a survey of top practitioners. *Public Affairs Review, 3,* 65-76.

Buchholz, R. A. (1985). *The essentials of public policy for management.* Englewood Cliffs: Prentice Hall.

Buchholz, R. A. (1988). Adjusting corporations to the realities of public interests and policy. In R. L. Heath (Ed.), *Strategic issues management: How organizations influence and respond to public interests and policies* (pp. 50-72). San Francisco: Jossey-Bass.

Burgoon, M., Pfau, M., & Birk, T. S. (1995). An inoculation theory explanation for the effects of corporate issue/advocacy advertising campaigns. *Communication Research, 22,* 485-505.

Burke, K. (1946, October 22). Letter to Malcolm Cowley, Burke File, Pennsylvania State University Pattee Library, University Park, PA.

Burke, K. (1951). Rhetoric—Old and new. *Journal of General Education, 5,* 202-209.

Burke, K. (1966). *Language as symbolic action.* Berkeley: University of California Press.

Burke, K. (1969a). *A grammar of motives.* Berkeley: University of California Press.

Burke, K. (1969b). *A rhetoric of motives.* Berkeley: University of California Press.

Burrough, B. (1983, August 1). Company's handling of radioactive items stirs a bitter fight with Texas regulators. *The Wall Street Journal*, pp. 17, 25.

Burton, T. M. (1995, June 22). Harvard study finds no major link between implants and immune illnesses. *The Wall Street Journal*, p. B11.

Camillus, J. C. (1986). *Strategic planning and management control: Systems for survival and success*. Lexington, MA: Lexington Books.

Cannell, W., & Otway, H. (1988). Audience perspectives in the communication of technological risks. *Futures, 20,* 519-532.

Capitalizing on social change. (1979, October 29). *Business Week,* 105-106.

Carbide's U.S. plant fined for violations. (1984, December 17). *Houston Post,* p. 3A.

Carbide was warned disaster possible. (1985, January 25). *Houston Post,* p. 5A.

Carroll, A. B. (1991). The pyramid of corporate social responsibility: Toward the moral management of organizational stakeholders. *Business Horizons, 34*(4), 39-48.

Carson, R. (1962). *Silent spring.* Boston: Houghton Mifflin.

Carson, T. L., Wokutch, R. E., & J. Cox, J. E., Jr. (1985). An ethical analysis of deception in advertising. *Journal of Business Ethics, 4,* 93-104.

Casarez, N. B. (1991). Corruption, corrosion, and corporate political speech. *Nebraska Law Review, 70,* 689-753.

Chaffee, S. H., & Roser, C. (1986). Involvement and the consistency of knowledge, attitudes, and behavior. *Communication Research, 13,* 373-399.

Chase, W. H. (1977). Public issue management: The new science. *Public Relations Journal, 32*(10), 25-26.

Chase, W. H. (1982, December 1). Issue management conference—A special report. *Corporate Public Issues and Their Management, 7,* 1-2.

Chase, W. H. (1984). *Issue management: Origins of the future.* Stamford, CT: Issue Action Publications.

Chemical Manufacturers Association. (1989). *Title III: One year later.* Washington, DC: Author.

Chemical risks: Fears, facts, and the media. (1985). Washington, DC: Media Institute.

Cheney, G. (1992). The corporate person (re)presents itself. In E. L. Toth & R. L. Heath (Eds.), *Rhetorical and critical approaches to public relations* (pp. 165-183). Hillsdale, NJ: Lawrence Erlbaum.

Cheney, G., & Dionisopoulos, G. N. (1989). Public relations? No, relations with publics: A rhetorical-organizational approach to contemporary corporate communications. In C. H. Botan & V. Hazleton, Jr. (Eds.), *Public relations theory* (pp. 135-157). Hillsdale, NJ: Lawrence Erlbaum.

Cheney, G., & Vibbert, S. L. (1987). Corporate discourse: Public relations and issue management. In F. M. Jablin, L. L. Putnam, K. H. Roberts, & L. W. Porter (Eds.), *Handbook of organizational communication: An interdisciplinary perspective* (pp. 165-194). Newbury Park, CA: Sage.

Chess, C., Salomone, K. L., Hance, B. J., & Saville, A. (1995). Results of a national symposium on risk communication: Next steps for government agencies. *Risk Analysis, 15,* 115-125.

Chickering, A. L. (1982, October/November). Warming up the corporate image. *Public Opinion, 5,* 13-15.

Chrisman, J. J., & Carroll, A. B. (1984). SMR forum: Corporate responsibility—Reconciling economic and social goals. *Sloan Management Review, 25*(4), 59-65.

Coates, J. F., Coates, V. T., Jarratt, J., & Heinz, L. (1986). *Issues management: How you can plan, organize and manage for the future.* Mt. Airy, MD: Lomond.

Cochran, P. L., & Nigh, D. (1990). Illegal corporate behavior and the question of moral agency: An empirical examination. In W. C. Frederick & L. E. Preston (Eds.), *Business ethics: Research issues and empirical studies* (pp. 145-163). Greenwich, CT: JAI.

Cochran, P. L., & Wood, R. A. (1984). Corporate social responsibility and financial performance. *Academy of Management Journal, 27*, 42-56.

Coe, B. J. (1983). The effectiveness challenge in issue advertising campaigns. *Journal of Advertising, 12*(4), 27-35.

Cohen, B. (1983). Nuclear journalism: Lies, damned lies, and news reports. *Policy Review, 26*(3), 70-74.

Cohen, D. (1982). Unfairness in advertising revisited. *Journal of Marketing, 46*(4), 73-80.

Cohn, V. (1990). *Reporting on risk: Getting it right in an age of risk.* Washington, DC: Media Institute.

Colemen, C. (1993). The influence of mass media and interpersonal communication on societal and personal risk judgment. *Communication Research, 20*, 611-628.

Condit, C. M., & Condit, D. M. (1992). Smoking OR health: Incremental erosion as a public interest group strategy. In E. L. Toth & R. L. Heath (Eds.), *Rhetorical and critical approaches to public relations* (pp. 241-256). Hillsdale, NJ: Lawrence Erlbaum.

Connor, M. J. (1975, May 14). Mobil's advocacy ads lead a growing trend, draw praise, criticism. *The Wall Street Journal,* pp. 1, 20.

Coombs, W. T. (1992). The failure of the Task Force on Food Assistance: A case study of the role of legitimacy in issue management. *Journal of Public Relations Research, 4*, 101-122.

Coombs, W. T. (1995). Choosing the right words: The development of guidelines for the selection of the "appropriate" crisis-response strategies. *Management Communication Quarterly, 8*, 447-476.

Copulos, M. (1985). It's effective—But is it safe? *Reason, 16*(3), 24-32.

Covello, V. T. (1992). Risk communication: An emerging area of health communication research. In S. A. Deetz (Ed.), *Communication yearbook 15* (pp. 359-373). Thousand Oaks, CA: Sage.

Covello, V. T., Sandman, P. M., & Slovic, P. (1988). *Risk communication, risk statistics, and risk comparisons: A manual for plant managers.* Washington, DC: Chemical Manufacturers Association.

Cowen, S. S., & Segal, M. G. (1981). In the public eye: Reporting social performance. *Financial Executive, 47*(1), 11-16.

Coyle, R. J., & Stephens, L. F. (1979). Why practitioners should master sampling and survey research. *Public Relations Journal, 35*(2), 14-16.

Crable, R. E., & Vibbert, S. L. (1983). Mobil's epideictic advocacy: "Observations" of Prometheusbound. *Communication Monographs, 50*, 380-394.

Crable, R. E., & Vibbert, S. L. (1985). Managing issues and influencing public policy. *Public Relations Review, 11*(2), 3-16.

Cutler, B. D., & Muehling, D. D. (1989). Advocacy advertising and the boundaries of commercial speech, *Journal of Advertising, 18*, 40-50.

Cutler, B. D., & Muehling, D. D. (1991). Another look at advocacy advertising and the boundaries of commercial speech. *Journal of Advertising, 20*(4), 49-52.

Cutlip, S. M. (1994). *The unseen power: Public relations. A history.* Hillsdale, NJ: Lawrence Erlbaum.

Cutlip, S. M. (1995). *Public relations history: From the 17th to the 20th century.* Hillsdale, NJ: Lawrence Erlbaum.

Cutlip, S. M., & Center, A. H. (1982). *Effective public relations* (5th ed.). Englewood Cliffs, NJ: Prentice Hall.

Daft, R. L., Sormunen, J., & Parks. D. (1988). Chief executive scanning, environmental characteristics, and company performance: An empirical study. *Strategic Management Journal, 9*, 123-139.

Davies, J. C., Covello, V. T., & Allen, F. W. (Eds.). (1987). *Risk communication.* Washington, DC: Conservation Foundation.

Davis, G. F., & Thompson, T. A. (1994). A social movement perspective on corporate control. *Administrative Science Quarterly, 39,* 141-173.

Davison, W. P. (1972). Public opinion research as communication. *Public Opinion Quarterly, 36,* 311-22.

Denbow, C. J., & Culbertson, H. M. (1985). Linkage beliefs and diagnosing an image. *Public Relations Review, 11*(1), 29-37.

Deveny, K. (1991, August, 23). Kraft USA settles contest gone awry for $10 million. *The Wall Street Journal,* p. B6.

DeWitt, J. B. (1983). Films can project your association's message. *Association Management, 35*(3), 85-91.

DiBacco, T. V. (1982, June 30). Business ethics: A view from the cloister. *The Wall Street Journal,* A30.

Dickie, R. B. (1984, January-March). Influence of public affairs offices on corporate planning and of corporations on government policy. *Strategic Management Journal, 5,* 15-34.

Dillman, D. A., & Christenson, J. A. (1974). Toward the assessment of public values. *Public Opinion Quarterly, 38,* 206-221.

Dinsmore, W. H. (1978). Can ideas be sold like soap? *Public Relations Quarterly, 23*(3), 16-18.

Dionisopoulos, G. N. (1986). Corporate advocacy advertising as political communication. In L. L. Kaid, D. Nimmo, & K. R. Sanders (Eds.), *New perspectives on political advertising* (pp. 82-106). Carbondale: Southern Illinois University Press.

Dionisopoulos, G. N., & Crable, R. E. (1988). Definitional hegemony as a public relations strategy: The rhetoric of the nuclear power industry after Three Mile Island. *Central States Speech Journal, 39,* 134-145.

Divelbiss, R. I., & Cullen, M. R., Jr. (1981). Business, the media, and the American public. *Michigan State University Business Topics, 29*(1), 21-28.

Dominick, J. R. (1981). Business coverage in network newscasts. *Journalism Quarterly, 58,* 179-185, 191.

Dougherty, P. H. (1983, November 30). Advertising: Grey's corporate survey. *New York Times,* p. 40.

Douglas, M. (1992). *Risk and blame.* London: Routledge.

Dozier, D. M., Grunig, L. A., & Grunig, J. E. (1995). *Manager's guide to excellence in public relations and communication management.* Mahwah, NJ: Lawrence Erlbaum.

Drake, B. H., & Drake, E. (1988). Ethical and legal aspects of managing corporate cultures. *California Management Review, 30,* 107-123.

Driskill, L. P., & Goldstein, J. R. (1986). Uncertainty: Theory and practice in organizational communication. *Journal of Business Communication, 23*(3), 41-57.

Druck, K. B. (1978). Dealing with exploding social and political forces. *Vital Speeches, 45*(4), 110-114).

DuBos, T. J. (1982, October 8). Letter to Jack Hart, School of Communication, University of Houston, Texas.

Duhe, S. F., & Zoch, L. M. (1994-1995). Framing the media's agenda during a crisis. *Public Relations Quarterly, 39*(4), 42-45.

Dunn, C. P. (1991). Are corporations inherently wicked? *Business Horizons, 34*(4), 3-8.

Dutton, J. E. (1993). Interpretations on automatic: A different view of strategic issue diagnosis. *Journal of Management Studies, 30,* 339-357.

Dutton, J. E., & Ashford, S. J. (1993). Selling issues to top management. *Academy of Management Review, 18,* 397-428.

Dutton, J. E., & Duncan, R. B. (1987). The creation of momentum for change through the process of strategic issue diagnosis. *Strategic Management Journal, 8,* 279-295.

Dutton, J. E., & Jackson, S. E. (1987). Categorizing strategic issues: Links to organizational action. *Academy of Management Review, 12*(1), 76-90.

Dutton, J. E., & Ottensmeyer, E. (1987). Strategic issue management systems: Forms, functions, and contexts. *Academy of Management Review, 12*(2), 355-365.

Dyer, S. C., Jr., Miller, M. M., & Boone, J. (1991). Wire service coverage of the Exxon Valdez crisis. *Public Relations Review, 17*(1), 27-36.

Edelman, J. M. (1964). *The symbolic uses of politics.* Urbana: University of Illinois Press.

Edelman, J. M. (1977) *Political language: Words that succeed and policies that fail.* New York: Academic Press.

Edelstein, A. S. (1993). Thinking about the criterion variable in agenda-setting research. *Journal of Communication, 43*(2), 85-99.

Editorial Board. (1995). A year of gridlock. *National Wildlife, 33*(2), 34-41.

Editors. (1985). Leading 100 business/industrial advertisers spend $420 million. *Business Marketing, 70*(4), 60-163.

Ehling, W. P., & Hesse, M. B. (1983). Use of "issue management" in public relations. *Public Relations Review, 9*(2), 18-35.

Ehrbar, A. F. (1978). The backlash against business advocacy. *Fortune, 98*(4), 62-64; 68.

Eisenberg, E. M. (1986). Meaning and interpretation in organizations. *Quarterly Journal of Speech, 72,* 88-113.

Elkington, J. (1994). Towards a sustainable corporation: Win-win-win business strategies for sustainable development. *California Management Review, 36*(2), 90-100.

Ellul, J. (1971). *Autopsy of revolution* (P. Wolf, Trans.). New York: Knopf.

Elmendorf, F. M. (1988). Generating grass-roots campaigns and public involvement. In R. L. Heath (Ed.), *Strategic issues management* (pp. 306-320). San Francisco: Jossey-Bass.

Environmental Protection Agency. (1988, April). *Seven cardinal rules of risk communication.* Washington, DC: Author.

Epstein, M. J., McEwen, R. A., & Spindle, R. M. (1994). Shareholder preferences concerning corporate ethical performance. *Journal of Business Ethics, 13,* 447-453.

Ewing, R. P. (1979). The uses of futurist techniques in issues management. *Public Relations Quarterly, 24*(1), 15-18.

Ewing, R. P. (1980). Evaluating issues management. *Public Relations Journal, 36*(6), 14-16.

Ewing, R. P. (1982). Advocacy advertising: The voice of business in public policy debate. *Public Affairs Review, 3,* 23-29.

Ewing, R. P. (1987). *Managing the new bottom line: Issues management for senior executives.* Homewood, IL: Dow Jones-Irwin.

Fidler, L. A., & Johnson, J. D. (1984). Communication and innovation implementation. *Academy of Management Review, 9,* 704-711.

Fink, S. (1986). *Crisis management: Planning for the inevitable.* New York: ANACOM.

Finn, D. (1981). The public relations role in coping with the information crisis. *Public Relations Quarterly, 26*(3), 5-7.

Fischhoff, B. (1985). Managing risk perceptions. *Issues in Science and Technology, 2*(1), 83-96.

Fischhoff, B. (1995). Risk perception and communication unplugged: Twenty years of process. *Risk Analysis, 15,* 137-145.

Fischhoff, B., Slovic, P., & Lichtenstein, S. (1978). How safe is safe enough? A psychometric study of attitudes toward technological risks and benefits. *Policy Sciences, 9,* 127-152.

Fishbein, M., & Ajzen, I. (1975). *Belief, attitude, intention, and behavior.* Reading, MA: Addison-Wesley.

Fisher, W. R. (1985). The narrative paradigm: An elaboration. *Communication Monographs, 52,* 347-367.

Fisher, W. R. (1987). *Human communication as narration: Toward a philosophy of reason, value, and action.* Columbia: University of South Carolina Press.

Fisher, W. R. (1989). Clarifying the narrative paradigm. *Communication Monographs, 56,* 55-58.

Fitzpatrick, K. R., & Rubin, M. S. (1995). Public relations vs. legal strategies in organizational crisis decision. *Public Relations Review, 21,* 21-33.

Fleming, J. E. (1980). Linking public affairs with corporate planning. *California Management Review, 23*(2), 35-43.

Fletcher, S. (1982, March 7). TV's coverage of oil crisis branded "superficial." *Houston Post,* p. 10D.

Foote, S. B. (1984). Corporate responsibility in a changing legal environment. *California Management Review, 26,* 217-228.

Ford, T. M. (1984, June). *Talk is too cheap.* Address given to the International Association of Business Communicators, Montreal, Canada.

Fox, J. F. (1983). Communicating on issues: The CEO's changing role. *Public Relations Review, 9*(11), 11-23.

Fram, E. H., Sethi, S. P., & Namiki, N. (1991). Newspaper advocacy advertising—A medium for discussing public issues? *Journal of Promotion Management, 1*(1), 77-97.

Franzen, R. S. (1977). An NBS internal communications study: A comment. *Public Relations Review, 3*(4) 83-88.

Fraser, E. A. (1982). Coalitions. In J. S. Nagelschmidt (Ed.), *The public affairs handbook* (pp. 192-199). New York: AMACOM.

Frederick, W. C. (1986). Toward CSR$_3$: Why ethical analysis is indispensable and unavoidable in corporate affairs. *California Management Review, 28*(4), 126-141.

Frederick, W. C., & Weber, J. (1990). In W. C. Frederick & L. E. Preston (Eds.), *Business ethics: Research issues and empirical studies* (pp. 123-144). Greenwich, CT: JAI.

Freeman, R. E. (1984). *Strategic management: A stakeholder approach.* Boston: Pitman.

Freudenberg, N. (1984). *Not in our backyards! Community action for health and the environment.* New York: Monthly Review Press.

Friedman, S. M. (1981, Spring). Blueprint for breakdown: Three Mile Island and the media before the accident. *Journal of Communication, 31,* 116-128.

Friendly, F. W. (1977). *The good guys, the bad guys and the first amendment: Free speech vs. fairness in broadcasting.* New York: Vintage.

Funkhouser, G. R. (1973). The issues of the sixties: An exploratory study in the dynamics of public opinion. *Public Opinion Quarterly, 37,* 62-75.

Galambos, L. (1975). *The public image of big business in America, 1880-1940: A quantitative study of social change.* Baltimore: Johns Hopkins University Press.

Galambos, L., & Pratt, J. (1988), *The rise of the corporate commonwealth.* New York: Basic Books.

Gamson, W. A. (1968). *Power and discontent.* Homewood, IL: Dorsey.

Gamson, W. A. (1975). *The strategy of social protest.* Homewood, IL: Dorsey.

Gandy, O. H., Jr. (1982). *Beyond agenda setting: Information subsidies and public policy.* Norwood, NJ: Ablex.

Gandy, O. H., Jr. (1992). Public relations and public policy: The structuration of dominance in the information age. In E. L. Toth & R. L. Heath (Eds.), *Rhetorical and critical approaches to public relations* (pp. 131-163). Hillsdale, NJ: Lawrence Erlbaum.

Garbett, T. (1981). *Corporate advertising: The what, the why, and the how.* New York: McGraw-Hill.

Garrett, D. E., Bradford, J. L., Meyers, R. A., & Becker, J. (1989). Issues management and organizational accounts: An analysis of corporate responses to accusations of unethical business practices. *Journal of Business Ethics, 8,* 507-520.

Gaudino, J. L., Fritsch, J., & Haynes, B. (1989). "If you knew what I knew, you'd make the same decision." A common misperception underlying public relations campaigns? In C. H.

Botan & V. Hazleton Jr. (Eds.), *Public relations theory* (pp. 299-308). Hillsdale, NJ: Lawrence Erlbaum.

Gaunt, P., & Ollenburger, J. (1995). Issues management revisited: A tool that deserves another look. *Public Relations Review*, 21, 199-210.

Gavaghan, P. F. (1983). Alcohol industry campaigns against alcohol abuse. *Public Relations Quarterly*, 28(2), 11-16.

Gay, C. D., & Heath, R. L. (1995). Working with experts in the risk communication infrastructure: Another challenge for public relations practitioners. *Public Relations Review*, 21(3), 211-224.

Gay, V. (1982). Mobil—They speak their mind. *Marketing & Media Decisions*, 17(1), 87-97.

Gerbner, G., Goss, L., Morgan, M., & Signorelli, N. (1984). Political correlates of television viewing. *Public Opinion Quarterly*, 48, 283-300.

Gergen, K. J., & Gergen, M. M. (1988). Narrative and the self as relationship. In L. Berkowitz (Ed.), *Advances in experimental social psychology* (Vol. 21, pp. 17-56). New York: Academic Press.

Gerloff, E. A., Muir, N. K., & Bodensteiner, W. D. (1991). Three components of perceived environmental uncertainty: An exploratory analysis of the effects of aggregation. *Journal of Management*, 17, 749-768.

Gildea, R. L. (1994-1995). Consumer survey confirms corporate social action affects buying decisions. *Public Relations Quarterly*, 39(4), 20-21.

Glasser, I. (1983). Introduction. In L. Siegel (Ed.), *Free speech, 1984: The rise of government controls on information, debate and communication* (pp. 1-2). New York: American Civil Liberties Union.

Gold, R. L. (1982). Accommodation preempts confrontation. *Public Relations Quarterly*, 27(3), 23-28.

Goldman, E., & Auh, T. S. (1979). Public policy issue analysis: A four-posted research design. *Public Relations Quarterly*, 24(4), 20-25.

Goldstein, A., Fischer, P., Richards, J., & Cretan, D. (1987). Relationship between high school student smoking and recognition of cigarette advertisements. *Journal of Pediatrics*, 110, 488-491.

Goodman, S. E. (1983). Why few corporations monitor social issues. *Public Relations Journal*, 39(4), 20.

Graber, D. A. (1982). The impact of media research on public opinion studies. In D. C. Whitney & E. Wartella (Eds.), *Mass Communication Review yearbook 3* (pp. 555-564). Beverly Hills, CA: Sage.

Grass, R. C. (1977). Measuring the effects of corporate advertising. *Public Relations Review*, 3(4), 39-50.

Green, J. C., & Guth, J. L. (1984). The party irregulars. *Psychology Today*, 18(10), 46-52.

Grier, P. (1984, December 26). Poisons in our midst are well-kept secret. *Rocky Mountain News*, p. 81.

Griffin, L. M. (1952). The rhetoric of historical movements. *Quarterly Journal of Speech*, 38, 184-188.

Griffin, R. J., Neuwirth, K., & Dunwoody, S. (1995). Using the theory of reasoned action to examine the impact of health risk messages. In B. R. Burleson (Ed.), *Communication yearbook 18* (pp. 201-228). Thousand Oaks, CA: Sage.

Grunig, J. E. (1977a). Evaluating employee communications in a research operation. *Public Relations Review*, 3(4), 61-82.

Grunig, J. E. (1977b). Measurement in public relations—An overview. *Public Relations Review*, 3(4), 5-10.

Grunig, J. E. (1978). Accuracy of communication from an external public to employees in a formal organization. *Human Communication Research, 5,* 40-53.

Grunig, J. E. (1979). Time budgets, level of involvement and use of the mass media. *Journalism Quarterly, 56,* 248-261.

Grunig, J. E. (1980). Communication of scientific information to nonscientists. In B. Dervin & M. J. Voigt (Eds.), *Progress in communication sciences* (Vol. 2, pp. 167-214). Norwood, NJ: Ablex.

Grunig, J. E. (1983). Communication behaviors and attitudes of environmental publics: Two studies. *Journalism Monographs, 81.*

Grunig, J. E. (1989a). Sierra club study shows who become activists. *Public Relations Review, 15,* 3-24.

Grunig, J. E. (1989b). Symmetrical presuppositions as a framework for public relations theory. In C. H. Botan & V. Hazleton, Jr. (Eds.), *Public relations theory* (pp. 17-44). Hillsdale, NJ: Lawrence Erlbaum.

Grunig, J. E. (1992a). Communication, public relations, and effective organizations: An overview of the book. In J. E. Grunig (Ed.), *Excellence in public relations and communication management* (pp. 1-18). Hillsdale, NJ: Lawrence Erlbaum.

Grunig, J. E. (Ed.). (1992b). *Excellence in public relations and communication management.* Hillsdale, NJ: Lawrence Erlbaum.

Grunig, J. E., & Grunig, L. S. (1989). Toward a theory of the public relations behavior of organizations: Review of a program of research. In J. E. Grunig & L. A. Grunig (Eds.), *Public Relations Research Annual* (Vol. 1; pp. 27-63). Hillsdale, NJ: Lawrence Erlbaum.

Grunig, J. E., & Hunt, T. (1984). *Managing public relations.* New York: Holt, Rinehart and Winston.

Grunig, J. E., & Repper, F. C. (1992). Strategic management, publics, and issues. In J. E. Grunig (Ed.), *Excellence in public relations and communication management* (pp. 117-157). Hillsdale, NJ: Lawrence Erlbaum.

Grunig, L. A. (1992a). Activism: How it limits the effectiveness of organizations and how excellent public relations departments respond. In J. E. Grunig (Ed.), *Excellence in public relations and communication management* (pp. 503-530). Hillsdale, NJ: Lawrence Erlbaum.

Grunig, L. A. (1992b). Toward the philosophy of public relations. In E. L. Toth & R. L. Heath (Eds.), *Rhetorical and critical approaches to public relations* (pp. 65-91). Hillsdale, NJ: Lawrence Erlbaum.

Grunig, L. A., Grunig, J. E., & Ehling, W. P. (1992). What is an effective organization? In J. E. Grunig (Ed.), *Excellence in public relations and communication management* (pp. 65-90). Hillsdale, NJ: Lawrence Erlbaum.

Guth, D. W. (1995). Organizational crisis and experience and public relations roles. *Public Relations Review, 21,* 123-136.

Gwyn, R. J. (1970). Opinion advertising and the free market of ideas. *Public Opinion Quarterly, 34,* 246-255.

Hadden, S. G. (1988). *A citizen's right to know.* Boulder, CO: Westview.

Hadden, S. G. (1989). Institutional barriers to risk communication. *Risk Analysis, 9,* 301-308.

Hahn, R. W. (1995, February 27). Regulatory reform—The whole story. *The Wall Street Journal,* p. A12.

Hainsworth, B., & Meng, M. (1988). How corporations define issue management. *Public Relations Review, 14*(4), 18-30.

Hansson, S. O. (1989). Dimensions of risk. *Risk Analysis, 9,* 107-112.

Haskell, F. K. (1984, December 23). Correcting the corporate myth. *Denver Post,* 4D.

Hattal, A. M., & Hattal, D. P. (1984). Videoconferencing. *Public Relations Journal, 40*(9), 21-24.

Hawkins, R. P., & Pingree, S. (1981). Using television to construct social reality. *Journal of Broadcasting, 25,* 347-364.

Hax, A. C., & Majluf, N. S. (1991). *The strategy concept and process: A pragmatic approach.* Englewood Cliffs, NJ: Prentice Hall.

Hazlett, T. W. (1989). The fairness doctrine and the First Amendment. *Public Interest, 96,* 103-116.

Hearit, K. M. (1994), Apologies and public relations crises at Chrysler, Toshiba, and Volvo. *Public Relations Review, 20,* 113-126.

Hearit, K. M. (1996). The use of counter-attack in apologetic public relations crises: The case of General Motors vs. Dateline NBC. *Public Relations Review, 22,* 233-248.

Heath, R. L. (1976). Variability in value system priorities as decision-making adaptation to situational differences. *Communication Monographs, 43,* 325-333.

Heath, R. L. (1979). Risk as a dimension of social movement vulnerability. In D. Nimmo (Ed.), *Communication yearbook 3* (pp. 491-505). New Brunswick, NJ: Transaction Books.

Heath, R. L. (1980). Corporate advocacy: An application of speech communication perspectives and skills—And more. *Communication Education, 29,* 370-377.

Heath, R. L. (1987-1988). Are focus groups a viable tool for PR practitioners to help their companies establish corporate responsibility? *Public Relations Quarterly, 32*(4), 24-28.

Heath, R. L. (Ed.). (1988a). *Strategic issues management: How organizations influence and respond to public interests and policies.* San Francisco: Jossey-Bass.

Heath, R. L. (1988b). The rhetoric of issue advertising: A rationale, a case study, a critical perspective—And more, *Central States Speech Journal, 39,* 99-109.

Heath, R. L. (1990). Corporate issues management: Theoretical underpinnings and research foundations. In J. E. Grunig & L. A. Grunig (Eds.), *Publication Relations Research Annual* (Vol. 2, pp. 29-65). Hillsdale, NJ: Lawrence Erlbaum.

Heath, R. L. (1991a). Effects of internal rhetoric on management response to external issues: How corporate culture failed the asbestos industry. *Journal of Applied Communication, 18*(2), 153-167.

Heath, R. L. (1991b). Public relations research and education: Agendas for the 1990s. *Public Relations Review, 17*(2), 185-194.

Heath, R. L. (1993). Toward a paradigm for the study and practice of public relations: A rhetorical approach to zones of meaning and organizational prerogatives. *Public Relations Review, 19*(2), 141-155.

Heath, R. L. (1994). *Management of corporate communication: From interpersonal contacts to external affairs.* Hillsdale, NJ: Lawrence Erlbaum.

Heath, R. L. (1995). Corporate environmental risk communication: Cases and practices along the Texas Gulf Coast. In B. R. Burleson (Ed.), *Communication yearbook 18* (pp. 255-277). Thousand Oaks, CA: Sage.

Heath, R. L., & Abel, D. D. (1996a). Proactive response to citizen risk concerns: Increasing citizens' knowledge of emergency response practices. *Journal of Public Relations Research, 8,* 151-171.

Heath, R. L., & Abel, D. D. (1996b). Types of knowledge as predictors of company support: The role of information in risk communication. *Journal of Public Relations Research, 8,* 35-55.

Heath, R. L., & Cousino, K. R. (1990). Issues management: End of first decade progress report. *Public Relations Review, 17*(1), 6-18.

Heath, R. L., & Douglas, W. (1990). Involvement: A key variable in people's reaction to public policy issues. In J. E. Grunig & L. A. Grunig (Eds.), *Public relations research annual* (Vol. 2, pp. 93-204). Hillsdale, NJ: Lawrence Erlbaum.

Heath, R. L., & Douglas, W. (1991). Effects of involvement on reactions to sources of messages and to message clusters. In L. A. Grunig & J. E. Grunig (Eds.), *Public relations research annual* (Vol. 3, pp. 179-193). Hillsdale, NJ: Lawrence Erlbaum.

Heath, R. L., Douglas, W., & Russell, M. (1995). Constituency building: Determining employees' willingness to participate in corporate political activities. *Journal of Public Relations Research, 7*(4), 273-288.

Heath, R. L., Liao, S., & Douglas, W. (1995). Effects of perceived economic harms and benefits on issue involvement, information use, and action: A study in risk communication. *Journal of Public Relations Research, 7,* 89-109.

Heath, R. L., & Nathan, K. (1991). Public relations' role in risk communication: Information, rhetoric and power. *Public Relations Quarterly, 35*(4), 15-22.

Heath, R. L., & Nelson, R. A. (1983a). An exchange on corporate advertising: Typologies and taxonomies. *Journal of Communication, 33*(Autumn), 114-118.

Heath, R. L., & Nelson, R. A. (1983b). Image/issue advertising tax rules: Understanding the corporate rights. *Public Affairs Review, 4,* 94-101, 104-105.

Heath, R. L., & Nelson, R. A. (1985). Image and issue advertising: A corporate and public policy perspective. *Journal of Marketing, 49*(1), 58-68.

Heath, R. L., & Nelson, R. A. (1986). *Issues management: Corporate public policymaking in an information society.* Beverly Hills, CA: Sage.

Heath, R. L., & Ryan, M. (1989). Public relations' role in defining corporate social responsibility. *Journal of Mass Media Ethics, 4*(1), 21-28.

Heerema, D. L., & Giannini, R. (1991). Business organizations and the sense of community. *Business Horizons, 34*(4), 87-93.

Herremans, I. M., Akathaporn, P., & McInnes, M. (1993). An investigation of corporate social responsibility reputation and economic performance. *Accounting, Organizations, & Society, 18,* 587-604.

Hiebert, R. E. (1991). Public relations as a weapon of modern warfare. *Public Relations Review, 17,* 107-116.

Hobbs, J. D. (1991, November). *"Treachery by any other name:" A case study of the Toshiba public relations crisis.* Paper presented at the meeting of the Speech Communication Association, Atlanta, GA.

Holsinger, R. L., & Dilts, J. P. (1997). *Media law* (4th ed.). New York: McGraw-Hill.

Honesty and ethical standards. (1983, July). *Gallup Report, 214,* p. 19.

Honesty and ethical standards. (1993, July). *Gallup Report, 334,* pp. 37-39.

Hosmer, L. T. (1991). Managerial responsibilities on the micro level. *Business Horizons, 34*(4), 49-55.

Huber, G. P., & Daft, R. L. (1987). The information environments of organizations. In F. M. Jablin, L. L. Putnam, K. H. Roberts, & L. W. Porter (Eds.), *Handbook of organizational communication: An interdisciplinary perspective* (pp. 130-164). Newbury Park, CA: Sage.

Hunger, J. D., & Wheelen, T. L. (1993). *Strategic management* (4th ed.). Reading, MA: Addison-Wesley.

Hush, M. (1983). Corporate advertising: Stacking the odds. *Grey Matter: Thoughts and Ideas on Advertising and Marketing* (Grey Advertising Inc.), *54,*(2), pp. 1-12.

Hwang, S. L. (1995, June 21). Philip Morris reassigns blame for its recall. *The Wall Street Journal,* pp. B1, B7.

Ingersoll, B. (1985, April 24). Annual meetings are much calmer affairs under changed SEC shareholder rules. *The Wall Street Journal,* p. 35.

Isaac, R. J., & Isaac, E. (1984, September 6). Subsidizing political hidden agendas. *The Wall Street Journal,* p. 28.

Iverson, A. C. (1982, April). *Advertising in a hostile environment.* Paper presented to The Popular Culture Association, Louisville, KY.

Jackson, B. (1984a, October 29). Democrats lead in PAC donations. *The Wall Street Journal,* p. 56.

Jackson, B. (1984b, November 6). Realtor, doctor PACs show clout. *The Wall Street Journal,* p. 56.

Jackson, P. (1982). Tactics of confrontation. In J. S. Nagelschmidt (Ed.), *The public affairs handbook* (pp. 211-220). New York: AMACOM.

Johnson, J. (1983). Issues management—what are the issues? An introduction to issues management. *Business Quarterly, 48*(3), 22-31.

Johnson, M. (1989, January 1). Baby alarms ring for Nestlé. *Marketing,* 18.

Jones, B. L., & Chase, W. H. (1979). Managing public issues. *Public Relations Review, 5*(2), 3-23.

Jones, J. F. (1975). Audit: A new tool for public relations. *Public Relations Journal, 31*(6), 6-8.

Juanillo, N. K., Jr., & Scherer, C. W. (1995). Attaining a state of informed judgments: Toward a dialectical discourse on risk. In B. R. Burleson (Ed.), *Communication yearbook 18* (pp. 278-299). Thousand Oaks, CA: Sage.

Kahn, H., & Weiner, A. J. (1967). *The year 2000: A framework for speculation on the next thirty-three years.* New York: Macmillan.

Kahn, H., Brown, W., & Martel, L. (1976). *The next 200 years: A scenario for America and the world.* New York: William Morrow.

Kaiser Aluminum & Chemical Corporation. (1980, August). *At issue: Access to television.* Oakland, CA: Author.

Kamm, T. (1984, December 26). French town with Union Carbide Corp. plant has dual concerns: Safety and unemployment. *The Wall Street Journal,* p. 15.

Kasperson, R. E. (1992). The social amplification of risk: Progress in developing an integrative framework. In S. Krimsky & D. Golding (Eds.), *Social theories of risk* (pp. 153-178). Westport, CT: Praeger.

Kelley, E. (1982). Critical issues for issue ads. *Harvard Business Review, 60*(4), 80-87.

Kelly, O. (1982, September 6). Corporate crime: The untold story. *U.S. News & World Report, 93,* pp. 25-29.

Klapper, J. T. (1960). *The effects of mass communication.* New York: Free Press.

Klein, W. J. (1983). Sponsored films. *Public Relations Journal, 39*(9). 20-21.

Kolko, G. (1967). *The triumph of conservatism: A reinterpretation of American history, 1900-1916.* Chicago: Quadrangle.

Kotcher, R. L. (1992). The technological revolution has transformed crisis communications. *Public Relations Quarterly, 37*(3), 19-21.

Krauskopf, A. M. (1979). Influencing the public: Policy considerations defining the tax status of corporate grassroots lobbying. *Catholic University Law Review, 28,* 313-357.

Krimsky, S. (1992). The role of theory in risk studies. In S. Krimsky & D. Golding (Eds.), *Social theories of risk* (pp. 3-22). Westport, CT: Praeger.

Krimsky, S., & Golding, D. (1992). Reflections. In S. Krimsky & D. Golding (Eds.), *Social theories of risk* (pp. 355-363). Westport, CT: Praeger.

Krippendorff, K., & Eleey, M. F. (1986). Monitoring a group's symbolic environment. *Public Relations Review, 12*(1), 13-36.

Kruckeberg, D., & Starck, K. (1988). *Public relations and community: A reconstructed theory.* New York: Praeger.

Lagerfeld, S. (1981, Summer). An anti-business business magazine. *Policy Review, 17,* 59-75.

Lauzen, M. M. (1994). Public relations practitioner role enactment in issues management. *Journalism Quarterly, 71,* 356-369.

Lauzen, M. M. (1995). Toward a model of environmental scanning. *Journal of Public Relations Research, 7,* 187-203.

Lauzen, M. M., & Dozier, D. M. (1994). Issues management mediation of linkages between environmental complexity and management of public relations function. *Journal of Public Relations Research, 6,* 163-184.

LeBon, G. (1925). *The crowd: A study of the popular mind.* New York: Macmillan.

Lee, I. L. (1907). Indirect service of railroads. *Moody's Magazine, 2,* 580-584.

Lentz, C. S. (1996). The fairness in broadcasting doctrine and the Constitution: Forced one-stop shopping in the "marketplace of ideas." *University of Illinois Law Review, 271*, 1-39.

Lerbinger, O. (1977). Corporate use of research in public relations. *Public Relations Review, 3*(4), 11-19.

Lerbinger, O. (1986). *Managing corporate crises.* Boston: Barrington.

Lesly, P. (1983). Policy, issues, and opportunities. In P. Lesly (Ed.), *Lesly's public relations handbook* (3rd ed., pp. 14-21). Englewood Cliffs, NJ: Prentice Hall.

Lesly, P. (1984). *Overcoming opposition: A survival manual for executives.* Englewood Cliffs, NJ: Prentice Hall.

Lesly, P. (1992). Coping with opposition groups. *Public Relations Review, 18*, 325-334.

Lichter, L. S., Lichter, S. R., & Rothman, S. (1982). How show business shows business. *Public Opinion, 5*(5), 10-12.

Lichter, L. S., Lichter, S. R., & Rothman, S. (1983). Hollywood and America: The odd couple. *Public Opinion, 5*(6), 54-58.

Lindenmann, W. K. (1977). Opinion research: How it works; how to use it. *Public Relations Journal, 33*(1), 12-14.

Lindenmann, W. K. (1983). Dealing with the major obstacles to implementing public relations research. *Public Relations Quarterly, 28*(3), 12-16.

Lipman, J. (1991a, March 4). Infomercial industry takes steps to clean up its late-night act. *The Wall Street Journal,* p. B4.

Lipman, J. (1991b, August 21). Sobering view: Alcohol firms put off public. *The Wall Street Journal,* p. B1, B6.

Lippmann, W. (1961). Drift and mastery: An attempt to diagnose the current unrest. Englewood Cliffs, NJ: Prentice Hall.

Littlejohn, S. E. (1986). Competition and cooperation: New trends in corporate public issue identification and resolution. *California Management Review, 29*(1), 109-123.

Liu, J. T., & Smith, V. K. (1990). Risk communication and attitude change: Taiwan's national debate over nuclear power. *Journal of Risk and Uncertainty, 3,* 331-349.

Loddeke, L. (1984, December 16). Legislative work under way in aftermath of India tragedy. *Houston Post,* p. 8B.

Long, L. W., & Hazleton, V., Jr. (1987). Public relations: A theoretical and practical response. *Public Relations Review, 13*(2), 3-13.

Lorange, P., & Vancil, R. F. (1976). How to design a strategic planning system. *Harvard Business Review, 54*(5), 75-81.

Lukasik, S. J. (1981). Information for decision making. *Public Relations Quarterly, 26*(3), 19-22.

Lundeen, R. W. (1983, October 28). *The media and industry: Two different worlds.* Address given to the Interstate National Gas Association, Columbia, MO.

MacEwen, E. C., & Wuellner, F. (1987). *Corporate communications and marketing: An integrated effort.* Paper presented at the ANA Corporate Advertising Workshop, New York, NY.

MacNaughton, D. S. (1976, December). Managing social responsiveness. *Business Horizons, 19,* 19-24.

Maher, P. (1982). Network TV warms up to issue advertisers. *Industrial Marketing, 67*(7), 33-39.

Mahon, J. F., & McGowan, R. A. (1991). Searching for common good: A process-oriented approach. *Business Horizons, 34*(4), 79-86).

Makeover, J. (1994). *Beyond the bottom line: Putting social responsibility to work for your business and the world.* New York: Simon & Schuster.

Mapes, L. V. (1984, November 1). For PACs it's the gift, not the thought, that counts. *The Wall Street Journal,* p. 28.

Marbach, W. D., Gibney, F., Gander, M., Tsuruoka, D., & Greenburg, N. F. (1984, December 17). A company in shock. *Newsweek, 104,* 37.

Marchand, R. (1987). The fitful career of advocacy advertising: Political protection, client cultivation, and corporate morale. *California Management Review, 29,* 128-156.

Marconi, J. (1992). *Crisis marketing: When bad things happen to good companies.* Chicago: Probus.

Marker, R. K. (1977). The Armstrong/PR data management system. *Public Relations Review, 3*(4), 51-59.

Markley, O. W. (1988). Conducting a situation audit: A case study. In R. L. Heath (Ed.), *Strategic issues management: How organizations influence and respond to public interests and policies* (pp. 137-154). San Francisco: Jossey-Bass.

Marx, T. G. (1986). Integrating public affairs and strategic planning. *California Management Review, 29*(1), 141-147.

Mathews, M. C. (1990). Codes of ethics: Organizational behavior and misbehavior. In W. C. Frederick & L. E. Preston (Eds.), *Business ethics: Research issues and empirical studies* (pp. 99-122). Greenwich, CT: JAI.

Mazur, A. (1981a, Spring). Media coverage and public opinion on scientific controversies. *Journal of Communication, 31,* 106-115.

Mazur, A. (1981b). *The dynamics of technical controversy.* Washington, DC: Communication Press.

McAdams, T. P., Jr. (1981, June 20). *How fair is broadcast news?* Address given to Texas UPI Broadcasters Meeting, San Antonio, TX.

McCombs, M. E. (1977). Agenda setting function of mass media. *Public Relations Review, 3*(4), 89-95.

McCombs, M. E. (1992). Explorers and surveyors: Expanding strategies for agenda-setting research. *Journalism Quarterly, 69,* 813-824.

McCombs, M. E., & Shaw, D. L. (1972). The agenda-setting function of the mass media. *Public Opinion Quarterly, 36*(2), 176-187.

McCoy, T. S. (1989). Revoking the fairness doctrine: The year of the contra. *Communications and the Law, 11*(3), 67-83.

McElreath, M. P. (1980). *Priority research questions in public relations for the 1980s.* New York: Foundation for Public Relations Research and Education.

McGinnis, M. A. (1984). The key to strategic planning: Integrating analysis and intuition. *Sloan Management Review, 26*(3), 45-52.

McGuire, J. W. (1990). Managerial motivation and ideology. In W. C. Frederick & L. E. Preston (Eds.), *Business ethics: Research issues and empirical studies* (pp. 51-75). Greenwich, CT: JAI.

McKenzie, R. B. (1983). *Using government power: Business against free enterprise.* Washington, DC: Competitive Economy Foundation.

McLaughlin, B. (Ed.) (1969). *Studies in social movements: A social psychological perspective.* New York: Free Press.

McLeod, D. M., & Perse, E. M. (1994). Direct and indirect effects of socioeconomic status on public affairs knowledge. *Journalism Quarterly, 71,* 433-442.

McLeod, J. M., & Chaffee, S. H. (1973). Interpersonal approaches to communication research. In S. H. Chaffee & J. M. McLeod (Eds.), Interpersonal perception and communication [Special issue]. *American Behavioral Scientist, 16,* 469-500.

McLuhan, M. (1969). *The Gutenberg galaxy.* New York: Signet.

Meadow, R. G. (1981). The political dimensions of nonproduct advertising. *Journal of Communication, 31*(3), 69-82.

Meier, B. (1985, February 8). Study by EPA finds laws may be insufficient to protect the public against toxic chemicals. *The Wall Street Journal,* p. 4.

Mendelsohn, H. (1973). Some reasons why information campaigns can succeed. *Public Opinion Quarterly, 37,* 50-61.

Meyers, R. A., Newhouse, T. L., & Garrett, D. E. (1978). Political momentum: Television news treatment. *Communication Monographs, 45,* 382-388.

Middleton, K. R. (1991). Advocacy advertising, the First Amendment, and competitive advantage: A comment on Cutler & Muehling. *Journal of Advertising, 20*(2), 77-81.

Miller, W. H. (1987, November 2). Issue management: "No longer a sideshow." *Industry Week, 235,* 125-129.

Mintzberg, H. (1984). Who should control the corporation? *California Management Review, 27*(1), 90-115.

Mitroff, I. I., & Pearson, C. M. (1993). *Crisis management.* San Francisco: Jossey-Bass.

Moore, M. (Ed.). (1989). *Health risks and the press. Perspectives on media coverage of risk assessment and health.* Washington, DC: Media Institute.

Moore, R. H. (1979). Research by the Conference Board sheds light on problems of semantics, issue identification and classification—And some likely issues for the '80s. *Public Relations Journal, 35*(11), 43-46.

Moore, R. H. (1982). The evolution of public affairs. In J. S. Nagelschmidt (Ed.), *The public affairs handbook* (pp. xiii-xv). New York: AMACOM.

Morgan, G. (1982). Cybernetics and organization theory: Epistemology or technique? *Human Relations, 35*(7), 521-537.

Morgan, G. (1986). *Images of organization.* Beverly Hills, CA: Sage.

Moskowitz, M. (1985, January 28). Shareholder protests not going to fade away. *Houston Post,* p. F4.

Mumby, D. K. (1987). The political function of narrative in organizations. *Communication Monographs, 54,* 113-127.

Murphy, P. (1992). The limits of symmetry: A game theory approach to symmetric and asymmetric public relations. In L. A. Grunig & J. E. Grunig (Eds.), *Public relations research annual* (Vol. 3, pp. 115-131). Hillsdale, NJ: Lawrence Erlbaum.

Murphy, P., & Dee., J. (1996). Reconciling the preferences of environmental activists and corporate policymakers. *Journal of Public Relations Research, 8,* 1-33.

Muskie, E. S., & Greenwald, D. J., III. (1986). The Nestlé Infant Formula Audit Commission as a model. *Journal of Business Strategy, 6*(4), 19-23.

Myers, K. N. (1993). *Total contingency planning for disasters: Managing risk, minimizing loss, and ensuring business continuity.* New York: John Wiley.

Nagelschmidt, J. S. (Ed.). (1982). *The public affairs handbook.* New York: AMACOM.

Naisbitt, J. (1982). *Megatrends: Ten new directions transforming our lives.* New York: Warner.

Nathan, K., & Heath, R. L. (1992, August). *Demographic factors and risk communication variables: Knowledge, benefits, control, involvement and uncertainty.* Paper presented at the Association of Educational Journalism and Mass Communication Convention, Montreal, Canada.

Nathan, K., Heath, R. L., & Douglas, W. (1992). Tolerance for potential environmental health risks: The influence of knowledge, benefits, control, involvement and uncertainty. *Journal of Public Relations Research, 4,* 235-258.

National Research Council. (1989). *Improving risk communication.* Washington DC: National Academy Press.

Nelson, R. A., & Heath, R. L. (1986). A systems model for corporate issues management. *Public Relations Quarterly, 31*(3), 20-24.

Nelson-Horchler, J. (1982, May 17). Why TV hates business. *Industry Week, 213,* 38-43.

Neuman, R. (1986). *The paradox of mass politics.* Cambridge, MA: Harvard University Press.

Newman, K. M. (1988). *Toxic chemical disclosures: An overview of new problems, new opportunities for the professional communicator.* New York: Public Relations Society of America.

Nimmo, D. D. (1974). *Popular images of politics: A taxonomy.* Englewood Cliffs, NJ: Prentice Hall.

Nimmo, D. D., & Combs, J. E. (1981). "The horror tonight:" Network television news and Three Mile Island. *Journal of Broadcasting, 25,* 289-293.

Nimmo, D. D., & Combs, J. E. (1982). Fantasies and melodramas in television network news: The case of Three Mile Island. *Western Journal of Speech Communication, 47,* 45-55.

Noah, T. (1993, December 29). Ethanol boon shows how Archer-Daniels gets its way in Washington with low-key lobbying. *The Wall Street Journal,* p. A10.

Noah, T. (1995, March 6). GOP's Rep. DeLay is working in every corner to exterminate regulations that bug business. *The Wall Street Journal,* p. A16.

Noah, T., & Carey, S. (1993, December 20). EPA irks Du Pont by acting to delay its plan to phase out CFC production. *The Wall Street Journal,* p. B8.

Noelle-Neumann, E. (1983). The effect of media on media effects research. *Journal of Communication, 33*(3), 157-165.

Noelle-Neumann, E. (1984). *The spiral of silence: Public opinion—Our public skin.* Chicago: University of Chicago Press.

Norris, F. (1903). *The pit: A story of Chicago.* New York: Doubleday, Page.

Nowlan, S. E., Shayon, D. R., & Contributing Editors from HRN. (1984). *Leveraging the impact of public affairs: A guidebook based on practical experience for corporate public affairs executives.* Philadelphia: HRN.

O'Shea, J. (1983, April 25). Drive to kill withholding bill shows power of banking lobby. *Houston Post,* p. 4C.

O'Toole, J. E. (1975a). Advocacy advertising act II. *Cross Currents in Corporate Communications, 2,* 33-37.

O'Toole, J. E. (1975b). Advocacy advertising shows the flag. *Public Relations Journal, 31*(11), 14-16.

Oberschall, A. (1973). *Social conflict and social movements.* Englewood Cliffs, NJ: Prentice Hall.

Oberschall, A. (1978). The decline of the 1960s social movements. In L. Kriegsberg (Ed.), *Research in social movements, conflict, and change: An annual compilation of research* (Vol. 1, pp. 257-289). Greenwich, CT: JAI.

Olasky, M. N. (1987). *Corporate public relations: A new historical perspective.* Hillsdale, NJ: Lawrence Erlbaum.

Olgeirson, I. (1993, April 16). Georgia-Pacific agrees to provide woodpecker shield. *The Wall Street Journal,* p. B10.

Opinion Research Corporation. (1981a, June). Priority analysis of 45 national issues. *Public Opinion Index, 39.*

Opinion Research Corporation. (1981b, March). The business climate. *Public Opinion Index, 39.*

Otten, A. L. (1984, December 31). States begin to protect employees who blow whistle on their firms. *The Wall Street Journal,* p. 11.

Otway, H. (1992). Public wisdom, expert fallibility: Toward a contextual theory of risk. In S. Krimsky & D. Golding (Eds.), *Social theories of risk* (pp. 215-228). Westport, CT: Praeger.

Owen, C., & Scherer, R. (1993). Social responsibility and market share. *Review of Business, 15*(1), 11-16.

Pagan, R. D., Jr. (1983, November 7). *Issue management: No set path* (Paper presented to the Issues Management Association, New York City). Washington, DC: Nestle Coordination Center for Nutrition.

Palmlund, I. (1992). Social drama and risk evaluation. In S. Krimsky & D. Golding (Eds.), *Social theories of risk* (pp. 197-212). Westport, CT: Praeger.

Paluszek, J. (1995). The rebirth of corporate social responsibility. *Public Relations Strategist, 1*(4), 48-51.

Parenti, M. (1986). *Inventing reality: The politics of the mass media.* New York: St. Martin's.

Pauchant, T. C., & Mitroff, I. I. (1992). *Transforming the crisis-prone organization.* San Francisco: Jossey-Bass.

Pearson, R. (1989). Business ethics as communication ethics: Public relations practice and the idea of dialogue. In C. H. Botan & V. Hazleton, Jr. (Eds.), *Public relations theory* (pp. 111-131). Hillsdale, NJ: Lawrence Erlbaum.

Pearson, R. (1990). Ethical systems or strategic values? Two faces of systems theory in public relations. In L. A. Grunig & J. E. Grunig (Eds.), *Public relations research annual* (Vol. 2, pp. 219-234). Hillsdale, NJ: Lawrence Erlbaum.

Pereira, J. (December 17, 1993). Toys 'R' Us decided to pull Night Trap from store shelves. *The Wall Street Journal,* p. A9.

Perspectives on current developments: Truth vs. provability at the FTC. (1983). *Regulation: AEI Journal of Government and Society, 7*(2), 4-6.

Petty, R. E., & Cacioppo, J. T. (1986). *Communication and persuasion: Central and peripheral routes to attitude change.* New York: Springer-Verlag.

Petzinger, T., Jr., & Burrough, B. (1984, December 14). U.S. cities and towns ponder the potential for chemical calamity. *The Wall Street Journal,* pp. 1, 6.

Pfeffer, J. (1981). *Power in organizations.* Boston: Pitman.

Phillips Petroleum Company. (1994). *1994 Health, Environmental and Safety Report.* Bartlesville, OK: Author.

Phillips, K. (1981). Business and the media. *Public Affairs Review, 2,* 53-60

Pierce, J., Gilpin, E., Burn., D. M., Whalen, E., Rosbrook, B., Shopland, D., & Johnson, M. (1991). Does tobacco advertising target young people to start smoking? Evidence from California. *JAMA, 266,* 3155-3157.

Pincus, J. D. (1980). Taking a stand on the issues through advertising. *Association Management, 32*(12), 58-63.

Pinsdorf, M. K. (1991). Flying different skies: How cultures respond to airline disasters. *Public Relations Review, 17*(1), 37-56.

Pires, M. A. (1983). Texaco: Working with public interest groups. *Public Relations Journal, 39*(4), 16-19.

Pires, M. A. (1988). Building coalitions with external constituencies. In R. L. Heath (Ed.), *Strategic issues management: How organizations influence and respond to public interests and policies* (pp. 1855-198). San Francisco: Jossey-Bass.

Plough, A., & Krimsky, S. (1987). The emergence of risk communication studies: Social and political context. *Science, Technology, & Human Values, 12*(3-4), 4-10.

Pool, I. D. (1983). *Technologies of freedom.* Cambridge, MA: Belknap Press of Harvard University Press.

Porter, W. M. (1992). The environment of the oil company: A semiotic analysis of Chevron's "People Do" commercials. In E. L. Toth & R. L. Heath (Eds.), *Rhetorical and critical approaches to public relations* (pp. 279-300). Hillsdale, NJ: Lawrence Erlbaum.

Post, J. E. (1978). *Corporate behavior and social change.* Reston, VA: Reston Publishing.

Post, J. E. (1979). Corporate response models and public affairs management. *Public Relations Quarterly, 24*(4), 27-32.

Post, J. E. (1985). Assessing the Nestle boycott: Corporate accountability and human rights. *California Management Review, 27,* 113-131.

Post, J. E., & Kelley, P. C. (1988). Lessons from the learning curve: The past, present, and future of issues management. In R. L. Heath (Ed.), *Strategic issues management: How organiza-*

tions influence and respond to public interests and policies (pp. 345-365). San Francisco: Jossey-Bass.

Post, J. E., Murray, E. A., Jr., Dickie, R. B., & Mahon, J. F. (1982). The public affairs function in American corporations: Development and relations with corporate planning. *Long Range Planning, 15*(2), 12-21.

Post, J. E., Murray, E. A., Jr., Dickie, R. B., & Mahon, J. F. (1983). Managing public affairs: The public affairs function. *California Management Review, 26,* 135-150.

Premeaux, S. R., & Mondy, R. W. (1993). Linking management behavior to ethical philosophy. *Journal of Business Ethics, 12,* 349-357.

Prior-Miller, M. (1989). Four major social scientific theories and their value to the public relations researcher. In C. H. Botan & V. Hazleton, Jr. (Eds.), *Public relations theory* (pp. 67-81). Hillsdale, NJ: Lawrence Erlbaum.

Private enterprise and public values. (1979). *Society, 16*(2), 18-19.

Public Affairs Council. (1978). *The fundamentals of issue management.* Washington, DC: Author.

Public Relations Society of America. (1987). Report of Special Committee on Terminology. *International Public Relations Review, 11*(2), 6-11.

Quintilian. (1920-1922). *The institutio oratorio* (H. E. Butler, Trans., Vols. 1-4). Cambridge, MA: Harvard University Press.

Raucher, A. R. (1968). *Public relations and business: 1900-1929.* Baltimore: Johns Hopkins University Press.

Rayner, S. (1992). Cultural theory and risk analysis. In S. Krimsky & D. Golding (Eds.), *Social theories of risk* (pp. 83-115). Westport, CT: Praeger.

Reese, S. D., & Danielian, L. H. (1994). The structure of news sources on television: A network analysis of "CBS News," "Nightline," "MacNeil/Lehrer," and "This week with David Brinkley." *Journal of Communication, 44*(2), 84-107.

Reeves, P. N. (1993). Issues management: The other side of strategic planning. *Hospital & Health Services Administration, 38*(2), 229-241.

Renfro, W. L. (1982). Managing the issues of the 1980s. *The Futurist, 16*(8), 61-66.

Renfro, W. L. (1993). *Issues management in strategic planning.* Westport, CT: Quorum.

Renn, O. (1992a). Concepts of risk: A classification. In S. Krimsky & D. Golding (Eds.), *Social theories of risk* (pp. 53-79). Westport, CT: Praeger.

Renn, O. (1992b). The social arena concept of risk debates. In S. Krimsky & D. Golding (Eds.), *Social theories of risk* (pp. 179-196). Westport, CT: Praeger.

Ressler, J. A. (1982). Crisis communications. *Public Relations Quarterly, 27*(3), 8-10.

Reuss, C., & Silvis, D. E. (Eds.). (1981). *Inside organizational communication.* New York: Longman.

Rhody, R. (1983). The public's right to know. *IPRA Review, 7*(11), 46-47.

Rice, R. E., & Atkin, C. K. (Eds.). (1990). *Public communication campaigns* (2nd ed.). Newbury Park, CA: Sage.

Rogers, E. M., Dearing, J. W., & Bregman, D. (1993). The anatomy of agenda-setting research. *Journal of Communication, 43*(2), 68-84.

Roloff, M. E. (1981). *Interpersonal communication: The social exchange approach.* Beverly Hills, CA: Sage.

Ronick, H. R. (1983). The F.T.C.: An overview. *Cases & Comment, 88*(4), 35-38.

Rosenblatt, R. (1984, December 17). All the world gasped. *Time, 124,* p. 20.

Ross, I. (1976). Public relations isn't kid glove stuff at Mobil. *Fortune, 94*(9), 106-111, 196-202.

Roth, T. (1984, December 17). Chemical firms may be facing new regulations. *The Wall Street Journal,* p. 4.

Rowan, F. (1984). *Broadcast fairness: Doctrine and practice.* New York: Longman.

Rowan, K. E. (1995). What risk communicators need to know: An agenda for research. In B. R. Burleson (Ed.), *Communication yearbook 18* (pp. 300-319). Thousand Oaks, CA: Sage.

Rowe, K., & Schlacter, J. (1978). Integrating social responsibility into the corporate structure. *Public Relations Quarterly, 23*(3), 7-12.

Rowland, R. C., & Rademacher, T. (1990). The passive style of rhetorical crisis management: A case study of the Superfund controversy. *Communication Studies, 41,* 327-343.

Rubin, D. M., & Sachs, D. P. (1973). *Mass media and the environment.* New York: Praeger.

Rumptz, M. T., Leland, R. A., McFaul, S. A., Solinski, R. M., & Pratt, C. B. (1992). A public relations nightmare: Dow Corning offers too little, too late. *Public Relations Quarterly, 37*(2), 30-32.

Ryan, M. (1986). Public relations practitioners' views of corporate social responsibility. *Journalism Quarterly, 63,* 740-747.

Ryan, M., & Martinson, D. L. (1983). The PR officer as corporate conscience, *Public Relations Quarterly, 28*(2), 20-23.

Ryan, M., & Martinson, D. L. (1984). Ethical values, the flow of journalistic information and public relations persons. *Journalism Quarterly, 61,* 27-34.

Ryan, M., & Martinson, D. L. (1985). Public relations practitioners, public interest and management. *Journalism Quarterly, 62,* 111-115.

Salamon, J. (1983, March 28). Fight over withholding splits banks. *The Wall Street Journal,* p. 21.

Salmon, C. (1989, Winter). Milking deadly dollars from the Third World. *Business & Society Review, 68,* 43-48.

Salmon, C. T. (1992). Bridging theory "of" and theory "for" communication campaigns: An essay on ideology and public policy. In S. A. Deetz (Ed.), *Communication yearbook 15* (pp. 346-358). Newbury Park, CA: Sage.

Salmon, C. T., Reid, L. N., Pokrywczynski, J., & Willett, R. W. (1985). The effectiveness of advocacy advertising relative to news coverage. *Communication Research, 12,* 546-567.

Sandman, P. M. (1986, November). *Explaining environmental risk: Some notes on environmental risk communication.* Washington, DC: Environmental Protection Agency.

Sawaya, R. N., & Arrington, C. B. (1988). Linking corporate planning with strategic issues. In R. L. Heath (Ed.), *Strategic issues management: How organizations influence and respond to public interests and policies* (pp. 73-86). San Francisco: Jossey-Bass.

Schellhardt, T. D. (1975, May 14). More regulation by government gets 56% backing in poll. *The Wall Street Journal,* p. 27.

Scherer, C. L., & Juanillo, N. K., Jr. (1992). Bridging together theory and praxis: Reexamining public health communication. In S. A. Deetz (Eds), *Communication yearbook 15* (pp. 312-345). Newbury Park, CA: Sage.

Schmertz, H. (1983, December 13). *The press and the public.* Address before the Annual Review Meeting, Gannett News Service, Washington, D.C.

Schmertz, H. (1986). *Good-bye to the low profile: The art of creative confrontation.* Boston: Little, Brown.

Schneider, M. D. (1996). Telecom act throws open competition in electronic mass media and telecommunications, *Communications Lawyer, 14*(2), 9-10.

Schorr, B., & Conte, C. (1984, August 27). Public-interest groups achieve higher status and some permanence. *The Wall Street Journal,* pp. A1, 8.

Schultz, D. L. (1989). Toxic chemical disclosure: Companies tackle the challenge. *Public Relations Journal, 45*(1), 13-19.

Schultze, Q. J. (1981). Advertising and public utilities: 1900-1917. *Journal of Advertising, 10*(4), 41-44, 48.

Schuman, H., & Presser S. (1977-1978). Attitude measurement and the gun control paradox. *Public Opinion Quarterly, 41,*427-438.

Schwartz, K. (1982). Communicating more effectively. In J. S. Nagelschmidt (Ed.), *The public affairs handbook* (pp. 123-134). New York: AMACOM

Schwenk, C. R. (1984). Cognitive simplification processes in strategic decision making. *Strategic Management Journal, 5,* 111-128.

Scott, R. L., & Smith D. K. (1969). The rhetoric of confrontation. *Quarterly Journal of Speech, 55,* 1-8.

Sethi, S. P. (Ed.). (1974). *The unstable ground: Corporate social policy in a dynamic society.* Los Angeles: Melville.

Sethi, S. P. (1976a). Dangers of advocacy advertising. *Public Relations Journal, 32*(11), 42, 46-47.

Sethi, S. P. (1976b, Summer). Management fiddles while public affairs flops. *Business and Society Review, 18,* 9-11.

Sethi, S. P. (1977). *Advocacy advertising and large corporations: Social conflict, big business image, the news media, and public policy.* Lexington, MA: D. C. Heath.

Sethi, S. P. (1979). Institutional/image advertising and idea/issue advertising as marketing tools: Some public policy issues. *Journal of Marketing, 43,* 68-78.

Sethi, S. P. (1981, November). *Advocacy advertising in America.* Keynote address given to the Advocacy Advertising Conference, Toronto, sponsored by the Conference Board of Canada.

Sethi, S. P. (1986, August 10). Beyond the fairness doctrine: A new war on corporate "propaganda." *The New York Times,* p. F3.

Sethi, S. P. (1987a). A novel communications approach to building effective relations with external constituencies. *International Journal of Advertising, 6,* 279-298.

Sethi, S. P. (1987b). *Handbook of advocacy advertising: Concepts, strategies and applications.* Cambridge, MA: Ballinger.

Shants, F. B. (1978). Countering the anti-nuclear activists. *Public Relations Journal, 34*(10), 10.

Sharlin, H. I. (1987). Macro-risks, micro-risks, and the media: The EDB case. In B. B. Johnson & V. T. Covello (Eds.), *The social and cultural construction of risk* (pp. 183-198). Dordrecht, The Netherlands: Reidel.

Sherif, C., Sherif, M., & Nebergall, R. (1965). *Attitude and attitude change: The social judgment-involvement approach.* Philadelphia: W. B. Saunders.

Shim, J. K., & McGlade, R. (1984). Current trends in the use of corporate planning models. *Journal of Systems Management, 35*(9), 24-31.

Simms, M. (1994). Defining privacy in employee health screening cases: Ethical ramifications concerning the employee/employer relationship. *Journal of Business Ethics, 13,* 315-325.

Simons, H. W. (1970). Requirements, problems, and strategies: A theory of persuasion for social movements. *Quarterly Journal of Speech, 56,* 1-11.

Simons, H. W. (1972). Persuasion in social conflicts: A critique of prevailing conceptions and a framework for future research. *Speech Monographs, 39,* 229-247.

Simons, H. W. (1974). The carrot and stick as handmaidens of persuasion in conflict situations. In G. R. Miller & H. W. Simons (Eds.), *Perspectives on communication in social conflict* (pp. 172-205). Englewood Cliffs, NJ: Prentice Hall.

Simons, H. W. (1976). Changing notions about social movements. *Quarterly Journal of Speech, 62,* 425-430.

Simons, H. W. (1983). Mobil's system-oriented conflict rhetoric: A generic analysis. *Southern Speech Communication Journal, 48,* 243-254.

Sims, R. R. (1992). The challenge of ethical behavior in organizations. *Journal of Business Ethics, 11,* 505-513.

Sinclair, U. (1906). *The jungle.* New York: Doubleday, Page.

Singer, E., & Endreny, P. (1987). Reporting hazards: Their benefits and costs. *Journal of Communication, 37*(3), 10-25.

Slovic, P. (1979). Rating the risks. *Environment, 21*(3), 14-39.

Slovic, P. (1987). Perception of risk. *Science, 230,* 280-285.

Slovic, P. (1992). Perception of risk: Reflections on the psychometric paradigm. In S. Krimsky & D. Golding (Eds.), *Social theories of risk* (pp. 117-152). Westport, CT: Praeger.

Slovic, P., Fischhoff, B., & Lichtenstein, S. (1987). Behavioral decision theory perspectives on protective behavior. In N. D. Weinstein (Ed.), *Taking care: Understanding and encouraging self-protected behavior.* (pp. 14-41). Cambridge, UK: Cambridge University Press.

Small, W. J. (1991). Exxon Valdez: How to spend billions and still get a black eye. *Public Relations Review, 17*(1), 9-25.

Smelser, N. J. (1963). *Theory of collective behavior.* New York: Free Press.

Smircich, L. (1983). Implications for management theory. In L. L. Putnam & M. E. Pacanowsky (Eds.), *Communication and organizations: An interpretive approach* (pp. 221-241). Beverly Hills, CA: Sage.

Smith, G., & Heath, R. L. (1990). Moral appeals in Mobil Oil's op-ed campaign. *Public Relations Review, 16*(4), 48-54.

Smith, N. C. (1995). Marketing strategies for the ethics era. *Sloan Management Review, 36*(4), 85-97.

Smith, T. W. (1980). America's most important problem—A trend analysis, 1946-1976. *Public Opinion Quarterly, 44,* 164-180.

Sneath, W. S. (1977). Managing for an uncertain future. *Vital Speeches, 43*(7), 196-199.

Solomon, C. (1993a, April 15). Exxon attacks scientific views of Valdez spill. *The Wall Street Journal,* pp. B1, B5.

Solomon, C. (1993b, March 29). What really pollutes? Study of a refinery proves an eye-opener. *The Wall Street Journal,* pp. A1, A6.

Solomon, J. B., & Russell, M. (1984, December 14). U.S. chemical disclosure-law efforts getting boost from tragedy in Bhopal. *The Wall Street Journal,* p. 18.

Spitzer, C. E. (1979). Where are we getting all this information and what are we doing with it? *Public Relations Journal, 35*(2), 8-11.

Sproule, J. M. (1989). Organizational rhetoric and the public sphere. *Communication Studies, 40,* 258-265.

Stamm, K. R. (1977). Strategies for evaluating public relations. *Public Relations Review, 3*(4), 120-128.

Starr, C. (1969). Social benefit versus technological risk. *Science, 165,* 1232-1238.

Steckmest, F. W. (with the Resource and Review Committee for the Business Roundtable). (1982). *Corporate performance: The key to public trust.* New York: McGraw-Hill.

Steffens, L. (1904). *The shame of the cities.* New York: McClure, Phillips.

Stephenson, D. R. (1982). How to turn pitfalls into opportunities in crisis situations. *Public Relations Quarterly, 27*(3), 11-15.

Stewart, C., Smith, C., & Denton, R. E., Jr. (1984). *Persuasion and social movements.* Prospect Heights, IL: Waveland.

Strenski, J. B. (1978). The communications audit: Primary PR measurement tool. *Public Relations Quarterly, 23*(4), 17-18.

Strenski, J. B. (1984). The communications audit—Basic to business development. *Public Relations Quarterly, 29*(1), 14-17.

Stridsberg, A. B. (1977). *Corporate advertising: How advertisers present points of view in public affairs.* New York: Hastings House.

Stroup, M. A. (1988). Identifying critical issues for better corporate planning. In R. L. Heath (Ed.), *Strategic issues management: How organizations influence and respond to public interests and policies* (pp. 87-97). San Francisco: Jossey-Bass.

Study sees too much emphasis on bad business news. (1984, March 19). *Broadcasting, 106,* 74-75.

Subramanian, R., Fernandes, N., & Harper, E. (1993). Environmental scanning in U.S. companies: Their nature and their relationship to performance. *Management International Review, 33,* 271-286.

Sullivan, A. (1993, August 31). Oil industry projects a surge in outlays to meet U.S. environmental standards. *The Wall Street Journal,* p. A2.

Tarbell, I. (1904). *The history of the Standard Oil Company.* New York: McClure, Phillips.

Tarde, G. (1922). *L'opinion et la foule.* Paris: Alcan.

Taylor, U. (1995). Some costs of lobbying may still be deductible. *Taxation for Accountants, 54*(2), 73-78.

Tedlow, R. S. (1979). *Keeping the corporate image: Public relations and business: 1900-1950.* Greenwich, CT: JAI.

The corporate image: PR to the rescue. (1979, January 22). *Business Week,* pp. 47-61.

The corporate imperative: Management of profit and policy. (1982, March 1). *Corporate Public Issues and Their Management, 7,* 1-4.

"The Dream" in danger. (1995). *Public Relations Strategist, 1*(1), 44-45.

Theberge, L. J. (Ed.). (1981). *Crooks, conmen, and clowns: Businessmen in TV entertainment.* Washington, DC: Media Institute.

Theberge, L. J., & Hazlett, T. W. (1982). *TV coverage of the oil crises: How well was the public served?* (3 vols.). Washington, DC: Media Institute.

Thomas, H. (1984). Mapping strategic management research. *Journal of General Management, 9*(3), 55-72.

Thomas, J. B., Clark, S. M., & Giola, D. A. (1993). Strategic sensemaking and organizational performance: Linkages among scanning, interpretation, action, and outcomes. *Academy of Management Journal, 36,* 239-270.

Thomas, K., Swaton, E., Fishbein, M., & Otway, H. J. (1980). Nuclear energy: The accuracy of policy makers' perceptions of public beliefs. *Behavioral Science, 25,* 332-344.

Thomas, S., & LeShay, S. V. (1992). Bad business? A reexamination of television's portrayal of businesspersons. *Journal of Communication, 42*(1), 95-105.

Thompson, D. B. (1981, February 23). Issue management: New key to corporate survival. *Industry Week, 208,* 77-80.

Thomsen, S. R. (1995). Using online databases in corporate issues management. *Public Relations Review, 21,* 103-122.

Tichenor, P. J., Donohue, G. A., & Olien, C. H. (1977). Community research and evaluating community relations. *Public Relations Review, 3*(4), 96-109.

Tirone, J. F. (1977). Measuring the Bell System's public relations. *Public Relations Review, 3*(4), 21-38.

Toch, H. (1965). *The social psychology of social movements.* Indianapolis, IN: Bobbs-Merrill.

Toth, E. L., & Heath, R. L. (Eds.). (1992). *Rhetorical and critical approaches to public relations.* Hillsdale, NJ: Lawrence Erlbaum.

Toulmin, S. E. (1964). *The uses of argument.* Cambridge, UK: Cambridge University Press.

Trost, C. (1985, January 7). Bhopal disaster spurs debate over usefulness of criminal sanctions in industrial accidents. *The Wall Street Journal,* p. 14.

Tucker, K., Broom, G., & Caywood, C. (1993). Managing issues acts as bridge to strategic planning. *Public Relations Journal, 49*(11), 38-40.

Tucker, K., & McNerney, S. L. (1992). Building coalitions to initiate change. *Public Relations Journal, 48*(1), 28-30.

Tucker, K., & Trumpfheller, B. (1993). Building an issues management system. *Public Relations Journal, 49*(11), 36-37.

Tversky, A., & Kahneman, D. (1986). Judgment under uncertainty: Heuristics and biases. In H. R. Arkes & K. R. Hammond (Eds.), *Judgment and decision making* (pp. 38-55). Cambridge, UK: Cambridge University Press.

U.S. Congress. (1962, September 4). Senate, *Congressional Record* (Vol. 108, 87th Cong., 2nd sess., pp. 17,362-17,363). Washington, DC: Government Printing Office.

U.S. Congress. (1978a). House of Representatives, Committee on Government Operations, *IRS administration of tax laws relating to lobbying* (95th Cong., 2nd sess.). Washington, DC: Government Printing Office.

U.S. Congress. (1978b). Senate, Committee on the Judiciary, Subcommittee on Administrative Practice and Procedure, *Sourcebook on corporate image and corporate advocacy advertising* (95th Congress, 2nd sess). Washington, DC: Government Printing Office.

Van Meter, J. R. (1983, October 28). TV didn't invent evil businessmen. *The Wall Street Journal*, p. 28.

Van Riper, R. (1976). The uses of research in public relations. *Public Relations Journal, 32*(2), 18-19.

Vasquez, G. M. (1993). A homo narrans paradigm for public relations: Combining Bormann's symbolic convergence theory and Grunig's situational theory of publics. *Journal of Public Relations Research, 5,* 201-216.

Vasquez, G. M. (1994). Testing a communication theory-method-message-behavior complex for the investigation of publics. *Journal of Public Relations Research, 6,* 267-291.

Vaughan, E. (1995). The significance of socioeconomic and ethnic diversity for the risk communication process. *Risk Analysis, 15,* 169-180.

von Winterfeldt, D. (1992). Expert knowledge and public values in risk management: The role of decision analysis. In S. Krimsky & D. Golding (Eds.), *Social theories of risk* (pp. 321-342). Westport, CT: Praeger.

Wallace, K. R. (1963). The substance of rhetoric: Good reasons. *Quarterly Journal of Speech, 49,* 239-249.

Wallack, L., Dorfman, L., Jernigan, D., & Themba, M. (1993). *Media advocacy and public health.* Newbury Park, CA: Sage.

Walty, W. (1981). Is issue advertising working? *Public Relations Journal, 37*(11), 29.

Waltzer, H. (1988). Corporate advocacy advertising and political influence. *Public Relations Review, 14*(1), 41-55.

Wanta, W., & Wu, Y. (1992). Interpersonal communication and the agenda-setting process. *Journalism Quarterly, 69,* 847-855.

Warner, K. E., Goldenhar, L. M., & McLaughlin, C. G. (1992). Cigarette advertising and magazine coverage of the hazards of smoking: A statistical study. *New England Journal of Medicine, 326,* 305-309.

Wartick, S. L., & Cochran, P. L. (1985). The evolution of corporate responsibility model. *Academy of Management Review, 10,* 759-769.

Wartick, S. L., & Mahon, J. F. (1994). Toward a substantive definition of the corporate issue construct. *Business & Society, 33,* 293-311.

Wartick, S. L., & Rude, R. E. (1986). Issues management: Corporate fad or corporate function? *California Management Review, 29*(1), 124-140.

Waz, J. (1983). Fighting the fair fight. *Channels, 2*(2), 66-69.

Weaver, P. H. (1988). The self-destructive corporation. *California Management Review, 30*(3), 128-143.

Weaver, R. M. (1970). *Language is sermonic* (R. L. Johannsen, R. Strickland, & R. T. Eubanks, Eds.). Baton Rouge: Louisiana State University Press.

Weick, K. E. (1988). Enacted sensemaking in crisis situations. *Journal of Management Studies, 25,* 305-317.

Weiner, R. (1994). Have database services replaced clipping services? *Public Relations Quarterly, 39*(2), 5-8.

Weinstein, A. K. (1979). Management issues for the coming decade. *University of Michigan Business Review, 31*(9), 29-32.

Weis, W. L., & Burke, C. (1986). Media content and tobacco advertising: An unhealthy addiction. *Journal of Communication, 36*(4), 59-69.

Weisendanger, B. (1994). Plug into a world of information. *Public Relations Journal, 50*(2), 20-23.

Weissman, G. (1984). Social responsibility and corporate success. *Business and Society Review, 51,* 67-68.

Weterings, R. A., & Eijndhoven, J. C. (1989). Informing the public about uncertain risks. *Risk Analysis, 9*(4), 473-482.

Whitaker, M., Mazumdar, S., Gibney, F., Jr., & Behr, E. (1984, December 17). It was like breathing fire. *Newsweek, 104,* 26-32.

Wiebe, R. H. (1967). *The search for order: 1877-1920.* New York: Hill & Wang.

Wiebe, R. H. (1968). *Businessmen and reform: A study of the progressive movement.* Chicago: Quadrangle.

Williams, D. E., & Olaniran, B. A. (1994). Exxon's decision-making flaws: The hypervigilant response to the Valdez grounding. *Public Relations Review, 20,* 5-18.

Williams, P. R. (1982). The new technology and its implications for organizational communicators. *Public Relations Quarterly, 27*(1), 15-16.

Winslow, R. (1984, July 18). Woman helps sink nuclear power plant that cost $4 billion. *The Wall Street Journal,* p. 1, 19.

Winslow, R. (1985a, January 28). Union Carbide moved to bar accident at U.S. plant before Bhopal tragedy. *The Wall Street Journal,* p. 6.

Winslow, R. (1985b, February 13). Union Carbide plans to resume making methyl isocyanate at its U.S. facility. *The Wall Street Journal,* p. 2.

Winters, L. C. (1988). Does it pay to advertise to hostile audiences with corporate advertising? *Journal of Advertising Research, 28*(3), 11-18.

Witte, K. (1995). Generating effective risk messages: How scary should your risk communication be? In B. R. Burleson (Ed.), *Communication yearbook 18* (pp. 229-254). Thousand Oaks, CA: Sage.

Woodyard, C. (1996, September 29). Maxxam to swap redwood forest. *Houston Chronicle,* pp. 1A, 24A.

Young, L. H. (1981). The media's view of corporate communications in the '80's. *Public Relations Quarterly, 26*(3), 9-11.

Young, S. (1990). Combating NIMBY with risk communication. *Public Relations Quarterly, 35,*(2), 22-26.

Zachary, G. P. (1992, February 6). All the news? *The Wall Street Journal,* pp. A1, A8.

Zentner, R. D. (1978). Measuring the effectiveness of corporate advertising. *Public Relations Journal, 34*(11), 24-25.

Zhu, J., Watt, J. H., Snyder, L. B., Yan, J., & Jiang, Y. (1993). Public issue priority formation: Media agenda setting and social interaction. *Journal of Communication, 43*(1), 8-29.

Zraket, C. A. (1981). New challenges of the information society. *Public Relations Quarterly, 26*(3), 12-15.

Legal References

American Broadcasting Co., 15 RR 2d 791 (1969).

Austin v. Michigan Chamber of Commerce, 494 U.S. 652 (1990).

Bigelow v. Virginia, 421 U.S. 809 (1975).

Board of Trustees v. Fox, 492 U.S. 469, (1989).

William F. Bolger et al. v. Young Drug Products Corp, USDC Dist Col, 526 FSupp, 823 (1981).

Brandywine-Main Line Radio, Inc., 14 RR 2d 1051 (1968).

Buckley v. Valeo, 424 U.S. 1 (1976).

Business Executives Move for Vietnam Peace v. FCC, and Democratic National Committee v. FCC, 414 U.S. 94, 93 S.Ct. 2080 (1973).

California Medical Association v. FEC, 453 U.S. (1981).

Central Hudson Gas & Electric Corp. v. Public Service Commission of New York, 447 U.S. 557 (1980).

Columbia Broadcasting System, Inc. v. Democratic National Committee; Federal Communications Commission v. Business Executives' Move for Vietnam Peace; Post-Newsweek Stations, Capital Area, Inc., v. Business Executives' Move for Vietnam Peace; and American Broadcasting Companies v. Democratic National Committee, 41 LW 4688 (1973).

Commarano v. United States, 246 F.2d 751 9th Cir. (1957).

Consolidated Edison Company of New York v. Public Service Commission, 447 U.S. 530 (1980).

Democratic National Committee v. FCC, 414 U.S. 94, 93 S.Ct.2080 (1973).

Edge Broadcasting, 113 S. Ct., 2703 (1989).

Fairness Doctrine, 30 RR 2d 1261 (1974).

Fairness Doctrine and the Public Interest Standards, 39 FR 26372 (1974).

First National Bank of Boston v. Bellotti, 435 U.S. 765 (1978).

Grosjean v. American Press Co., 297 U.S. 233 (1936).

The Miami Herald Publishing Company, v. Pat L. Tornillo, 418 U.S. 241-62 (1974).

Muller v. Oregon, 208 U.S. 412 (1908).

Munn v. Illinois, 94 U.S. 113 (1877).

National Commission on Egg Nutrition v. FTC, 570 F. 2d. (1978).

National Football League Players Association, 27 RR 2d 179 (1973).

New York Times Co. v. Sullivan, 376 U.S. 254 (1964).
Radioactive Waste Policy, 52 RR 2d 481 (1982).
Radio Station KKHI, 47 RR 2d 839 (1980).
Red Lion Broadcasting Co. v. FCC, 395 U.S. 367 (1969).
Report on the Handling of Public Issues Under the Fairness Doctrine and the Public Interest
    Standards of the Communications Act, 48 FCC 2d a (1974).
Syracuse Peace Council v. WTVH-TV, 99 FCC.2d 1389 (1984); 2F.C.C.Rcd 5043 (1987).
Virginia State Board of Pharmacy v. Virginia Citizens Consumer Council, 425 U.S. 748 (1976).
George R. Walker, 20 RR 2d 264 (1970).
WCMP Broadcasting Co., 27 RR 2d 1000 (1973).

Author Index

Subject Index

About the Author

ROBERT L. HEATH is Professor of Communication at the University of Houston. He is Director of the Institute for the Study of Issues Management and the Advisory Director of Research for Churchill Group, Inc., in Houston and part of World Communication Group. With coeditor Dr. Elizabeth Toth, he won the PRIDE Award from the Public Relations Division, Speech Communication Association in 1992 for Rhetorical and Critical Approaches to Public Relations (Lawrence Erlbaum Publications). He won the 1995 PRIDE award for outstanding research article with coauthors Shu-Huei Liao and William Douglas. He won the Pathfinder Award in 1992 from the Institute for Public Relations Research and Education. In 1996, he won the National Research Award from the International Association of Business Communicators.

His other books are *Management of Corporate Communication: From Interpersonal Contacts to External Affairs* (1994), *Human Communication Theories and Research: Concepts, Contexts, and Challenges* (1992) with Jennings Bryant, *Strategic Issues Management* (1988), *Realism and Relativism: A Perspective on Kenneth Burke* (1986), and *Issues Management: Corporate Public Policymaking in an Information Society* (1986) with Richard Alan Nelson.